International Conference on Image Processing, Computer Vision, & Pattern Recognition (IPCV'19)

Las Vegas, Nevada, USA
29 July – 1 August 2019

Editors:

Hamid R. Arabnia
Leonidas Deligiannidis
Fernando G. Tinetti
Ashu M.G. Solo

ISBN: 978-1-7138-5323-7

Printed from e-media with permission by:

Curran Associates, Inc.
57 Morehouse Lane
Red Hook, NY 12571

Some format issues inherent in the e-media version may also appear in this print version.

Printed by Curran Associates, Inc. (2022)

For permission requests, please contact CSREA Press
at the address below.

CSREA Press
ATTN: Hamid R. Arabnia
1060 Long Creek Drive
Watkinsville, GA 30677
USA

Phone: (706) 542-3480

hra@cs.uga.edu

Additional copies of this publication are available from:

Curran Associates, Inc.
57 Morehouse Lane
Red Hook, NY 12571 USA
Phone: 845-758-0400
Fax: 845-758-2633
Email: curran@proceedings.com
Web: www.proceedings.com

Contents

SESSION: IMAGING SCIENCE, MACHINE LEARNING, DEEP NETWORKS AND VARIATIONS + SENSOR TECHNOLOGIES

SESSION: IMAGING SCIENCE, NOVEL ALGORITHMS AND APPLICATIONS

SESSION: LATE BREAKING PAPERS: IMAGING SCIENCE AND APPLICATIONS

PROCEEDINGS OF THE 2019 INTERNATIONAL CONFERENCE ON IMAGE PROCESSING, COMPUTER VISION, & PATTERN RECOGNITION

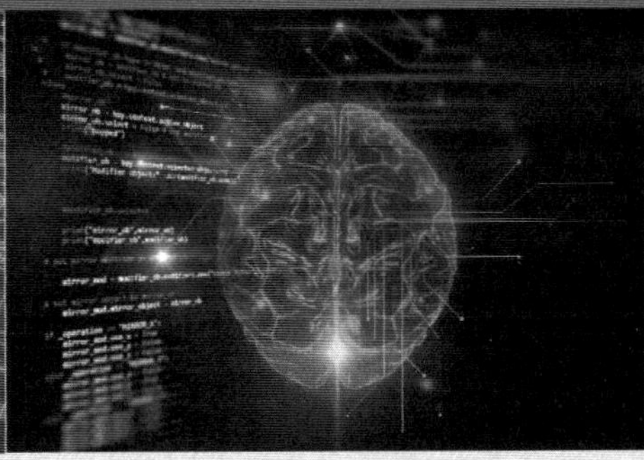

IPCV'19

Editors

Hamid R. Arabnia

Leonidas Deligiannidis, Fernando G. Tinetti

Associate Editor

Ashu M. G. Solo

Publication of the 2019 World Congress in Computer Science, Computer Engineering, & Applied Computing (CSCE'19)
July 29 - August 01, 2019 | Las Vegas, Nevada, USA
https://americancse.org/events/csce2019

This volume contains papers presented at the 2019 International Conference on Image Processing, Computer Vision, & Pattern Recognition. Their inclusion in this publication does not necessarily constitute endorsements by editors or by the publisher.

American Council on Science and Education (ACSE)

Printed in the United States of America
https://americancse.org/events/csce2019/proceedings

Foreword

It gives us great pleasure to introduce this collection of papers to be presented at the 2019 International Conference on Image Processing, Computer Vision, & Pattern Recognition (IPCV'19), July 29 - August 1, 2019, at Luxor Hotel (a property of MGM Resorts International), Las Vegas, USA. The preliminary edition of this book (available in July 2019 for distribution on site at the conference) includes only a small subset of the accepted research articles. The final edition (available in August 2019) will include all accepted research articles. This is due to deadline extension requests received from most authors who wished to continue enhancing the write-up of their papers (by incorporating the referees' suggestions). The final edition of the proceedings will be made available at https://americancse.org/events/csce2019/proceedings .

An important mission of the World Congress in Computer Science, Computer Engineering, and Applied Computing, CSCE (a federated congress to which this conference is affiliated with) includes *"Providing a unique platform for a diverse community of constituents composed of scholars, researchers, developers, educators, and practitioners. The Congress makes concerted effort to reach out to participants affiliated with diverse entities (such as: universities, institutions, corporations, government agencies, and research centers/labs) from all over the world. The congress also attempts to connect participants from institutions that have* ***teaching*** *as their main mission with those who are affiliated with institutions that have* ***research*** *as their main mission. The congress uses a quota system to achieve its institution and geography diversity objectives."* By any definition of diversity, this congress is among the most diverse scientific meeting in USA. We are proud to report that this federated congress has authors and participants from 57 different nations representing variety of personal and scientific experiences that arise from differences in culture and values. As can be seen (see below), the program committee of this conference as well as the program committee of all other tracks of the federated congress are as diverse as its authors and participants.

The program committee would like to thank all those who submitted papers for consideration. About 62% of the submissions were from outside the United States. Each submitted paper was peer-reviewed by two experts in the field for originality, significance, clarity, impact, and soundness. In cases of contradictory recommendations, a member of the conference program committee was charged to make the final decision; often, this involved seeking help from additional referees. In addition, papers whose authors included a member of the conference program committee were evaluated using the double-blinded review process. One exception to the above evaluation process was for papers that were submitted directly to chairs/organizers of pre-approved sessions/workshops; in these cases, the chairs/organizers were responsible for the evaluation of such submissions. The overall paper acceptance rate for regular papers was 24%; 18% of the remaining papers were accepted as poster papers (at the time of this writing, we had not yet received the acceptance rate for a couple of individual tracks.)

We are very grateful to the many colleagues who offered their services in organizing the conference. In particular, we would like to thank the members of Program Committee of IPCV'19, members of the congress Steering Committee, and members of the committees of federated congress tracks that have topics within the scope of IPCV. Many individuals listed below, will be requested after the conference to provide their expertise and services for selecting papers for publication (extended versions) in journal special issues as well as for publication in a set of research books (to be prepared for publishers including: Springer, Elsevier, BMC journals, and others).

- *Prof. Emeritus Nizar Al-Holou (Congress Steering Committee); Professor and Chair, Electrical and Computer Engineering Department; Vice Chair, IEEE/SEM-Computer Chapter; University of Detroit Mercy, Detroit, Michigan, USA*
- *Dr. Mahmood Al-khassaweneh; University of Detroit Mercy, Detroit, Michigan, USA*
- *Prof. Hamid R. Arabnia (Congress Steering Committee); Graduate Program Director (PhD, MS, MAMS); The University of Georgia, USA; Editor-in-Chief, Journal of Supercomputing (Springer); Fellow, Center of Excellence in Terrorism, Resilience, Intelligence & Organized Crime Research (CENTRIC).*
- *Prof. Dr. Juan-Vicente Capella-Hernandez; Universitat Politecnica de Valencia (UPV), Department of Computer Engineering (DISCA), Valencia, Spain*
- *Prof. Juan Jose Martinez Castillo; Director, The Acantelys Alan Turing Nikola Tesla Research Group and GIPEB, Universidad Nacional Abierta, Venezuela*

- *Prof. Emeritus Kevin Daimi (Congress Steering Committee); Director, Computer Science and Software Engineering Programs, Department of Mathematics, Computer Science and Software Engineering, University of Detroit Mercy, Detroit, Michigan, USA*
- *Prof. Zhangisina Gulnur Davletzhanovna; Vice-rector of the Science, Central-Asian University, Kazakhstan, Almaty, Republic of Kazakhstan; Vice President of International Academy of Informatization, Kazskhstan, Almaty, Republic of Kazakhstan*
- *Prof. Leonidas Deligiannidis (Congress Steering Committee); Department of Computer Information Systems, Wentworth Institute of Technology, Boston, Massachusetts, USA; Visiting Professor, MIT, USA*
- *Dr. Trung Duong; Research Faculty at Center for Advanced Infrastructure and Transportation (CAIT), Rutgers University, the State University of New Jersey, New Jersey, USA*
- *Prof. Mary Mehrnoosh Eshaghian-Wilner (Congress Steering Committee); Professor of Engineering Practice, University of Southern California, California, USA; Adjunct Professor, Electrical Engineering, University of California Los Angeles, Los Angeles (UCLA), California, USA*
- *Prof. Byung-Gyu Kim (Congress Steering Committee); Multimedia Processing Communications Lab.(MPCL), Department of Computer Science and Engineering, College of Engineering, SunMoon University, South Korea*
- *Prof. Tai-hoon Kim; School of Information and Computing Science, University of Tasmania, Australia*
- *Prof. Dr. Guoming Lai; Computer Science and Technology, Sun Yat-Sen University, Guangzhou, P. R. China*
- *Prof. Hyo Jong Lee; Director, Center for Advanced Image and Information Technology, Division of Computer Science and Engineering, Chonbuk National University, South Korea*
- *Dr. Muhammad Naufal Bin Mansor; Faculty of Engineering Technology, Department of Electrical, Universiti Malaysia Perlis (UniMAP), Perlis, Malaysia*
- *Dr. Andrew Marsh (Congress Steering Committee); CEO, HoIP Telecom Ltd (Healthcare over Internet Protocol), UK; Secretary General of World Academy of BioMedical Sciences and Technologies (WABT) a UNESCO NGO, The United Nations*
- *Prof. Aree Ali Mohammed; Head, Computer Science Department, University of Sulaimani, Kurdistan, Iraq*
- *Prof. Dr., Eng. Robert Ehimen Okonigene (Congress Steering Committee); Department of Electrical & Electronics Engineering, Faculty of Engineering and Technology, Ambrose Alli University, Nigeria*
- *Prof. James J. (Jong Hyuk) Park (Congress Steering Committee); Department of Computer Science and Engineering (DCSE), SeoulTech, Korea; President, FTRA, EiC, HCIS Springer, JoC, IJITCC; Head of DCSE, SeoulTech, Korea*
- *Prof. Dr. R. Ponalagusamy; Department of Mathematics, National Institute of Technology, India*
- *Dr. Akash Singh (Congress Steering Committee); IBM Corporation, Sacramento, California, USA; Chartered Scientist, Science Council, UK; Fellow, British Computer Society; Member, Senior IEEE, AACR, AAAS, and AAAI; IBM Corporation, USA*
- *Ashu M. G. Solo (Publicity), Fellow of British Computer Society, Principal/R&D Engineer, Maverick Technologies America Inc.*
- *Prof. Dr. Ir. Sim Kok Swee; Fellow, IEM; Senior Member, IEEE; Faculty of Engineering and Technology, Multimedia University, Melaka, Malaysia*
- *Prof. Fernando G. Tinetti (Congress Steering Committee); School of CS, Universidad Nacional de La Plata, La Plata, Argentina; also at Comision Investigaciones Cientificas de la Prov. de Bs. As., Argentina*
- *Prof. Hahanov Vladimir (Congress Steering Committee); Vice Rector, and Dean of the Computer Engineering Faculty, Kharkov National University of Radio Electronics, Ukraine and Professor of Design Automation Department, Computer Engineering Faculty, Kharkov; IEEE Computer Society Golden Core Member; National University of Radio Electronics, Ukraine*
- *Dr. Haoxiang Harry Wang (CSCE); Cornell University, Ithaca, New York, USA; Founder and Director, GoPerception Laboratory, New York, USA*
- *Prof. Shiuh-Jeng Wang (Congress Steering Committee); Director of Information Cryptology and Construction Laboratory (ICCL) and Director of Chinese Cryptology and Information Security Association (CCISA); Department of Information Management, Central Police University, Taoyuan, Taiwan; Guest Ed., IEEE Journal on Selected Areas in Communications.*
- *Prof. Layne T. Watson (Congress Steering Committee); Fellow of IEEE; Fellow of The National Institute of Aerospace; Professor of Computer Science, Mathematics, and Aerospace and Ocean Engineering, Virginia Polytechnic Institute & State University, Blacksburg, Virginia, USA*
- *Prof. Jane You (Congress Steering Committee); Associate Head, Department of Computing, The Hong Kong Polytechnic University, Kowloon, Hong Kong*

We would like to extend our appreciation to the referees, the members of the program committees of individual sessions, tracks, and workshops; their names do not appear in this document; they are listed on the web sites of individual tracks.

As Sponsors-at-large, partners, and/or organizers each of the followings (separated by semicolons) provided help for at least one track of the Congress: Computer Science Research, Education, and Applications Press (CSREA); US Chapter of World Academy of Science; American Council on Science & Education & Federated Research Council (http://www.americancse.org/). In addition, a number of university faculty members and their staff (names appear on the cover of the set of proceedings), several publishers of computer science and computer engineering books and journals, chapters and/or task forces of computer science associations/organizations from 3 regions, and developers of high-performance machines and systems provided significant help in organizing the conference as well as providing some resources. We are grateful to them all.

We express our gratitude to keynote, invited, and individual conference/tracks and tutorial speakers - the list of speakers appears on the conference web site. We would also like to thank the followings: UCMSS (Universal Conference Management Systems & Support, California, USA) for managing all aspects of the conference; Dr. Tim Field of APC for coordinating and managing the printing of the proceedings; and the staff of Luxor Hotel (Convention department) at Las Vegas for the professional service they provided. Last but not least, we would like to thank the Co-Editors of IPCV'19: Prof. Hamid R. Arabnia, Prof. Leonidas Deligiannidis, Prof. Fernando G. Tinetti, and Associate Editor, Ashu M. G. Solo.

We present the proceedings of IPCV'19.

Steering Committee, 2019
http://americancse.org/

SESSION

IMAGING SCIENCE, MACHINE LEARNING, DEEP NETWORKS AND VARIATIONS + SENSOR TECHNOLOGIES

Chair(s)

TBA

Unsupervised Object Discovery and Inference with Deep Latent Similarity Model

Shuanglu Dai and Hong Man
Department of Electrical and Computer Engineering, Stevens Institute of Technology,
1 Castle Point on Hudson, NJ07030, Hoboken, U.S.A.

Abstract— *In this paper, an end-to-end unsupervised object discovery and inference method is introduced based on a novel deep latent similarity model (DLSM). The method is able to locate potential objects in a complex visual scene and group them with latent categorical structure in a fully automated and unsupervised fashion. The region proposal network (RPN) introduced by Faster R-CNN is used as the frontend object proposal generator. A deep network based distance metric is introduced to capture the non-linear similarities between every pair of object proposals. This similarity affinity is embedded with latent categorical structures. Propagation on the deep similarity affinity identifies object exemplars and associated latent similarities. More importantly, the network distances, the exemplars and the latent similarities are modeled in a joint distribution conditioned on the object proposal inputs. The exemplar of each new object proposal will be inferred by maximizing this joint distribution, which will then determines the latent categories of this new input. Extensive experiments on Pascal-VOC 07 and Pascal07-6x2 have shown that DLSM outperforms many state-of-the-art unsupervised methods in object discovery, and its performance in object detection is competitive with many best supervised object detection methods.*

Keywords: Object discovery; object detection; deep unsupervised learning; affinity propagation

1. Introduction

Visual object detection is a classic computer vision task that has been studied for decades. Supervised region-based convolutional neural networks have shown promising performance in detecting objects given a fixed groups of object categories. However, the extensively design and training of these networks restrict their capabilities to the exact categories given by the training data. To mitigate this problem, object discovery has been recently studied for summarizing image topics based on dominant objects. Unfortunately, the discovered objects can not be marked by categories or latent categories. While fully-supervised object detectors becomes prevalent, unsupervised object detection remains challenging due to the uncertainty of object categories.

Recent developments on supervised object detector have been focused more on nature language descriptions in addition to identifications of object categories. Besides competitive performances, state-of-the-art object detection methods such as deformable part-based model [1], single-shot multi-box detector (SSD) and de-convolution SSD [2], Fast and Faster region-based convolutional neural networks (RCN) [3], [4], residual network with RCN [5] and class activation mapping [6] exhibit various properties that can be helpful in summarizing visual topics and structure language-based descriptions. However the generated languages are restricted to finite object categories, as these methods depend on exhaustive data training. Obviously, these current supervised detectors are not able to discover object categories that are not included in the training data.

Rather than fully-supervised object detection, object discovery determines dominant objects by weakly-supervised or unsupervised models [7]. Recently, the study of visual object discovery has been attractive in visual understanding since language models such as topic relational model [8], [9] and latent Dirichlet allocation [10], [11] are introduced to bridge visual objects with language topics. More interestingly, the exploration of latent topical relations identifies potential object groups without strong supervision on specific object categories [12].

This paper proposes a deep latent similarity model (DLSM) for unsupervised object inference. The proposed method is able to discover object regions and infer object categories to certain extent. This model embeds the deep distance network with a joint distribution. A similarity function is introduced as prior to generate the deep distance and infer latent categories. A latent category structure based on affinity propagation [13] is introduced to penalize the similarity function. The affinity propagation algorithm will be able to identify object exemplars among input object candidates (or proposals) and associate every new object proposal with a particular exemplar. Therefore object proposals are categorized by these unlabeled object exemplars. The exemplar labeling based on similarity function generates scores for object proposals to measure how likely an object proposal really locates an object with a latent category. The network and similarity priors are optimized by statistical inference. Object categories are not required to be specified, and the whole learning process does not require any image training. The proposed method is evaluated in unsupervised object detection and unsupervised object discovery tasks. Promising results demonstrates the effectiveness of the proposed method for unsupervised object discovery and detection.

The major contributions are summarized as follows. First, a deep latent similarity model (DLSM) is introduced, which effectively integrates a deep network distance metric with the affinity propagation algorithm to capture categorical non-linear similarities; Second, the deep network distances, the exemplar selections and the latent similarities are modeled in a unique joint distribution, and it is maximized for every new object proposal that achieves category inference and model update simultaneously; Third, an end-to-end unsupervised object discovery method incorporating region proposal network (RPN) [3] with the DLSM is developed and has shown competitive performance in extensive experiments on Pascal-VOC 07 and Pascal07-6x2 datasets.

2. Deep Latent Similarity Model

Given a data set $\boldsymbol{X}=\{X_i\}_{i=1,...,N}$ with samples drawn from some data hypothesis $X_i \in \mathcal{X}$, a deep network distance between $X_i, X_j \in \mathcal{X}\times\mathcal{X}$ can be defined by

$$d_f(X_i, X_j) = ||f_W(X_i) - f_W(X_j)||_2 \quad (1)$$

where f is a non-linear mapping constructed by a deep network with linear mapping W at the last layer, where W is square root matrix, that is, WW^T is a full rank symmetric matrix. d_f computes a Mahalanobis distance on a non-linearly projected space of the data pairs (X_i, X_j) with metric WW^T. It thus embeds implicit non-linear data similarity in an unscaled space $\mathbb{R}_+$. By definition, the network distance between any data pair varies due to the network variable f and linear mapping W. Rather than controlling the variations of these variables separately, we propose to model the distribution of the network distance by introducing a latent similarity function $\boldsymbol{S}=\{s_{ij}\in\mathbb{R}_+, \forall i, j\in\mathcal{N}\times\mathcal{N}\}$ based on affinity propagation [13]. The affinity propagation algorithm attempts to identify a subset of the original data samples as the "exemplars" that become the most representative cluster centers, and then associate each data sample with its closest exemplar. Given the set of exemplars $\boldsymbol{C}=\{c_i\}_{i=1,...,N}$, where c_i is a data sample selected from $\boldsymbol{X}$ and is the exemplar of the X_i sample, $s_{c_i,c_j} = p(c_j|c_i)$ introduces a non-metric similarity between the exemplar of the X_i sample and the exemplar of the X_j sample.

We assume the negative distance between any pair of samples follows a normal distribution given by

$$-d_f(X_i, X_j) + \tau \sim N(s_{i,j}, 1), X_i, X_j \in \mathcal{X}\times\mathcal{X} \quad (2)$$

The parameter $\tau > 0$ is introduced to provide a similarity boundary. To achieve a network distance with highest probability, $d_f(X_i, X_j)$ optimally converges to 0 for $s_{ij}\geq\tau$ and converges to infinity for $s_{ij}<\tau$. The proposed distribution forces the similarity negatively related to the distance. Furthermore, this paper extends the energy functional in affinity propagation [13] to the following Gibbs distributions.

$$\begin{aligned} s_{i,c_i} &\sim Gibbs(c_i), \forall i \\ \boldsymbol{c}_{1:N} &\sim Gibbs(\delta_1(\boldsymbol{c}_{1:N}), ..., \delta_N(\boldsymbol{c}_{1:N})) \end{aligned} \quad (3)$$

where $\boldsymbol{c}_{1:N}=\{c_1, ..., c_N\}$. Penalty functions $\boldsymbol{\delta}=\{\delta_1, ..., \delta_N\}$ are introduced by a prior distribution. The joint distribution of the similarity, exemplar and network distance $P(\boldsymbol{S}, \boldsymbol{c}_{1:N}, d_f|\boldsymbol{X})$ can be obtained by following the conditional distributions given by eq.2 and 3.

For effective visual representation, this paper constructs the non-linear mapping f using residual convolution blocks [5] with an implicit self-expressive layer [14]. The proposed deep metric $d_f(Z_1, Z_2)$ measures the closeness of pairs of samples (X_1, X_2) in their self-expressive subspaces (Z_1, Z_2). The network structure of d_f is illustrated in figure 1.

2.1 Inference

Given a collection of N data samples $\boldsymbol{X}$ and a group of M new data samples $\boldsymbol{X}^{new} = \{X_i^{new}\}_{i=1,...,M}$, the inference task of DLSM is to identify the deep network distance d_f and similarity function $\boldsymbol{S}$ with a structured exemplar set $\boldsymbol{c}_{1:N+M}$. A marginal maximum a posterior (MAP) inference is introduced on the joint distribution $P(\boldsymbol{S}, \boldsymbol{c}_{1:N+M}, d_f|\boldsymbol{X}, X^{new})$.

$$\begin{aligned} max &\sum_{\boldsymbol{c}_{1:N+M}} P(\boldsymbol{S}, \boldsymbol{c}_{1:N+M}, d_f|\boldsymbol{X}, \boldsymbol{X}^{new}) \\ &= P(d_f|S) \sum_{\boldsymbol{c}_{1:N+M}} P(\boldsymbol{S}|\boldsymbol{c}_{1:N+M})P(\boldsymbol{c}_{1:N+M}) \\ &\propto P(d_f|\boldsymbol{S})Z(\boldsymbol{S}) \end{aligned} \quad (4)$$

where $Z(\boldsymbol{S})$ is a partition function of the random field distribution $P(\boldsymbol{c}_{1:N+M}|\boldsymbol{S})$.

$$Z(\boldsymbol{S}) = \sum_{\boldsymbol{c}_{1:N+M}} exp\{\sum_i s_{i,c_i}^2 + \sum_k \delta_k(\boldsymbol{c}_{1:N+M})\} \quad (5)$$

The exemplar labeling of DLSM is to update the optimal exemplar for every past data samples and identify the optimal exemplar for every new data sample $(\boldsymbol{X}, \boldsymbol{X}^{new})$. This problem can be described as a marginal MAP inference of the exemplars $\boldsymbol{c}_{1:N+M}$. Given similarity measure $\boldsymbol{S}$, the exemplars can be inferred by maximizing the conditional random field $P(\boldsymbol{c}_{1:N+M}|\boldsymbol{S})$, where

$$\begin{aligned} &P(\boldsymbol{c}_{1:N+M}|\boldsymbol{S})\propto P(\boldsymbol{c}_{1:N+M}, \boldsymbol{S})\propto exp\{\sum_i s_{i,c_i}^2+\sum_k \delta_k(\boldsymbol{c}_{1:N+M})\} \\ &\max P(\boldsymbol{c}_{1:N+M}|\boldsymbol{S}) \Leftrightarrow \max\{\sum_i s_{i,c_i}^2 + \sum_k \delta_k(\boldsymbol{c}_{1:N+M})\}, \forall i \end{aligned} \quad (6)$$

This is in the form of an affinity propagation using the squared similarity as metrics.

3. Implementations

In this work, DLSM is applied to unsupervised visual object inference. We introduce object inference as a relaxed problem of object detection. Object detection provides the location and the category label for each detected object from all object proposals. Object inference aims at indicating

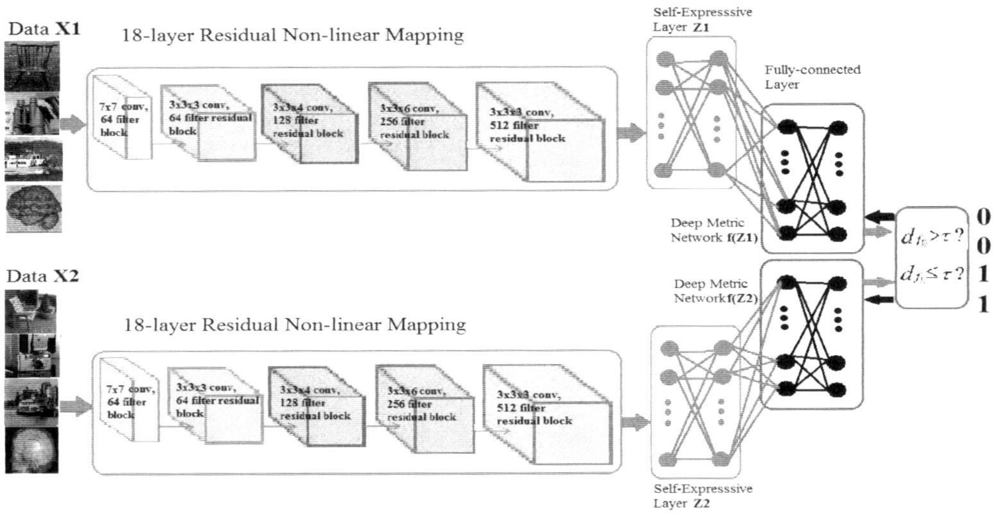

Fig. 1: Metric network structure for visual representation

how likely the object from an object proposal belongs to a specific but unlabeled object category. More specifically, an object proposal method will produce 1 score for each object proposal indicating how likely this proposal is locating an object, while object inference method will provide N scores for each proposal to indicate how likely the proposal is locating an object belonging to each of the N possible categories.

Object inference has broad applications as they can be evaluated as weak object detection and object discovery. Object discovery is a vision task that identifying dominant visual objects that summarizing the underlying topics presented by an image. The discovery of objects is often evaluated by object localizations. In recent years, unsupervised object discovery has caught great interests in topic relational modeling as it bridges latent visual semantics with language models.

As discussed in the previous section, the proposed model embeds latent categorical structure from an unlabeled data set. This past data set can be viewed as a "knowledge dataset". The inference further groups new samples to latent exemplars as "pseudo" categories. In object inference experiments, a subset images is randomly selected from the image data set as the knowledge data set, and the object proposals generated from test images, excluding the images in the knowledge data set, are used as new data samples. The similarities are estimated by the proposed inference method. An average K local similarity neighbors is used to score the proposals, where each proposal is scored by the average of its top K similarities. This scoring scheme is introduced based on our observation that many object proposals are often locating the same object in an image. $K = 5$ is adopted in this paper.

To obtain a well optimized deep network structure on the experimental data sets, the proposed distance network is pre-trained on the object regions localized by Pascal-VOC 07. The localized object regions are taken as a set of images to construct the knowledge set. It should be stressed that this pre-training is only introduced to obtain an initialization of network parameters, and the label information of these localized image regions is never used in the object inference procedure. A minimum squared error (MSE) loss is used as the loss function

$$\min_{f} \mathcal{E}_{X_i}\mathcal{E}_{X_j|X_i}(\tau(l(X_i, X_j) - 1) + d_f(X_i, X_j))^2 \quad (7)$$

where the similarity label $l(X_i, X_j) = 1$ if two images X_i, X_j are similar and 0 otherwise. The similarity margin $\tau = 1000$ is used. $\mathcal{E}_{X_i}, \mathcal{E}_{X_j|X_i}$ denote the expectation of the i-th image X_i and the expectation of the j-th image X_j given the i-th image.

A detailed procedure of the proposed object inference is described in algorithm 1. As an unsupervised method, only images without labels are used as input to our model and there is no supervised training. The inference of DLSM optimizes the network distance d_f and the similarity iteratively to maximize the joint probability distribution $P(\boldsymbol{S}, \boldsymbol{c}_{1:N+M}, d_f|\boldsymbol{X}, \boldsymbol{X}^{new})$. Started with an initialization of d_f, this optimization is solved by repeatedly using d_f to estimate $\boldsymbol{S}$ and using $\boldsymbol{S}$ to estimate d_f, which follows an alternating maximization scheme. No object labels and supervised training are used to learn the deep distance network. After inference, the exemplar labeling of DLSM generates 20 scores for each proposal to indicate 20 latent object categories. The region proposal network proposed by [3] is used to generate object proposals.

4. Experiments

4.1 Evaluation Tasks and Comparative Studies

The experiments evaluate the proposed visual object inference method as an unsupervised object discovery method

Algorithm 1 Similarity Clustering with Optimized Metric (Optim-MSC)

procedure DEEPSIM(Image I,Knowledge data X, region proposal network F_p, similarity margin τ, similarity neighbor K)
    Initialize distance network d_f.
    Generate proposal regions as group of new images $\boldsymbol{X}^{new} \leftarrow F_p(I)$.
    while $P(\boldsymbol{S}, \boldsymbol{c}_{1:N+M}, d_f|\boldsymbol{X}, \boldsymbol{X}^{new})$ not converge **do**
        Compute similarities $\boldsymbol{S}=\{s_{ij}|i,j=1,...N+M\}$.
        Optimize distance network d_f.
    Generate 20 latent categories using affinity propagation on $\boldsymbol{S}$ and $\boldsymbol{c}$.
    Compute average K similarity scores for proposals.
    return similarity scores for $\boldsymbol{X}^{new}$

and an unsupervised object detector. While supervised object detector has been benefited from deep image classifier and region proposals, unsupervised object detection remains challenging due to the unspecified categorical spaces, intra-category variations, background clutters and occlusions in real-world images.

Benchmark and state-of-the-art methods for unsupervised object discovery are evaluated. These methods are mainly implemented based on variations of topic relational models and visual feature matching. Methods based on topic relational models using latent Dirichlet allocation with Dirichlet forest (LDA-DF) [15], the topic relational model proposed by [16], latent Dirichlet allocation learnt from web images (LDA-Web) and latent Dirichlet allocation with mixture of Dirichlet trees (LDA-MDT) [10] are evaluated as the state-of-the-art methods. The latent Dirichlet allocation on topic model (LDA) is evaluated as a benchmark method based on topic relational modeling [7]. Methods based on visual feature matching proposed by [9], [17], unsupervised object discovery and localization (UODL) [18], [19], [20], [11], [21], [8], [12] and structure contrast based method [22] are evaluated as the most recent state-of-the-art methods, where variants of UODL are evaluated as a benchmark method based on visual feature matching. The comparative feature matching based methods can be divided into 3 types according to the kinds of labeled images used in the supervised learning, which include positive images (P), negative images (N) and additional (A) images. While both positive and negative data are used by weakly-supervised localization methods in [11], [19]–[21], [23], positive data supervision is mainly used by co-localization methods in [8], [18]. In contrast to those methods, the structure contrast based method [22] and the proposed unsupervised object discovery method do not use any data supervision.

On object detection, since there lacks of existing method for unsupervised detection, the proposed unsupervised detector is compared with fully-supervised benchmark and state-of-the-art object detectors using region-based convolutional neural network (RCN) and feature pyramids. While comparing the proposed unsupervised detector with those supervised detectors is not a fair and equivalent comparison, the purpose of this evaluation is to examine the effectiveness of the proposed unsupervised method in categorizing unlabeled objects according to their true state of nature. It should be noted that the proposed method will produce a set of object categories and place all detected objects into these categories, it will not provide the specific labels to these categories, since these labels never appeared in the learning and test process. With this understanding, it is easy to see that although some exhaustively supervised RCN detectors may outperform the proposed unsupervised detector, the analysis of the competitiveness of the proposed unsupervised detector is still valid. The supervised object detectors including Deformable part model (DPM) [24], RCN version of DPM [1], region-based convolutional neural network (RCNN-BB) and Fast-RCNN (FRCN) [4], single-shot multibox detectors (SSD) [2] are evaluated as state-of-the-art methods. While DPM and its RCN version are evaluated as benchmark supervised detectors. The Faster RCNN proposed in [3] is not evaluated as the network of Faster RCNN is similar to FRCN and its performance is close to FRCN.

4.2 Databases and Evaluation Metrics

The proposed method is evaluated mainly on Pascal-VOC 07 and Pascal07-6x2. Pascal-VOC 07 is an image data set collected in realistic scenes, which includes 5011 training images and 4092 test images labelled by 20 categories. These categories are following different semantic hierarchies, including "person" with "person", "Animal" with "bird", "cat", "cow", "dog", "horse", "sheep", "Vehicle" with "aeroplane", "bicycle", "boat", "bus", "car", "motorbike", "train" and "Indoor" with "bottle", "chair", "dining table", "potted plant", "sofa", "tv/monitor". The object locations are labelled by rectangle boxes and pose labels of the objects are provided. The PASCAL07-6x2 is subset of the PASCAL07 train+val data, which consists of 463 images labelled by 6 categories from the left and right viewpoints. These categories include "aeroplane", "bicycle", "boat", "bus", "horse", and "motorbike". Each of the 12 class/viewpoint combinations contains between 21 and 50 images for a total of 463 images.

Unsupervised object discovery is evaluated on Pascal-VOC 2007 and Pascal07-6x2 data sets. The correct localization (CorLoc) rate is introduced as an evaluation metric for object discovery, which is also widely used by the comparative methods [9], [10], [17], [18]. The intersection of union (IoU) is introduced to measure if an object is correctly localized. The standard PASCAL-VOC criterion is used to compute IoU, where IoU>0.7 is considered as a correct localization. This metric is adequate for images labeled with single objects category. As images in Pascal-VOC 07 may contain different object categories, this experiment further introduces average precision (AP) to evaluate the localization of objects labeled with multiple categories. The performances of object detection are evaluated on Pascal-VOC 07 data set by AP. Pascal07-6x2 data set is not evaluated in object detection tasks as it was not evaluated as a standard benchmark by comparative methods.

4.3 Evaluations on Unsupervised Object Discovery

Firstly, the class-by-class AP and corLoc obtained by the comparative methods based on topic relational models are recorded in table 1 and 2. Again, although the class labels are listed in the tables, these are not the outcomes of all these unsupervised object discovery methods. These methods only place object proposals into the set of unlabeled categories, which correspond to the true labeled categories. The proposed method outperforms the comparative relational models in terms of AP and corLoc. As observed from table 1, the proposed method obtains worse object localizations on "bicycle", "boat" and "bus" than the other categories. This shows the knowledge image set constructed from object boxes with different sizes are not scaled well for model inference, which subsequently leads to error exemplar labeling. The corLocs recorded in table 2 provides a detailed class-by-class analysis on Pascal-VOC 6x2 data set. As observed from table 2, the proposed method outperforms the comparative methods on the classes and their poses in terms of corLoc. By examining the AP and corLoc from table 1 and 2, it can be observed that the proposed method obtains competitive corLoc but relatively lower AP on Pascal-VOC 6x2 data set. This shows the proposed method is able to achieve competitive "top-K" scores for single object discovery and localization but it detects many extra wrongly boxes as object regions, which reduces AP.

Secondly, the class-by-class AP and corLoc obtained by the comparative feature matching based methods are recorded in table 3 and 4. The benchmark method UODL is evaluated class-by-class on Pascal-VOC 6x2 data set and all the comparative feature matching based methods are comprehensively evaluated on PascalVOC07 with all 20 classes in term of corLoc. For a detailed feature and model analysis, UODL is also evaluated by eliminating the use of multiple object regions (UODL-MOR), substituting probabilistic hough matching with appearance-based matching (UODL-PHM), replacing the standout score with the maximum confidence (UODL-STO) and keeping full model (UODL-full). It can be observed from table 3 that the standout score and probabilistic hough matching contribute the most to UODL but it is still too heuristic to identify effective components in this method. Compared to UODL and other comparative methods, the proposed method is able to optimize deep network and affinity propagation in an end-to-end fashion and thus obtains better performance. Furthermore, it can be observed from table 4 that the proposed method outperforms the other feature matching based methods in terms of AP. This result show that the proposed method can generate proposal box scores that related to the locations of ground truth boxes.

4.4 Evaluations on Object Detection

This experiment further examines the effectiveness of the proposed method for unsupervised object detection. The proposed unsupervised method is compared with well-known fully-supervised RCN based object detectors. The APs obtained by those supervised detector and the proposed unsupervised detector are recorded in table 5. It should be noted again that the proposed unsupervised method only produces categorization without labeling. The training set is specified by "None" as the proposed detector does not need training. As observed from table 5, the proposed unsupervised detector obtains the second best mAP among the comparative detectors. This promising result may be benefited by the end-to-end optimization of the ResNet-18 structure upon the proposed graphical model. This shows the proposed model is effective for unsupervised object detection and may be improved in the future for better performances.

4.5 Visualization of Latent Exemplar Images

Since the latent exemplars are interpretable intermediate results from the proposed object inference method, some of these exemplar images from Pascal-VOC 6x2 data set are shown in figure 2. This analysis evaluates the capability of unsupervised topic summarization using the deep latent similarity model. This evaluation further explains how the proposed model effectively identifies object categories. As observed from figure 2, the generated latent exemplars exhibit three major attributes. First, the latent exemplars capture the essential parts of the objects with different appearances, such as colors. This can be obviously observed from the exemplar images of "horse". White, brown and black horses are all captured as exemplars of the same category. Second, the latent exemplars incorporate different poses and scenes. It can be observed from figure 2 that scenes such as a boat in front of buildings, people talking in front of bus, horse riding on the road and grass are captured. It is also obvious that different poses such as front, rear, left and right are all captured by those exemplars in each class. Third, the latent exemplars are robust to image scales and singletons. As figure 2 shows, exemplar images in relatively smaller resolution compared to the other images are captured. While unexpected scenes are also captured by the proposed method as singletons. For example, the last "bicycle" exemplar image shows a person is blocking the target bicycle; the last "horse" exemplar image shows a horse head in the fence. With these three major properties, the latent exemplars provide a robust and comprehensive

Table 1: Evaluation of object discovery with comparative methods based on topic relational models on Pascal-VOC 6x2 data set in term of class-by-class AP(%).

Methods	Aeroplane	Bicycle	Boat	Bus	Horse	Motorbike
Russell et al. (LDA)	34.60	61.27	39.31	35.74	43.78	47.33
LDA+Web	35.50	57.30	38.44	31.34	45.92	48.76
Andrzejewski et al. (LDA-DF)	34.75	62.12	41.07	36.29	44.25	47.73
Kim et al.	45.74	40.33	31.01	35.44	29.10	30.23
Faktor et al.	41.57	44.62	45.73	34.51	50.31	41.40
Niu et al.(LDA-MDT)	36.71	62.93	46.84	45.39	46.61	53.59
proposed	**88.90**	**68.43**	**67.43**	**69.62**	**76.34**	**79.55**

Table 2: Evaluation of object discovery with comparative methods based on topic relational models on Pascal-VOC 6x2 data set in term of CorLoc (%).

Methods	Aeroplane		Bicycle		Boat		Bus		Horse		Motorbike	
	Left	Right	Left	Right	Left	Right	Left	Right	Left	Right	Left	Right
Russell et al.	40.47	58.97	16.66	23.91	11.90	17.50	14.28	34.78	27.65	31.11	40.54	51.51
LDA+Web	41.67	58.15	15.87	26.08	11.36	18.34	15.93	30.31	37.21	32.28	41.15	52.33
Andrzejewski et al.	47.61	71.79	25.00	26.08	14.28	22.50	33.33	43.47	38.29	40.00	54.05	63.63
Tang et al.	41.86	51.28	25.00	24.00	11.36	11.63	38.10	56.52	43.75	52.17	51.28	64.71
Cho et al.	62.79	66.67	54.17	56.00	18.18	18.60	42.86	69.57	70.83	71.74	69.23	44.12
Niu et al.(LDA-MDT)	64.28	87.17	35.41	39.13	16.66	30.00	42.86	60.86	46.80	53.33	59.45	75.75
proposed	**88.24**	**87.27**	**89.41**	**94.87**	**77.42**	**71.64**	**87.23**	**85.25**	**78.05**	**78.57**	**85.71**	**84.38**

Table 3: Evaluation of object discovery with the benchmark visual feature matching based method on Pascal-VOC 6x2 data set in term of CorLoc (%).

Methods	Aeroplane		Bicycle		Boat		Bus		Horse		Motorbike	
	Left	Right	Left	Right	Left	Right	Left	Right	Left	Right	Left	Right
UODL-full	62.79	71.79	77.08	62.00	25.00	32.56	66.67	91.30	83.33	86.96	82.96	70.59
UODL-MOR	62.79	74.36	52.08	42.00	15.91	27.91	61.90	91.30	85.42	76.09	48.72	8.82
UODL-PHM	39.53	38.46	54.17	60.00	6.82	9.30	42.86	73.91	68.75	82.61	33.33	2.94
UODL-STO	34.88	0.0	2.08	0.0	0.0	4.65	0.0	8.70	64.58	30.43	2.56	0.0
proposed	**88.24**	**87.27**	**89.41**	**94.87**	**77.42**	**71.64**	**87.23**	**85.25**	**78.05**	**78.57**	**85.71**	**84.38**

Table 4: Evaluation of object discovery with comparative methods based on visual feature matching in term of class-by-class AP(%). Testing images in Pascal-VOC07 with all 20 classes are used. The success localization is evaluated at IoU>0.7.

Method	data used	aero	bk	brd	boa	bot	bus	car	cat	chr	cow	dtab	dog	hos	mtbk	per	plnt	shp	sofa	tr	tv	Av.
siva, Xiang	P+N	42	47	18	09	03	41	73	45	05	31	19	34	49	65	08	09	17	32	55	06	30.4
siva et al.	P+N	46	22	31	20	05	38	41	52	07	30	28	41	42	47	24	12	28	33	49	09	30.2
shi et al.	P+N	67	54	34	18	01	47	61	69	03	32	16	59	52	65	18	03	21	35	63	06	36.2
cinbis et al.	P+N	57	58	29	21	07	55	69	21	09	51	10	29	58	61	37	19	57	12	55	59	38.8
cho et al.	P	50	41	30	19	04	62	65	43	09	49	12	44	64	57	15	09	31	34	62	32	36.6
Wang et al.	P+N+A	80	64	52	15	21	56	74	44	26	53	16	57	58	70	14	38	59	47	49	61	48.5
Dai et al.	**None**	58	88	24	25	44	76	69	18	19	33	25	28	52	72	51	34	60	7	35	33	43.2
proposed	**None**	89	68	61	67	60	70	53	82	76	64	88	60	76	80	59	66	43	82	78	72	**69.7**

Table 5: Comparisons of the class-by-class mAPs(%) obtained by benchmark supervised and deep object detector. Testing images in Pascal VOC07 with all 20 classes are evaluated.

Methods	model/train set	aero	bk	brd	boa	bot	bus	car	cat	chr	cow	dtab	dog	hos	mtbk	per	plnt	shp	sofa	tr	tv	Av.
DPM	Latent SVM/07	37	62	12	18	29	55	60	26	21	26	27	15	61	51	45	14	22	38	49	44	35.4
DPM	RCNN/07	68	73	57	43	37	66	74	68	34	64	55	61	69	69	59	33	63	51	63	65	58.5
FRCN	VGG/07	75	78	69	53	37	77	78	82	41	73	68	80	79	73	69	30	65	70	76	66	66.9
RCN-BB	VGG/07	73	77	63	45	45	75	78	80	41	74	62	79	78	73	64	36	67	67	70	71	66.0
SSD300	VGG/07	73	78	64	59	39	75	81	79	46	68	69	77	82	77	73	41	64	69	78	69	68.0
SSD512	VGG/07	75	81	70	61	46	83	85	84	49	75	67	82	84	79	77	45	70	69	78	72	71.6
proposed	**DeepSim/ None**	89	68	61	67	60	70	53	82	76	64	88	60	76	80	59	66	43	82	78	72	69.7

image topic summarization. Exemplar labeling based on the summarization enables DLSM to obtain effective object category identification.

Fig. 2: Discovered latent exemplar images from Pascal-VOC 6x2 that summarizing the latent visual topics. Rows 1-6: "Aeroplane","Bicycle","Boat","Bus","Horse","Motorbike"

5. Conclusions

This paper proposed a deep latent similarity model for unsupervised object inference. The deep distance network is first modeled with a similarity prior and optimized upon a joint probability distribution. A latent categorical similarity function is embedded to structure the categorization. The inference of the model provides similarity scores to indicate how likely a proposal image region localizes an object belonging to a particular category. The proposed object inference outperforms current state-of-the-art unsupervised methods for object discovery. The promising results compared to full-supervised deep object detectors have also shown the effectiveness of the proposed method for unsupervised object detection.

References

[1] R. Girshick, F. Iandola, T. Darrell, and J. Malik, "Deformable part models are convolutional neural networks," in *Proceedings of the IEEE conference on Computer Vision and Pattern Recognition*, 2015, pp. 437–446.

[2] W. Liu, D. Anguelov, D. Erhan, C. Szegedy, S. Reed, C.-Y. Fu, and A. C. Berg, "Ssd: Single shot multibox detector," in *European conference on computer vision*. Springer, 2016, pp. 21–37.

[3] S. Ren, K. He, R. Girshick, and J. Sun, "Faster r-cnn: Towards real-time object detection with region proposal networks," in *Advances in neural information processing systems*, 2015, pp. 91–99.

[4] R. Girshick, J. Donahue, T. Darrell, and J. Malik, "Rich feature hierarchies for accurate object detection and semantic segmentation," in *Proceedings of the IEEE conference on computer vision and pattern recognition*, 2014, pp. 580–587.

[5] K. He, X. Zhang, S. Ren, and J. Sun, "Deep residual learning for image recognition," in *Proceedings of the IEEE conference on computer vision and pattern recognition*, 2016, pp. 770–778.

[6] B. Zhou, A. Khosla, A. Lapedriza, A. Oliva, and A. Torralba, "Learning deep features for discriminative localization," in *Proceedings of the IEEE Conference on Computer Vision and Pattern Recognition*, 2016, pp. 2921–2929.

[7] B. C. Russell, W. T. Freeman, A. A. Efros, J. Sivic, and A. Zisserman, "Using multiple segmentations to discover objects and their extent in image collections," in *2006 IEEE Computer Society Conference on Computer Vision and Pattern Recognition (CVPR'06)*, vol. 2. IEEE, 2006, pp. 1605–1614.

[8] A. Joulin, K. Tang, and L. Fei-Fei, "Efficient image and video co-localization with frank-wolfe algorithm," in *European Conference on Computer Vision*. Springer, 2014, pp. 253–268.

[9] K. Tang, A. Joulin, L.-J. Li, and L. Fei-Fei, "Co-localization in real-world images," in *Proceedings of the IEEE conference on computer vision and pattern recognition*, 2014, pp. 1464–1471.

[10] Z. Niu, G. Hua, L. Wang, and X. Gao, "Knowledge-based topic model for unsupervised object discovery and localization," *IEEE Transactions on Image Processing*, vol. 27, no. 1, pp. 50–63, 2018.

[11] Z. Shi, T. M. Hospedales, and T. Xiang, "Bayesian joint topic modelling for weakly supervised object localisation," in *Computer Vision (ICCV), 2013 IEEE International Conference on*. IEEE, 2013, pp. 2984–2991.

[12] C. Wang, W. Ren, K. Huang, and T. Tan, "Weakly supervised object localization with latent category learning," in *European Conference on Computer Vision*. Springer, 2014, pp. 431–445.

[13] B. J. Frey and D. Dueck, "Clustering by passing messages between data points," *science*, vol. 315, no. 5814, pp. 972–976, 2007.

[14] P. Ji, T. Zhang, H. Li, M. Salzmann, and I. Reid, "Deep subspace clustering networks," in *Advances in Neural Information Processing Systems*, 2017, pp. 24–33.

[15] D. Andrzejewski, X. Zhu, and M. Craven, "Incorporating domain knowledge into topic modeling via dirichlet forest priors," in *Proceedings of the 26th annual international conference on machine learning*. ACM, 2009, pp. 25–32.

[16] G. Kim, C. Faloutsos, and M. Hebert, "Unsupervised modeling of object categories using link analysis techniques," in *2008 IEEE Conference on Computer Vision and Pattern Recognition*. IEEE, 2008, pp. 1–8.

[17] A. Faktor and M. Irani, ""clustering by composition"-unsupervised discovery of image categories," *IEEE transactions on pattern analysis and machine intelligence*, vol. 36, no. 6, pp. 1092–1106, 2014.

[18] M. Cho, S. Kwak, C. Schmid, and J. Ponce, "Unsupervised object discovery and localization in the wild: Part-based matching with bottom-up region proposals," in *Proceedings of the IEEE Conference on Computer Vision and Pattern Recognition*, 2015, pp. 1201–1210.

[19] M. Pandey and S. Lazebnik, "Scene recognition and weakly supervised object localization with deformable part-based models," in *Computer Vision (ICCV), 2011 IEEE International Conference on*. IEEE, 2011, pp. 1307–1314.

[20] P. Siva and T. Xiang, "Weakly supervised object detector learning with model drift detection," in *Computer Vision (ICCV), 2011 IEEE International Conference on*. IEEE, 2011, pp. 343–350.

[21] R. G. Cinbis, J. Verbeek, and C. Schmid, "Multi-fold mil training for weakly supervised object localization," in *Computer Vision and Pattern Recognition (CVPR), 2014 IEEE Conference on*. IEEE, 2014, pp. 2409–2416.

[22] S. Dai, P. Su, and H. Man, "Object discovery and localization via structural contrast," in *2018 25th IEEE International Conference on Image Processing (ICIP)*. IEEE, 2018, pp. 2760–2764.

[23] P. Siva, C. Russell, and T. Xiang, "In defence of negative mining for annotating weakly labelled data," in *European Conference on Computer Vision*. Springer, 2012, pp. 594–608.

[24] P. F. Felzenszwalb, R. B. Girshick, D. McAllester, and D. Ramanan, "Object detection with discriminatively trained part-based models," *IEEE transactions on pattern analysis and machine intelligence*, vol. 32, no. 9, pp. 1627–1645, 2010.

A Short Review on Image Caption Generation with Deep Learning

*Soheyla Amirian**, *Khaled Rasheed*†, *Thiab R. Taha*‡, *Hamid R. Arabnia*§

The University of Georgia
Athens, Georgia, USA

Abstract

Methodologies that utilize Deep Learning offer great potential for applications that automatically attempt to generate captions or descriptions about images. Image captioning is considered to be one of the intellectually challenging problems in imaging science. The application domains include: automatic caption (or description) generation for images for people who suffer from various degrees of visual impairment; the automatic creation of metadata for images (indexing) for use by search engines; general purpose robot vision systems; and many others. Each of these application domains can positively and significantly impact many other task-specific applications. This paper is not meant to be a comprehensive review of image captioning; rather, it is a concise review of image captioning methodologies based on deep learning, strengths and limitations, the datasets and the evaluation metrics used in automatic image captioning. Finally, a quick discussion about the software and hardware requirements for implementing an image captioning method is presented.

Index Terms— Deep Learning, Image Captioning, Long Short Term Memory (LSTM), Graphics Processing Unit (GPU), Tensor Processing Unit (TPU).

1. Introduction

Image processing has played and will continue to play an important role in science and industry. Its applications spread to many areas, including visual recognition [1] and scene understanding [2], to name a few. Before the advent of Deep Learning, most researchers used imaging methods that worked well on rigid objects in controlled environments with specialized hardware [3, 4, 5, 6, 7, 8, 9, 10, 11, 12]. In recent years, deep learning based convolutional neural networks has positively and significantly impacted the field of image captioning allowing a lot more flexibility. In this paper, we attempt to highlight recent advances in the field of image captioning in the context of deep learning. Since 2012, many researchers have participated in advancing the deep learning model design [13], applications and interpretation [14]. The science and methodology behind deep learning have been in existence for decades, but an increasing abundance of digital data and the involvement of powerful GPUs has accelerated the development of deep learning research in recent years. Convenient development libraries such as TensorFlow and PyTorch, the open source community, large labeled datasets (e.g. MSCOCO, Flicker, and...) [15, 16], and splendid demonstrations simulate the explosive growth of the deep learning field.

Describing a scene in an image is a highly demanding task for humans. To create machines with this capability, computer scientists have been exploring methods to connect the science of understanding human language with the science of automatic extraction and analysis of visual information. Image captioning captioning need more effort than image recognition, because of the additional challenge of recognizing the objects and actions in the image and creating a succinct meaningful sentence based on the contents found. The advancement of this process opens up enormous opportunities in many application domains in real life, such as aid to people who suffer from various degrees of visual impairment, self-driving vehicles, sign language translation, human-robot interaction, and more. This paper surveys the state of the art approaches with a focus on deep learning models for image captioning. The models and generated captions are evaluated by using BLEU, METEOR, CIDEr [17, 18, 19], and other metrics.

This paper is a concise review of image captioning methodologies based on deep learning. This review begins by introducing the Image Captioning in Section 2. Then, a few recent methods of Image Captioning, the Datasets and Metrics are discussed in Section 3. Finally, Required Software and Hardware Platforms for implementing a model are mentioned in Section 4.

2. Image Captioning

Image captioning is the process of generating a concise description of an input picture/ image (See Figure 1). Typically, such functions are done manually. Automating this process

*Ph.D. Candidate, Department of Computer Science.
†Director, Institute of Artificial Intelligence; Professor, Department of Computer Science.
‡Professor and Head, Department of Computer Science.
§Professor and Graduate Program Director, Department of Computer Science.

would be a significant contribution. A lot of research has been done on image captioning [20, 21, 22, 23] that are quite impactful. A system that automatically generates image captions can be utilized in many applications. Examples include: enhancing the accuracy of search engines; recognition and vision applications; enriching and creating new image datasets; enhancing the functionality of systems similar to Google Photos; and enhancing the optical system analysis of self-driving vehicles.

Fig. 1. These are a few examples of captions that has been generated for images.

For image captioning there are some challenges in how to extract visual information from the input and how to transform the visual information into a proper and meaningful language. Captioning research started with the classical retrieval and template based [20, 24] approaches in which Subject, Verb, and Object are detected separately and then joined using a sentence template. However, the advent of Deep Learning and the tremendous advancements in Natural Language Processing have equally affected the area of captioning. Hence, latest approaches follow deep learning based architectures that encode the visual features with Convolutional Neural Networks and decode with a language based model, which translates the features and objects given by an image based model to a meaningful sentence.

3. Image Captioning Methodologies

Automatically generating natural language sentences describing an image generally has two components: extracting the visual information, and describing it in a grammatically correct natural language sentence. Figure 2 depicts a simple Encoder-Decoder deep learning based captioning framework for image captioning. By convolutional Neural Network the objects and features are extracted from the image, then we need a network to generate a natural sentence based on the information that we have.

Convolutional Neural Network: There is a need for a model with a large learning capacity to learn about thousands of objects from a large number of images [14]. Deep learning presents computational models that are composed of multiple processing layers to learn representations of data in images [13, 25]. Deep learning based Convolutional Neural Networks play a key role in many applications, one of which is image recognition. Image recognition is used to perform a large number of visual tasks, such as understanding the content of images. There are several well-known models [13] in the field of CNNs based on object detection [1, 26, 27] and segmentation [28].

Recurrent Neural Networks: Sequence models like recurrent neural network (RNN) [29] have widely been utilized in speech recognition, natural language processing, and other areas. Sequence models can address supervised learning problems like machine translation [30], name entity recognition, DNA sequence analysis, and sentiment classification.

Gated Recurrent Unit: Gated recurrent unit (GRU) is a gating mechanism in RNN, introduced in 2014 by Cho et al. [30]. The basic RNN algorithm runs into vanishing gradient problem (a difficulty in training artificial neural networks). The gated recurrent units are an effective solution for addressing the vanishing gradient problem. They allow neural networks to capture a much longer range dependencies [29]. The advantage of the GRU is that it is a simple model and so it is actually easy to build a big network. Also, it only has two gates, so it computes quickly.

Long Short Term Memory: LSTM, as a special RNN structure, has proven to be stable and powerful for modeling long-range dependencies in various studies. LSTM can be adopted as a building block for complex structures. The complex unit in Long Short Term Memory is called a memory cell. Each memory cell is built around a central linear unit with a fixed self-connection [31]. LSTM is historically proven more powerful and more effective than a regular RNN since it has three gates (forget, update, and output). Long Short Term Memory recurrent neural networks can be used to generate complex sequences with long-range structure [32, 33].

3.1. Recent Deep Learning based Models:

There are many methods for image captioning. Earlier methods, prior to deep neural networks (DNNs), were retrieved-based [20] or template-based [24] models. Recent methods are based on deep neural networks. Generating an automatic caption for describing an image has two stages. First, the information needs to be extracted from the image and put it in a feature vector. This stage focuses on visual recognition by deep learning models. Then the feature vector is fed into the

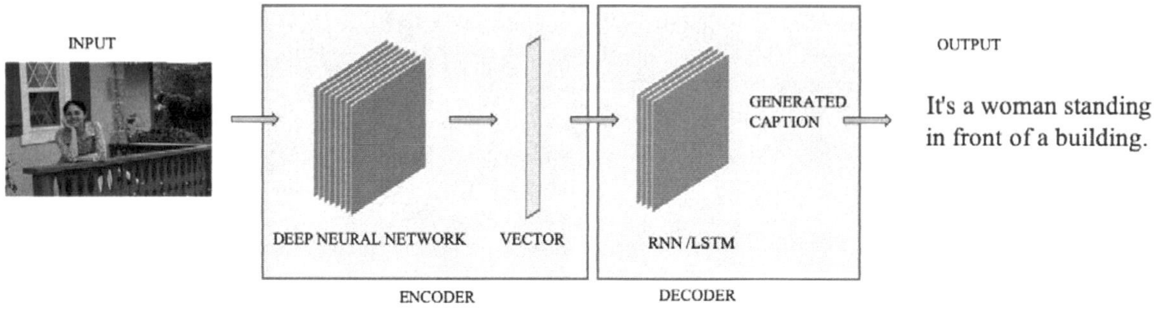

Fig. 2. This is an overall encoder-decoder structure for image captioning models. A deep learning model encodes the image into a feature vector. The language model takes the input vector to generate a sentence that describes the image.

second stage. The second stage is caption generation which is describing what is extracted in a grammatically correct natural language sentence. Figure 2 depicts an overall encoder-decoder structure for image captioning methods. So, we classified DNN-based methods on the basis of the main framework into subcategories that they respectively use. Here, a review of recent deep learning based methods for automatic image captioning is discussed. All are summarized in Table 1.

A major breakthrough in image captioning occurred in 2014 through the application of encoder-decoder models. Kiros et al. introduced an encoder-decoder pipeline model in which an encoder network takes the image as an input and extracts a fixed-size feature vector that a decoder network maps to a sequence of words. They set new best results when using the 19-layer Oxford convolutional network. They were also developing an attention-based model that jointly learns to align parts of captions to images. The generated descriptions are arguably the nicest ones to date [32]. The attention model is one of the models used in deep learning got from one of the most curious facets of the human visual system. Attention-based model learns to focus on different parts of the image. This is important when there is a lot of clutter in an image. However, this may cause losing information which could be useful for richer and more descriptive captions [17].

Xu et al. proposed the attention based approach that gives the state of the art performance on three benchmark datasets using the BLEU and METEOR metric (See section 3.3). They also showed how the learned attention can be exploited to give more interpret ability to the model generation process, and demonstrate that the learned alignments correspond very well to human intuition. Their model encourages future work in using visual attention [17].

You et al. also proposed a model of semantic attention. The algorithm combines top-down and bottom-up strategies to extract richer information from the image, and fuses them with a RNN that can selectively attend on rich semantic attributes detected from the image. They performed their method on the Microsoft COCO and the Flickr30K, and captioning system was implemented based on LSTM network. The image feature vector is extracted from the last 1024 dimensional convolutional layer of the GoogleNet [13] CNN model. Furthermore, their framework employs attention at both input and output layers to the RNN module. Their effort was exploiting abundant fine-grain visual semantic aspects, and fusing global and local information for generating a better caption. The experimental results show that the algorithm significantly outperforms the state-of-the-art approaches consistently across different evaluation metrics [21].

Fu et al. proposed the image caption system that exploits the parallel structures between images and sentences. One contribution of this system is that it aligns the process of generating captions and the attention shifting among the visual regions. Another is that it introduces the scene-specific contexts to LSTM that adapt language models for word generation to specific scene types. The architecture is that, an image is first analyzed and represented with multiple visual regions from which visual features are extracted. The visual feature vectors are then fed into a LSTM network, which predicts both the sequence of focusing on different regions and the sequence of generating words based on the transition of visual attention. The neural network model is also governed by a scene vector, a global visual context extracted from the whole image. Intuitively, it selects a scene-specific language model for generating text. This has been tested on several popular datasets, including MSCOCO, Flickr8K, and Flickr30K. They evaluated captions in BLEU-n, METEOR, ROUGE-L and CIDEr-D metrics (See Table 1). Either region-based attention or scene-specific contexts alone improve performance, but combining the two provides a further improvement [34].

In 2018, Aneja et al. developed a convolutional image captioning technique with existing LSTM techniques and also analyzed the differences between RNN based learning and their method. This technique contains three main components. The first and the last components are input and output word embedding respectively. However, while the middle component contains LSTM or GRU units in the RNN case, masked convolutions are employed in their CNN-based ap-

Table 1. The summary of a few recent works for Image Caption (All the results have been converted to percentages).

Model	Architecture	Evaluation
(2014, Kiros et al.)	CNN+LSTM encoder–decoder Attention-based	Image Annotation result R@1 R@5 R@10 Med r 23.0 50.7 62.9 5 (OxfordNet) on Flickr30K. R@K is Recall@K (high is good). Med r is the median rank (low is good).
(2015, Xu et al.)	CNN+RNN Attention-based	BLEU-1 BLEU-2 BLEU-3 BLEU-4 METEOR 71.8 50.4 35.7 25.0 23.04 Hard attention on MSCOCO
(2016, You et al.)	CNN+RNN Attention-based	BLEU-1 BLEU-2 BLEU-3 BLEU-4 METEOR 70.9 53.7 40.2 30.4 24.3 Using the ground-truth visual attributes on MSCOCO
(2017, Fu et al.)	Region-based attention and scene-specific contexts VGG/Alex/ResNet + LSTM Attention-based	ENSEMBLE result BLEU-1 BLEU-2 BLEU-3 BLEU-4 METEOR ROUGE-L CIDEr-D 72.4 55.5 41.8 31.3 24.8 53.2 95.5 on MSCOCO
(2018, Aneja et al.)	CNN+LSTM ResNet152	BLEU-1 BLEU-2 BLEU-3 BLEU-4 METEOR ROUGE-L CIDEr 72.5 55.5 41 29.9 25.1 53.2 97.2 on MSCOCO
(2018, Anderson et al.)	CNN+LSTM Faster R-CNN;ResNet101 Attention-based	BLEU-1 BLEU-2 BLEU-3 BLEU-4 METEOR ROUGE-L CIDEr SPICE 80.2 64.1 49.1 36.9 27.6 57.1 117.9 21.5 on MSCOCO

proach. This component is feed-forward without any recurrent function. Their CNN with attention (Attn) achieved comparable performance. They also experimented with an attention mechanism by attention parameters using the conv-layer activations. The results of CNN+Attn method were increased rather than the LSTM baseline. For better performance on the MSCOCO they used ResNet features and the results show ResNet boosts their performance on the MSCOCO. The results on the MSCOCO with Resnet101 and Resnet152 were comparable to previous works. Table 1 shows that the METEOR and CIDEr results are outstanding [35].

Anderson et al. proposed a combined bottom-up and top-down attention mechanism that enables attention to be calculated at the level of objects and other salient image regions. The bottom-up attention uses Faster R-CNN with ResNet-101 [13], which represents a natural expression of a bottom-up attention mechanism. The top-down mechanism uses task-specific context to predict an attention distribution over the image regions. The attended feature vector is then computed as a weighted average of image features over all regions. Their results on the MSCOCO dataset present a new state-of-the-art for the task, achieving CIDEr, BLEU-4 scores of 117.9 and 36.9, respectively. Demonstrating the broad applicability of the method, applying the same approach to Visual Question Answering they obtained first place in the 2017 VQA Challenge [36].

3.2. Image Captioning Datasets:

There are a few datasets that are widely used to evaluate and compare image captioning methods: Flickr8K [23], Flickr9K [17], Flickr30k [17, 23] and Microsoft COCO [17, 18].

Flickr: The Flickr8K, 9k, and 30k datasets contain more than 8000, 9000, and 30000 images, respectively. Each image is annotated using Amazon Mechanical Turk with 5 independent sentences. The Flickr8K dataset mainly contains human and animal images, while the Flickr30k dataset contains humans involved in everyday activities and events. For each image, five sentences are provided [17, 23].

COCO: Microsoft Common Objects in COntext (MS-COCO) is a large-scale object detection, segmentation, and captioning dataset that contains 91 object categories, 328K images and five assigned captions to each image [17, 18, 37].

3.3. Image Captioning Evaluation Metrics:

Captions are evaluated using the BLEU, METEOR, CIDEr, and other metrics [17, 18, 19]. These metrics are common for comparing the different image captioning models, and have varying degrees of similarity with human judgment [38].

BLEU: BiLingual Evaluation Understudy is a method of automatic machine translation evaluation that is a precision-based metric, correlates highly with human evaluation, and has a little marginal cost per run [17, 39]. BLEU has different n-grams based versions for candidate sentences with respect to the reference sentences.

METEOR: Metric for Evaluation of Translation with Explicit ORdering is an automatic metric that evaluates translation hypotheses. It is based on a generalized concept of unigram matching between the machine-produced translation and human-produced reference translations [17, 18, 40, 41].

CIDEr: Consensus-based Image Description Evaluation enables an objective comparison of machine generation approaches based on their human-likeness, without having to make arbitrary calls on weighing content, grammar, saliency, etc. with respect to each other [19]. CIDEr was first developed specifically for evaluating image captioning tasks, but it is also used in video captioning methods.

ROUGE: Recall-Oriented Understudy for Gisting Evaluation determines the quality of a summary by comparing it to other summaries created by humans. ROUGE, similar to BLEU, has different n-grams based versions [42].

SPICE: Anderson et al. introduced Semantic Propositional Image Captioning Evaluation, a novel semantic evaluation metric that measures how effectively image captions recover objects, attributes, and the relations between them. It correlates more with human judgment of semantic quality as compared to previously reported metrics [43].

WMD: Word Mover's Distance measures the dissimilarity between two text documents. Therefore, the sensitivity of this metric when compared to BLUE, ROUGE, and CIDEr, is low about word order or synonym swapping, but, like CIDEr and METEOR, provides high correlation with human judgments [44].

3.4. Discussion:

In this section, we briefly reviewed a few methods, according to the common approaches that they have used. For fair comparison of the models, Table 1 shows the results of attention-based methods on the MSCOCO dataset, the common dataset that they have utilized. We could state that Anderson et al. performed better on the MSCOCO dataset. This method outperformed previous works. The reason is that it uses the attention mechanism which focuses only on relevant objects of the image. Also, We found that the performance of a technique can vary across different metrics, parameters and datasets. Here, we tried to compare them based on the common performance criteria. However, image captioning still has a long way to go in improving the accuracy of captioning the events in images (See Figure 3).

Fig. 3. Image captioning still have a big room in improving the accuracy of describing the events and objects in images.

4. The Required Platform for Implementation:

Deep Learning has dramatically improved the accuracy of image recognition. Image recognition is considered to be one of the most challenging problems in image science. In recent years, deep learning based convolutional neural networks have positively and significantly impacted the field of image recognition allowing a lot of flexibility. Deep Learning is responsible for many of the recent breakthroughs in image science, such as image captioning. Despite Deep Learning's popularity, it is difficult to accurately predict the time that it takes to train a deep learning network to solve a given problem. The training time can be seen as the product of the training time per epoch and the number of epochs which need to be performed to reach the desired level of accuracy. We define the features which could influence the prediction of execution time while performing the training. We categorize these features into layer, implementation, and hardware features. Each of these categories can contain almost an endless list of features. Layer (Algorithm or model) Features include Activation Function (ReLU, Softmax, Tanh,...), Optimizer (Gradient Descent, Momentum, Adam,...), Batch Size (the number of training samples which are processed together as part of the same batch), Number of inputs to the layer, the neurons within the layer, Matrix, Kernel, Stride, and Padding size. Hardware Features include CPU, GPU or TPU technology (memory, clock, speed, bandwidth,...) [45].

4.1. Software Requirement:

Tensorflow: TensorFlow is an end-to-end open source platform for machine learning. TensorFlow is developed by Google and has integrated the most common units in deep learning frameworks. It supports many up-to-date networks such as CNN and RNN with different settings. TensorFlow is designed for remarkable flexibility, portability, and high efficiency of equipped hardware [46].

PyTorch: PyTorch is a Python-based scientific computing package that serves two purposes: as a replacement for NumPy to use the power of GPUs and as a deep learning research platform that provides maximum flexibility and speed[1] [35].

Keras: Keras is a high-level neural network API, written in Python and capable of running on top of TensorFlow, CNTK, or Theano. It was developed with a focus on enabling fast experimentation. Being able to go from idea to result with the least possible delay is the key to doing good research. Keras allows for easy and fast prototyping (through user friendliness, modularity, and extensibility). Keras supports both convolutional networks and recurrent networks, as well as a combination of both. Keras runs seamlessly on CPU and GPU[2].

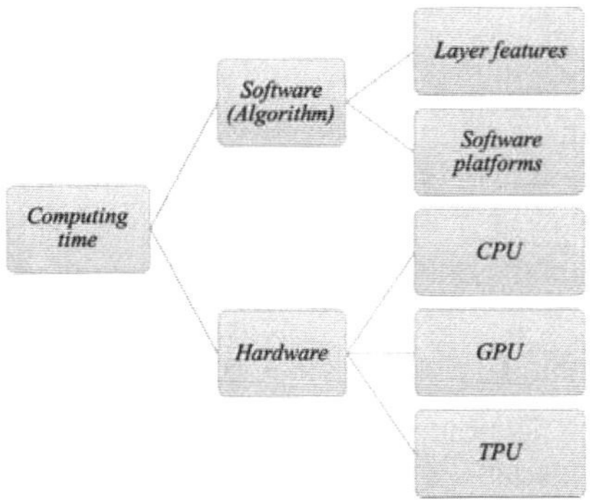

Fig. 4. Computing time dependencies

4.2. Hardware Requirement:

The science and methodology behind deep learning have been in existence for decades. In recent years, however, there has been a significant acceleration in the utilization of deep learning due to an increasing abundance of digital data and the involvement of the powerful hardware.

GPU: Compared to CPU, the performance of matrix multiplication on Graphics Processing Unit is significantly better. With GPU computing resources, all the deep learning tools mentioned achieve much higher speedup when compared to their CPU-only versions [46]. GPUs have become the platform of choice for training large, complex Neural Network-based systems because of their ability to accelerate the systems. For example, it used to take a few days to train AlexNet (the work of Krizhevsky et al. [14] which outperformed all other image recognition approaches at the time [13]) on the ImagetNet dataset with a NVIDIA K40 machine. Now with DGX-2, NVIDIA group are able to train AlexNet in a few minutes[3]. Shi et al. worked to evaluate the running time performance of a set of modern deep learning software tools and see how they perform on different types of neural networks and different hardware platforms. They showed that all tested tools can make good use of GPUs to achieve significant speedup over their CPU counterparts. There is no single software tool that can consistently outperform others, however, which implies that there exist some opportunities to further optimize the performance [46].

TPU: Tensor Processing Unit (Domain-Specific Architecture) is a custom chip that has been deployed in Google data centers since 2015. DNNs are dominated by tensors, so the architects created instructions that operate on tensors of data rather than one data element per instruction [47]. To reduce the time of deployment, TPU was designed to be a coprocessor on the PCI Express (PCIe) I/O bus rather than be tightly integrated with a CPU, allowing it to plug into existing servers just as a GPU does. The goal was to run whole inference models in the TPU to reduce I/O between the TPU and the host CPU. Minimalism is a virtue of domain-specific processors. Jouppi et al. show in their paper that the TPU leverages its advantages to run 15 times as fast as the K80 GPU, resulting in a performance/ Watt advantage of 29 times. While future CPUs and GPUs will surely run inference faster, a redesigned TPU using circa-2015 GPU memory would go three times faster and boost the performance/ Watt advantage to nearly 70 over the K80 and 200 over Haswell CPU [33, 47].

5. Conclusion and Future Work

There are many models that have already been presented to generate meaningful captions for images. These models are quite good, but have some constraints. Image captioning still have a long way to go in improving the accuracy of captioning the events in images (See Figure 3). We reviewed some of the recent deep learning based works, and it is hard to compare different works due to the different combination of structures, using different parameters and implying various datasets. We also noticed that there is a lot of room for improvement in accuracy.

Researchers attempt to give sight to the machines. First, machines learn to see. Then, they help us to see better. We will not only use the machines because of their intelligence, we will also collaborate with them in ways that we cannot even imagine. By improving image captioning models, we can further aid people with hearing or sight impairments as well as improving search engines.

[1] https://pytorch.org/tutorials/beginner/blitz/tensor-tutorial.html
[2] https://keras.io/
[3] https://devblogs.nvidia.com/tensor-core-ai-performance-milestones/

6. Acknowledgement

We gratefully acknowledge the support of NVIDIA Corporation with the donation of the Titan V GPU used for this research.

7. References

[1] Joseph Redmon and Ali Farhadi, "Yolov3: An incremental improvement," *arXiv preprint arXiv:1804.02767*, 2018.

[2] Marius Cordts, Mohamed Omran, Sebastian Ramos, Timo Rehfeld, Markus Enzweiler, Rodrigo Benenson, Uwe Franke, Stefan Roth, and Bernt Schiele, "The cityscapes dataset for semantic urban scene understanding," in *Proceedings of the IEEE conference on computer vision and pattern recognition*, 2016, pp. 3213–3223.

[3] Hamid R Arabnia and Martin A Oliver, "Fast operations on raster images with simd machine architectures," in *Computer Graphics Forum*. Wiley Online Library, 1986, vol. 5, pp. 179–188.

[4] SM Bhandarkar and Hamid R Arabnia, "Parallel computer vision on a reconfigurable multiprocessor network," *IEEE Transactions on Parallel and Distributed Systems*, vol. 8, no. 3, pp. 292–309, 1997.

[5] Homayoun Valafar, Hamid R Arabnia, and Gita Williams, "Distributed global optimization and its development on the multiring network," *Neural, Parallel & Scientific Computations*, vol. 12, no. 4, pp. 465–490, 2004.

[6] David Luper, Delroy Cameron, John Miller, and Hamid R Arabnia, "Spatial and temporal target association through semantic analysis and gps data mining.," in *IKE*, 2007, vol. 7, pp. 25–28.

[7] Rabia Jafri and Hamid R Arabnia, "Fusion of face and gait for automatic human recognition," in *Information Technology: New Generations, 2008. ITNG 2008. Fifth International Conference on*. IEEE, 2008, pp. 167–173.

[8] Hamid R Arabnia, Wai-Chi Fang, Changhoon Lee, and Yan Zhang, "Context-aware middleware and intelligent agents for smart environments," *IEEE Intelligent Systems*, vol. 25, no. 2, pp. 10–11, 2010.

[9] Rabia Jafri, Syed Abid Ali, and Hamid R Arabnia, "Computer vision-based object recognition for the visually impaired using visual tags," in *Proceedings of the International Conference on Image Processing, Computer Vision, and Pattern Recognition (IPCV)*. The Steering Committee of The World Congress in Computer Science, Computer Engineering and Applied Computing (WorldComp), 2013, p. 1.

[10] Leonidas Deligiannidis and Hamid R Arabnia, "Parallel video processing techniques for surveillance applications," in *Computational Science and Computational Intelligence (CSCI), 2014 International Conference on*. IEEE, 2014, vol. 1, pp. 183–189.

[11] Ebrahim Parcham, Neda Mandami, A Nicki Washington, and Hamid R Arabnia, "Facial expression recognition based on fuzzy networks," in *Computational Science and Computational Intelligence (CSCI), 2016 International Conference on*. IEEE, 2016, pp. 829–835.

[12] Ahmad P Tafti, Ahmadreza Baghaie, Mehdi Assefi, Hamid R Arabnia, Zeyun Yu, and Peggy Peissig, "Ocr as a service: An experimental evaluation of google docs ocr, tesseract, abbyy finereader, and transym," in *International Symposium on Visual Computing*. Springer, 2016, pp. 735–746.

[13] Soheyla Amirian, Zengyan Wang, Thiab R. Taha, and Hamid R. Arabnia, "Dissection of deep learning with applications in image recognition," in *Computational Science and Computational Intelligence; "Artificial Intelligence" (CSCI-ISAI); 2018 International Conference on. IEEE*, 2018, pp. 1132–1138.

[14] Alex Krizhevsky, Ilya Sutskever, and Geoffrey E Hinton, "Imagenet classification with deep convolutional neural networks," in *Advances in Neural Information Processing Systems 25*, F. Pereira, C. J. C. Burges, L. Bottou, and K. Q. Weinberger, Eds., pp. 1097–1105. Curran Associates, Inc., 2012.

[15] Michaela Regneri, Marcus Rohrbach, Dominikus Wetzel, Stefan Thater, Bernt Schiele, and Manfred Pinkal, "Grounding action descriptions in videos," *Transactions of the Association for Computational Linguistics*, vol. 1, pp. 25–36, 2013.

[16] Anna Rohrbach, Atousa Torabi, Marcus Rohrbach, Niket Tandon, Christopher Pal, Hugo Larochelle, Aaron Courville, and Bernt Schiele, "Movie description," *International Journal of Computer Vision*, vol. 123, no. 1, pp. 94–120, 2017.

[17] Kelvin Xu, Jimmy Ba, Ryan Kiros, Kyunghyun Cho, Aaron Courville, Ruslan Salakhudinov, Rich Zemel, and Yoshua Bengio, "Show, attend and tell: Neural image caption generation with visual attention," in *International conference on machine learning*, 2015, pp. 2048–2057.

[18] Xinlei Chen, Hao Fang, Tsung-Yi Lin, Ramakrishna Vedantam, Saurabh Gupta, Piotr Dollár, and

C Lawrence Zitnick, "Microsoft coco captions: Data collection and evaluation server," *arXiv preprint arXiv:1504.00325*, 2015.

[19] Ramakrishna Vedantam, C Lawrence Zitnick, and Devi Parikh, "Cider: Consensus-based image description evaluation," in *Proceedings of the IEEE conference on computer vision and pattern recognition*, 2015, pp. 4566–4575.

[20] Ali Farhadi, Mohsen Hejrati, Mohammad Amin Sadeghi, Peter Young, Cyrus Rashtchian, Julia Hockenmaier, and David Forsyth, "Every picture tells a story: Generating sentences from images," in *European conference on computer vision*. Springer, 2010, pp. 15–29.

[21] Quanzeng You, Hailin Jin, Zhaowen Wang, Chen Fang, and Jiebo Luo, "Image captioning with semantic attention," in *Proceedings of the IEEE conference on computer vision and pattern recognition*, 2016, pp. 4651–4659.

[22] Qi Wu, Chunhua Shen, Lingqiao Liu, Anthony Dick, and Anton van den Hengel, "What value do explicit high level concepts have in vision to language problems?," in *Proceedings of the IEEE conference on computer vision and pattern recognition*, 2016, pp. 203–212.

[23] Andrej Karpathy, Armand Joulin, and Li F Fei-Fei, "Deep fragment embeddings for bidirectional image sentence mapping," in *Advances in neural information processing systems*, 2014, pp. 1889–1897.

[24] Siming Li, Girish Kulkarni, Tamara L Berg, Alexander C Berg, and Yejin Choi, "Composing simple image descriptions using web-scale n-grams," in *Proceedings of the Fifteenth Conference on Computational Natural Language Learning*. Association for Computational Linguistics, 2011, pp. 220–228.

[25] Yann LeCun, Yoshua Bengio, and Geoffrey Hinton, "Deep learning," *nature*, vol. 521, no. 7553, pp. 436, 2015.

[26] Ross Girshick, Jeff Donahue, Trevor Darrell, and Jitendra Malik, "Rich feature hierarchies for accurate object detection and semantic segmentation," in *Proceedings of the IEEE conference on computer vision and pattern recognition*, 2014, pp. 580–587.

[27] Ross Girshick, "Fast r-cnn," in *Proceedings of the IEEE international conference on computer vision*, 2015, pp. 1440–1448.

[28] Bernardino Romera-Paredes and Philip Hilaire Sean Torr, "Recurrent instance segmentation," in *European Conference on Computer Vision*. Springer, 2016, pp. 312–329.

[29] Junyoung Chung, Caglar Gulcehre, KyungHyun Cho, and Yoshua Bengio, "Empirical evaluation of gated recurrent neural networks on sequence modeling," *arXiv preprint arXiv:1412.3555*, 2014.

[30] Kyunghyun Cho, Bart Van Merriënboer, Caglar Gulcehre, Dzmitry Bahdanau, Fethi Bougares, Holger Schwenk, and Yoshua Bengio, "Learning phrase representations using rnn encoder-decoder for statistical machine translation," *arXiv preprint arXiv:1406.1078*, 2014.

[31] Sepp Hochreiter and Jürgen Schmidhuber, "Long short-term memory," *Neural computation*, vol. 9, no. 8, pp. 1735–1780, 1997.

[32] Ryan Kiros, Ruslan Salakhutdinov, and Richard S Zemel, "Unifying visual-semantic embeddings with multimodal neural language models," *arXiv preprint arXiv:1411.2539*, 2014.

[33] Yonghui Wu, Mike Schuster, Zhifeng Chen, Quoc V Le, Mohammad Norouzi, Wolfgang Macherey, Maxim Krikun, Yuan Cao, Qin Gao, Klaus Macherey, et al., "Google's neural machine translation system: Bridging the gap between human and machine translation," *arXiv preprint arXiv:1609.08144*, 2016.

[34] Kun Fu, Junqi Jin, Runpeng Cui, Fei Sha, and Changshui Zhang, "Aligning where to see and what to tell: Image captioning with region-based attention and scene-specific contexts," *IEEE transactions on pattern analysis and machine intelligence*, vol. 39, no. 12, pp. 2321–2334, 2017.

[35] Jyoti Aneja, Aditya Deshpande, and Alexander G Schwing, "Convolutional image captioning," in *Proceedings of the IEEE Conference on Computer Vision and Pattern Recognition*, 2018, pp. 5561–5570.

[36] Peter Anderson, Xiaodong He, Chris Buehler, Damien Teney, Mark Johnson, Stephen Gould, and Lei Zhang, "Bottom-up and top-down attention for image captioning and visual question answering," in *Proceedings of the IEEE Conference on Computer Vision and Pattern Recognition*, 2018, pp. 6077–6086.

[37] Tsung-Yi Lin, Michael Maire, Serge Belongie, James Hays, Pietro Perona, Deva Ramanan, Piotr Dollár, and C Lawrence Zitnick, "Microsoft coco: Common objects in context," in *European conference on computer vision*. Springer, 2014, pp. 740–755.

[38] Gunnar A Sigurdsson, Gül Varol, Xiaolong Wang, Ali Farhadi, Ivan Laptev, and Abhinav Gupta, "Hollywood in homes: Crowdsourcing data collection for activity understanding," in *European Conference on Computer Vision*. Springer, 2016, pp. 510–526.

[39] Kishore Papineni, Salim Roukos, Todd Ward, and Wei-Jing Zhu, "Bleu: a method for automatic evaluation of machine translation," in *Proceedings of the 40th annual meeting on association for computational linguistics*. Association for Computational Linguistics, 2002, pp. 311–318.

[40] Michael Denkowski and Alon Lavie, "Meteor universal: Language specific translation evaluation for any target language," in *Proceedings of the ninth workshop on statistical machine translation*, 2014, pp. 376–380.

[41] Satanjeev Banerjee and Alon Lavie, "Meteor: An automatic metric for mt evaluation with improved correlation with human judgments," in *Proceedings of the acl workshop on intrinsic and extrinsic evaluation measures for machine translation and/or summarization*, 2005, pp. 65–72.

[42] Chin-Yew Lin, "Rouge: A package for automatic evaluation of summaries," *Text Summarization Branches Out*, 2004.

[43] Peter Anderson, Basura Fernando, Mark Johnson, and Stephen Gould, "Spice: Semantic propositional image caption evaluation," in *European Conference on Computer Vision*. Springer, 2016, pp. 382–398.

[44] Matt Kusner, Yu Sun, Nicholas Kolkin, and Kilian Weinberger, "From word embeddings to document distances," in *International Conference on Machine Learning*, 2015, pp. 957–966.

[45] Daniel Justus, John Brennan, Stephen Bonner, and Andrew Stephen McGough, "Predicting the computational cost of deep learning models," in *2018 IEEE International Conference on Big Data (Big Data)*. IEEE, 2018, pp. 3873–3882.

[46] Shaohuai Shi, Qiang Wang, Pengfei Xu, and Xiaowen Chu, "Benchmarking state-of-the-art deep learning software tools," in *2016 7th International Conference on Cloud Computing and Big Data (CCBD)*. IEEE, 2016, pp. 99–104.

[47] Norman Jouppi, Cliff Young, Nishant Patil, and David Patterson, "Motivation for and evaluation of the first tensor processing unit," *IEEE Micro*, vol. 38, no. 3, pp. 10–19, 2018.

Improved Stereo Matching based on Convolutional Neural Network

Yingnan Geng[1,2], Mi Lu[2], Baixiu Ding[2,3], Wenrui Zhang[2], and Yindong Hua[2]
[1]Electrical and Information Engineering, Changchun Institute of Technology, Changchun, Jilin, China
[2]Electrical and Computer Engineering, Texas A&M University, College Station, Texas, USA
[3]Electrical Engineering and Computer, Jilin Jianzhu University, Changchun, Jilin, China

Abstract— *The MC-CNN (as Matching Cost Convolutional Neural Network) based on Convolutional Neural Network (CNN) obtains good results in stereo matching. However, it often takes tremendous time to run algorithms by GPU, because stereo images are big and the training module takes a lot of samples. In this paper, T-CNN, a stereo matching algorithm consisting of two main modules: training and testing is proposed. For the training module, fewer samples from the stereo image patches are trained in order to reduce the running time. For the testing module, we combine the values from the MC-CNN network, color information and gradient information to obtain cost matching function. In our experiments, the matching costs of T-CNN are compared with that of MC-CNN networks, showing that our algorithm T-CNN outperforms the MC-CNN.*

Keywords: stereo matching, convolutional neural network, disparity map, color similarity, gradient similarity

1. Introduction

Stereo matching, finding corresponding pixels and obtaining disparity map from stereo images: reference image and target image, is always a basic problem in stereo vision and has been used in many fields such as 3D scene reconstruction, autonomous driving and intermediate view generation. For pixel (x, y) in the reference image and pixel $(x - d, y)$ in the target image, the difference d in horizontal location of an pixel is called the disparity. Then the depth Z_{depth} can be computed by equation (1). And 3D coordinates (X, Y, Z) can be obtained from (2), where f is the focal length of the camera and B is the distance between the camera centers. As depth and 3D coordinates can be obtained by disparity values, a stereo matching system aims to produce an accurate dense disparity map[1].

$$Z_{depth} = \frac{fB}{d} \quad (1)$$

$$\begin{cases} X = \dfrac{Bx}{d} \\ Y = \dfrac{By}{d} \\ Z = \dfrac{Bf}{d} \end{cases} \quad (2)$$

*This work was supported by the Science Foundation of education department of Jilin Province during '13rd Five-year plan'(JJKH20191255KJ).

Stereo matching algorithms consist of four steps: matching cost computation, cost aggregation, disparity optimization, and disparity refinement[2]. Among the approaches of stereo matching including global approaches, local approaches and learning approaches, CNN-based approaches as learning approaches are mainly used in two steps for stereo matching: matching cost computing and disparity refinement.

To compute the matching cost, traditional cost metrics, including the sum of absolute or squared difference (SAD/SSD), normalized cross correlation (NCC), gradient-based measure and adaptive support-weights metrics[3], compute matching cost in image patches directly. For CNN-based approaches, pairs of small image patches are trained, where the true disparities are known. The disparities are chosen based on the output values of a network. Zbontar[4] presented a siamese network with two shared-weight sub-networks. The cosine similarity measure were used to compute two output vectors from sub-networks and the final output values of network was obtained. Han[5] presented a MatchNet system which extracted features from patches and computed a similarity between the extracted features. Mayer[6] proposed the basic architecture DispNet for disparity estimation. Chen[7] learned a deep embedding model with fewer parameters and shallower network structures to extract discriminative features from patches in stereo pairs. Chang[8] added global context information to form a cost volume.

In disparity refinement, confidence measure is used to eliminate unreliable disparity values after computing the disparity maps. Confidence is classified into four groups: matching cost-based confidence measures, disparity-based confidence measures, image-based confidence measures, and prior-based confidence measures. In [9], the effective confidence measures in the random forest framework are selected to build a better prediction model. Pang[10] used residual learning across multiple scales, referenced as DispResNet to obtain more effective refinement. Shaked[11] proposed a new highway network architecure and the network outputs a disparity map, which replaces the convolutional "winner takes all".

Although CNN-based approaches are booming recently, big data and complex computation for stereo matching are still of problems. GPU is needed to run the programs, and training and testing take many hours. In this paper, we will

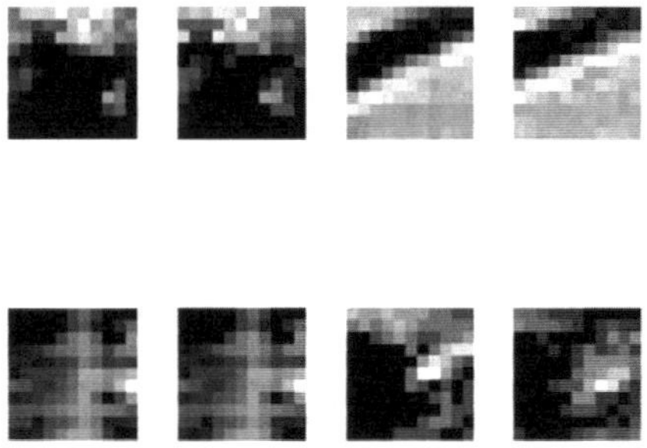

Fig. 1: Four pairs of training images with 11*11: left: reference image patches, right: constructed target image patches

focus on the matching cost from a rectified image pair. According to the MC-CNN model proposed[4], we use fewer samples for the training module. In the testing procedure, color and gradient information are combined with the output values of MC-CNN network between image patches in order to choose the final disparity.

2. MC-CNN Algorithm

The matching cost of MC-CNN is

$$C_{CNN}(p_0, d) = -s(< \boldsymbol{P}_L(p_0), \boldsymbol{P}_R(p_0 - d) >) \quad (3)$$

where C_{CNN} is the output of network when run on input reference patches with center pixel p_0 and target patches with center pixel $(p_0 - d)$.

The training network is a Siamese network. The stereo images are normalizated and partitioned into 11*11 patches. As shown in Fig. 1, there are four pairs of stereo image patches. In each pair, the left image patch is the reference image patch, and the right one is the reconstructed target image patch, which is computed as in (4).

$$q_{new}(x_{new}, y) = p_0(x - d, y) \quad (4)$$

where q_{new} is the rebuilt target pixel. p_0 is the reference pixel, and d is the groundtruth disparity value of p_0.

The network is shown in Fig. 2. From reference image patches and reconstructed image patches, some samples are selected to be input to the network. Each pair goes through four convolutional layers with kernel size 3*3 and the number of filter 112, followed by a rectified linear unit in each layer. Then the two vectors are concatenated and go through three dense layers with units 384, followed by a rectified linear unit. At last, the dense layer with sigmoid nonlinearity is added and the similarity score is obtained. The correct disparity corresponds to a big output value.

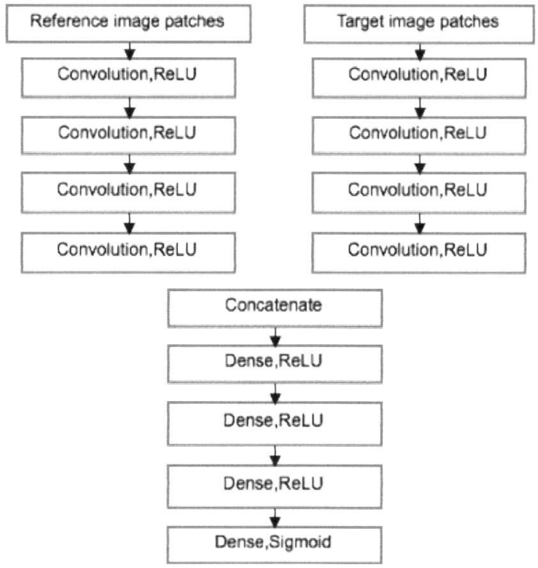

Fig. 2: Flowchart of MC-CNN

3. T-CNN Algorithm

As we all know, stereo matching methods based on learning are complex. Stereo images are often big. It usually takes a lot of time to run an algorithm by GPU. Consider data from KITTI 2012 for example. The size of color stereo images are 375*1240*3. If images are partitioned into size 11*11 image patches with each pixel centered in the reference image, there are 375*1240 = 465000 image patches. If in the reference image each image patch finds the corresponding image patches with possible disparities which are from 0 to 200 for KITTI 2012, there are 465000*200 = 93000000 possible matching patches for training in the target image. If all the samples are input to the network for the training, it is very time-consuming.

Is there any algorithm which can use fewer samples to obtain accurate dense disparity values? We propose a method referenced as T-CNN to combine the learning methods and traditional methods. Traditional methods including local algoirthms and global algorihtms, which obtain dense disparity maps, have been used for many years. If the cost of CNN values, as a new item, can be incorporated into the traditional algorithms, it will improve the performance of algorithm.

The flowchart of T-CNN is shown in Fig. 3. Stereo images are partitioned into small image patches with size 11*11. For a reference image patch with center pixel $p_0(x_0, y_0)$, the corresponding image patch in target image patch is centered as pixel $q_0(x_0 - d, y_0)$, $d \in [d_{min}, d_{max}]$. While finding the correspondence between reference image patches and target image patches, color difference, gradient difference and MC-CNN values are considered together as given in (5). Then the best disparities of each pixel correspond to the max cost values. At last, a new target image is reconstructed based on

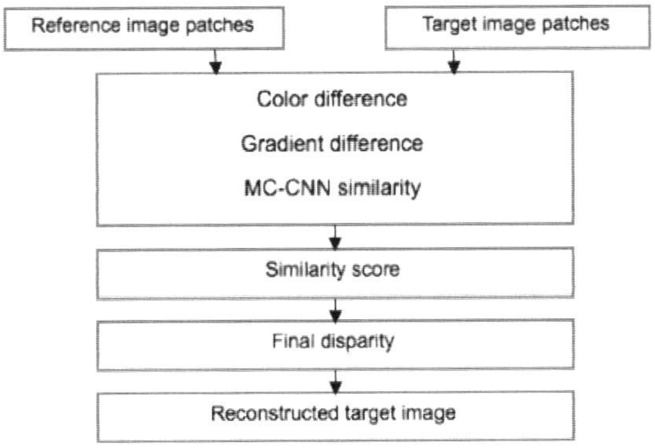

Fig. 3: Flowchart of T-CNN

the disparities and the reference image.

$$cost = \sum_{p \in W} exp(-\frac{dif_{color}}{a} - \frac{dif_{gradient}}{b}) + c \cdot V_{MC} \quad (5)$$

where dif_{color} and $dif_{gradient}$ are the color difference and the gradient difference between two image patches respectively, computed by the Euclidean distance shown in (6) and (7). V_{MC} is the output of MC-CNN network. a, b and c are constants.

$$dif_{color} = \sqrt{(\boldsymbol{I}_{reference}(p) - \boldsymbol{I}_{target}(q))^2} \quad (6)$$

$$dif_{gradient} = \sqrt{(\boldsymbol{G}_{reference}(p) - \boldsymbol{G}_{target}(q))^2} \quad (7)$$

where $\boldsymbol{I}$ are RGB values of an pixel. p is any pixel in an reference image patch with center pixel p_0, and q is any pixel in an target image patch with center pixel q_0. W is a set for all pixels in an reference image patch. $\boldsymbol{G}$ are the gradient values of an pixel including gradient values along x-axis and y-axis[3].

4. Experimental Results

4.1 Training

Training is the first step of learning methods. There are 465000 image patches for a pair of stereo image from KITTI 2012. In section 2 of MC-CNN, some image patches are extracted as samples to be trained. And the relationship between different sample numbers for the training module, and accurate training are listed in Table I.

In Table I, test score is the value of loss function which is $binary - crossentropy$. The times of training for different sample numbers are shown in "Time" column. From Table I, we can see that as the sample number is increasing, the test score is decreasing and the test accuracy is bigger, but the training takes longer time. In this paper, 10000 samples are used to train.

Table 1: Training with different sample

Sample number	Test score	Test accuracy	Time(s)
1000	0.78	0.50	508.22
3000	0.50	0.65	772.30
4000	0.48	0.66	772.30
5000	0.49	0.65	852.85
10000	0.25	0.86	1916.46
20000	0.27	0.86	4814.77

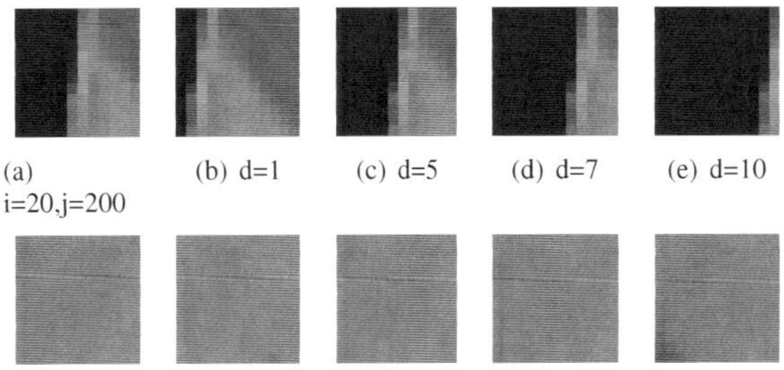

(a) i=20,j=200 (b) d=1 (c) d=5 (d) d=7 (e) d=10

(f) i=20,j=230 (g) d=1 (h) d=5 (i) d=7 (j) d=10

Fig. 4: Image patches with 11*11 size

4.2 MC-CNN

MC-CNN values are utilized to test if they can be utilized in stereo matching methods. Take two pairs of image patches centered at $p(20, 200)$ and $p(20, 230)$ for example, which belong to the edge area and smooth area in the reference image respectively. Reference image patches and their corresponding patches with different disparities in the target image are shown in Fig. 4, where d is the disparity value. Fig. 4(a) and (f) give reference image patches. Fig. 4(b-c) and Fig. 4(g-j) are target image patches with difference disparities. In Fig. 5, MC-CNN values are related to stereo image pairs with different disparities.

From Fig. 4 and Fig. 5, we can see that for the image patch centered at $p(20, 200)$, the best disparity is around $d = 5$. The MC-CNN value for $d = 5$ is the smallest. For the image patch centered at $p(20, 230)$, the best disparity is below $d = 10$ and the MC-CNN values are smaller undered $d = 10$.

Therefore, the MC-CNN network values can be used to match stereo image patches, and better dispairty correponds to smaller vaules. Because MC-CNN network values are small, they have to be normalizated to a range from 0 to 1.

4.3 Reconstructed target images

Stereo images 'Sawtooth' and 'Venus' from Middlebury stereo benchmark are used to evaluate our algorithm T-CNN. The hyper-parameters of T-CNN are as follows: a = 40, b = 20, c = 0.5. Rebuilt target images are used to compare the performance of algorithms shown in Fig. 6. Fig. 6(a) and Fig. 6(d) are the target images for 'Venus' and 'Sawtooth'.

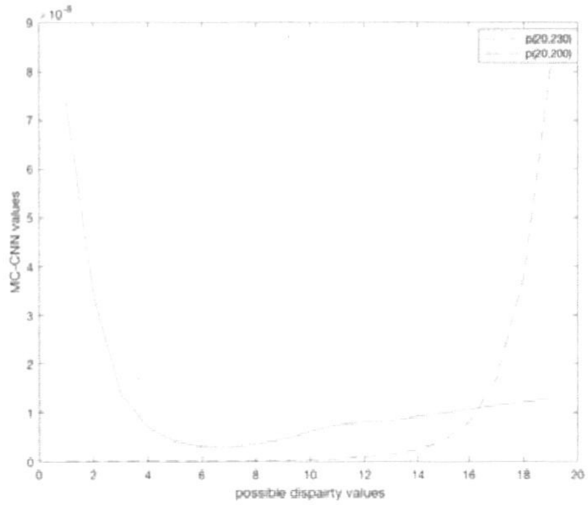

Fig. 5: MC-CNN values for the image patches $p(20, 200)$ and $p(20, 230)$

(a) target image for 'Venus'

(b) MC-CNN

(c) T-CNN

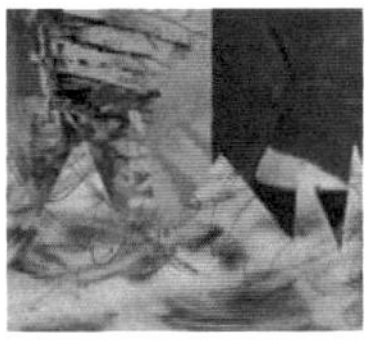

(d) target image for 'Sawtooth'

(e) MC-CNN

(f) T-CNN

Fig. 6: Rebuilt target image

Fig. 6(b) and Fig. 6(e) are rebuilt target images by MC-CNN. Fig. 6(c) and Fig. 6(f) are reconstructed target images by T-CNN. From Fig. 6, we can see that the edge areas rebuilt by T-CNN are more similar to that in target images.

The PSNR and SSIM values of rebuilt target images by T-CNN are also compared with those by MC-CNN. The PSNR and SSIM values are given in Table II and Table III respectively. The bigger the two values, the better the perceived quality of images. From Table II and Table III, we can see that the rebuilt target images by T-CNN are better than that by MC-CNN.

Table 2: PSNR Results

stereo images	T-CNN	MC-CNN
Venus	25.26	17.58
Sawtooth	23.57	16.68

Table 3: SSIM Results

stereo images	T-CNN	MC-CNN
Venus	0.8435	0.4712
Sawtooth	0.8043	0.3790

5. Conclusion

We have proposed a new stereo matching algorithm aimed at matching cost, which combines the learning methods with the traditional methods. The algorithms consists of two main modules: training and testing. By reducing the time of training, and combining color information and gradient information with MC-CNN values, a better matching cost can be obtained. In our experiment the matching cost extracted from MC-CNN is compared with that of our algorithm. Using the matching cost, dense disparity values are obtained by "winner takes all". By disparity values and the reference image, target images are rebuilt. From image visual quality, PSNR and SSIM results, T-CNN obtains the better disparity and better performance.

References

[1] Liang, Zhengfa, et al. "Learning for disparity estimation through feature constancy." *Proceedings of the IEEE Conference on Computer Vision and Pattern Recognition*. 2018.

[2] Scharstein, Daniel, and Richard Szeliski. "A taxonomy and evaluation of dense two-frame stereo correspondence algorithms." *International journal of computer vision* 47.1-3 (2002): 7-42.

[3] Geng, Yingnan, Yan Zhao, and Hexin Chen. "Stereo matching based on adaptive support-weight approach in RGB vector space." *Applied optics* 51.16 (2012): 3538-3545.

[4] Zbontar, Jure, and Yann LeCun. "Stereo Matching by Training a Convolutional Neural Network to Compare Image Patches." *Journal of Machine Learning Research* 17.1-32 (2016): 2.

[5] Han, Xufeng, et al. "Matchnet: Unifying feature and metric learning for patch-based matching." *Proceedings of the IEEE Conference on Computer Vision and Pattern Recognition*. pp. 3279-3286. 2015.

[6] Mayer, Nikolaus, et al. "A large dataset to train convolutional networks for disparity, optical flow, and scene flow estimation." *Proceedings of the IEEE Conference on Computer Vision and Pattern Recognition*. pp. 4040-4048. 2016.

[7] Chen, Zhuoyuan, et al. "A deep visual correspondence embedding model for stereo matching costs." *Proceedings of the IEEE International Conference on Computer Vision*. pp . 972-980. 2015.

[8] Chang, Jia-Ren, and Yong-Sheng Chen. "Pyramid stereo matching network." *Proceedings of the IEEE Conference on Computer Vision and Pattern Recognition*. pp . 5410-5418. 2018.

[9] Park, Min-Gyu, and Kuk-Jin Yoon. "Learning and selecting confidence measures for robust stereo matching." *IEEE transactions on pattern analysis and machine intelligence* 41.6 (2018): 1397-1411.

[10] Pang, Jiahao, et al. "Cascade residual learning: A two-stage convolutional neural network for stereo matching." *Proceedings of the IEEE International Conference on Computer Vision*. pp. 887-895. 2017.

[11] Shaked, Amit, and Lior Wolf. "Improved stereo matching with constant highway networks and reflective confidence learning." *Proceedings of the IEEE Conference on Computer Vision and Pattern Recognition*. pp. 4641-4650. 2017.

Vehicle Crashes: Early Detection Through Image Recognition

Laura Malis, Abigail Payne, Myles McLeroy, Travis Atkison
Department of Computer Science, University of Alabama, Tuscaloosa, AL, USA

Abstract— *The ability to identify collisions of two vehicles could lead to emergency services being dispatched immediately when a car accident occurs. If both drivers are incapacitated and no witnesses around, delay in emergency services could lead to an unnecessary fatality. As a first step, a dataset of point collisions were collected representing vehicles as center of masses. This project uses TensorFlow, and is trained for binary classification with categorizes containing positive or negative collision events. After training, transfer learning will be used on a data set of car collisions to determine the accuracy of the point mass model. Future applications include determining if vehicles will crash given their proximity, this can extend into other areas including reckless or dangerous driving.*

Keywords: neural networks, image analysis, image classification, transportation industry, event detection

1. Introduction

In the event of a vehicle crash where the drivers are incapacitated and unable to call for help, having a witness available that can make that call can be vital. On highly trafficked roads during popular times of the day, there is often someone who fits in as a witness. Unfortunately, during other times of the day and on rural roads, there is a smaller chance of there being someone who witnessed the accident. This method attempts to be an alternative to the normal human bystander. If a camera is positioned on a light post or traffic light, a constant video stream can be analysed for images of crashes. If a crash is detected, it can be sent to a traffic management center for human verification and then emergency services can be dispatched. This process should happen in a faster manner than hoping that a human bystander happens across the accident.

Collecting data to train this model proved to be quite difficult. Hours of road camera footage was examined to get images of vehicles immediately preceding a crash, during the crash, and immediately post the crash. However, since a crash happens so quickly, each event only results in a couple of usable images. There are also 3 major crash types: front end, rear end, and t-bone. These types of crashes are different enough that the original idea was to create a multi-classification where we see which of the types of crash it is. However, we did not get enough data to do this.

The idea of crashes however is not unique to vehicles. In everyday life we can see collisions, such as two balls crashing together. This can be extrapolated to our problem of vehicle crashes. In this paper, we represented each vehicle by a point mass. This point mass would act as the center of gravity of the vehicle. By using point masses to represent vehicles, data is more easily generated. This also turns the multiple class classification problem into one of binary classification, simply, are the masses in a positive crash event or not. For our purposes, we defined a positive crash event as the two point masses touching and a negative crash event as the two point masses not touching.

From here we are able to have very intuitive next steps. The first of which would to be to change the definition of a positive crash event. Since, we have the point masses representing the center of gravity of each vehicle, it is very unlikely that the actual centers of gravity would collide. The definition of positive crash event would need to be changed to point masses are sufficiently close that there is an increased likelihood of them being in a crash. With this change, we would also have to consider point mass direction. If two point masses are sufficiently close together, but headed away from each other, this would be considered a negative crash event.

Following these changes to the data set and appropriate tuning to the algorithm, we would apply the trained model a vehicle data set. Through this we would see how closely vehicles crashes can be modeled by point mass collisions. As described below, we were able to attain a very encouraging prediction rate.

2. Background

Understanding why car accidents happen, how to prevent them, and how to properly prosecute those who instigate them have become important topics within the scientific community in recent years. There has been much trial and error about how to best go about answering these questions, which is evident in how many different models are being used to attempt similar lines of research. The majority of the work done in the field of image detection as it pertains to traffic has been in road sign recognition. In a study surrounding applying a visual attention mechanism to traffic sign recognition, Rodrigues, et al., [1], acquired images from a moving vehicle and then performed detection and classification from that collected data. In order to gather the initial test data, researchers used a bottom-up visual attention mechanism and previously gathered research on machine trained traffic signs [1]. Expanding on that research, Kuo, et al. [2] proposed a two-stage recognition and detection method and classification strategy. First, the geometric characteristics are used to pinpoint the exact position of the road sign. In the second stage, a radial basis function (RBF) neural network is used to recognize the signs. Road signs were detected and recognized with the accuracy of 95.5% [2].

Straying from the standard methods of image detection, Saharan, et al. [3] uses Genetic Algorithms to address the clustering that occurs during accidents or pileups. They based this on an extensive previous study that showed that genetic algorithms were successful in finding minority classes in a greater-sized data set. What this study ultimately identified were the factors that may be most significantly contributing to road accidents [3]. In another study concerned with analyzing the largest contributors to vehicle collisions, Olutayo, et al. [4] uses Artificial Neural Networks and Decision Trees as data analysis techniques to analyze historical data about a particular crash-ridden roadway in Nigeria. This research also focuses on empirical research on the large number of data mining algorithmic solutions that exist, but little or no empirical research has been done on comparing their efficiency on road accident data sets. In order to categorize data efficiently, this research takes into account where human attempts have been made to reduce accidents, such as remodeling roadways [4]. The following research (Xie, et al. [5]) compares three types of Bayesian neural network (BNN) models and their efficiency in modeling highway safety. Ultimately, this model predicts whether or not highway crashes will occur. The research also attempted to ascertain which model could be best extended to determine other factors in traffic safety, such as accident modification factors [5]. Broadening the types of models researched, the next article takes into account the Support Vector Machine (SVM) models for predicting motor vehicle crashes. This particular model is based on the statistical learning theory, and ultimately predicted crashes more effectively than the commonly used Negative Binomial (NB) regression. Building upon the use of the SVM model, Lie, et al. [6] uses this model for crash severity injury analysis. The SVM model was also analyzed for evaluating the impacts of external factors on crash injury severity's in comparison with the ordered probit (OP) and showed to create more reasonable outcomes than the OP model [6]. Omar, et al. [7] focuses on frontal crashes, specifically taking into account the initial velocity and structural characteristics of the car in question. This study ultimately found that the recurrent artificial neural networks (ANN) captures the characteristics of a frontal crash structure and predicts the crash performance of the same structure in any other crash scenario [7].

Crash injury prediction has also been a prevalent motive for a large portion of research in this field. In this study, Chong, et al. [8] aimed to model the severity of injury resulting from traffic accidents using artificial neural networks and decision trees. The author ultimately found that the decision tree outperforms the neural network. This particular paper concluded that driver's seat belt usage, light condition of the roadway, and driver's alcohol usage were the most significant factors as to whether a crash would occur [8]. Zeng, et al. [9] uses a convex combination (CC) algorithm to train a neural network for crash injury severity prediction. This course of action aims to stray from the typical linear statistical model that is typically employed in this field, and optimize currently in use neural networks by decreasing the number of nodes in use, but maintaining estimation accuracy [9]. Recently, Halim, et al. [10] presented a study that analyzed the current methods of research used to detect unsafe driving habits and predict accidents based on these habits. Within that, the study also researched the statistical methods used to predict these accidents [10].

Moving away from injury prediction, many researchers are currently invested in how the construction of roadways affects the probability of a car accident occurring. Hossain, et al. [11] presents a new framework for real-time crash prediction model building, specifically for basic freeway segments. The means for accomplishing this employ a random multinomial logit model, and then use a Bayesian belief net to build the crash predictions [11]. Montella, et al. [12] tests various crash prediction models for estimating the safety of rural motorways. The generalized linear model technique was used to fit the models and implemented a negative binomial distribution error structure. The most important result of this study was the indication of how much design consistency in roadways significantly affected road safety[12]. Expanding on the notion of the construction of roadways, Tarko, et al. [13] focuses on the topic of safety-conscious road planning as it pertains to calibrating safety prediction models. A major issue that is discussed is the lack of consistency in roadways worldwide and how that would make implementing a universal solution difficult. The solution proposed by researchers is to use a generalized version of the existing calibration procedure that has been utilized in the past for individual crash prediction models [13]. In the following study, Huang, et al. [14] developed an optimized radial basis function neural network (RBFNN) to approximate the nonlinear relationships between prominent risk factors and crash frequency. The output of this model was compared with the output of the traditional negative binomial (NB) and back-propagation neural network (BPNN), and it was ultimately concluded that the RBFNN model has better fitting and prediction performance than NB and BPNN models [14].

Specifically focusing on roadways containing intersections, Wang, et al. [15] analyzed longitudinal intersection crash data and the models that accompany modern analysis. The author found that using the basic negative binomial regression leads to invalid statistical inference and standard errors, so they utilized generalized estimating equations (GEE) to provide an extension to generalized linear models. What was ultimately concluded by the study was that intersections with more exclusive right-turn lanes and a partial left-turn protection phase decreased crash rates [15]. Building upon utilizing GEEs as previously introduced, Abdel-Aty, et al. [16] looked into spatially correlated crash frequency data fitted through the use of GEE models. Signalized intersections, particularly along a certain stretch of road are spatially correlated, and researchers set out to prove the respects in which they are correlated in relation to the probability of an accident occurring on a particular stretch of road [16]. Continuing along the path of signalized intersections, Harnen, et al. [17] established a mathematical model to predict motorcycle crashes and four-arm signalized intersections. Two models were compared against each other, the Poisson regression model and the negative binomial model. The binomial model, in this case, was ultimately found to be more suitable given the data [17].

In an attempt to put image recognition software into active use, Patent no. US08/375,249 is a crash predicting device that is mounted to the car for collecting images as the driver is operating the vehicle. The device takes into account potentially dangerous objects on the roadway and then predicts the probability of a crash occurring given the present state of the roadway. The device is originally pre-trained prior to being mounted in the vehicle, but constantly picks up data as the device is in use and adds to the training images [18].

In a broader sense and in regards to implementation of image detection software, Xu, et al. [19] focuses mainly on event detection in mediums such as security, surveillance, or some other constrained live video, which could ultimately serve to be beneficial, considering our current course of action[19]. In relation to the best research method to go about image recognition, Huang, et al. [20] attempted to account for the fundamental lacking of traditional crash prediction models, such as generalized linear regression models. He states that these models are incapable of taking into account the multilevel data structure, which is prevalent in crash data. In comparison, the study demonstrated the flexibilities and effectiveness of the Bayesian hierarchical model in comparison to the tradition crash prediction models. This type of lacking is evident in several of the references previously mentioned. The typical standard of the negative binomial (NB) model has consistently been proven sub-standard to more recent models, as Thompson describes [20].

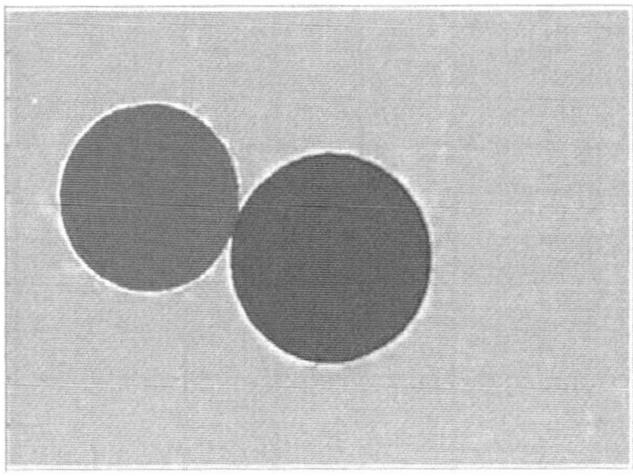

Fig. 1
AN EXAMPLE OF A POSITIVE CRASH EVENT. DESIGNATED BY TWO POINT MASSES TOUCHING EACH OTHER IN THE IMAGE TO BE ANALYSED.

Fig. 2
AN EXAMPLE OF A NEGATIVE CRASH EVENTS. THIS IS DESIGNATED AS SUCH AS THE TWO POINT MASSES ARE NOT TOUCHING.

3. Methodology

3.1 Problem

The over arching problem trying to be solved is to determine if two vehicles have collided when given a captured image of two vehicles. There are three main types of vehicle collisions, the t-bone, the front-end, and the rear-end. Each of these collisions look very different and should be separately categorized in image recognition. The added categorization can lead to increased information that can be relayed to emergency services in the event that the tool detects a crash.

The idea of vehicle collisions can be thought of in a broader sense. Every day, we see things colliding. Whether its as significant and detrimental as a vehicular collision or as simple and harmless as a high five between friends. Regardless of what is colliding it can be simplified into the idea of two objects of mass colliding. Here, we generalize that two vehicles colliding can be seen as two point masses colliding where the point masses represent the center of gravity of the vehicles.

For these experiments, circles were used to represent the point masses. The circles purposefully varied in size to represent a comparison between size and weights of the vehicles they represent. Figure 1[1] shows a positive collision event. A positive collision event occurs when two of the point masses are touching or overlapping. Figures 2 and 3 represent negative collision events. In Figure 3, the point masses are incredibly close, but because they are not physically touching this is not considered a positive collision event. Figure 2's categorization is much more apparent to the casual observer as a negative collision event because the point masses are spaced drastically apart.

3.2 Convolutional Neural Networks

A Convolutional Neural Network is a deep learning tool popularized in 2012. A Neural Network (Figure 4) is a network of functions which connect forward and backward propagation to manipulate weights to in turn assign a categorization to an image. Neural Networks have been inspired by the idea of neurons that appear in the brain and how they connect and pass impulses. While related, the computation neurons still

[1] We we able to get data from a variety of sites collisions from balls or circles. Images were pulled from: https://www.youtube.com/watch?v=3XSh79yfi0M, https://www.youtube.com/watch?v=RXB0Cvcldaw, https://www.youtube.com/watch?v=pPpQoCDS_tw, https://www.youtube.com/watch?v=po_nJFABUsA, https://www.youtube.com/watch?v=SBesU12g58I, and https://www.youtube.com/watch?v=2UHS883_P60

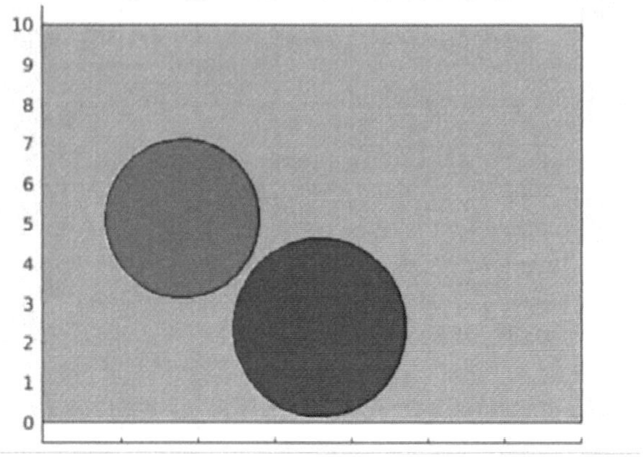

Fig. 3
AN EXAMPLE OF A NEGATIVE CRASH EVENT. WHILE POTENTIALLY NOT APPARENT TO THE CASUAL OBSERVER, THE POINT MASSES ARE NOT TOUCHING, THERE MORE NOT A IN A COLLISION. IN FUTURE WORK, THIS WOULD BE AN EXAMPLE OF SOMETHING THAT COULD BE CONSIDERED SUFFICIENTLY CLOSE FROM ASSUMING THESE ARE THE CENTER OF GRAVITY.

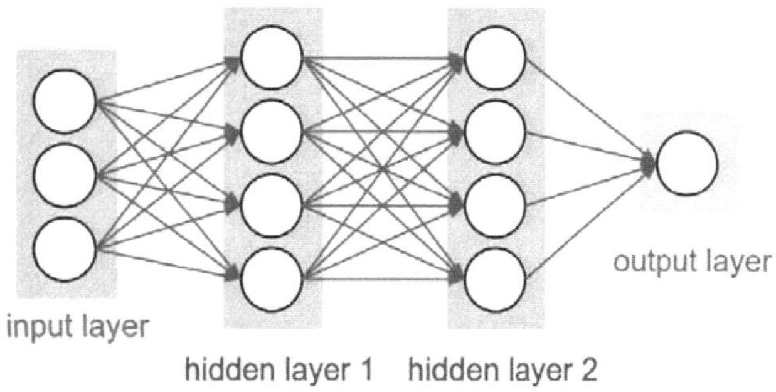

Fig. 4
HERE THE INPUT LAYER IS THE INPUT IMAGE THAT THE MODEL IS TRAINING ON. HIDDEN LAYER ONE AND TWO BOTH REPRESENT CONVOLUTIONAL LAYERS IN THE NETWORK WHERE THE NETWORK IS LEARNING FROM THE SAMPLE DATA. THE OUTPUT LAYER IS THE FINAL FULLY CONNECTED LAYER WHERE THE MODEL MAKES THE FINAL PREDICTION OF THE CLASS. [21]

differ a lot from a biological neuron, as the neurons are much more complicated and have many more factors that influence them then the computation neurons in a neural network [21].

A Convolutional Neural Network (CNN) is a Neural Network made of a series of convolutional and activation layers, but in many cases will include pooling and dropout layers to increase accuracy of the network. A convolutional layer is one that learns things about the shapes in the image. The first few layers in the network will earn the most basic details such as lines and edges, but as more layers are added more high level and specific details are learned by the model.

Following each of the convolutional layers, a linear layer is applied. In the case of this model of neural networks, a Rectified Linear Units (ReLU) activation layer is applied. ReLU is one of the less complicated mathematical activation algorithms. Due to this, it converges faster than other algorithms and makes it less computationally expensive which makes it ideal for basic use [22].

After each convolutional and activation pair, the model applied a pooling layer. In a pooling layer, the image is made smaller by down sampling. This is so that the image becomes more manageable as there are less features and it becomes less computationally expensive to compute further convolutions. While there are several ways to apply pooling, the specific method used in this model was max pooling. In max pooling, a filter is slid over the image. The filter is a matrix smaller than the input image. The filter is analyzed at each stride and the cell with the highest value is passed to the next layer.

The last layer from a covolutional neural network is a fully connected layer, which can also be called the output layer. This is where the model takes the information from the weights and the previously applied layers and makes a prediction about what the image contains.

	Predicted Crash	Predicted Not Crash
Actual Crash	158	1
Actual Not Crash	15	126

Table 1
A CONFUSION MATRIX FROM AN EXPERIMENT ON THE DATA SET. THE FIRST CELL REPRESENTS THE NUMBER OF TRUE POSITIVES. THE SECOND CELL REPRESENTS THE NUMBER OF FALSE NEGATIVES. THE THIRD CELL REPRESENTS THE NUMBER OF FALSE POSITIVES. THE FOURTH CELL REPRESENTS THE NUMBER OF TRUE NEGATIVES.

4. Results

Through our experiments, we were able to get a 94% accuracy. Table 1 shows a confusion matrix for one of our experimental runs. This matrix shows that the model achieved an accuracy rate of 94 %, sensitivity of 99.37 % and specificity of 8.67%.

Since this algorithm would be constantly executed over road footage and sending positive crash events for human verification and dispatch. It is more important that the sensitivity of the algorithm is high. Sensitivity means that there are very few false negative compared to the total number of positive crash events. In this test, we achieved only one (1) false negative. While it would be ideal that no positive crash event goes undetected, only having one false negative is very good. Figure 5 shows the image that created a false negative. In this case, it is clear that the point masses have collided, but part of one of the point masses is cut off. To decrease the chance of this being incorrectly categorized again, we will include more images where the point masses are in a positive collision event, but where some of either one or both of the point masses is cut off to give the algorithm more experience with this kind of data. The algorithm only incorrectly predicted negative crash

Fig. 5

THE IMAGE THAT WAS INCORRECTLY CLASSIFIED AS A NEGATIVE CRASH EVENT WHEN PREDICTED WITH THE MODEL.

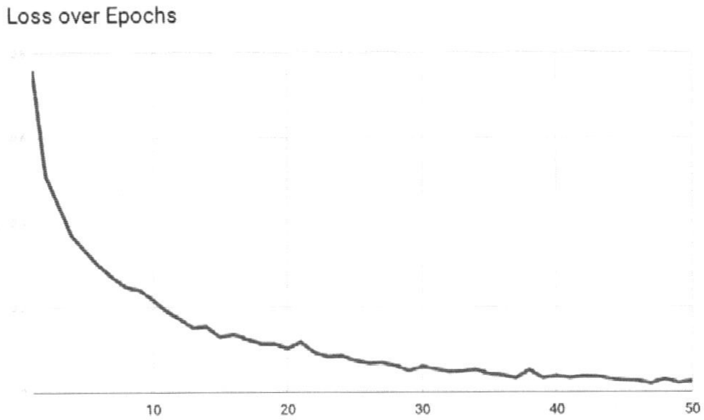

Fig. 6

A GRAPH DETAILING THE LOSS ON EACH EPOCH OF TRAINING. THIS GRAPH HAS A STEEP DECLINE UNTIL EPOCH 10. THE GRAPH BEGINS TO PLATEAU AT 45 EPOCHS. THIS SHOWS THAT THE LEARNING RATE SHOULD BE LOWERED TO HAVE THE GRAPH STEEPLY DECREASE FOR LONGER. THEN THE TRAINING SHOULD BE RUN FOR MORE EPOCHS TO HAVE A LONGER PLATEAU.

events incorrectly 8.76% of the time. In a real application this would not be ideal due to the inefficiency of sending negative collision events for human verification. However, one would rather having to verify that events are not positive crash events then potentially missing fatal positive crash events.

Figure 6 shows a graph of the loss at each epoch. This graph represents a trend as expected, steeply falling and then plateauing off. From this however, we can see that our learning rate may be able to be tuned to a more effective value. This can be seen as the the steep decline begins to taper of at about ten (10) epochs, but is a bit sooner than expected for an appropriate learning rate.

5. Conclusion

In conclusion, the difficult problem of having two vehicles collide was simplified into the more abstract idea of two point masses colliding. From that point, the effort generated a wide data set of images including various sizes and positions of point masses participating in either a positive or negative collision event. For this effort, a convolutional neural network was used and gained a prediction level of 94% accuracy when determining if two point masses have collided or not.

6. Future Works

In the immediate future, the model will be further tuned and then compared to other standard binary classification algorithms. Once satisfied having found the best model for determining positive versus negative collision events for point masses, we need to reevaluate the definition for a positive collision event.

An early assumption was made that the point masses represent the center of gravity of the vehicles that we are extrapolating to. In the event of a real vehicular collision, it is unlikely that the centers of gravity will actually collide. Instead we will need to redefine a positive collision event as two point masses that are sufficiently close. The tool will then be ran to see its accuracy on the new data set and likely retrained and tuned. Research will also have to be done to determine how close is sufficiently close.

From there, directionality will also have to be considered. In Figure 7, arrows represent the direction of the masses. Here, they are pointed towards each other, so since the point masses are sufficiently close, based on their position and their direction, it is likely a collision would actually occur. In Figure 8, one point mass has an arrow pointed toward the other while the other can be assumed to be stationary. In the case of point masses, it can be assumed that they will collide. However, we must closely evaluate the idea of significantly close, because when thought about in the vehicle domain, it could be seen as a car about to stop behind another vehicle or a rear-end collision event about to happen.

Once finished with the generalization of point masses, we will use transfer learning to see how the point mass model predicts vehicle collisions. From there we will confirm that point masses are a useful generalization and one that can be applied to this and other data sets. Depending on the accuracy of the transfer learning, we can run the algorithm over roadway footage to separate out still that might contain a collision and then through hand annotation, we can verify and create a robust data set to train a more specialized model to determine if two vehicles have collided.

Immediate next steps are to train on a variety of image recognition models to find a more efficient training method that maintains or improves current accuracy. The method currently being used sorts of images with the process known as bottle-necking. However, with the sub-problem of point masses, there are now a wider variety of models available that are applicable to the training being attempted. Secondary steps will be to apply the point mass trained model on to a data set with various types of car crashes and see how the model performs without extra training. The performance of the point

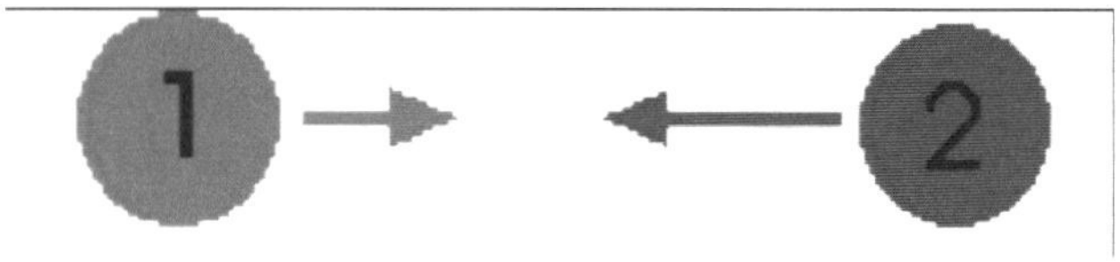

Fig. 7
THIS IS AN EXAMPLE OF TWO POINT MASSES THAT COULD BE SEEN AS SUFFICIENTLY CLOSE TO BE CONSIDERED A POSITIVE VEHICLE COLLISION. THE DIRECTIONALITY OF THE ARROWS POINTING AT EACH OTHER WOULD ALSO ALLOW YOU TO ASSUME THAT THIS WOULD RESULT IN A COLLISION

Fig. 8
AN EXAMPLE OF TWO POINT MASSES THAT ARE LIKELY TO COLLIDE BASED ON DIRECTION AND BEING SUFFICIENTLY CLOSE. HOWEVER, WHEN THOUGHT OF IN THE VEHICLE DOMAIN, IT COULD REPRESENT EITHER A VEHICLE STOPPING BEHIND ANOTHER, OR MOMENTS BEFORE A REAR-END COLLISION

mass trained algorithm will be further improved with images of vehicle crashes. Given this, our next steps will be to test this theory as to if point masses couple in the data with car accidents improve image recognition accuracy

Determining whether a collision has occurred between two vehicles can be helpful in predicting the likelihood of two cars colliding given their proximity. Being able to consistently predict the proximity of vehicles is the first step into being able to determine if a vehicle is driving recklessly or dangerously. This would allow law enforcement to be dispatched before a crash occurs and can potentially lead to fewer crashes overall.

References

[1] F. A. Rodrigues and H. M. Gomes, "Applying a visual attention mechanism to the problem of traffic sign recognition," in *Proceedings. XV Brazilian Symposium on Computer Graphics and Image Processing*. IEEE, 2002, p. 415.

[2] W.-J. Kuo and C.-C. Lin, "Two-stage road sign detection and recognition," in *2007 IEEE international conference on multimedia and expo*. IEEE, 2007, pp. 1427–1430.

[3] S. Saharan and R. Baragona, "A cluster analysis on road traffic accidents using genetic algorithms," in *AIP Conference Proceedings*, vol. 1830, no. 1. AIP Publishing, 2017, p. 030002.

[4] V. Olutayo and A. Eludire, "Traffic accident analysis using decision trees and neural networks," *International Journal of Information Technology and Computer Science*, vol. 2, pp. 22–28, 2014.

[5] Y. Xie, D. Lord, and Y. Zhang, "Predicting motor vehicle collisions using bayesian neural network models: An empirical analysis," *Accident Analysis & Prevention*, vol. 39, no. 5, pp. 922–933, 2007.

[6] Z. Li, P. Liu, W. Wang, and C. Xu, "Using support vector machine models for crash injury severity analysis," *Accident Analysis & Prevention*, vol. 45, pp. 478–486, 2012.

[7] T. Omar, A. Eskandarian, and N. Bedewi, "Vehicle crash modelling using recurrent neural networks," *Mathematical and computer Modelling*, vol. 28, no. 9, pp. 31–42, 1998.

[8] M. M. Chong, A. Abraham, and M. Paprzycki, "Traffic accident analysis using decision trees and neural networks," *arXiv preprint cs/0405050*, 2004.

[9] Q. Zeng and H. Huang, "A stable and optimized neural network model for crash injury severity prediction," *Accident Analysis & Prevention*, vol. 73, pp. 351–358, 2014.

[10] Z. Halim, R. Kalsoom, S. Bashir, and G. Abbas, "Artificial intelligence techniques for driving safety and vehicle crash prediction," *Artificial Intelligence Review*, vol. 46, no. 3, pp. 351–387, 2016.

[11] M. Hossain and Y. Muromachi, "A bayesian network based framework for real-time crash prediction on the basic freeway segments of urban expressways," *Accident Analysis & Prevention*, vol. 45, pp. 373–381, 2012.

[12] A. Montella, L. Colantuoni, and R. Lamberti, "Crash prediction models for rural motorways," *Transportation Research Record*, vol. 2083, no. 1, pp. 180–189, 2008.

[13] A. P. Tarko, "Calibration of safety prediction models for planning transportation networks," *Transportation research record*, vol. 1950, no. 1, pp. 83–91, 2006.

[14] H. Huang, Q. Zeng, X. Pei, S. Wong, and P. Xu, "Predicting crash frequency using an optimised radial basis function neural network model," *Transportmetrica A: transport science*, vol. 12, no. 4, pp. 330–345, 2016.

[15] X. Wang, M. Abdel-Aty, and P. A. Brady, "Crash estimation at signalized intersections: significant factors and temporal effect," *Transportation Research Record*, vol. 1953, no. 1, pp. 10–20, 2006.

[16] M. Abdel-Aty and X. Wang, "Crash estimation at signalized intersections along corridors: analyzing spatial effect and identifying significant factors," *Transportation Research Record*, vol. 1953, no. 1, pp. 98–111, 2006.

[17] S. Harnen, S. Wong, R. R. Umar, and W. W. Hashim, "Motorcycle crash prediction model for non-signalized intersections," *IATSS research*, vol. 27, no. 2, pp. 58–65, 2003.

[18] T. Nishio, "Vehicle crash predictive and evasive operation system by neural networks," July 30 1996, uS Patent 5,541,590.

[19] D. Xu and S.-F. Chang, "Video event recognition using kernel methods with multilevel temporal alignment," *IEEE Transactions on Pattern Analysis and Machine Intelligence*, vol. 30, no. 11, pp. 1985–1997, 2008.

[20] H. Huang, H. C. Chin, M. Haque, *et al.*, "Bayesian hierarchical analysis on crash prediction models," in *87th Annual Meeting of Transportation Research Board (TRB)*. Transportation Research Board, 2008.

[21] [Online]. Available: http://cs231n.github.io/neural-networks-1/

[22] V. Nair and G. E. Hinton, "Rectified linear units improve restricted boltzmann machines vinod nair," vol. 27, 06 2010, pp. 807–814.

SRGAN: Training Dataset Matters

Nao Takano and Gita Alaghband

Computer Science and Engineering University of Colorado, Denver

Abstract

Generative Adversarial Networks (GANs) in supervised settings can generate photo-realistic corresponding output from low-definition input (SRGAN). Using the architecture presented in the SRGAN original paper [2], we explore how selecting a dataset affects the outcome by using three different datasets to see that SRGAN fundamentally learns objects, with their shape, color, and texture, and redraws them in the output rather than merely attempting to sharpen edges. This is further underscored with our demonstration that once the network learns the images of the dataset, it can generate a photo-like image with even a slight hint of what it might look like for the original from a very blurry edged sketch. Given a set of inference images, the network trained with the same dataset results in a better outcome over the one trained with arbitrary set of images, and we report its significance numerically with Fréchet Inception Distance score [22]. Keywords: GAN, SRGAN, FID.

1. Introduction

Generative Adversarial Networks are a type of deep neural networks that are used to generate images by using two networks; the generator and the discriminator. The generator attempts to generate images from an array of often smaller size, and the discriminator determines whether the generated images are real or fake by finding the Nash equilibrium of a game [7, 8]. GANs have shown to be very effective methods for Super Resolution imaging (SR), also referred to as Single image super-resolution (SISR), which is a class of techniques that enhances the resolution of an imaging system. It aims to refine and convert an image of low-resolution to that of high-resolution. Following the work by Dong et al. [25], Ledig et al. [2] demonstrated that using the Generative Adversarial Network as well as pre-trained VGG network [26] improve the performance of SR (SRGAN).

SRGAN has achieved generating high resolution images by training rather general image sets, i.e., any arbitrary image set can be used for training. But if one is to enhance a particular type of image, such as that of human face, a building, or furniture, should the network be trained with the given specific features that will appear in the inference images? The question of how the selection of training data affects the SRGAN has not been well studied.

This paper explores effective ways of training to achieve super-resolution and other applications, using various datasets in SRGAN. In order to answer a question such as *"If we want to reconstruct high-resolution face images from low-resolution ones using SRGAN, should we train it with the dataset of face images, or does it matter what kind of images we train?"*, we use three different datasets for training and measure the effects on the resulting images. In other words, this study attempts to uncover how SRGAN uses neural networks to generate super-resolution images by learning other similar images.

Our main contributions are as follows:

- With FID, we show numerically that for the best result one should use the same image-type dataset that will be used at inference time.
- Demonstrate examples of other usages of SRGAN, such as Coloring and Edges to Photo, as applications of image-to-image translation.

After Section 2, Related Work, we describe the dataset and the network architecture, along with the experimental methods in Section 3. Section 4 describes the results of the experiments in Section 3. In Section 5, we explore usages of SRGAN beyond super-resolution, coloring and edges to photo, and the paper concludes with Section 6.

2. Related Work

2.1 Unsupervised Training

With Generative Adversarial Networks, along with Variational AutoEncoders (VAE) [20] and other techniques, a random noise is often used as an input to draw images in an unsupervised manner. Since its inception in 2014 [7], GAN has evolved within this domain for generating clearer images and more stable training, with the input of a sample from a Gaussian distribution z. Radford et al. [10] successfully generated convincing images by using a convolutional neural network that has no fully connected layers and replaced max-pooling with strided convolutions. Arjovsky et al. [11] demonstrated a stable training by measuring divergence with Earth Mover (EM) distance, a distance between two probability distributions that is to be minimized continuously. It was followed by Gulrajani et al. [12], which proposes weight regularization rather than weight clipping. Mao et al. [13] introduced a least-squares loss for slower saturation of the loss function. And Berthelot et al. [14] proposed a loss derived from the Wasserstein distance with an auto-encoder based training as a discriminator. Meanwhile, with increasing members of the GAN family, efforts have been made to organize, sort, and evaluate different flavors of GANs [18].

2.2 Supervised Training

On the other hand, attempts to control the output more precisely by way of supervised training settings took place. The training is conducted by feeding an image to the network as an input (as opposed to the random noise z), and form a one-to-one mapping with the corresponding output image. Our work focuses on this area. SRGAN [2] is one of the prominent works of one-to-one mapping.

Conditional GAN (cGAN) [15, 16, 17] inserts a condition in the network and tries to generate an output with specific attributes. Notably, in close relation to our work, Isola et al. [3] showed that cGANs can achieve image-to-image translation. In this regard, SRGAN is a part of the broader term of Conditional GANs.

The supervised nature of these GANs requires paired training data, which is often difficult to obtain except in the case where one can generate input images from the original ones, as demonstrated in this paper. CycleGAN [9] eliminates this requirement; it can translate images in one domain to another without pairs of training data.

3. Methods and Experimental Settings

3.1 Dataset

We use three different datasets:

1. CelebA for faces – we use the "aligned" version, which has been compiled from the original version of "in the wild". Every image is a uniform size of 178 x 218 and contains all peoples' faces in the center of the frame. (Total number of images: 202,599) [27]
2. Lsun Dining Room – consisting of dining tables, chairs, etc., representing indoor furniture (657,571) [28]
3. Lsun Tower – architectural buildings in the outdoors (708,264) [28]

The idea of selecting these three datasets is to contrast them to each other, where each dataset representing unique characteristics of images of a similar kind (faces, towers, furnished rooms). We created three different pre-trained networks, corresponding to respective datasets. When the trainings are completed, each of which should have learned human faces, indoor furniture, and buildings outdoor, respectively. For our experiment, a single training consists of 200,000 images, which are selected randomly from one of the datasets and run for 10 epochs.

Note that the aligned CelebA contains faces in the frame consistent in all the images in such a way that we can simply center-crop and resize them in the same ratio, while Lsun images are taken from the wild, and objects are placed randomly in an image. Thus, naturally the network learns faces more easily than dining rooms or towers. All the images are resized (CelebA) or randomly cropped (Dining Room and Tower) to be 128×128 in size.

3.2 Network Architecture

3.2.1 Architecture

We used code from Github [1] which closely presents the original SRGAN [2] and made very few changes to the network itself. We used different datasets for comparison. The generator of the network has eight residual blocks (the original SRGAN uses 16 blocks), each of which consists of Conv, BN, and Parametric ReLU, followed by layers of PixelShufflers, which are inserted to accommodate various upscale ratios (The original SRGAN has two PixelShufflers to facilitate 4×4 upscaling factors). The discriminator also contains eight convolutional layers, consisting of Conv, BN, and Leaky ReLU, but with more feature maps than those of the generator. Both networks use the kernel size 3 and no max-pooling is used. In order to properly measure the effects of the choice of datasets, we used the fixed network architecture throughout the experiments. (Figure 1)

Although the study of the network construction is beyond the scope of our work, a few points should be made. There are discussions as to which network between the generator and discriminator should be more powerful, such as how fast the generator learns than the discriminator does, or vice versa. Despite suggestions that the parameters of the discriminator should be updated more frequently than the generator, many implementations use the same frequency of parameter updates between the two networks. We follow the latter. In terms of the network size, the discriminator in our network is several times larger than its counter-part.

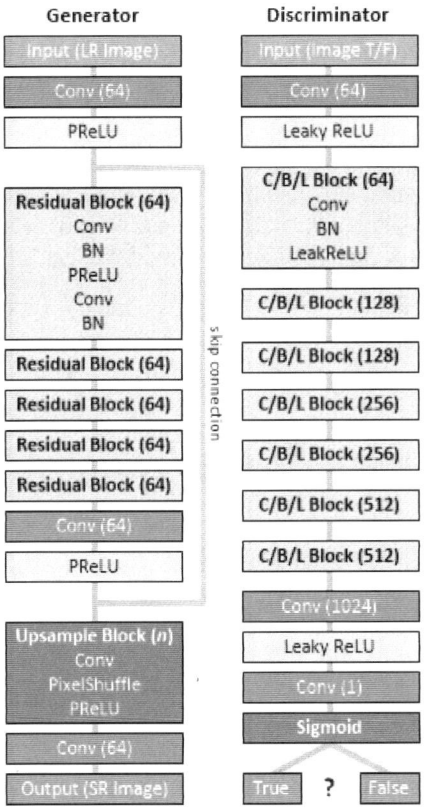

Figure 1: Architecture of the network. The numbers in the parenthesis indicate the number of feature maps.

3.2.2 Loss function

With a pair of training images, the discriminator calculates the loss function – pixel-wise distances between the target image and the input image. This is a straight forward way to minimize the loss in image-to-image translation. The original SRGAN paper [2] uses Mean Squared Error (MSE, or L2) loss in its content loss calculation. While we also used L2 loss for the majority of experiments, in Section 5 we used both L1 and L2 losses for comparison. In general, the L2 function performs well as long as outliers (noise in the image) are not present in the input.

$$L_{L1}(G) = \sum_{x=1}^{W}\sum_{y=1}^{H} \left\| I_{x,y}^{target} - G\left(I^{input}\right)_{x,y} \right\|$$

$$L_{L2}(G) = \sum_{x=1}^{W}\sum_{y=1}^{H} \left(I_{x,y}^{target} - G\left(I^{input}\right)_{x,y} \right)^2$$

As part of the content loss, 16 layer VGG network [26] was used throughout the experiments along with L1 or L2 loss.

3.2.3 Batch Normalization

Batch Normalization (BN) is a normalization technique used on the input of each layer to reduce covariance shift (changing of distribution of activations in intermediate layers) [5]. Wang, et al. [4] claims that removing the BN improves the image quality, but it is also known to allow a wider range of the selections for hyper-parameters. Determining hyper-parameters increases the experimental budget exponentially when we change the image size, and BN helps alleviate this cost. Using Batch Normalization helps the network to converge more easily.

The network adopted in this paper uses Batch Normalization at each layer in all experiments.

4. Super-Resolution with 4×4 Up-Scaling Images

4.1 Method

The up-scale ratio we use in this section is 4×4, as is typically done in SRGAN. We create three trained-networks by training three datasets, namely, CelebA [27], Lsun Dining Room [28], and Lsun Tower [28]. Given a target image of 128×128, an input image is created by resizing the target image by 4×4 with bi-cubic interpolation, resulting in a 32×32 low resolution (LR) image. This input is then passed to the generator, resulting in an image with the original size of 128×128, yet still low resolution, at which point we have a pair of images; one is the original HR image (target), the other is the LR output by the generator, both the same size. Now, the loss is calculated between the pair which is to be minimized during the training. This process is repeated with 200,000 different pairs, consisting of one epoch.

We trained 10 epochs for each of three networks. With Nvidia GTX 1080 Ti, using a single GPU it takes approximately one hour for an epoch, thus about 10 hours to finish training. After creating the three trained networks, each with trained with faces, dining rooms, and towers, we then test each for inference with the test sets of the three datasets of face, dining room and tower, totaling 9 tests.

4.1.1 Evaluation of the performance metrics

The image-to-image translation involves the supervised training of two images; original or target, and the corresponding image generated from the LR input, to be measured its fidelity to the original. Thus, direct comparison of two images between the original and the generated image would make sense. We can measure the Euclidean distance, often as MSE, of every pixel between pairs of the two images, then average them over the entire test set. Peak

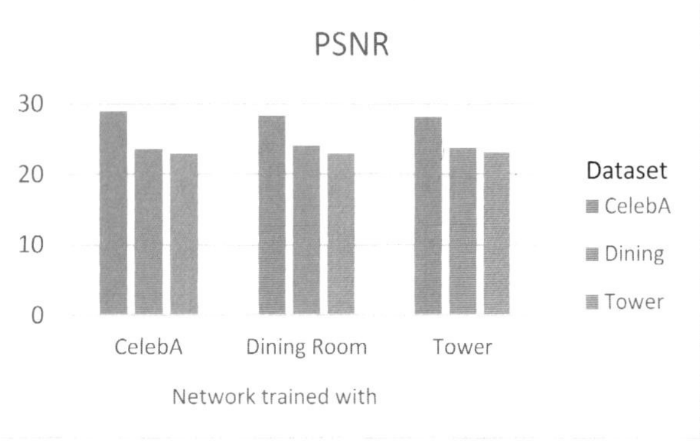

Chart 1: Pixel-wise Euclidean Distance Metrics – PSNR. The higher the value, the better.

Chart 2: Pixel-wise Euclidean Distance Metrics – SSIM. The higher the value, the better.

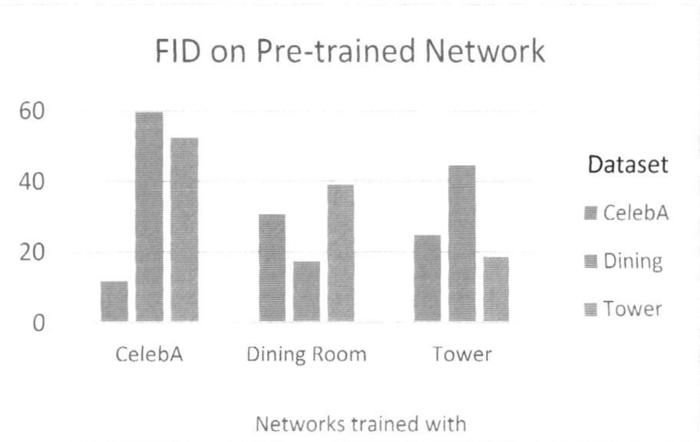

Chart 3: Each pre-trained network that has been trained with CelebA, Dining Room, and Tower is tested against three datasets. The lower the value is, the better.

Signal to Noise Ratio (PSNR) and Structural Similarity Index (SSIM) are derivatives of MSE metrics. PSNR represents a measure of the peak error (noise). The lower the value, the lower the error. SSIM gives a value of 1.0 if the two images are identical. The lower the SSIM value, the bigger the difference. Traditionally they have been used to measure image qualities in the reconstruction of image compression, however, for GANs those measurements do not represent the true quality of the generated output [2, 4, 6, 8, 18, 21, 22]. The reason they do not represent visual perception is well described in Theis et al. [21]. Even for a pair of identical images, a shift by only one pixel on one of the images causes a large increase in the distance of the metrics. Nevertheless, Chart 1 and 2 show these MSE-based quantitative results and will be compared to Fréchet Inception Distance (FID) [22], which corresponds to more realistic qualitative measure

Fréchet Inception Distance uses a pre-trained Inception network [24] and calculates Fréchet distance between two multivariate Gaussian distributions with mean μ and covariance Σ,

$$\mathrm{FID}(x, g) = \left\|\mu_x - \mu_g\right\|^2 + \mathrm{Tr}\left(\Sigma_x + \Sigma_g - 2\left(\Sigma_x \Sigma_g\right)^{1/2}\right)$$

where x, g are the activations of the pool_3 layer of the Inception-v3 net for real samples and generated samples, respectively. We take 2,599 images from test set, and generate the corresponding inference images through one of our pre-trained networks, resulting in two sets that are to be measured by the FID calculator [23]; 2,599 test images and 2,599 output images. Note that the number of images comes from the CelebA dataset, whose total is 202,599, of which we used 200,000 for training, thus leaving 2,599 for testing. The sample size must be consistent throughout the measurements, thus we randomly select 2,599 images from each of test sets of Dining Room and Tower as well.

Measuring FID appropriately shows that an image of CelebA, Dining Room, or Tower is best inferred through the network that has been trained with CelebA, Dining Room, or Tower, respectively, as seen in the [Chart 3]. FID measures can better support what we observe visually in Figure 2 as described in the next section.

4.1.2. Visual analysis of the outputs

More obvious differences can be observed in actual images shown in Figure 2. For example, the top three images are CelebA images and we can see that the networks trained with Dining Room and Tower never learned the shape of eyes, whereas the network that has been trained with faces clearly shows pupil/iris (dark area in the center of an eye) and sclera (white area surrounding iris).

The 4th and 5th rows are Dining Room images. In the 4th row, the edge of the white table is more clearly shown, inferred by the network trained with Dining Room. Similarly, the image in the 5th row shows columns of the chair (vertical wooden back support) more clearly through the network trained with it. On the other hand, in the images with the network trained with Tower, one can observe bricks and window-like texture on the surface of the buildings more clearly (rows 6 and 7).

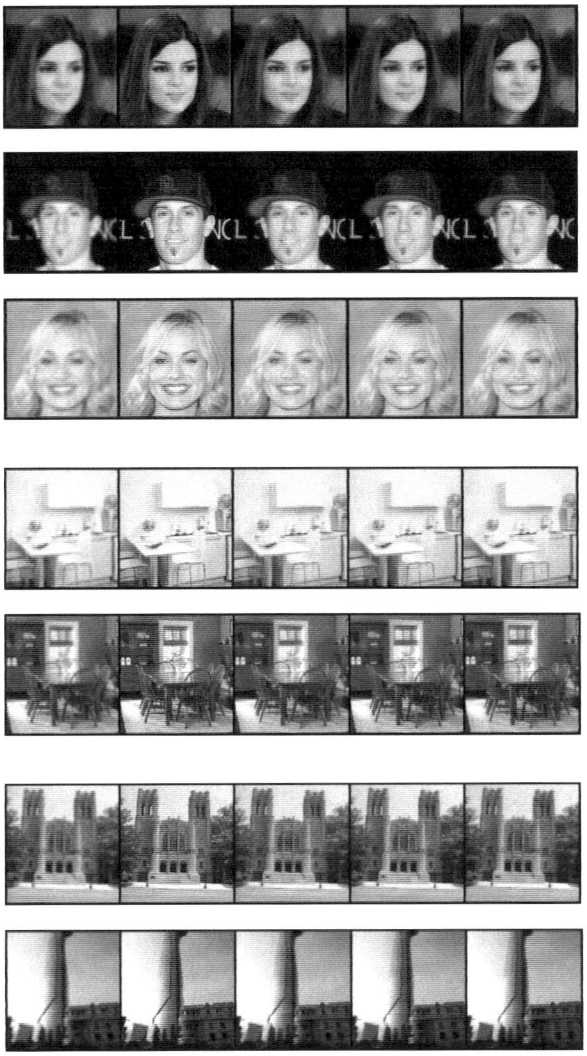

Figure 2: Top 3 rows: CelebA images. Center 2 rows: Dining Room. Bottom 2 rows: Tower.
From left to right: Input LR image, Target Image,
Output inference by pre-trained network with CelebA,
Output inference by pre-trained network with Dining Room,
Output inference by pre-trained network with Tower.

5. Coloring and Edges to Photo

5.1 Coloring

There have been various methods of coloring single channel images – i.e., grayscale and edged. But CNN architectures, along with Transposed/Fractionally-Strided Convolutions (or deconvolutions), have been used more recently [3, 19]. We used this image-to-image translation with L2 loss function for the colorization with the same architecture of the network used for SRGAN. We used upscale ratio 1 (No blurring operation in the inputs) for all the trainings.

For inference, we only used corresponding pre-training networks; i.e. for the inference of face images, we used the network trained by face dataset only, for dining room images we used the network trained by dining room dataset only. Before the training, we prepared the input data with gray-scale images using OpenCV.

5.1.1. Face

Figure 4 shows the result of our experiment for face coloring. As can be seen, regardless of race the difference in skin color of human faces is relatively small. However in the testing, the network properly redraws the original skin color in the output images. Note that the network never learned the color of the background, and more generic beige color is used for it (3rd and 4th rows on Figure 4).

5.1.2. Dining Room

Figure 5 shows the result of our experiment for dining room coloring. Many training images contain tables and chairs, and very often if the color of the table is white, the chairs are brown, and vice versa. Two examples of those color combinations are presented. It appears the network detects the texture of materials to determine the color of furniture.

5.1.3. Tower

As shown in Figure 6, the buildings in the dataset do not exhibit a common color, but other elements, such as the sky or illumination of the building at night, will be regenerated in the output, which indicates that the network picks up colors of the most common denominator found in the training images.

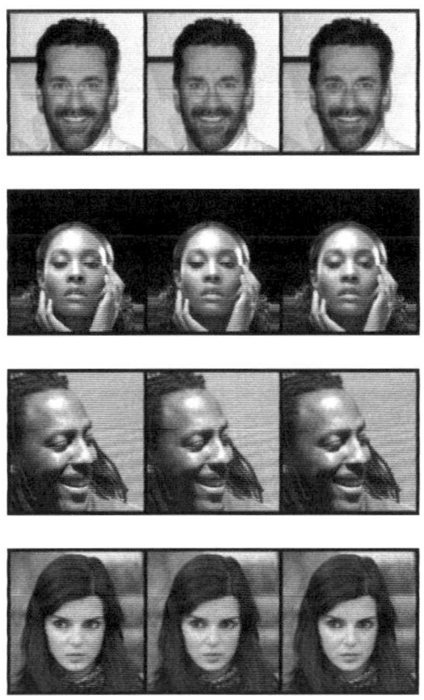

Figure 4: Converting Gray-Scale to Color (Face)
Left: black and white, Center: original, Right: output.

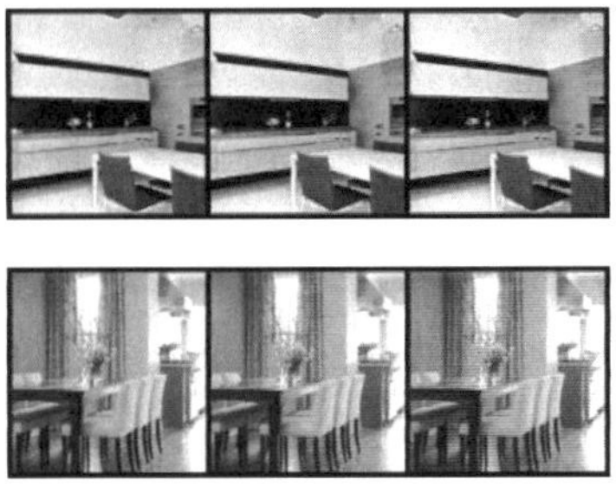

Figure 5: Converting Gray-Scale to Color (Dining Room)
Left: black and white, Center: original, Right: output.

Figure 6: Converting Gray-Scale to Color (Tower)
Left: black and white, Center: original, Right: output.

5.2 Edges to Photo

In this section, we conducted additional experiments with two loss functions described in Section 3.2.2, as well as several upscale values, to see how blurry edge images can generate corresponding colored images. We were able to generate images only for CelebA; the network did not converge for Dining Room or Tower in training. In the CelebA datasets, the objects (faces) are placed roughly at the center of the frames, but Lsun images contain multiple objects "in the wild", not aligned in any way as in CelebA, blurring a focal point to learn a single object. We used OpenCV to generate edged images with its Canny edge detector before training.

Setting the upscale value 1 (input and target images have the same size) induces artifacts, although the output image has better resolution than that of the upscale value of 2 or greater. As we blur the input, the artifacts disappear in the output and smooths out the details. In the very blurry output, such as ×8 and ×16, the network still draws human faces, indicating what it has learned by the training. In terms of the loss functions L1 or L2, we observe clear differences, but it is hard to say which one is better than the other for all cases (Figure 7).

The way the artifacts show up in the output draws an attention. Our experimental results and observations suggest that in most cases, either experimental or practical, the objective of the type of exercise presented in this section is a general restoration of the original object, per se, so the features in objects in the input should be in such a way that they represent a general guideline, like DNA, to represent the original. Neural network of SRGAN and Image-to-Image translation learns to capture these features, it seems, in the form of the guideline to reproduce the original image. For a pre-trained network, the more articulate the guideline is, the better it produces the image. However, if the guideline in the input is overly articulated, there will be artifacts in the output. The greater the detail the input is depicted, the more amplified the artifacts will be, in which case it appears the output fails to generalize the original object.

×1 (176×176 => 176×176)

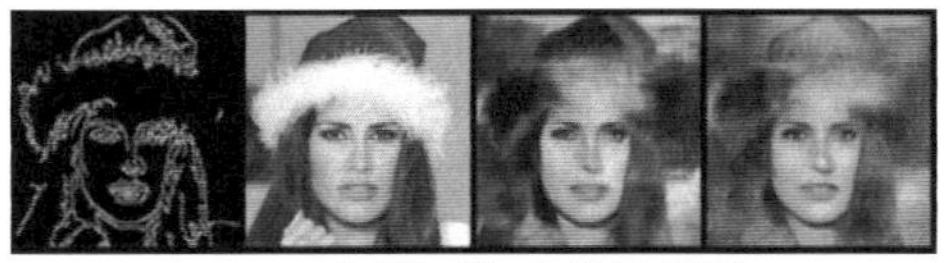

×2 (88×88 => 176×176)

×4 (44×44 => 176×176)

×8 (22×22 => 176×176)

×16 (11×11 => 176×176)

Figure 7: Converting Edges to Photo
From left to right: Input, Target, Output L1, and Output L2

6. Conclusion

In all the experiments conducted in this paper, we used a fixed network architecture of the GANs. We showed that given a set of inference images, the network trained with the same dataset results in a better outcome. This is numerically presented in FID scores. SRGAN fundamentally learns objects, with their shape, color, and texture, and redraws them in the output rather than attempting to sharpen edges.

We also showed that one-to-one mapping of image translation inherent in supervised training can be used in coloring and converting edges to photo. Once the network learns objects, it can regenerate them from a very faint sketch that suggests the original. The question remains as to whether the result presented here is consistent with all other architectures of the network. We further need to investigate the artifacts presented in the previous section in future work.

References

[1] https://github.com/leftthomas/SRGAN

[2] Christian Ledig, Lucas Theis, Ferenc Huszár, Jose Caballero, Andrew Cunningham, Alejandro Acosta, Andrew Aitken, Alykhan Tejani, Johannes Totz, Zehan Wang, Wenzhe Shi, *Photo-Realistic Single Image Super-Resolution Using a Generative Adversarial Network.* 2017 IEEE Conference on CVPR

[3] Phillip Isola, Jun-Yan Zhu, Tinghui Zhou, Alexei A. Efros, *Image-to-Image Translation with Conditional Adversarial Networks.* IEEE Conference on Computer Vision and Pattern Recognition (CVPR), July 2017, ISSN: 1063-6919

[4] Xintao Wang, Ke Yu, Shixiang Wu, Jinjin Gu, Yihao Liu, Chao Dong, Chen Change Loy, Yu Qiao, Xiaoou Tang, *ESRGAN: Enhanced Super-Resolution Generative Adversarial Networks.* preprint arXiv:1809.00219v2, Sep 2018.

[5] Sergey Ioffe and Christian Szegedy, *Batch Normalization: Accelerating Deep Network Training by Reducing Internal Covariate Shift.* PMLR, pp.448–456, 2015.

[6] Tero Karras, Timo Aila, Samuli Laine, Jaakko Lehtinen, *Progressive Growing of GANs for Improved Quality, Stability, and Variation.* ICLR 2018.

[7] Ian J. Goodfellow, Jean Pouget-Abadie, Mehdi Mirza, Bing Xu, David Warde-Farley, Sherjil Ozair, Aaron Courville, Yoshua Bengio, *Generative Adversarial Nets.* Advances in Neural Information Processing Systems 27, Curran Associates, Inc. pp.2672–2680, 2014

[8] Tim Salimans, Ian Goodfellow, Wojciech Zaremba, Vicki Cheung, Alec Radford, and Xi Chen, *Improved techniques for training GANs.* Advances in Neural Information Processing Systems, pp.2234–2242, 2016

[9] Jun-Yan Zhu, Taesung Park, Phillip Isola, and Alexei A. Efros, *Unpaired Image-to-Image Translation using Cycle-Consistent Adversarial Networks.* 2017 IEEE International Conference on Computer Vision (ICCV), ISSN: 2380-7504

[10] A. Radford, L. Metz, and S. Chintala. *Unsupervised representation learning with deep convolutional generative adversarial networks.* In ICLR, 2016.

[11] Martin Arjovsky, Soumith Chintala, and L´eon Bottou, *Wasserstein GAN.* International Conference on Machine Learning (ICML), 2017

[12] Ishaan Gulrajani, Faruk Ahmed, Mart´ın Arjovsky, Vincent Dumoulin, and Aaron C. Courville. *Improved training of Wasserstein GANs.* Advances in Neural Information Processing Systems (NIPS), 2017

[13] Xudong Mao, Qing Li, Haoran Xie, Raymond YK Lau, Zhen Wang, and Stephen Paul Smolley. *Least squares generative adversarial networks.* International Conference on Computer Vision (ICCV), 2017

[14] David Berthelot, Tom Schumm, and Luke Metz. *BEGAN: Boundary equilibrium generative adversarial networks.* preprint arXiv:1703.10717, 2017

[15] Emily Denton, Soumith Chintala, Arthur Szlam, and Rob Fergus, *Deep Generative Image Models using a Laplacian Pyramid of Adversarial Networks.* Advances in Neural Information Processing Systems (NIPS) pp.1486–1494, 2015

[16] J. Gauthier. *Conditional generative adversarial nets for convolutional face generation.* Class Project for Stanford CS231N: Convolutional Neural Networks for Visual Recognition, Winter semester, 2014

[17] M. Mirza and S. Osindero. *Conditional generative adversarial nets.* arXiv:1411.1784, 2014

[18] Mario Lucic, Karol Kurach, Marcin Michalski, Olivier Bousquet, and Sylvain Gelly, *Are GANs Created Equal? A Large-Scale Study.* NeurIPS, pp.698–707, 2018

[19] Richard Zhang, Phillip Isola, and Alexei A. Efros, *Colorful Image Colorization.* Computer Vision - ECCV 2016, pp.649–666

[20] Carl Doersch, *Tutorial on Variational Autoencoders.* arXiv:1606.05908v2, Aug 2016

[21] Lucas Theis, Aäron van den Oord, and Matthias Bethge, *A note on the evaluation of generative models.* CVPR, 2017

[22] Martin Heusel, Hubert Ramsauer, Thomas Unterthiner, Bernhard Nessler, and Sepp Hochreiter, *GANs trained by a two time-scale update rule converge to a local Nash equilibrium.* In Advances in Neural Information Processing Systems, 2017

[23] https://github.com/bioinf-jku/TTUR

[24] Christian Szegedy, Vincent Vanhoucke, Sergey Ioffe, Jonathon Shlens, *Rethinking the Inception Architecture for Computer Vision*, 2016 IEEE Conference on Computer Vision and Pattern Recognition (CVPR), ISSN: 1063-6919, 2016

[25] Chao. Dong, Chen Change Loy, Kaiming He, and Xiaoou Tang, *Image super-resolution using deep convolutional networks.* IEEE Transactions on Pattern Analysis and Machine Intelligence, 38(2):295–307, 2016.

[26] Karen Simonyan and Andrew Zisserman, *Very deep convolutional networks for large-scale image recognition.* In International Conference on Learning Representations (ICLR), 2015. 2, 3, 4, 5

[27] http://mmlab.ie.cuhk.edu.hk/projects/CelebA.html

[28] Fisher Yu, Ari Seff, Yinda Zhang, Shuran Song, Thomas Funkhouser, Jianxiong Xiao, *LSUN: Construction of a Large-Scale Image Dataset using Deep Learning with Humans in the Loop.* CoRR, abs/1506.03365, 2015

On the Agreement of Commodity 3D Cameras

Johan Hagelbäck[1], Alisa Lincke[1], Welf Löwe[1], and Eduard Rall[2]
[1]DISA, Linnaeus University, Växjö/Kalmar, Sweden
[2]AIMO AB, Stockholm, Sweden

Abstract— *The advent of commodity 3D sensor technology has, amongst other things, enabled the efficient and effective assessment of human movements. Machine learning approaches do not rely manual definitions of gold standards for each new movement. However, to train models for the automated assessments of a new movement they still need a lot of data that map recorded movements to expert judgments. As camera technology changes, this training needs to be repeated if a new camera does not agree with the old one. The present paper presents an inexpensive method to check the agreement of cameras, which, in turn, would allow for a safe reuse of trained models regardless of the cameras. We apply the method to the Kinect, Astra Mini, and Real Sense cameras. The results show that these cameras do not agree and that the models cannot be reused without an unacceptable decay in accuracy. However, the suggested method works independent of movements and cameras and could potentially save effort when integrating new cameras in an existing assessment environment.*

Keywords: 3D camera agreement, human movement assessment

1. Introduction

Healthcare is becoming more and more value centered optimizing patient value (best possible health achieved) and system value (effective treatments at efficient costs). Until recently, measuring value, e.g., clinical outcomes, was not a capability of hospital or health IT [1]. With inexpensive sensor technologies and data analytics becoming increasingly available, it is nowadays possible to collect data on the clinical activities of healthcare, the health status of a patient and the change of this status after a treatment. We contribute with an automated objective method for the assessment of physical health of the human musculoskeletal system to help diagnose, predict or prevent related pain, injuries and long-lasting diseases. We use commodity 3D camera technology, such as the Microsoft Kinect.[1]

Any effective and efficient method for the assessment of human movements should be independent of the actual movement and the underlying camera technology. It should be possible to add new movements and new cameras with little expertise in the correct movement execution and without any expertise in the camera technology. This way new movements, e.g., for the assessment of insufficiencies or risks in specific professions or sports, and new cameras, e.g., Orbbec's Astra Mini,[2] and Intel's Real Sense,[3] could be added swiftly by the medical and physiotherapist experts without any technical support. With machine learning (ML) based approaches, adding new movements has become quite efficient and accurate [2]. Experts assess and score some representative executions of a new movement, which trains a model that is then used for all executions of this movement.

However, getting the necessary data points, i.e., a representative sample of movement executions and corresponding expert scores, is still expensive. It requires one to two days of recordings and five to ten days of expert scoring, let away the effort for organizing recordings with a representative sample of the population and managing medical experts in specific human movements. To date, this procedure needs to be repeated for each new camera integrated in the assessment environment, since, the input to the trained ML model from the camera might have changed. If, however, the cameras agree, i.e., they produce the same input to the model or any differences can systematically be compensated, the old trained model can be reused also with the new camera. This saves the effort of retraining involving new recordings and expert scorings.

The paper contributes with (i) an extensive study of methods for validating 3D cameras against a ground truth or testing their agreement, (ii) an efficient and effective statistical method for assessing the agreement of 3D cameras without a ground truth at hand, and (iii) an instantiation of this method for testing the agreement of three commodity 3D camera systems: Kinect, Astra Mini, and Real Sense. It is organized as follows: Section 2 discusses related methods for validating 3D cameras. Section 3 establishes the foundations of the subsequent discussions. Section 4 suggest a method to test the agreement of 3D cameras without knowing the ground truth. Section 5 applies this method to check the agreement of Kinect, Astra Mini, and Real Sense. Finally, Section 6 concludes the paper and shows directions of ongoing and future work.

2. Related Work

We separately discuss related work that *indirectly* validates 3D camera technologies by validating their *usage* in an application context and related work that *directly* compares

[1]https://en.wikipedia.org/wiki/Kinect

[2]https://orbbec3d.com/astra-mini

[3]https://realsense.intel.com

the output of 3D camera technologies with some ground truth (validations) or with each other (agreement).

2.1 Indirect Camera Validation

Quite a few studies research the recognition of human movements using a technology stack consisting of a commodity 3D camera providing input to software computing a skeleton avatar [3]–[10]. Their goal is the *classification* of different movements and not their quality assessment. Classification abstracts quite a bit from the features of a skeleton avatar. Even inaccurate camera/skeleton avatar technology may lead to quite accurate classifications.

The same technology stack has also been used in movement quality assessment [11]–[14]. However, these studies aim at *qualitative* assessments or at identifying different abnormal movement patterns rather than at *quantitatively* scoring the quality of a movement. Again, qualitative assessment abstracts from the skeleton avatar, which lowers the accuracy requirements of the camera/skeleton avatar technology stack.

Zhao et al. assess the feasibility of using the Kinect indirectly by examining a set of correctness rules defined for each exercise. They use logical invariants of each exercise that are independent of the camera system used [15].

Dressler et al. [16], [2] validate an automated, quantitative assessment of human movements based on the Kinect camera against expert scores. Their automated assessment even localizes the quality issue. This level of abstraction of this application is lower than classifications and qualitative assessments. It allows for the indirect conclusion that the camera/skeleton avatar technology is quite accurate.

2.2 Direct Camera Validation

In a pre-study for validating the agreement of Kinect and Astra Mini, Progressive Sports Technologies and AIMO excluded interference between these two cameras and between them and a Vicon motion capture system [17]. All three systems are infrared signal based. Kinect and Astra Mini are marker free while the Vicon relies on reflecting markers. Descriptive statistics (mean, standard deviation) of the joint position is used. This does not yet imply an agreement between the camera systems. In contrast this study, Naeemabadi et al. found an impact of a marker based motion capture system consisting of eight Qualisys Oqus cameras on the skeleton computation algorithm of the Kinect [18].

Lopez et al. found an agreement of joint angles measured with the skeleton avatar software of the Kinect and with goniometers. They evaluated the data with Bland-Altman plots and concluded the interchangeability of both measurement techniques [19].

Fern'ndez-Baena et al. conducted a comparison study of the precision of joint angles between Kinect and a marker based optical motion capture system and obtained a range of disparity that guaranties enough precision for most clinical rehabilitation treatments [20]. They use mean error and mean error relative to the range of motion for assessing the agreement of the systems.

Baldewijns et al. validated step length and time determined by the Kinect against the GAITRite walkway system as a ground truth [21]. They use Spearman's correlation coefficient for this validation. Müller et al. confirmed these results by showing an agreement of the Kinect with the Vicon motion capture system [22]. Therefore, Pearson's correlation coefficient and Bland-Altman statistics were used. In contrast to these results, Geerse et al. found significant differences in foot placement locations and step lengths and evidence for nonequivalence when comparing the Kinect based results with a gold-standard motion-registration system using two Optotrak cameras [23]. They use repeated-measures ANOVAs, agreement statistics and two one-sided t-tests to test agreement.

Ma et al. complemented these results by confirming the accuracy of the Kinect skeleton model in upper-body movements using a Vicon system [24]. The spatial accuracy was evaluated using Pearson's correlation coefficient, signal to noise ratio and 3D distance differences. For measurement validity, the accuracy was evaluated using mean and standard error of the difference, percentage error, Pearson's correlation coefficient and intra-class correlation.

Gray et al. validated the Kinect as a screening tool for identifying anterior cruciate ligament (ACL) injury risks by comparing relevant variables with a Vicon system as a gold standard [25]. This study demonstrated good agreement between the Kinect and the Vicon systems. The intra-class correlation coefficient (ICC) (two-way, single measure, absolute agreement) was used to assess the degree of agreement.

Kim et al. validated the Kinect for human abduction-adduction motion analysis by showing high agreement with a Vicon motion capture system [26]. Therefore, they used Pearson's correlation coefficient and limit of agreement analysis. They also showed that the Kinect camera was more effective for motion analysis than an inertial measurement unit (IMU) sensor.

Plantard et al. assessed the agreement of the Kinect skeleton avatar with the Vicon motion capture system in order to validate an ergonomic assessment method in real workplace conditions [27]. For the agreement test under lab conditions, they assess the root mean square error of the joint angles of both systems. In a second phase they validated their ergonomic assessment method under real world conditions against human experts, which is an *indirect* camera validation in our conceptual context, cf. Section 2.1.

Eltoukhy et al. validated the Kinect for the measurement of lower extremity jump landing and squatting kinematics establishing an agreement with an 8 camera BTS Smart 7000DX motion analysis system. However, Kinect values were improved by applying a corrective factor.

Even other studies that evaluate the agreement of Kinect to traditional 3D motion analysis systems in physiotherapist settings: Cippitelli et al. validated the Kinect for sit-to-stand analysis [28]. Eltoukhy et al. established the validity of the Kinect for static and dynamic balance assessment [29]. They analyze intra-class correlation coefficients showing consistency and agreement.

2.3 Discussion

The studies introduced in Section 2.1 need to be redone for every new camera technology in order to transfer their results. This is quite some effort and hampers the adoption of new technologies. However, if it can be shown that the new technology agrees with the one used in the studies, this effort can be saved. To this end, these studies are beneficiaries of the method discussed in the present paper.

The studies discussed Section 2.2 open up a wide range of methods for validating the agreement between cameras. However, they all show the validation against a ground truth, using exact measurements with special devises or expensive motion capturing technology. Repeating these studies with new camera technology can follow the suggested methods but would requires quite some effort. Moreover, most studies are done with an application in mind, e.g., gait analysis, sit-to-stand analysis, abduction-adduction motion analysis etc. Results are therefore only valid for the tested application. To this end, the method discussed in the present paper is an inexpensive alternative to the ones of these related studies.

3. Foundations

A *sequence* is a list of frames from a recording of a human movement. A sequence is *static* if the recorded movement is actually a posture, i.e., the recorded person does not intend to move, e.g., he/she stands still. Otherwise, a sequence is called *dynamic*, e.g., if the recorded movement is a deep squat. Each *frame* is a record of features and describes the body posture at a specific point in time during a movement. Each *feature* describes an aspect of the body posture at a specific point in time. A feature is called *direct* if it is directly measured by the 3D camera/skeleton avatar software or *indirect* if it is computed from the direct or other indirect features. The direct features include the x, y, and z coordinates of skeleton joints. Indirect features include angles between limbs and the axes of the 3D coordinate system. An *aggregated sequence* is a list of aggregated frames. An *aggregated frame* aggregates two or more frames into one. It is a vector, with an element for each feature, containing the mean of the respective feature values of the aggregated frames.

It is natural to understand features as real-valued random variables. We assess the sample distributions of feature values using descriptive statistics, such as (sample) mean and standard deviation. We do not make any assumption about the kind of the distributions, e.g., their normality.

Additionally, we assess the agreement between two measurement methods with the *linear* correlation between their feature values using the Pearson correlation coefficient. Altman and Bland argue that a high correlation is necessary but not sufficient for concluding an agreement between two measurement methods and suggest an additional analysis of the differences [32]. Accordingly, we assess the differences of feature values and their distributions. Finally, we use Bland-Altman plots to visually check the nature of relations between feature values.

Matching corresponding phases of two *dynamic* movement sequences is an important subproblem of testing the agreement of cameras. Approaches based on *Dynamic Time Wrapping* (DTW) [30] and *Hidden Markov Models* (HMM) [31] are arguably predominant in addressing this problem. DTW approaches are used, e.g., in [4], [11], [12], [7], HMM approaches in [5], [14]. None of the two approaches can ignore irrelevant leading and trailing subsequences. *Sequence Alignment* is a DTW generalization able to find an optimal matching of *relevant subsequences* automatically [2].

4. Testing the Agreement of Cameras

We suggest testing the agreement of the complete technology stack consisting of a 3D camera and the software computing a skeleton avatar in four straightforward steps: (1) Exclude interference between the systems. (2) Check the agreement of direct features from the two systems. (3) Check the agreement of indirect features from the two systems used in an application area. (4) Check the agreement of the two systems in an application. Each step shows either (a) an agreement, (b) a systematic disagreement that can compensated for, or (c) a random disagreement. We only check for linear correlation. Consequently, systematic disagreement refers to the *linear* predictor function $Y = f(X) = aX + b$ whose parameters a, b are estimated from the feature values X, Y in a linear regression analysis.

For showing an agreement, we try to exclude interference in Step (1) and to show case (a) or (b) in the subsequent Steps (2)-(4). If we don't succeed in one step, we still can try with the next one since, each step is an abstraction of the feature values of the previous one: If we succeed in Step (2), we conclude an agreement of the camera technology stacks. If we don't succeed in Step (2) but in Step (3), we conclude an agreement of the cameras for the assessment of all movements that only rely on the analyzed indirect features. If we don't succeed in Steps (2) and (3) but in Step (4), we conclude an agreement of the cameras for the assessment of the analyzed movement.

4.1 Excluding Interference of Systems

Step (1) tries to exclude two symmetric cases: camera system A (resp. B) is impacted if camera system B (resp.

A) is recording simultaneously. We only discuss one case. The symmetric case is handled identically.

Similar to [17], we suggest to record static and dynamic sequences. However, we don't have a ground truth from a professional motion capturing system. Therefore, we have to deviate from their method.

For the static sequence, we alter fixed time intervals where only system A is recording (condition A) and where both systems A and B are recording (condition AB). We are only interested in the recordings of system A under both conditions. For each direct feature, we compute two distributions of feature values, one for A and one for AB. We expect differences of the mean and the standard deviations of the two corresponding distributions to be negligible.

As [17], we suggest to record a complex movement, such as a deep squat, for assessing dynamic sequences. We alter complete movements where only system A is recording (condition A) and where both systems A and B are recording (condition AB). Again, we are only interested in the recordings of system A under both conditions. For each direct feature *and each phase* of the movement, we compute two distributions of feature values, one for A and one for AB. We expect differences of the mean and the standard deviations of the two corresponding distributions to be negligible.

For the dynamic sequences, it is however not trivial to separate the phases of a continuous movement. This is necessary in order to add the feature values of a frame to the distributions belonging to the right phase. In order to map each frame to the right phase, we first select a sequence recording a movement instance with high quality under condition A. This *master* sequence is split into phases of 10 subsequent frames each. All other sequences are matched to the master sequence using *Sequence Alignment* [16]. This results in a mapping of each frame f_r of a recorded sequence to one or more subsequent frames F_m of the master sequence. f_r belongs to the phase that the frames in F_m belong to. If a frame is mapped to more than one master frame and these master frames belong to two subsequent phases, then f_r belongs to both phases.

4.2 Agreement of (In-)Direct Features

Steps (2) and (3) are handled in a similar way. The only difference is that the assessment method is applied first to the direct features (2) and then to the indirect features (3) that are computed in a preprocessing step for each frame of direct features.

Having excluded mutual interference of the systems A and B, we suggest to record dynamic sequences simultaneously with both systems. For each instance of a movement, we get two sequences, one with system A and another with system B. For the matching frames of the two sequences, we expect the values of the same features to correlate and their differences to be negligible.

Sequence Alignment computes a matching of frames in a similar way as described in Section 4.1. However, we only compute a pairwise matching of the sequences A and B recording the same movement instances. After matching, we aggregate the frames of both sequences separately: a frame f_A of sequence A mapped to k frames $f_B^1, \ldots, f_B^k$ of sequence B triggers an aggregation of $f_B^1, \ldots, f_B^k$ in sequence B. Likewise, a frame in sequence B mapped to more than one frame in sequence A triggers an aggregation of these frames in sequence A. This way both sequences A and B have the same number of aggregated frames and the i-th aggregated frame of sequence A matches the i-th aggregated frame of sequence B.

4.3 Agreement in an Application

In Step (4), we again record dynamic sequences simultaneously with both systems A and B. We assume the application computes either a class or a score.

For a classification application, we expect an agreement of the classes c_A and c_B computed based on the sequences A and B recording the same movement instances. That is, we expect a high accuracy (the number of agreeing over all classifications is close to 1), and for each class C, a high precision (number of $c_A = c_B = C$ over $c_B = C$ close to 1) and a high recall (number of $c_A = c_B = C$ over $c_A = C$ close to 1).

For a scoring application, we expect an agreement of the scores s_A and s_B computed based on the sequences A and B recording the same movement instances. That is, we expect a high correlation of the scores (Pearson's coefficient r of correlation close to 1) and negligible differences $s_A - s_B$.

5. Kinect, Astra Mini, and Real Sense

We test the agreement of Microsoft's Kinect (v2) using the Kinect for Windows SDK[4] for skeleton avatar computation and two alternative systems, Orbbec's Astra Mini and Intel's Real Sense both using the NuiTrack SDK[5] for skeleton avatar computation.

5.1 Excluding Interference of Systems

As for Step (1), there is no interference between Kinect and Astra Mini [17]. Therefore, we do not assume interference between Kinect and Real Sense either but excluding interference formally is left to future work.

5.2 Agreement of (In-) Direct Feature Values

For Steps (2) and (3), we recorded 14 deep squat movement instances simultaneously with a Kinect and an Astra Mini camera and 7 instances with a Kinect and a Real Sense. Some initial linear transformations of the joint vectors compensated for potential differences between the cameras

[4]https://developer.microsoft.com/en-us/windows/kinect
[5]https://nuitrack.com

Table 1: Joint Agreement with Kinect (Direct Features)

Joints	Astra Mini		Real Sense	
	r	$\mu_d \pm \Delta$	r	$\mu_d \pm \Delta$
AnkleLeft	0.95	0.04 ±0.47	0.93	0.04 ±0.54
AnkleRight	0.96	0.07 ±0.37	0.94	0.11 ±0.44
ElbowLeft	0.55	-0.04 ±0.74	0.75	0.04 ±0.61
ElbowRight	0.55	0.02 ±0.72	0.72	0.03 ±0.66
Head	0.99	0.01 ±0.06	0.99	0 ±0.09
HipLeft	0.51	-0.04 ±0.32	0.46	-0.05 ±0.36
HipRight	0.55	0.04 ±0.27	0.51	0.08 ±0.31
KneeLeft	0.87	0 ±0.46	0.75	0.06 ±0.49
KneeRight	0.82	0.12 ±0.32	0.80	0.13 ±0.32
Neck	0.99	0 ±0.06	0.99	0 ±0.05
ShoulderLeft	0.80	-0.03 ±0.48	0.80	-0.01 ±0.52
ShoulderRight	0.81	0 ±0.50	0.80	0.1 ±0.50
SpineBase	0.90	0 ±0.04	0.79	0 ±0.05
SpineMid	0.97	0.01 ±0.08	0.95	0.01 ±0.10
SpineShoulder	0.99	0 ±0.06	0.98	0.01 ±0.05
WristLeft	0.76	-0.03 ±0.65	0.85	-0.03 ±0.62
WristRight	0.70	0.07 ±0.69	0.79	0.05 ±0.65
μ_r, μ_Δ	0.80	±0.37	0.81	±0.37
σ_r, σ_Δ	0.17	±0.24	0.15	±0.22
$\min_r, \max_\Delta$	0.51	±0.74	0.46	±0.66

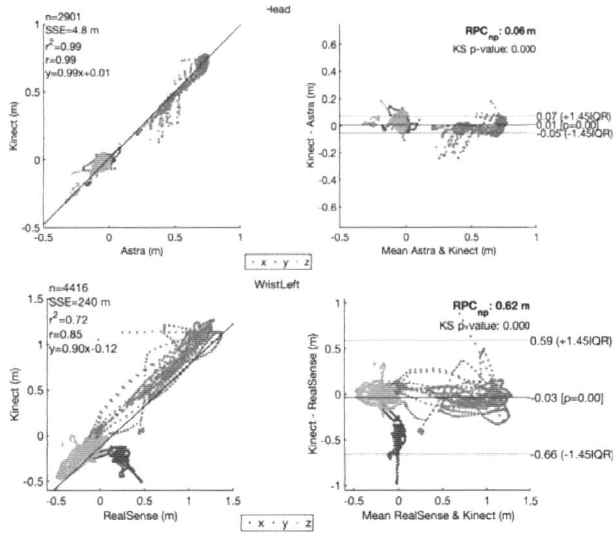

Fig. 1: Bland-Altman plots: x, y, z positions (left) and their differences (right) of Kinect and Astra Mini for Head (top) and Kinect and Real Sense for Wrist Left (bottom)

and SDKs. The transformations move the spine base of the first frame to the center of the 3D coordinate system and let the skeletons "face" the camera, cf. [16] for the details.

5.2.1 Agreement of Direct Features

As for Step (2), the direct features are the x, y, z positions of 17 joints that all three systems have in common. These joints are listed in the first column of Table 1. The other columns list correlations and differences of Astra Mini (Real Sense) feature values to the corresponding Kinect feature values. The correlations are given as the Pearson coefficient r. The differences are given in *meters*. For each feature, we list the mean μ_d of the pairwise differences d and the difference confidence interval $\Delta = \pm 2\sigma_d$ in which 95% of the differences are expected. At the bottom of the table, we list mean μ and standard deviation σ of r and Δ together with the minimum correlation r and the maximum Δ.

On average the correlation between the joint positions recorded with Kinect and Astra Mini (resp. Real Sense) is quite high: the mean correlation $\mu_r \geq 0.8$. For the left hip joint (HipLeft), both alternative cameras show the lowest correlation with the Kinect, $r = 0.51$ ($r = 0.46$), followed by the right hip (HipRight), $r = 0.55$ ($r = 0.51$). This does not come as a surprise as the Kinect SDK systematically differs from the NuiTrack SDK in estimating the hip joints.

For each joint, the mean of the differences μ_d of the joint positions recorded with Kinect and Astra Mini (resp. Real Sense) is quite low: at most $12cm$ ($13cm$) for the right knee for the Astra Mini (Real Sense). However, the confidence intervals Δ are large, up to $74cm$ for the Astra Mini ($66cm$ for the Real Sense).

Figure 1 shows selected Bland-Altman plots showing the correlation of x, y, z positions (left) and their respective differences d (right). We choose the head features measured with Kinect and Astra Mini (top) showing a good agreement, and the left wrist features measured with Kinect and Real Sense (bottom) showing a bad agreement, especially, in the x coordinate.

The results (Table 1 and Figure 1) confirm a high agreement only for some "joints", such as, the head, the neck, the spine, whereas an agreement cannot be concluded for most of the joints and, hence, neither for the systems as a whole.

5.2.2 Agreement of Indirect Features

As for Step (3), the indirect features are the angles between limbs adjacent to the same joint. These angles are listed in the first column of Table 2 followed by the correlations r and differences d of the angles of Astra Mini (Real Sense) and the corresponding Kinect angles. Differences are in *degrees* (°). The average correlations of the alternative cameras with the Kinect are modest, $\mu_r = 0.54$ for the Astra Mini (0.48 for the Real Sense), only high for the left ($r = 0.94$) and the right ($r = 0.97$) knee angles of Astra Mini and Kinect. For the hip angles, we even have a negative correlation.

The mean differences μ_d can neither be ignored: up to 32° for the Astra Mini (25° for the Real Sense). The intervals Δ in which 95% of all differences are expected are up to 39° for the Astra Mini (72° for the Real Sense).

Figure 2 shows selected Bland-Altman plots—correlation (left) and differences (right)—of the neck angles measured with Kinect vs. Astra Mini (top) and of the left elbow angles measured with Kinect vs. Real Sense (bottom). The plots visually confirm the low agreement of the angles measured

Table 2: Angle Agreement with Kinect (Indirect Features)

Limb Angle	Astra Mini		Real Sense	
	r	$\mu_d \pm \Delta$	r	$\mu_d \pm \Delta$
Hip-**Knee**-Ankle (left)	0.94	-5.4 ±9.1	0.76	11 ±33
Hip-**Knee**-Ankle (right)	0.97	0.6 ±11	0.65	12 ±42
Shoulder-**Elbow**-Wrist (left)	0.25	20 ±39	0.58	8.4 ±16
Shoulder-**Elbow**-Wrist (right)	0.42	21 ±36	0.76	12 ±26
SpineBase-**Hip**-Knee (left)	-0.88	-18 ±30	-0.63	-16 ±72
SpineBase-**Hip**-Knee (right)	-0.86	-22 ±35	-0.36	-17 ±59
SpineBase-**SpineMid**-SpineShoulder	0.28	11 ±8.3	0.07	5.2 ±12
SpineMid-**SpineBase**-Hip (left)	0.70	-31 ±8.2	0.62	-22 ±37
SpineMid-**SpineBase**-Hip (right)	0.68	-32 ±9.1	0.59	-25 ±35
SpineMid-**SpineShoulder**-Neck	0.06	-2.2 ±1.5	0.5	-2.3 ±0.7
SpineShoulder-**Neck**-Head	0.16	-2 ±11	0.01	3.6 ±24
SpineShoulder-**Shoulder**-Elbow (left)	0.61	9.2 ±24	0.39	13 ±18
SpineShoulder-**Shoulder**-Elbow (right)	0.21	8.9 ±21	0.31	13 ±18
μ_r, μ_Δ	0.54	±18.7	0.45	±30.2
σ_r, σ_Δ	0.31	±12.3	0.23	±18.7
$\min_r, \max_\Delta$	0.06	±39	0.01	±72

with the Kinect and the alternative cameras as already concluded from the correlation coefficients and difference interval sizes.

The results (Table 2 and Figure 2) show a high agreement between Astra Mini and Kinect for the knee angles, whereas an agreement cannot be concluded for all other angles and, hence, neither for the systems as a whole in Step (3).

5.3 Agreement in an Application

For Step (4), we assess the 37 deep squat movement instances simultaneously recorded with Kinect and Astra Mini (29 instances with Kinect and Real Sense) with a manually implemented and tuned deep squat movement scoring app that agrees with human experts [16]. We retrained this scoring app with the original training data but with 3 instead of 15 phases, which only gives marginally lower agreement with the expert scoring.

For all movement instances, Table 3 shows the correlations and differences of Astra Mini (Real Sense) scores to the corresponding Kinect scores. The correlation is quite low for Real Sense camera ($r = 0.12$), but higher than expected for the Astra Mini ($r = 0.29$) given the results of Steps (2) and (3). However, we cannot conclude an agreement of the systems in Step (4).

6. Conclusions and Future Work

The paper discusses (i) the state of the art in assessing the agreement between 3D camera/skeleton avatar systems. It distinguishes related work that indirectly validates 3D camera technologies by validating their usage in an application context from related work that directly compares the output of 3D camera technologies with some ground truth or with each other. It also lists the different assessment methods used.

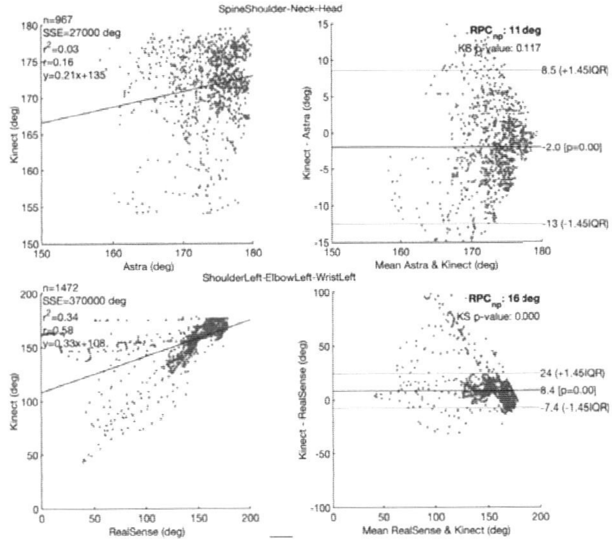

Fig. 2: Bland-Altman plots: SpineShoulder-**Neck**-Head Angles of Kinect and Astra Mini (top), Left Shoulder-**Elbow**-Wrist Angles of Kinect and Real Sense (bottom)

Table 3: Deep Squat Quality Score Agreement with Kinect

Deep Squat	Astra Mini		Real Sense	
	r	$\mu_d \pm \Delta$	r	$\mu_d \pm \Delta$
Quality score	0.29	-0.2 ±0.15	0.12	-0.1 ±0.10

Based on this analysis of the state of the art, the paper suggests (ii) a method that assesses the agreement of camera systems without a ground truth from a professional motion capturing system (or other trusted measurements) at hand. The method works in four steps: (1) exclusion of interference, (2) agreement test of direct features, (3) agreement test of indirect features, and (4) test of agreement in a client application.

Finally, the paper uses the suggested method to (iii) assess the agreement of Kinect v2 with Astra Mini and Real Sense, three comparably inexpensive 3D camera systems. For the Kinect v2, the Kinect SDK provides the skeleton avatar, for Astra Mini and Real Sense, the NuiTrack SDK. We cannot confirm their agreement.

The negative implication of the results is that movement assessment engines designed for or trained with the Kinect cannot simply be reused when adopting the alternative camera systems Astra Mini and Real Sense. The positive implication of the result is that the assessment method, and the test framework that was built as a side effect, can be reused when assessing new emerging camera technology.

This objectifies and simplifies future camera technology adoption decisions.

The two evaluated SDKs place some joints systematically differently, which leads to the low agreement in these joints. We currently work on an automatic compensation of these differences in order to improve the overall the skeleton agreement. Moreover, we currently apply the method to test the agreement of Kinect (projected to 2D) and the key points recognized by PoseNet [33], [34]. While it is too early to report result, we find that the method suggested in this paper is well applicable to this new case.

Future work aims at a systematic literature review of the field with the related work review (i) as a starting point. It also aims at applying the assessment method (ii) to more cases to confirm that it works effectively and efficiently also to hopefully see in cases with positive outcome. Finally, it aims at making the assessment framework prototype available for general reuse.

References

[1] J. Elton and A. O'Riordan, *Healthcare Disrupted: Next Generation Business Models and Strategies*. Wiley, 2016.

[2] D. Dressler, P. Liapota, and W. Löwe, "Data driven human movement assessment," *11th Int. Conf. Innovation in Knowledge Based and Intelligent Engineering Systems, (KES), Invited Session Digital Health, Distance Learning and decision support for eHealth*, 2019.

[3] J. Wang, Z. Liu, Y. Wu, and J. Yuan, "Mining actionlet ensemble for action recognition with depth cameras," *IEEE Conf. Computer Vision and Pattern Recognition*. IEEE Computer Society, 2012.

[4] J. Wang and H. Zheng, "View-robust action recognition based on temporal self-similarities and dynamic time warping," *IEEE Int. Conf. Computer Science and Automation Engineering (CSAE)*, vol. 2, 2012.

[5] L. Xia, C.-C. Chen, and J. K. Aggarwal, "View invariant human action recognition using histograms of 3d joints," *CVPR Workshops*. IEEE Computer Society, 2012.

[6] A. Yao, J. Gall, and L. Van Gool, "Coupled action recognition and pose estimation from multiple views," *Int. J. Computer Vision*, vol. 100, no. 1, 2012.

[7] R. Vemulapalli, F. Arrate, and R. Chellappa, "Human action recognition by representing 3d skeletons as points in a lie group," *IEEE Conf. Computer Vision and Pattern Recognition*, 2014.

[8] M. Jiang, J. Kong, G. Bebis, and H. Huo, "Informative joints based human action recognition using skeleton contexts," *Signal Processing: Image Communication*, vol. 33, 2015.

[9] H. Pazhoumand-Dar, C.-P. Lam, and M. Masek, "Joint movement similarities for robust 3d action recognition using skeletal data," *J. Visual Communication and Image Representation*, vol. 30, 2015.

[10] R. Slama, H. Wannous, M. Daoudi, and A. Srivastava, "Accurate 3d action recognition using learning on the grassmann manifold," *Pattern Recognition*, vol. 48, no. 2, 2015.

[11] R. Wang, G. Medioni, C. J. Winstein, and C. Blanco, "Home monitoring musculo-skeletal disorders with a single 3d sensor," *IEEE Conf. Computer Vision and Pattern Recognition Workshops*, 2013.

[12] N. M. Khan, S. Lin, L. Guan, and B. Guo, "A visual evaluation framework for in-home physical rehabilitation," *IEEE Int. Symp. Multimedia*, 2014.

[13] A. Paiement, L. Tao, M. Camplani, S. Hannuna, D. Damen, and M. Mirmehdi, "Online quality assessment of human motion from skeleton data," *Proceedings of the British Machine Vision Conference*. BMVA Press, 2014.

[14] L. Tao, A. Paiement, D. Damen, M. Mirmehdi, S. Hannuna, M. Camplani, T. Burghardt, and I. Craddock, "A comparative study of pose representation and dynamics modelling for online motion quality assessment," *Computer Vision and Image Understanding*, vol. 148, 2016.

[15] W. Zhao, D. D. Espy, and A. Reinthal, "A validation study of rehabilitation exercise monitoring using kinect," *Advanced Methodologies and Technologies in Medicine and Healthcare*, D. Mehdi Khosrow-Pour, Ed. IDG Global, 2017.

[16] D. Dressler, P. Liapota, and W. Löwe, "Towards an automated assessment of musculoskeletal insufficiencies," in *11th Int. Conf. Innovation in Knowledge Based and Intelligent Engineering Systems, (KES), Invited Session Data Selection in Machine Learning*, 2019.

[17] P. S. Technologies, "AIMO – 3D Body Tracking Validation," Loughborough University Sports Technology Institute, Tech. Rep., 04 2018.

[18] M. Naeemabadi, B. I. Dinesen, O. K. Andersen, and J. Hansen, "Influence of a marker-based motion capture system on the performance of microsoft kinect v2 skeleton algorithm," *IEEE Sensors J.*, vol. 19, 2019.

[19] N. Lopez, E. Perez, E. Tello, A. Rodrigo, and M. E. Valentinuzzi, "Statistical validation for clinical measures: Repeatability and agreement of kinect™-based software," *BioMed Research Int.*, 2018.

[20] A. Fern'ndez-Baena, A. Susín, and X. Lligadas, "Biomechanical validation of upper-body and lower-body joint movements of kinect motion capture data for rehabilitation treatments," *4th Int. Conf. Intelligent Networking and Collaborative Systems*, 2012.

[21] G. Baldewijns, G. Verheyden, B. Vanrumste, and T. Croonenborghs, "Validation of the kinect for gait analysis using the gaitrite walkway," *36th Annual Int. Conf. of the IEEE Engineering in Medicine and Biology Society, EMBC*, 2014.

[22] B. Müller, W. Ilg, M. A. Giese, and N. Ludolph, "Validation of enhanced kinect sensor based motion capturing for gait assessment," *PLOS ONE*, vol. 12, no. 4, 2017.

[23] D. Geerse, B. Coolen, D. Kolijn, and M. Roerdink, "Validation of foot placement locations from ankle data of a kinect v2 sensor," *Sensors*, vol. 17, no. 10, 2017.

[24] M. Ma, R. Proffitt, and M. Skubic, "Validation of a kinect v2 based rehabilitation game," *PLOS ONE*, vol. 13, no. 8, 2018.

[25] A. D. Gray, J. M. Marks, E. E. Stone, M. C. Butler, M. Skubic, and S. L. Sherman, "Validation of the microsoft kinect as a portable and inexpensive screening tool for identifying acl injury risk," *Orthopaedic J. Sports Medicine*, vol. 2, no. 7 (suppl.), 2014.

[26] C. Y. Kim, J. S. Hong, and K. J. Chun, "Validation of feasibility of two depth sensor-based microsoft kinect cameras for human abduction-adduction motion analysis," *Int. J. Precision Engineering and Manufacturing*, vol. 17, no. 9, 2016.

[27] P. Plantard, H. P. Shum, A.-S. L. Pierres, and F. Multon, "Validation of an ergonomic assessment method using kinect data in real workplace conditions," *Applied Ergonomics*, vol. 65, 2017.

[28] E. Cippitelli, S. Gasparrini, S. Spinsante, E. Gambi, F. Verdini, L. Burattini, F. Di Nardo, and S. Fioretti, "Validation of an optimized algorithm to use kinect in a non-structured environment for sit-to-stand analysis," *37th Annual Int. Conf. of the IEEE Engineering in Medicine and Biology Society (EMBC)*, 2015.

[29] M. A. Eltoukhy, C. Kuenze, J. Oh, and J. F. Signorile, "Validation of static and dynamic balance assessment using microsoft kinect for young and elderly populations," *IEEE J. Biomedical and Health Informatics*, vol. 22, no. 1, 2018.

[30] H. Sakoe and S. Chiba, "Dynamic programming algorithm optimization for spoken word recognition," *IEEE Transactions Acoustics, Speech, and Signal Processing*, vol. 26, no. 1, 1978.

[31] L. E. Baum and T. Petrie, "Statistical inference for probabilistic functions of finite state markov chains," *The Annals of Mathematical Statistics*, vol. 37, no. 6, 1966.

[32] D. G. Altman and J. M. Bland, "Measurement in medicine: the analysis of method comparison studies," *The Statistician*, vol. 32, 1983.

[33] G. Papandreou, T. Zhu, N. Kanazawa, A. Toshev, J. Tompson, C. Bregler, and K. P. Murphy, "Towards accurate multi-person pose estimation in the wild," *CoRR*, vol. abs/1701.01779, 2017.

[34] G. Papandreou, T. Zhu, L. Chen, S. Gidaris, J. Tompson, and K. Murphy, "Personlab: Person pose estimation and instance segmentation with a bottom-up, part-based, geometric embedding model," *CoRR*, vol. abs/1803.08225, 2018.

On Stationary Periodic Kernels

Hongjun Su[1] **and Hong Zhang**[2]
[1]Department of Electrical Engineering, Georgia Southern University, Savannah, GA 31419, U.S.A.
[2]Department of Computer Science, Georgia Southern University, Savannah, GA 31419, U.S.A.

Abstract - *Kernels as similarity measures are key components of machine learning algorithms such as Support Vector Machine and Gaussian Process. For attributes with periodic property, it is advantageous to apply a kernel that is periodic. We propose a general family of periodic kernels and prove that all stationary periodic kernels belong to this family. The results are extended to d- dimensional spaces.*

Keywords: Kernel, Machine learning, Periodic function, Fourier transform, Bochner's theorem

1 Introduction

A kernel is a similarity measure that is the key component of support vector machines ([2]) and other machine learning techniques ([5],[8],[9]). Often the performance of a machine learning system depends highly on the effectiveness of the kernel to represent the similarity between objects. Capturing the special structural information of the data in the kernel can be useful in improving the system performance.

One special property in the attributes of the data is periodicity. Examples of periodic attributes include the "time of day", "day of year", and "position of a wave". Applications involving seasonal economics data, environmental attributes, and astronomical data can all be linked naturally to periodic structures. Many image processing and recognition applications may also involve elements of periodic nature. To recognize the label on a cylindrical can, for example, the image can be naturally treated as a periodic function defined on a cylinder. In analyzing image objects of simply connected regions, such as chromosome images [7], the data defined along the contour of a region is also naturally a periodic function.

The standard kernel functions such as the RBF kernel do not have the periodic property and could produce inaccurate measures of similarity. For example, the time stamp of 2:00 is closer to 23:00 than to 10:00 because of the period of 24 hours. This fact will not be reflected in a standard kernel function: $e^{-(2-23)^2} < e^{-(2-10)^2}$.

There are kernels that exhibit periodic property. One commonly used periodic kernel is ([4])

$$k(x,y) = e^{-\frac{\sin^2 2\pi(x-y)/T}{l^2}}$$

The following is another simple kernel function that provides proper measures for periodic data of period T.

$$k(x,y) = \cos\frac{2\pi}{T}(x-y)$$

This is a valid kernel function because

$$\cos\frac{2\pi}{T}(x-y) = \cos\frac{2\pi}{T}x\cos\frac{2\pi}{T}y + \sin\frac{2\pi}{T}x\sin\frac{2\pi}{T}y$$

A function of the form $f(x)f(y)$ is a kernel, and a positive linear combination of two kernels is a kernel. This kernel function faithfully reflects the periodic nature of the data. For example, in the time of day case this periodic kernel provides more reasonable measures:

$$\cos\frac{2\pi}{24}(2-23) = \frac{\sqrt{2}}{2} > -\frac{1}{2} = \cos\frac{2\pi}{24}(2-10)$$

In this paper, we provide a characterization of stationary periodic kernels, in terms of their Fourier series.

This paper is organized as follows. Section 2 introduces 1-dimentional periodic kernels and their characterization in terms of Fourier series. In Section 3, the results are generalized to d-dimensional spaces. Experimental results comparing the periodic kernels to standard kernels on Gaussian mixture distributions are presented in Section 4. Finally, Section 5 provides conclusions and proposals for future studies.

2 Periodic Kernels

A kernel is a real valued function on two variables that is symmetric and positive definite.

$$K(x,y) = K(y,x)$$

$$\sum_{i,j=1}^{n} K(x_i,x_j)c_ic_j \geq 0$$

A shift invariant or stationary kernel satisfies the condition

$$K(x,y) = k(x-y)$$

We call a 1-dimensional stationary kernel periodic of period T if

$$K(x,y) = k(x-y+T) = k(x-y)$$

We will show that a general 1-dimensional stationary kernel of period T can be expressed as

$$K(x,y) = k(x-y)$$

$$= \sum_{n=0}^{\infty} a_n \cos\frac{2\pi n}{T}(x-y),\ a_n \geq 0 \quad (1)$$

We will apply Fourier transform ([6]) and Bochner's theorem ([3]) to derive the result.

Let G be a locally compact abelian group. A character $\chi(x)$ is a continuous group homomorphism from G to the circle group $\mathbb{T}$. The dual group is the set of all characters on G, denoted $\hat{G}$, along with the multiplication operation. Let f be a function on G. The Fourier transform of f is defined as a function on $\hat{G}$:

$$\hat{f}(\chi) = \int_G f(x)\overline{\chi(x)}dv(x)$$

where v is the Haar measure on G.

Bochner's theorem states that for a locally compact abelian group G with dual group $\hat{G}$, and a positive definite function f

$$f(x) = \int_{\hat{G}} \chi(x)d\mu(\chi)$$

where μ is a positive finite measure.

Theorem 1. The function defined in Equation (1) is a stationary periodic kernel. A stationary periodic kernel must be of the form defined in Equation (1).

Proof. Using a trigonometric identity, we can rewrite the function as

$$K(x,y) = k(x-y) = \sum_{n=0}^{\infty} a_n \cos\frac{2\pi n}{T}(x-y)$$

$$= \sum_{n=0}^{\infty} a_n \left[\cos\frac{2\pi n}{T}(x)\cos\frac{2\pi n}{T}(y) + \sin\frac{2\pi n}{T}(x)\sin\frac{2\pi n}{T}(y)\right]$$

$$= \sum_{n=0}^{\infty} \left[\sqrt{a_n}\cos\frac{2\pi n}{T}(x)\sqrt{a_n}\cos\frac{2\pi n}{T}(y) + \sqrt{a_n}\sin\frac{2\pi n}{T}(x)\sqrt{a_n}\sin\frac{2\pi n}{T}(y)\right]$$

Therefore the function is a covariance kernel. It is clearly periodic with period T.

Conversely, if k is a periodic kernel, consider the Fourier series of $k(x-y)$. Since k is real, the Fourier series can be written as a series of sin and cos functions.

$$k(x-y) = \sum_{n=0}^{\infty} a_n \cos\frac{2\pi n}{T}(x-y) + b_n \sin\frac{2\pi n}{T}(x-y)$$

Since k is an even function, the Fourier series contains only cos terms.

$$k(x-y) = \sum_{n=0}^{\infty} a_n \cos\frac{2\pi n}{T}(x-y)$$

Now we only need to show that $a_n \geq 0$. Since k is positive definite, by Bochner's theorem,

$$k(x-y) = \int_{\hat{G}} \chi(x-y)d\mu(\chi)$$

In this case, the group G is the circle group. The dual group is the group of integers $\mathbb{Z}$. The positive measure μ corresponds the Fourier coefficients a_n. Therefore, $a_n \geq 0$.

3 Generalization to d-Dimensional Spaces

The results can be extended to kernel functions on d-dimensional Euclidean spaces $\mathbb{R}^d$, by using the similar Fourier analysis as the 1-dimensional case. A stationary kernel function on $\mathbb{R}^d$ is periodic if it is periodic with respect to each of its dimensions.

$$k\big(x-y+(0,0,\dots,T_j,\dots 0)\big) = k(x-y), \qquad j = 1,2,\dots,d$$

where T_j is the period for the dimension j.

The domain of such a function is the direct product of d circles $\mathbb{T}^d$, which is a locally compact abelian group. The dual group is the direct product of the integer group $\mathbb{Z}^d$. Using the Fourier analysis on the group, we can show that such a kernel can be expressed as the following series of products of cos functions.

$$K(x,y) = k(x-y)$$

$$= \sum_{n\geq 0} a_n \prod_{j=1}^{d} \cos\frac{2\pi n_j}{T_j}(x_j - y_j),\ a_n \geq 0 \tag{2}$$

where $n = (n_1, n_2, \ldots, n_j, \ldots, n_d) \in \mathbb{Z}^d$.

Theorem 2. A stationary kernel on $\mathbb{R}^d$ is periodic if and only if it is defined in Equation (2).

Proof. Each term in Equation (2) is a product of kernels and hence a kernel. Since the coefficients are positive, the sum is also a kernel.

Conversely, consider the Fourier transform of k on T^d

$$\hat{k}(\chi) = \int_G k(x) \prod_{j=1}^{d} \exp\left(-\frac{2\pi n_j}{T_j} i x_j\right) dv(x)$$

By using the inversion formula, the function k can be expressed as a series over the dual group $\mathbb{Z}^d$. Since k is real, the Fourier series can be written as a series of sin and cos functions. Since k is an even function, the Fourier series contains only cos terms.

$$k(x-y) = \sum_{n\geq 0} a_n \prod_{j=1}^{d} \cos\frac{2\pi n_j}{T_j}(x_j - y_j)$$

Since k is positive definite, by Bochner's theorem,

$$k(x-y) = \int_{\hat{G}} \chi(x-y) d\mu(\chi)$$

The positive measure μ corresponds to the Fourier coefficients a_n. Therefore, $a_n \geq 0$.

4 Experimental Results and Discussions

A 2-dimensional example is used to compare a periodic kernel with a standard RBF kernel. The space is considered periodic in both dimensions, so it is topologically a torus. A two-class classification problem is formulated with each class following a Gaussian mixture distribution ([1]). The positive class has two centers at the middle of the two identified edges. The negative class has two centers at the four corners and the middle of the space. A sample from the distribution is shown in Figure 1.

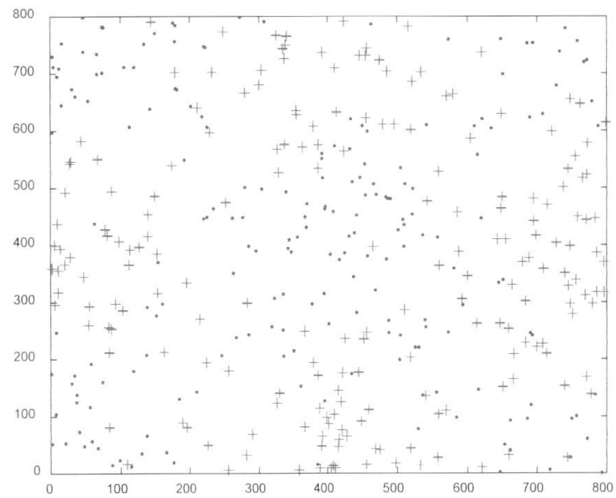

Figure 1. Gaussian mixtures on a torus

The top and bottom edges are identified and so are the left and right edges. When plotted in a plane, the sample appears to be fragmented. Gaussian process is used to classify the data. Two kernels, a standard RBF kernel and a periodic kernel, are applied to the same data set to compare the performance of classification.

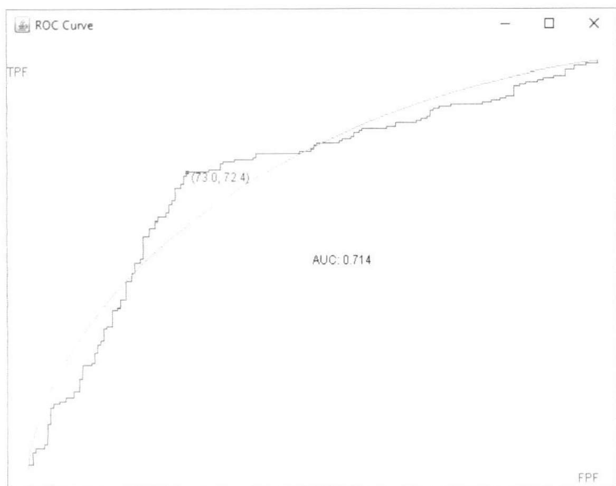

Figure 2. ROC curve for classification with standard RBF kernel

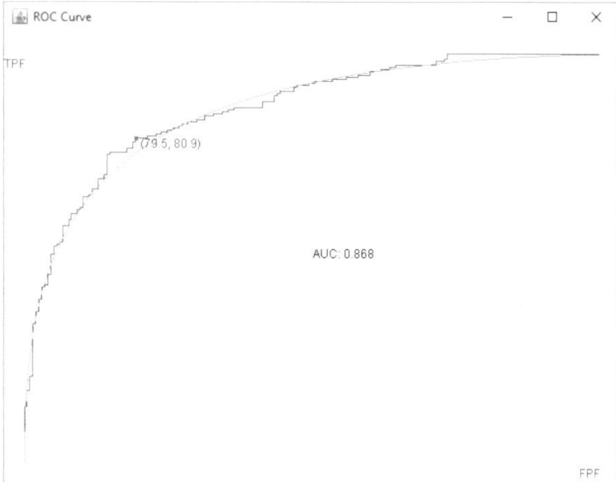

Figure 3. ROC curve for classification with periodic kernel

The ROC (Receiver Operating Characteristic) curve for the performance with RBF kernel is shown in Figure 2. The ROC curve for the periodic kernel is Figure 3.

It is clear that the periodic kernel outperforms the RBF kernel. By incorporating the topology of torus, the periodic kernel is benefited in measuring the similarity in the more faithful representation of the underlying structure.

When the underlying periodic structure is ignored as in the RBF kernel, the fragmented distributions could make the learning more difficult. A learning system might still be able to learn the class distribution as disconnected components. However, learning the more complex classes will require the increased capacity of the learning system, which may lead to overfitting and reduced performance in generalization.

5 Conclusions and Future Work

In this paper, we presented a complete characterization of stationary periodic kernels in terms of explicit cos series.

The main technique applied in this study is the Fourier transform on locally compact abelian groups. The Bochner's theorem provided the tool for the characterization of the positive definite kernel functions.

For future work, we will consider other locally compact abelian groups and their Fourier transforms in relation to kernel structures. We will also study the efficacy of the different periodic kernels on practical machine learning applications.

6 References

[1] Bishop, Christopher, Pattern recognition and machine learning. New York: Springer, (2006).

[2] Boser, B. E.; Guyon, I. M.; Vapnik, V. N., "A training algorithm for optimal margin classifiers". Proceedings of the fifth annual workshop on Computational learning theory - COLT '92. p. 144, (1992).

[3] Gihman, I. I. and Skorohod, A. V., The Theory of Stochastic Processes, volume 1. Springer-Verlag, (1974).

[4] MacKay, D. J. C., Introduction to Gaussian Processes. In Bishop, C. M., editor, Neural Networks and Machine Learning. Springer-Verlag, (1998).

[5] Rasmussen, C.E. and Christopher K. I. Williams, Gaussian Processes for Machine Learning, The MIT Press, (2006).

[6] Rudin, W., Fourier analysis on groups, Wiley-Interscience, (1962).

[7] Su, H.; Zhang, H., "Detecting Object Bending with Complex Polynomial Fitting," Proceedings of the 2013 International Conference on Image Processing, Computer Vision, & Pattern Recognition, IPCV'13, (2013).

[8] Su, H.; Zhang, H., "Distances and Kernels Based on Cumulative Distribution Functions," Emerging Trends in Image Processing, Computer Vision and Pattern Recognition, Chapter 36, Morgan Kaufmann, (2014).

[9] Su, H.; Zhang, H., "Efficient Computation of Distribution Kernels and Distances," Proceedings of the 2015 International Conference on Image Processing, Computer Vision, & Pattern Recognition, IPCV'15, (2015).

A Convolutional Neural Network Based Smart Parking System

Andres Estebanez
Department of Computer Engineering
California State University, Sacramento
Sacramento, USA
andresxestebanez@csus.edu

Praveen Meduri
Electrical and Electronics Engineering
California State University, Sacramento
Sacramento, USA
praveen.meduri@csus.edu

***Abstract*—The issue of parking in cities and campuses has become ever more pressing as the number of drivers on the road continues to increase. At the same time, new breakthroughs in the fields of internet-of-things and machine learning have opened up new opportunities for maximizing parking efficiency. In this paper, we will present out results for an implementation of our convolutional neural network-based smart-parking image-recognition system. We found our method to be extremely effective and computationally cheap.**

Keywords—smart parking, convolutional neural networks (CNN), object recognition, computer vision, deep learning

1. Introduction

Our world is becoming increasingly urban with around 54% of the world's population currently living in cities. By 2050, this figure is projected to compound up to 66% [1]. To ensure that quality of life is not degraded for its denizens, a future city should be well equipped with numerous smart solutions to the multitude of problems that arise from scaling. The particular problem of parking management is a persistent one. Researchers at UCLA reported that an average of 30% of drivers struggle to find parking during busy times of the day [2]. In this paper, we explore smart parking solutions in university setting, using CNNs.

Currently, on many university campuses across the United States, parking is a significant issue. Much of the campus' area is dedicated to parking spaces for students, faculty, and labor. The logistics of parking are additionally handled in a very inefficient manner; Cars pass over metal inductors at the entrance and exits to the parking areas, and the inductive coils will register the passing of each car. This method, however, is extremely imprecise with many false negatives. Moreover, it does not provide any information about which parking spaces themselves are occupied.

In place of this, we envision a system which utilizes many camera nodes set-up around a university campus which all will deploy a learning classifier. These nodes will all be responsible for accurately assessing the occupation status of their allotted parking spaces, and relaying this information to a phone based application which can guide users to the empty spots[3]. We expect that these nodes will be composed of Raspberry Pi or field programmable gate arrays (FPGA) for computation and implementations of convolutional neural networks (CNN) for parking space classification.

CNNs have become increasingly common of late for image recognition problems. CNNs are considered the state-of-the-art since AlexNet won the ImageNet image classification competition in 2012 [4]. AlexNet was trained on 1.2 million images to classify into 1,000 categories, and achieved the lowest error rate in the competition with only 15.2%, with the second best being 26.2% [5]. This was no accident, as CNNs possess a variety of characteristics which make them well-suited for image recognition problems

- They are very robust. CNNs deal with problems such as occlusions, different weather conditions, and operating at different times of day in different levels of sun light very well, with little loss of accuracy [3].
- The classification portion is not computation heavy [4] and can be implemented on a Raspberry Pi. Amato et al. [4] accomplished a classification speed of 15 seconds per iteration using a Raspberry Pi model 2. Another effective way of implementing a CNN-based classifier is the FPGA, which has been shown to implement CNN-based classifiers very well [6].
- The architecture of CNNs is very conducive to image recognition problems as the receptive fields and spatial sub-sampling take advantage of the spatial locality of image-based problems [7]. Local correlations in the data, meaning ones that have a close proximity in space, will form features. The CNN takes advantage of this in a way that a fully connected neural network cannot, as the numerous connections are not as efficient for image-based problems.
- Improvements in the arithmetic units of computers have made CNN training times become tractable[8]. Specifically, improvements made in graphics processing unit (GPU) technology have brought about an age where the training of extremely large

and deep CNNs on very high resolution images is now possible.

The rest of the paper will follow the following format: section 2 will discuss our methods for conducting the experiment, section 3 will be our results, section 4—our conclusions, and section 5—future work

2. METHODS

For our experiment, we opted to use a modified LeNet architecture for our CNN. The LeNet architecture is one of the earliest and simplest of all the common architectures and is shown in figure – 1. The simplicity of its design allows for very short classification times, which are necessary if we wish to do our computations on simple devices on the network edge.

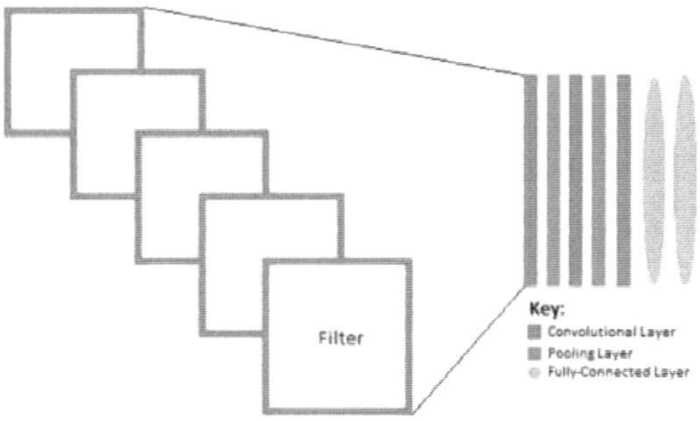

Figure – 1 LeNet-5 Architecture

Our LeNet architecture is shallower than the original one—banishing the final convolutional layer, as shown in figure – 2. This is possible because our categorization problem is relatively simple—only having two possible output categories compared to the original LeNet architecture, which required one output for every letter of the alphabet. Our design has two convolutional layers, each followed by a pooling layer. We removed the third convolutional layer as it was unnecessary. We then utilized a fully connected layer followed by a ReLu activation layer. Activation layers are important to break up the linearity of the classifier and more easily classify non-linearly separable data. The ReLu activation function specifically is used because it significantly lowers the computation needed for gradient descent relative to other activation functions such as tanh, and therefore training and classification time in general[5]. There is a final fully connected layer with two outputs—one for each class. This layer is a softmax layer, which is meant to output a result similar to a probability, in which the "guesses" for each class should all be decimal numbers which sum to unity. The architecture of our CNN is shown in the figure below.

We selected a learning rate of .001, which was borne out to be the most effective empirically. This was then dropped by a factor of ten after each training epoch. We then trained for 10 epochs, and the final network was chosen based on which training iteration showed the smallest loss.

Our dataset was comprised of 89,417 images of occupied parking spaces and 84,285 vacant parking spaces. These images were drawn from the first five days worth of data from each parking lot subdirectory in PKLot. That is to say, each of the three component parking lots in PKLot are separated into three different weather conditions, and then divided by day. We drew from the first five days of each of these subclasses. The data were then divided into training and validation sets randomly in proportions of 9:1. The images received no preprocessing save for all being resized to a uniform 150x150 size.

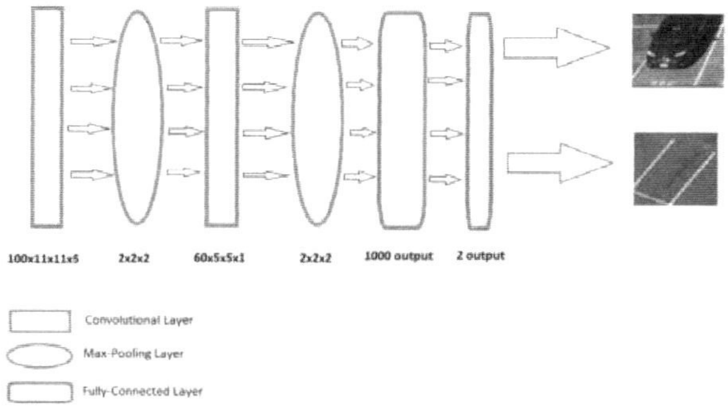

Figure – 2 Modified LeNet Implemented in this work

The training was conducted on a laptop computer with an 8-core Intel i7. The shallowness of the neural network meant that the time it took to train was by no means prohibitive. In fact, it only took two hours for the algorithm to converge on a solution. The implementation for the network was done using the Caffe framework with the Python extension. Caffe offers a straightforward and simple way to specify parameters and train the CNN.

Testing was done on images from several parking lots. These lots include the three lots from PKLot, the two lots from CNRPark, and one consisting of images gathered from CSU Sacramento campus. The images from CSU Sacramento, however, only consisted of occupied parking spots. The three parking lots of PKLot consist of PUC, UF4, and UF5. PUC is the most populous of the lots, making up [some percent] of PKLot. The other two (though they are technically two cameras of a single lot) consist of fewer images and at oblong angles compared to PKLot. CNRPark is divided into lots 'A' and 'B'. Lot A possesses fewer occlusions and more regularity in data, making it an easier lot to test on, much like lot PUC in the PKLot.

3. Results And Discussion

Our results for the different experiments are shown below in figure – 3. We achieved very high accuracy on our principal training lot of PUC with over 97%. However, as we move to other lots, this performance degrades considerably. Performance especially seems to suffer not on the occupied, but the unoccupied spaces of the other parking lots. In fact, in all cases except PUC, the classifier's performance degraded considerably on the unoccupied class relative the occupied class of test data.

Parking Lot	Experimental Accuracy		
	Occupied	Unoccupied	Total
PUC	97.54%	97.32%	97.43%
UFPR04	92.30%	69.52%	78.10%
UFPR05			
CNRPark A	87.10%	76.16%	82.60%
CNRPark B	79.06%	53.31	72.51%
CSUS Lot	97.12%	N/A	N/A

Figure – 3 Accuracy of our approach on different datasets

Experiment:	Best Accuracy:	
	Intra-dataset	Inter-dataset
Cazamias et al. 2016	99.97%	80.70%
Valipour et al. 2018	99.97%	95.00%
Vu et al. 2017	99.23%	N/A
Xiang et al. 2017	95.00%	N/A
Nyambal et al. 2017	95.49%	N/A
Amato et al. 2016	99.60%	90.70%

Figure – 4 Accuracy of existing approaches

Though we have yet to surpass the best results attained in the field parking space occupancy detection, we have achieve results among the best. We are comparing our best results from the PKLot PUC lot to the best results on others' respective test lots, and our best result, which was on the CNRPark A, with those of other studies. Our 97.4% accuracy was firmly in the middle of other experiments, and we achieved this with a relatively simple LeNet implementation.

4. Conclusion And Future Work

In the general deep learning for image recognition, there is significant cause for optimism but also significant challenges. The field has made immense strides over a short period of time and problems which once seemed the domain of science fiction are becoming tractable for scientists world-wide through the use of these tools. Similarly, our experiment shows great promise and cause for optimism, as well as significant challenges moving forward.

There is great promise to be drawn from the fact that we achieved over 97% on the principal training lot—PUC—of our experiment. In addition, on our positive set of parked cars from the CSU Sacramento campus—the location in which we hope to implement our smart parking system—we similarly achieved above 97% accuracy on our positive test set. This means that the realization of a smart-parking system there is tantalizingly close.

There are, however, still significant challenges. Questions still remain about the ease with which the trained neural networks can be generalized to work on a variety of different parking lots in different settings. Parking lots with cameras at different angles, occlusions, inclement weather, and other factors remain significant obstacles. Another issue would be the tedious process of delineating each parking space for testing. As it stands now, parking spaces must be delineated through manual cropping.

We have made significant strides so far and wish to pursue further lines of inquiry in pursuit of the smart parking system. Currently, our CNN system still shows great room for improvement. We wish to try additional means of data preprocessing and manipulation as well as different network architectures in order to improve our results. Another interesting question would be the efficacy of using ensemble learning—using multiple CNNs to vote on the state of the parking spot as well as using other machine learning algorithms in conjunction.

5. ACKNOWLEDGEMENTS

The authors would like to thank the Research and Creative Activity (RCA) Subcommittee of California State University At Sacramento for providing the funding to carryout this research. This work is funded through the RCA grant for the academic year 2018 – 2019.

6. References

[1] "World Urbanization Prospects", United Nations Organization, 2014. [Online]. Available: http://www.un.org/en/development/desa/news/population/world-urbanization-prospects-2014.html. [Accessed 09 30 2018].

[2] D. C. Shoup, "The high cost of free parking", Chicago: Planners Press, American Planning Association, 2005.

[3] P. Meduri and E. Telles, "A Haar-Cascade classifier based Smart Parking System", 2018 International Conference IP, Computer Vision, and Pattern Recognition, pp. 66-70.

[4] Giuseppe Amato, Fabio Carrara, Fabrizio Falchi, Claudio Gennaro, and Claudio Vairo, "Car parking occupancy detection using smart camera networks and

Deep Learning," 2016 IEEE Symposium on Computers and Communication (ISCC), June 2016.

[5] A. Krizhevsky, I. Sutskever, G. E. Hinton, "Imagenet classification with deep convolutional neural networks", Advances in neural information processing systems, pp. 1097-1105, 2012.

[6] K. Abdelouahab, M. Pelcat, F. Berry, and J. Sérot, "Accelerating CNN inference on FPGAs: A Survey," HAL Id: hal-01695375. [Online].

Available: https://hal.archives-ouvertes.fr/hal-01695375/file/hal-accelerating-cnn.pdf. [Accessed: 30-Sep-2018].

[7] X. Xiang, N. Lv, M. Zhai, and A. El Saddik, "Real-Time Parking Occupancy Detection for Gas Stations Based on Haar-AdaBoosting and CNN ," IEEE Sensor Journal, vol. 17, no. 19, pp. 6360–6367, Oct. 2017.

[8] Y. Lecun, L. Bottou, Y. Bengio, and P. Haffner, "Gradient Based Learning Applied to Document Recognition," http://yann.lecun.com/. [Online]. [Accessed: 01-Oct-2018].

http://yann.lecun.com/exdb/publis/pdf/lecun-01a.pdf.

[9] J. Cazamias and M. Marek, "Parking Space Classification and Convolutional Neural Networks," stanford.edu. [Online].

Available:
http://cs231n.stanford.edu/reports/2016/pdfs/280_Report.pdf.

[10] Almeida, P., Oliveira, L. S., Silva Jr, E., Britto Jr, A., Koerich, A., "PKLot – A robust dataset for parking lot classification", Expert Systems with Applications, 42(11):4937-4949, 2015.

[11] J. Nyambal and R. Klein, "Automated parking space detection using convolutional neural networks ," 2017 Pattern Recognition Association of South Africa and Robotics and Mechatronics (PRASA-RobMech) , Nov. 2017.

[12] S. Valipour, M. Siam, E. Stroulia, and M. Jagersand, "Parking Stall Vacancy Indicator System Based on Deep Convolutional Neural Networks," arxiv.org. [Online].

Available:https://arxiv.org/pdf/1606.09367.pdf. [Accessed: 01-Oct-2018].

[13] H. T. Vu and C.-C. Huang, "A multi-task convolutional neural network with spatial transform for parking space detection," 2017 IEEE International Conference on Image Processing (ICIP).

[14] K. Danilyuk, "ConvNets Series. Spatial Transformer Networks – Towards Data Science," Towards Data Science, 19-Sep-2017. [Online].

[15] P. Viola and M. Jones, "Rapid object detection using a boosted cascade of simple features", Proceedings of the 2001 IEEE Computer Society Conference on Computer Vision and Pattern Recognition. CVPR 2001, 2001, pp. I-511-I-518 vol.1.

[16] R. Fusek, K. Mozdˇreˇn, M. Surkala, and E. Sojka, "AdaBoost for Parking Lot Occupation Detection"
https://pdfs.semanticscholar.org/2963/3712a36c3efc77ce3a9844a2e9a029daf310.pdf

MetaNet: A Boosting-Inspired Deep Learning Image Classification Ensemble Technique

Junyi He[1], Ian Pedroza[1], and Qingzhong Liu[2]
[1]The Woodlands College Park High School, The Woodlands, TX 77382, USA
[2]Department of Computer Science, Sam Houston State University, Huntsville, TX 77341, USA

ABSTRACT

The researchers proposed MetaNet, a new ensembling technique for improved image classification. A common machine learning ensembling technique, known as boosting has been effective at improving an ensemble of weak models' performance. However, the researchers modified the training process through proposing "complement blocks" to extend boosting to deep learning applications. Through complement blocks, models are trained and later stacked to form what is called "MetaNet". On the popular CiFAR10 dataset and a breast cancer histopathology dataset, MetaNet outperformed the baseline models by between 3-4% and traditional ensembles by 0.5-2% in f1-score or accuracy. The initial validation suggests that this ensembling technique can improve researchers' and institutions' abilities to classify images or data across multiple fields, from everyday objects to medical images.

Keywords

Boosting, Ensemble, Image classification, Deep Learning

1. Introduction

Model ensembling is a popular method to improve algorithms' performance at various tasks. In machine learning, bagging and decision trees are very popular [2, 3]. Boosting involves creating multiple small models, commonly known as stumps, that each learn the data that the previous stumps fail to learn from [6]. Each stump is assigned a weight based on the proportion of the training data they correctly classify [6]. Adaboost is a popular manifestation of boosting [6]. Stacking is a form of meta-learning in which multiple models are trained, and their confidence values for any given prediction are fed to a final model, commonly a neural network, which learns the optimal way to make predictions based on the confidence values of the learners [5].

There are some recent works for improving ensembles. One example is i.Boosting, but the procedure is limited to the realms of feature-extracted datasets [11]. Other works inspired by boosting are limited in their application to one model architecture, i.e. BoostResNet, which is not an ensemble [7]. The Hydra ensemble applies ResNet feature extractors and different fully connected layers to create faster ensembles, but does not utilize boosting-concepts [9].

Ensembling is a relatively unpopular technique that researchers use to solve deep learning challenges. When used, very basic procedures such as soft voting using complex models as the constituent models are employed [4]. Bejnordia et al., developed a stacking procedure for providing a clinically-realistic framework that determines the benign/malignant status of a breast cancer tumor as well as the invasive/noninvasive state of such histopathology sample using context awareness on whole image slides [1]. This is different from a boosting inspired approach that can generalize to all image datasets.

2. MetaNet & Setup

2.1 Ensemble Description

Figure 1 illustrates the MetaNet concept.

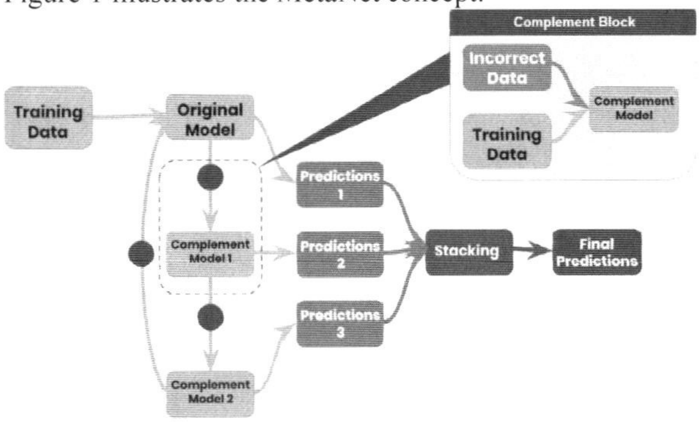

Figure 1: MetaNet- An ensemble of 3 models trained using complement blocks.

Each model can be any deep learning architecture. Most hyperparameters such as the optimizer, model size, etc., can vary based on the application. However, the authors suggest using a categorical_crossentropy loss function for all applications to maximize stacking effectiveness.

The complement block contains two parts: two datasets and a compliment model. Said model is initially trained using the subsection of the training images that the previous model fails to classify after a given number of epochs (authors suggest greater than 20). The model is then finetuned using the entire original training data to increase generalizability (authors suggest the same or slower learning rate and over 20 epochs).

Note: the original model is refinetuned with the wrong images of the third model (complement model 2) and finetuned once more with the entire dataset. This process will be referred to as MetaNet refinetuning in this paper.

After the complement blocks, the next procedure in MetaNet is to gather the confidence values of the predictions on the training data from each model. The values are fed into a meta-learner (such as an Artificial Neural Network). To make predictions, image(s) are shown to each model and respective confidence values are compiled, which the meta-learner uses to make the final prediction.

2.2 Datasets

To validate the MetaNet process, multiple image datasets were used: the popular CiFAR10 dataset [8] and a kaggle breast cancer histopathology dataset (BCHD) [10]. Note, only 20,000 images, with roughly the same number of images from the two classes, from the BCHD were used by the models.

2.3 Data Pre-processing

The train and test sets of CiFAR10 were 50,000 and 10,000 images respectively. All images were normalized by dividing all pixel values by 255 and subtracting the mean values from each pixel value before dividing by the standard deviation. All images from the BCHD were preprocessed before retrieval.

2.4 Data Augmentation

All CiFAR10 train images were subject to the same augmentation techniques, including rotating the images within 15 degrees, shifting the image horizontally within 10%, shifting the image vertically within 10%, and flipping the image horizontally.

The BCHD train images were augmented by zooming in within 20%, flipped horizontally, and all disappeared pixels were filled with the nearest pixels.

2.5 Architecture Descriptions

The CiFAR10 model hyperparameters are: 7 layered CNNs, with 6 convolution layers and one fully connected layer. The models were trained on 20 epochs, the optimizer was rmsprop with a learning rate of 0.001, and the loss was cateogircal_crossentropy.

The BCHD model was a ResNet50 pretrained on imagenet. GlobalAveragePooling2D and three hidden layers were used instead of the imagenet fully connected layers. The ouput layer had 2 neurons with a softmax activation function. The learning rate varied based on the number of epochs. The loss function was categorical_crossentropy and the optimizer was rmsprop with learning rate decay.

The normal ensemble models used to compare MetaNet with had altered hyperparameters but same learning configuration as the models in MetaNet. Additionally, while the MetaNet models were trained with complement blocks, while the normal ensemble never trained on complement data (only the entire dataset).

2.6 Google Colaboratory

A Tesla K80 GPU was used through the Google Colaboratory web platform.

3. Results

3.1 MetaNet Overall Performance

The figures below illustrates how MetaNet compares to a single model and an ensemble of models created under conditions that are most commonly practiced (stacking diverse models) for image classification deep learning problems.

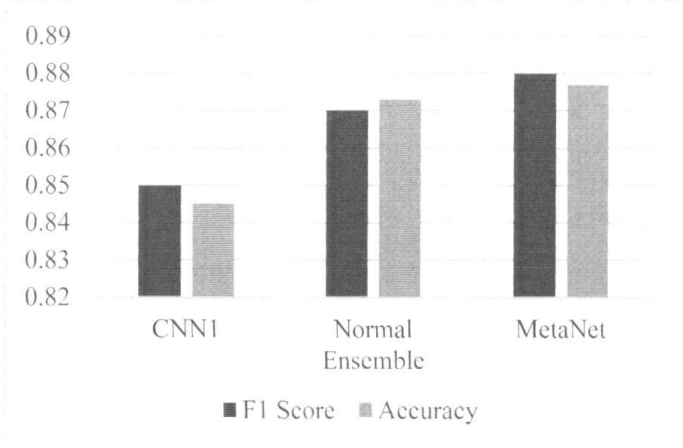

Figure 2(a) - CiFAR10 Performance Comparison

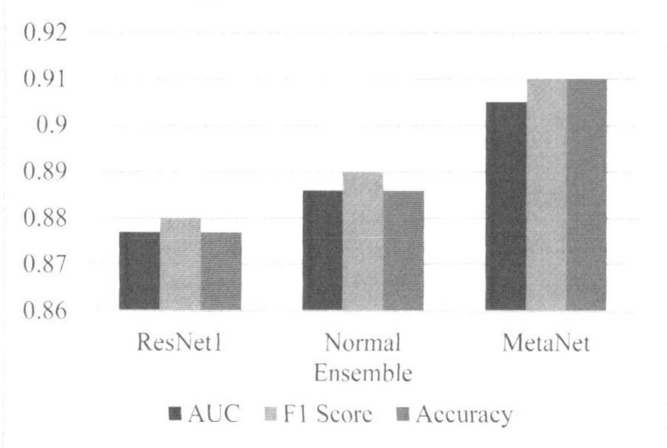

Figure 2(b) - BCHD Performance Comparison

3.2 MetaNet Constituent Model Performances

The tables list the model performances for both CiFAR10 and MetaNet models. For CiFAR10, the researchers experimented with combining the first (with and without refinetuning), second, and third CNNs, first and second CNNs, second and third CNNs, and so on.

After discovering that optimal results were obtained with 3 models, the same procedure was not performed on the BCHD dataset, where it is assumed that MetaNet refers to ResNet1 refinetuned, ResNet2, and ResNet3 as constituent models. Note, CiFAR10 illustrates that without the CNN1 refinetuning, the ensemble would only obtain an f1 score of .87 instead of .88.

Table 1(a) Performance (F1-Score) of constituent or combinations of constituent models on CiFAR10 dataset

MetaNet on CiFAR		
	Train	Test
CNN1	0.87	0.85
CNN2	0.88	0.85
CNN3	0.86	0.84
CNN4	0.87	0.84
CNN1 (refinetuned)	0.88	0.85
MetaNet1-3 (no refinetuning)	0.9	0.87
MetaNet1-3 (refinetuned)	0.92	0.88
MetaNet1&2	0.88	0.85
MetaNet2&3	0.88	0.85
MetaNet1&3	0.87	0.84
MetaNet1-4	0.87	0.86
Metanet1-4 (refinetuned)	0.92	0.88

Table 1(b) Performance (F1-Score) of constituent or combinations of constituent models on the BCHD

	Train	Test	Test 2
ResNet1	0.88	0.87	0.87
ResNet2	0.94	0.9	0.9
ResNet3	0.89	0.88	0.88
ResNet1 Refinetuned	0.92	0.88	0.89

3.3 Normal Ensemble Performances

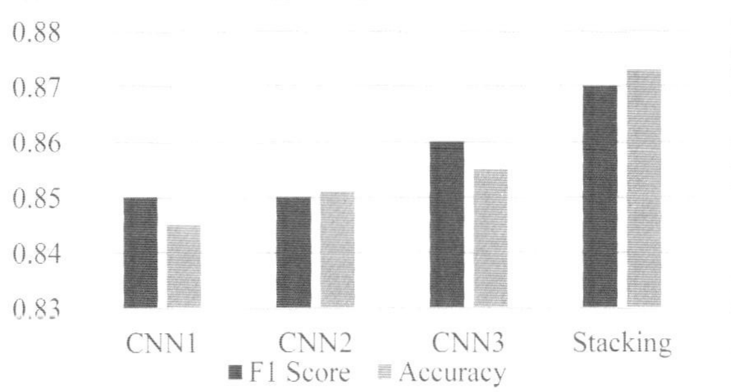

Figure 3(a) CiFAR10 Constituent Models of Diverse Traditional Ensembling Method

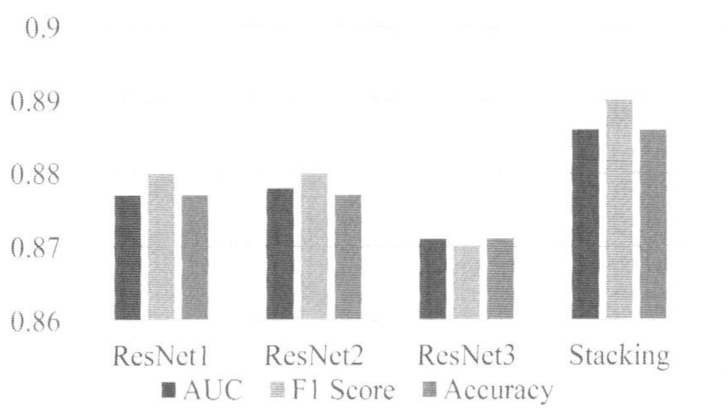

Figure 3(b) BCHD Constituent Models of Diverse Traditional Ensembling Method

3.4 Effect of Finetuning

The graph below indicates the f1 score obtained by each complement model on the previous models' wrong images before and after finetuning on the training data.

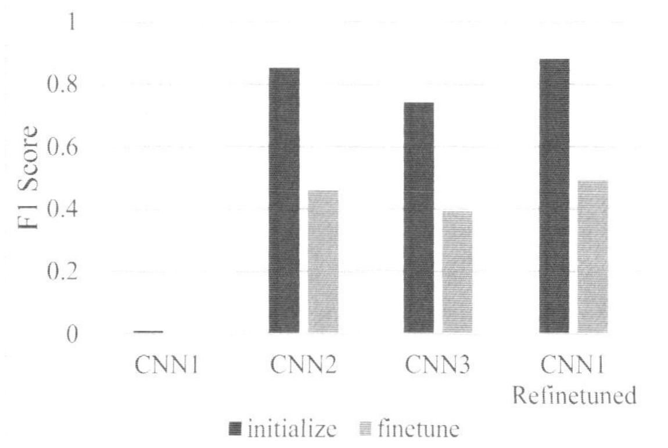

Figure 4(a) CiFAR10 complement models' performances on the previous models' wrong images before and after finetuning on the entire training data

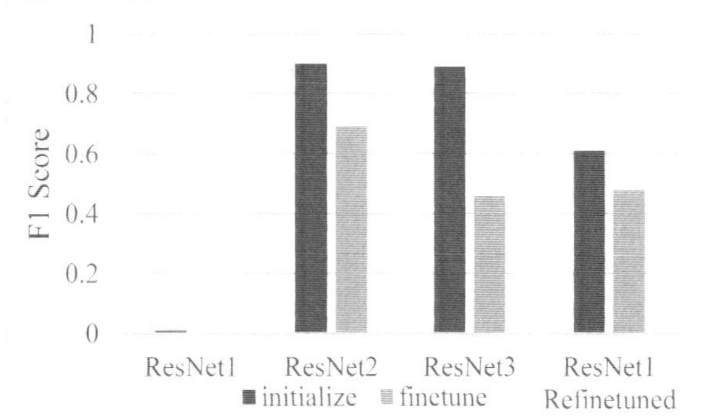

Figure 4(b) BCHD complement models' performances on the previous models' wrong images before and after finetuning on the entire training data

After initializing each deep learning complement model on the previous model's wrongly classified images, the models demonstrated high levels of skill to predict those wrong images. However, after finetuning the models on the entire dataset to increase generalizability, each model's ability to recognize those same wrong images is reduced (by a factor of between 1/3 and ½).

3.5 Model Averaging Improvement

Below is a table that illustrates the number of images from the test dataset that were missed by each model. For guidance, here is a sample interpretation of Table 2(a). 721 images were missed by the first CNN. The CNN1 made 500 and 502 incorrect predictions on the images that the CNN2 and CNN3 got wrong respectively. The CNN2 made 253 unique incorrect predictions that CNN1 did not get wrong, and of those, the CNN3 missed 89 of those images and 140 unique ones that CNN2 did not.

Table 2(a) BCHD Normal Ensemble Model Averaging Analysis

Breast Cancer Normal Ensemble- Model Averaging				
Model 1	721			
Model 2	500	253		
Model 3	502	89	140	
	(608) 113	-89	0	**24**

Table 2(b) BCHD MetaNet Model Averaging Analysis

Breast Cancer MetaNet- Model Averaging				
Model 1	778			
Model 2	382	185		
Model 3	368	98	257	
	(465) 313	-98	0	**215**

The results suggest that the normal ensemble increased the number of correctly classified test images by 24 (0.96% of the test data) through just averaging the constituent models' votes while MetaNet increased the number by 215 (3.6% of the test data).

4. Conclusions & Future Work

In this work, the researchers proposed the concept of complement blocks, which were used in MetaNet. It was discovered that finetuning complement models on the entire dataset was valuable to increase generalizability while maintaining model diversity. Through validation using the popular CiFAR10 and Breast Cancer Histopathology datasets, the researchers suggested that a modified boosting concept can be beneficial for deep learning.

The intention of this study was not to set a milestone state-of-the-art result on these datasets. Rather, it was to suggest that MetaNet could outperform the baseline constituent model or normal ensembling procedures through complement blocks and stacking.

In the future, the authors have identified two main ideas for further study.

First, up to 20 models could be trained on the data using complement blocking and stacked to assess MetaNet's performance.

Second, state-of-the-art architectures will be used on these datasets to determine whether MetaNet can use complement blocks to further improve state-of-the-art results.

5. References

[1] Bejnordi, B. E., Zuidhof, G., Balkenhol, M., Hermsen, M., Bult, P., Ginneken, B. V., Laak, J. V. (2017). Context-aware stacked convolutional neural networks for classification of breast carcinomas in whole-slide histopathology images. *Journal of Medical Imaging, 4*(04), 1. doi:10.1117/1.jmi.4.4.044504

[2] Breiman, L. (1996). Bagging predictors. *Machine Learning, 24*(2), 123-140. doi:10.1007/bf00058655

[3] Cutler, A. (2014). Random Forests. *Wiley StatsRef: Statistics Reference Online.* doi:10.1002/9781118445112.stat06520

[4] Eeti, L., and Buddhiraju, K., "A modified class-specific weighted soft voting for bagging ensemble," *2016 IEEE International Geoscience and Remote Sensing Symposium (IGARSS)*, Beijing, 2016, pp. 2622-2625. doi: 10.1109/IGARSS.2016.7729677

[5] Enesco, M., & Dhandhania, K. (2018). Ensemble Methods (Part 3): Meta-learning, Stacking and Mixture of Experts. Retrieved from https://www.commonlounge.com/discussion/1697ade39ac142988861daff4da7f27d

[6] Freund, Y., & Schapire, R. E. (1997). A Decision-Theoretic Generalization of On-Line Learning and an Application to Boosting. *Journal of Computer and System Sciences, 55*(1), 119-139. doi:10.1006/jcss.1997.1504

[7] Huang, F., Schapire, R., Langford, J., & Ash, J. (2017). Learning Deep ResNet Blocks Sequentially using Boosting Theory. *ICML 2018*. Retrieved February 28, 2019.

[8] Krizhevsky, A. (2009). The CIFAR-10 dataset. Retrieved from https://www.cs.toronto.edu/~kriz/cifar.html

[9] Minetto, R., & Segundo, M. P. (2019). Hydra: An Ensemble of Convolutional Neural Networks for Geospatial Land Classification. *IEEE TRANSACTIONS ON GEOSCIENCE AND REMOTE SENSING*. Retrieved April 18, 2019.

[10] Mooney, P. (2017, December 19). Breast Histopathology Images. Retrieved from https://www.kaggle.com/paultimothymooney/breast-histopathology-images

[11] Lu, Y., Zhang, T. and Tian, Q., "i.Boosting for Image Classification," *2007 IEEE International Conference on Multimedia and Expo*, Beijing, 2007, pp. 1711-1714. doi: 10.1109/ICME.2007.4284999

Modality Detection and Classification of Biomedical Images with Deep Transfer Learning and Feature Extraction

Jose Dixon
Computer Science Department
Morgan State University
Baltimore, Maryland, USA
jodix5@morgan.edu

Mahmudur Rahman
Computer Science Department
Morgan State University
Baltimore, Maryland, USA
md.rahman@morgan.edu

***Abstract*—Classification of medical images of diverse modalities is an important first step for many applications in biomedical domain, such as computer aided diagnosis (CAD) and retrieval. However, the descriptiveness and discriminative power of features extracted from medical images are critical to achieve good classification and retrieval performances. Recently, Deep learning algorithms, such as convolutional neural networks (CNN) seem to be effective in supplying better accuracy. CNN trained on large-scale data sets such as ImageNet have demonstrated to be excellent at the task of transfer learning. These networks learn a set of rich, discriminating features to recognize 1,000 separate object classes. CNNs not only give state-of-the-art results when trained for a specific task, but experiments have shown that the filters learned over the ImageNet dataset are generic and useful for other image tasks that the CNN was not originally trained for. Using a pre-trained CNN as a feature extractor also provides an alternative to the hand-crafted features based on learning a transformation of raw data input to a representation that can be effectively exploited in general machine learning tasks, such as Random Forest or Support Vector Machine (SVM) Classifiers. This work is focusing on extracting such features from medical images by applying deep transfer learning with pre-trained VGG16 network as feature extractors, and also exploring data augmentation to address the limitation of small training set. The experimental results in a medical data set of 5000 images of 30 different categories based on modalities, body parts, orientations, and specific visual features showed that this approach obtained the best accuracy (97%).**

Keywords: Classification, Modality Detection, Convolutional Neural Networks, Deep learning, Feature extraction, Deep feature extraction.

I. INTRODUCTION

The Deep learning is the subfield of machine learning that is devoted to building algorithms that explain and learn a high and low level of abstractions of data that traditional machine learning algorithms often cannot. Convolutional neural networks (also called ConvNet) leverage spatial information and are therefore very well suited for classifying images [1]. These nets use an ad hoc architecture inspired by biological data taken from physiological experiments done on the visual cortex. In the last 20 years, computer vision research has focused on manually defined pipelines for extracting good image features. For a while, image feature extractors such as LBP and HOG were the standard. Recent developments in deep learning research have extended the reach of traditional machine learning models by incorporating automatic feature extraction in the base layers. They replace manually defined feature image extractors with manually defined models that automatically learn and extract features.

II. TRANSFER LEARING METHODS

Transfer learning reuses knowledge from past related tasks to ease the process of learning to perform a new task (Donges, 2018). The goal of transfer learning is to leverage previous learning and experience to more efficiently learn novel, but related, concepts, compared to what would be possible without this prior experience. The utility of transfer learning is typically measured by a reduction in the number of training examples required to achieve a target performance on a sequence of related learning problems, compared to the number required for unrelated problems [2]

Convolutional neural networks (CNNs) trained on large-scale datasets such as ImageNet have demonstrated to be excellent at the task of transfer learning. These networks learn a set of rich, discriminating features to recognize 1,000 separate object classes. CNNs not only give state-of-the-art results when trained for a specific task, but experiments have shown that the filters learned over the ImageNet dataset are generic and useful for other image tasks that the CNN was not originally trained for [3,4]

Data augmentation is about accumulating more data than what is already available [5]. The process of performing these transformations on existing training images to generate new images is called data augmentation. Another advantage of using data augmentation is that you are able to increase the size of your training dataset (when used with data generators, we can get infinite images).

Each type CNN utilizes its own layers, kernels, training, and feature extraction techniques. Deep learning architectures can be composed of several types of layers (Casari & Zheng, 2018). Fully connected layers are so named because every input can be used in every output. In contrast to fully connected layers, a convolutional layer uses only a subset of inputs for each output. A pooling layer combines multiple inputs into a single output.

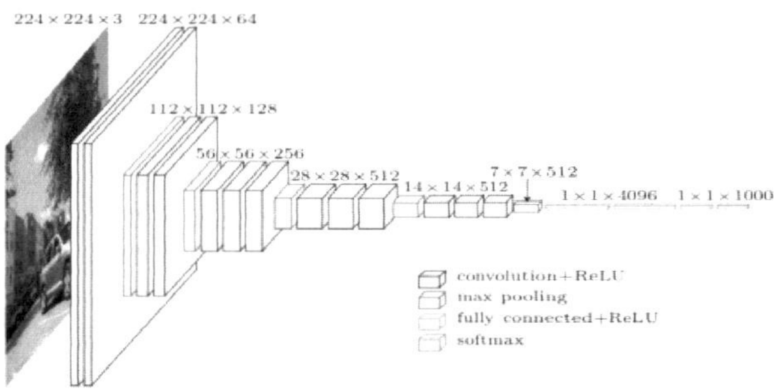

Figure 1: A representation of VGG16 architecture

VGGNet is a network based 3x3 convolutional layers stacked and alternated with max pooling, two 4096-connected layers stacked and alternated with max pooling, two 4096 fully-connected layers followed by a softmax classifier [4]. Prior to VGG the initial convolutional layers of a network used filters with large receptive fields, such as 7 x 7. Additionally, the networks usually had alternating single convolutional and pooling layers. Figure 1 shows how VGGNet architecture looks like of a convolutional layer in VGGNet with a large filter size can be replaced with a stack of two or more convolutional layers with smaller filters (factorized convolution). VGGNet architecture with very small (3 × 3) filters can be trained to increasingly higher depths (16-19 layers) and obtain state-of-the-art classification [7].

III. DEEP FEATURE EXTRACTOR

Using a pretrained CNN as a feature extractor rather than training a CNN from scratch is attractive as it transfers learning (i.e. filters) from other domains where more training data is available, and avoids a time consuming training process.

In this work, we loaded all the images from the training and test sets, extract their features using a pre-trained 16-layer VGG mode [4]l, and store the extracted features keyed on the image id to a new file in HDF5 dataset format that is later loaded and used as input for training with few general machine learning classifiers, such as Logistic Regression, Random Forest, SVM, etc. Here, we at first pre-processed the images (e.g. 3 channel 224 x 224 pixel image) for the VGG model (without the output layer) trained on ImageNet dataset [3] and used the extracted features predicted by this model as input.

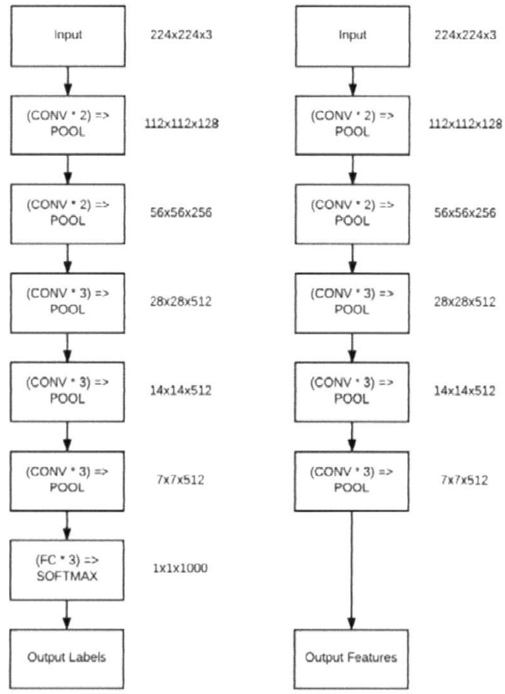

(a) (b)

Figure 2 (a) The original VGG16 network architecture (b) VGG16 network as feature extractor [7]

When treating the VGG16 networks (Fig. 2) as a feature extractor, we essentially "chop off" the network prior to the fully-connected layers. The last layer of the network is a max pooling layer (Figure 2(a)), which will have the output shape of 7 x 7 x 512 implying there are 512 filters each of size 7 x 7. If we were to forward propagate an image through this network with its FC head removed, we would be left with 512, 7x7 activations that have either activated or not based on the image contents. Therefore, we can actually take these 7 x 7 x 512 = 25,088 values and treat them as a feature vector that quantifies the contents of an image [7].

After repeating this process for the entire dataset of images (including datasets that VGG16 was not trained on), we are left with a design matrix of N images, each with 25,088 columns used to quantify their contents (i.e., feature vectors). Given our feature vectors, we can train an off-the-shelf machine learning model such SVM, Logistic Regression classifier, Random Forest, etc. on top of these features to obtain a classifier that recognizes new classes of images. Hence, the VGG16 network is used here as an intermediary feature extractor. The downstream machine learning classifier will take care of learning the underlying patterns of the features extracted from the CNN.

IV. Experiments

For experiments, we used a subset (5000 images) of the ImageCLEFMed dataset [9] with 30 different medical modalities (Figure 3). 50% of the 5,000 images are used for testing and training vice versa. The dataset comprises of different classes of medical modalities of compound or multi pane images, diagnostic images, and generic biomedical illustrations. The diagnostic images consists of radiology, visible light photography, microscopy, 3D reconstructions, and printed signals or waves. The generic biomedical illustrations are not related to medical imaging.

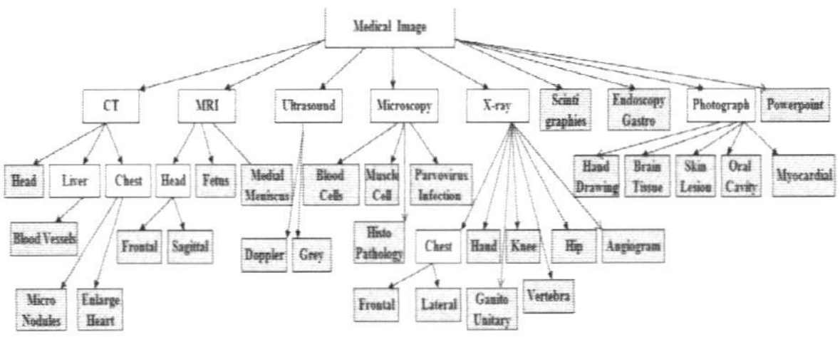

Figure 3: Different classes and categories used for ImageCLEFMed dataset.

The medical modalities are organized into different classes and subclasses that are relevant to medical imaging hierarchy map as shown in Figure 3 [6].

V. Results and Discussion

Figure 4 and 5 show VGGNet based classification results of different categories and histogram graph of accuracy results based on applying data augmentation technique. It is observed that data augmentation feature can help significantly to improve the feature extraction processing for a convolutional neural network such as VGGNet.

	precision	recall	f1-score	support
Angiogram_Budd_Chiari	0.98	0.81	0.89	58
Brain_Limb_Alzheimer	0.97	0.88	0.92	34
CT_Chest	1.00	1.00	1.00	36
CT_Head	0.89	0.89	0.89	27
CT_Liver_BloodVessels	0.90	0.94	0.92	48
CT_Mediastinal	0.94	1.00	0.97	32
Endoscopy_Gastro	1.00	1.00	1.00	62
Handdrawn_Illustration	0.81	0.97	0.88	35
MRI_Fetus	1.00	0.69	0.82	13
MRI_Frontal_Head	0.98	0.87	0.92	53
MRI_Medial_Meniscus	0.88	1.00	0.94	60
MRI_Sagittal_Head	0.86	1.00	0.92	36
Microscopic_Bacterial_Meningitis	0.48	1.00	0.65	32
Microscopic_BloodSmears	0.94	0.87	0.90	97
Microscopic_HistoPathology	0.75	0.63	0.69	38
Microscopic_MuscleCell	0.83	0.91	0.87	32
Microscopic_Parvovirus_Infection	0.88	0.66	0.76	68
Patho_Gross_Miocardial_Infarction	0.91	0.84	0.87	25
Patho_Oral_Cavity	0.90	1.00	0.95	28
Powerpoint	0.91	0.91	0.91	22
Scintigraphies	0.95	0.69	0.80	29
Skin_Lesion	1.00	0.91	0.96	47
US_Doplar	0.89	0.83	0.86	30
US_Grey	0.94	0.96	0.95	53
Xray_Chest_Frontal	0.99	0.97	0.98	71
Xray_Chest_Lateral	0.93	1.00	0.96	26
Xray_GenitoUnitary	0.94	0.98	0.96	47
Xray_Hand	1.00	0.96	0.98	25
Xray_Head	0.92	1.00	0.96	11
Xray_Hip	0.97	0.92	0.95	38
Xray_Knee	0.89	0.96	0.93	26
Xray_Vertebral_Osteophytes	0.95	0.95	0.95	22
avg / total	0.92	0.90	0.91	1261

Figure 4: Results of VGGNet (with Data Augmentation) Classification

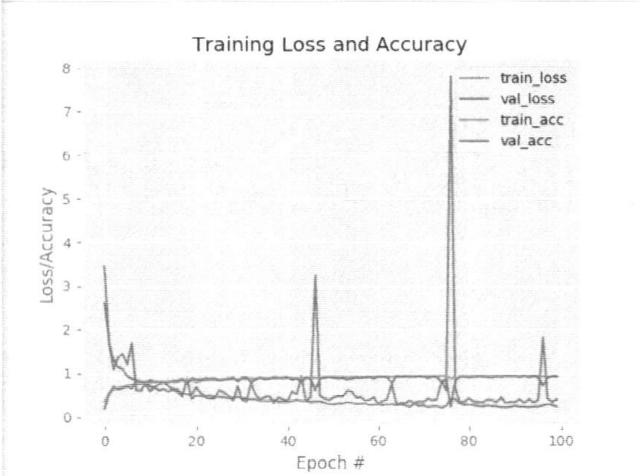

Figure 5: Histogram graph of Accuracy Results from the VGGNet (with Data Augmentation) Classification

Table 1: Classification Results (Test set)

Classifier	Precision	Recall	F1-Score
VGGNet w/oDA	0.63	0.57	0.64
VGGNet w/DA	0.92	0.90	0.91
VGGNet (Deep Feature)	0.97	0.97	0.97

From Table 1, it is observed that without the data augmentation feature, VGGNet has the worst results for the deep learning classification in the experiment. With data augmentation, it achieved around 92% accuracy. However, we obtained the best accuracy (97%) after extracting the deep features based on using VGG16 model as transfer learning and performing a logistic linear regression based classification on this feature space. Hence, it proves to be effective to extract deep features at first and perform ordinary classification, such as linear regression, support vector machine (SVM) at a later stage.

VI. CONCLUSIONS

Modality detection is an essential task to enhance the performance of a medical image retrieval system. This paper present modality detection/classification of medical images based on applying deep transfer learning (VGGNet) with different approaches. It is found that the best classification accuracy is obtained when the deep feature is extracted by applying a transfer leaning approach and later general machine learning based classification (linear regression) is performed in that deep feature space instead of fine tuning the classifier. In future, we will try to explore other deep learning models and use ensemble of classifiers as classifier combination approach.

ACKNOWLEDGMENT

This research was supported by an NSF HBCU-UP Research Initiation Award (RIA) grant (Award Id: 1601044).

REFERENCES

[1] Mishra, C., & Gupta, D. L. (2017). Deep machine learning and neural networks: An overview. IAES International Journal of Artificial Intelligence, 6(2), 66-73. Retrieved from https://search-proquest-com.proxy-ms.researchport.umd.edu/docview/1924958782?accountid=12557
"Modern Machine Learning Algorithms: Strengths and Weaknesses." (2018, May 20). https://elitedatascience.com/machine-learning-algorithms (accessed 6 August 2018)

[2] Donges, N., & Donges, N. (2018, April 23). Transfer Learning. Retrieved from https://towardsdatascience.com/transfer-learning-946518f95666

[3] O. Russakovsky et al., "ImageNet large scale visual recognition challenge," IJCV, 2015.

[4] Karen Simonyan and Andrew Zisserman. "Very Deep Convolutional Networks for Large- Scale Image Recognition". In: CoRR abs/1409.1556 (2014). URL: http://arxiv.org/abs/1409.1556 (cited on

[5] Guillou, P., & Guillou, P. (2019, January 23). Data Augmentation by fastai v1. Retrieved May 8, 2019, from https://medium.com/@pierre_guillou/data-augmentation-by-fastai-v1-84ca04bea302

[6] Rahman, M., Antani, S. K., & Thoma, G. R. (2010). A classification-driven similarity matching framework for retrieval of biomedical images. 2010 Proceedings of the International Conference on Multimedia Information Retrieval, 147-154.

[7] Rosebrock, A. Deep Learning for Computer Vision Practitioner Bundle https://www.pyimagesearch.com/deep-learning-computer-visionpython- book/ , pg. 31-47 (accessed 26 August 2018)

[8] Zocca, V., Roelants, P., Spacagna, G., Slater, D., & Vasilev, I. (n.d.). Python Deep Learning - Second Edition. Retrieved January, 2019, from https://learning.oreilly.com/library/view/python-deep-learning/9781789348460/96fa5814-e23e-4b62-8103-e1c097f3eaa7.xhtml

[9] H. M¨uller, J. Kalpathy-Cramer, I. Eggel, S. Bedrick, Jr. J. Reisetter, C. E. K., and W. R. Hersh, W. R. "Overview of the CLEF 2010 Medical Image Retrieval Track", CLEF 2010 Evaluation Labs and Workshop, On-line Working Notes. Padua, Italy, Sep. 2010.

Traffic Sign Detection using Region Based Convolutional Neural Networks

Allaboina Sai Praneeth, saipraneeth.a84@jntuh.ac.in;
Ganapuram Vaishnavi, vaishuganapuram@jntuh.ac.in;
Cherukuri Hima, himabindu1997@gmail.com;
Dr.Makkena Madhavi Latha, mmadhavilatha@jntuh.ac.in;
Digital Signal Processing team, Department of Electronics and Communication Engineering, JNTUH College of Engineering Hyderabad, Telangana, India

Abstract—**Aiming at the safety of automobile users, many advanced technologies have been invented to avoid accidents.These inventions broadly deal with lane detection, obstacle detection and traffic sign recognition.This paper deals with the detection of traffic signs, which is being neglected inspite of being a significant cause for most of the accidents. Traffic signs are designed to alert an automobile user of any possible aberrations in his/her way. But humans are prone to neglect these signs, thereby creating a necessity to caution the user. The RCNN system in this paper was tested on German data sets for the detection of traffic signs but a personally developed data set was added to the above network and then trained to achieve efficacy.**

Keywords: Object detection, Region proposals, Region based Convolutional Neural Networks (RCNN), Mean average precision (mAP).

I. Introduction

In the recent years, it is seen that road fatalities have been increasing. It cannot be denied that over speeding and not being aware of the surrounding traffic signs are among the majority of the reported reasons for the accidents. Making drivers aware of their surroundings could help ameliorate the situation. According to the Annual Global Road Crash Statistics an average of 3287 people die every day, which amounts to 1.25 million people every year and an additional 20-50 million are disabled or injured.These statistics led to the creation of technology involving traffic signal detection and recognition. Traffic sign detection involves two process namely localization and classification. Localization is the process of identifying the location of the object. Classification is the process of predicting the object in an image by identifying its class, type or category. If images can be categorized by the classifier into more than one class, it is called a multi-label classifier. Hence, Object Detection is the process of predicting the location of the object and its corresponding class. Instead of the single output of a label of the class, there are now two outputs, namely the class and the bounding box. There have been many approaches to object detection of which the Haar Cascades approach proposed by Viola and Jones in 2001 is a prominent one. Initially, object detection was modelled as a classification problem where windows of fixed sizes were taken from input images at all the possible locations. Each window was fed to the classifier which predicted the class of the object in the window.This approach had a problem as objects were capable of having varying sizes and a fixed size window could not always contain the object. To solve this problem, an image pyramid was created by scaling the image. The image was re-sized at multiple scales and the chosen window would completely contain the object in one of these re-sized images.Then, all these windows were fed to a classifier to detect the object of interest. This method is the root base for object detection, which holds a prominent position in present day technologies.

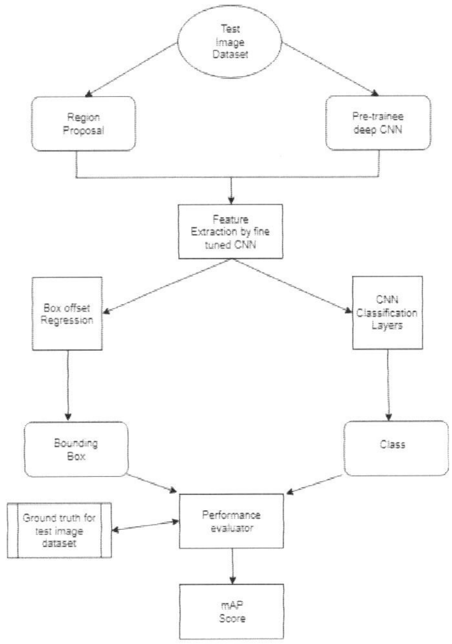

Fig. 1. Block Diagram

Traffic sign detection can be improvised using deep learning technological approaches. Deep learning techniques can perform end-to-end object detection without having specifically defined features and are typically based on convolutional neural networks. When CNNs became highly popular and their feature extraction capabilities became apparent, a sliding window detector was used in combination with them for object detection. Overfeat was one such system and its performance was poor. Hence, region proposal algorithms were used for successful object detection instead of sliding window approach as this method combines region proposals with CNNs, it was called region based convolutional neural network.

II. Methodology

The processes involved in the region based convolutional neural network can be explained breifly.

Region Proposals When an image is fed to an RCNN to extract information about the location and the class of one or more objects in the image, the network first extracts the region proposals from the given input image, which are then re-sized to the input image size of the network.Then the network extracts features of various region proposals. In the [Reference paper[1]], selective search algorithm was used to extract 2000 region proposals. Some other algorithms that can be used include category-independent object proposals, constrained parametric min cuts(CPMC), multi-scale combinatorial grouping, etc. Here edge boxes algorithm has been used in the Matlab implementation.

Training an RCNN One of the major bottlenecks in detection is having limited data available to work with. For a classification task, a Convolutional neural network requires a minimum of ten thousand images. Obtaining labeled data of that magnitude is quite a tough task for detection problems. One good approach for that is to perform training in two steps, which include supervised pre-training and domain specific fine tuning.In supervised pre-training, CNN is trained on a large data set containing generalized images. In domain specific fine tuning, the network is adopted to perform the detection task. In fine tuning, the classification layer is replaced by a new classification layer of N+1 classes, where N is number of classes in the detection task and a one is added for the background class. The CNN is now trained on the warped region proposals which are now classified into positive and negative training samples. This classification is based on Intersection over Union(IoU) threshold, which is an important parameter used in training, testing and object detection. It is used to quantify the detectors performance of localization while testing and to judge a sample as positive or negative during training. High IoU indicates a close match between the ground truth and the predicted bounding boxes. In the [Reference paper[1]], an IoU threshold of 0.5 is considered to differentiate the positive and negative training samples. Then N binary linear SVMs are to be trained for each class. They are trained on the feature vectors extracted from CNN. For each class, positive and negative samples are to be defined. This classification is based on a threshold different from that of the fine tuning step. Here a threshold of 0.3 is considered i.e. the negative samples are defined as those whose IoU with a ground truth box is less than 0.3. Later a regressor, which aims to learn the transformation that predicts a ground truth box from the predicted box using a feature vector that has been extracted, is trained to improve the accuracy of prediction of the object location.

Implementation The R-CNN that has been implemented, differs from the one used in the [Reference paper[1]] in a few ways. The region proposal algorithm used here is that of edge boxes and not selective search. However, the number of proposals per image remains same at 2000. This R-CNN does not use SVM to classify the region proposals from its features. Rather, it uses Softmax layer of the base Convolutional network as a classifier. In the [Reference paper[1]], since different IoU thresholds have been used, the positive and negative training samples for fine tuning and training the SVM are different. Same samples are used for both the IoU thresholds are not varied. The networks that have been used to test the performance are CIFAR10NET and Alexnet. CIFAR10NET is a network defined, consisting of 15 layers. It has three Convolutional Layers consisting of Relu and maxpooling layers after each of these three layers. This network takes an input image of size 32x32x3. This network is pre-trained using CIFAR10 dataset consisting of 50,000 images belonging to 10 categories. Alexnet is a pre-trained network that has been trained on more than a million images from the ImageNet database. This network can classify images into 1000 categories and this network can take an input image of size 227x227. Two data sets have been used to train and test the networks. First one is the German Traffic Sign Detection Benchmark. This dataset contains 600 training images and 300 test images. Ground truth information was available for both. These signs were distributed over 43 classes. The second dataset is a collection of 503 images gathered from the internet and personal data, which belongs to 41 classes. All these classes are present in the German Dataset. This data set has been referred to as a Collected Dataset.

Testing RCNN In the fine-tuning step, the network has been trained using SGDM (Stochastic Gradient Descent with Momentum) with initial learn rate of 0.001 and a mini batch size of 128. Different combinations of network and datasets were analyzed to obtain the best performance .

(1) Initially, CIFAR10NET has been trained on German training dataset and tested on German test dataset. In this, 300 detected images were analyzed and the poor performance was a result of low classification accuracy of CIFAR10NET. A number of background images were reported as traffic signs and also the localization capability of the network was poor.

Fig. 2. Speed limit 70 sign and Priority road sign are detected correctly. Localisation is poor and a lot of background is detected incorrectly.

(2) Alexnet is trained on German training data set and tested on German test data set. After training, from the detected images, it was found that incorrect background

detections decreased significantly compared to the previous CIFAR10NET. Also, localization performance of the network has been improved.

Fig. 3. Priority road sign is identified correctly but speed limit 70 sign is identified as speed limit 30 sign. Localisation is better than Fig.1 and there are no background detections.

(3) As the images in the German Training Data set were not very clear and training with such hazy pictures could affect the performance of the detector, a new data set was collected i.e. Collected Data set. All the images in this Data set were sharp and Alexnet was trained on this Collected Data set and tested on the German Test Data set. Here the incorrect background detections were eliminated upto the maximum possible extent. However the classes were predicted incorrectly for many traffic signs. This infers a trade off between correct classification and incorrect background detection.

Fig. 4. Priority road sign is not identified and speed limit 70 sign is identified as speed limit 30 sign. There are no background detections compared to Fig.1.

(4) Observing the drop in performance from training on the Collected Dataset, it was attempted to combine both the datasets while training in the hope of eliminating the background detection and improving the correct detections of traffic signs. So, Alexnet has been trained on the combined dataset and tested on German Dataset. While the background detections were close to the previous one, the identification capability was not as good as the second combination of network that has been analyzed before.

Fig. 5. Priority road sign is identified as Give way and speed limit 70 sign is identified as speed limit 50. There are no background detections compared to Fig.1.

(5) To improve the detection, a few more images were added to the Collected Dataset and was split into Collected Train and Collected Test datasets containing 432 and 161 images respectively. Now, these training and test datasets were applied to Alexnet. Replacing the test dataset helped to understand the relevance of correlation between the test and training datasets. In this case, a large number of traffic signs were detected properly and the background detections were the least.

Fig. 6. Image with No entry, Give way and Priority road signs is detected correctly

Mean Average Precision (mAP) Mean Average Precision is a metric used to evaluate object detector performance. To address these needs, average precision was used. Mean Average Precision is calculated by taking mean of average precision over all the classes.

III. Results

Mean Average Precision was calculated for all the above mentioned combinations of base networks and train data sets.

Table:

Base Network	Training Dataset	testing Dataset	mAP
CIFAR10NET	German Training Dataset	German Test Dataset	0.0684
ALEXNET	Collected Dataset	German Test dataset	0.0253
ALEXNET	Combined Dataset	German Test data set	0.1881
ALEXNET	German Training Dataset	German Test dataset	0.1921
ALEXNET	Collected Dataset	Collected Test dataset	0.5952

Table.1. Presentation of mAP scores.

It can be inferred from the above Tabular form, that the resulting mAP score of 0.5952 for the Collected Data set is higher when compared to the other combinations of data sets.

IV. Conclusion

Hence better results are obtained by the addition of the new data set. These results are theorized on the basis of the improvements in the system mentioned below. The increase in the number of negative samples improved the training process. Positive samples are to be clear and large enough for the RCNN to learn the symbol in the sign. RCNN system fails to recognize signs when the sign occupies a large part of the image and when the signs occupy a very tiny part of the image and such problems in real time systems translate to signs being recognized at an optimum distance, not very far or very close to the image capturing device. The RCNN, if trained on a proper data set, which is especially designed keeping these requirements in mind, could give very good results. Our personal data set is one of many such diverse data sets possible which resulted in high efficiency in detecting the traffic sign boards.

References

[1] Ross Girshick, Jeff Donahue, Trevor Darrell, Jitendra Malik,Rich feature hierarchies for accurate object detection and semantic segmentation, 2014 IEEE Conference on Computer Vision and Pattern Recognition.

[2] J. Stallkamp, M. Schlipsing, J. Salmen, C. Igel, The German Traffic Sign Recognition Benchmark: A multi-class classification competition, 2011 International Joint Conference on Neural Networks

[3] Hee Seok Lee, Kang Kim, Simultaneous Traffic Sign Detection and Boundary Estimation using Convolutional Neural Network,IEEE Transactions on Intelligent Transportation Systems (Volume: 19, Issue: 5 May 2018) .

[4] Shaoqing Ren, Kaimimng He, Ross Girshick, Jian Sun,"Faster R-CNN:Towards Real-Time Object Detection with Region Proposal Networks" arXiv:1506.01497v3 [cs.CV] on 6th january 2016.

[5] Ross Girshick, "Fast R-CNN", in IEEE International conferance on Computer Vision (ICCV) arXiv:1504.08083v2 [cs:CV] on 27th september 2015.

[6] J.R.Uijlings, K.E.Van de Sande, T.Gevers and A.W.Smeulders, "Selective Search for Object Recognition", International Journal of Computer Vision (IJCV), 2013.

[7] C.L.Zitnick and P.Dollar, " Edge boxes: Locating object proposals from edges", in European Conference on Computer Vision (ECCV), 2014

SESSION

IMAGING SCIENCE, NOVEL ALGORITHMS AND APPLICATIONS

Chair(s)

TBA

Integrated Application for Computer-Aided Image Stitching, Navigation, and Analysis for Large-Scale Whole-Slide Osteosarcoma Images

Regular Research Paper

Bogdan Armaselu
barmaselub@gmail.com
Harish Arunachalam
dr.harish.arunachalam@gmail.com
Rashika Mishra, Saloni Agarwal, and Ovidiu Daescu
Department of Computer Science, University of Texas at Dallas, Dallas, Texas, USA
{rashika.mishra, saloni.agarwal1, daescu}@utdallas.edu

Abstract— *Osteosarcoma is one of the most common forms of bone cancer found in children. For assessing treatment outcome pathologists dissect and scan the affected bone into a low-resolution gross map. The bone is divided into regions, which are then manually labeled on the gross map. All these labeled regions of the bone are sliced and scanned at high-resolution, and large-scale SVS whole-slide images (WSIs) are produced for each of them. Tumor necrosis is known to be a good bio-marker for predicting remission in osteosarcoma. To allow the pathologist to evaluate tumor necrosis, we design an algorithm to stitch the separate WSIs together into a whole-bone WSI resembling the gross map, which improves the performance of the previous algorithms. A novel tumor mapping module is also developed, which takes the output of a manual or automatic tumor classification on each WSI, and maps it to the whole-bone WSI.*

Keywords: osteosarcoma ; image stitching ; whole-slide image ; gross map ; computer-aided

1. Introduction

Osteosarcoma is one of the most common childhood cancers arising in the bone. For the purpose of assessing treatment efficiency, the affected bone is surgically cut and scanned into a low-resolution JPEG image up to several million pixels (Mp). This image is called the *gross map* (Figure 1, top). The gross map is then divided into *regions* which are labeled. Each of these regions is then sliced, H&E-stained, scanned at high resolution (40X), and converted to digital *whole-slide images* (WSI, Figure 2). The input WSIs are in SVS format and have very high resolutions, namely in the order of gigapixels (Gp) and a maximum resolution of 40X. Tumor necrosis is known to be an important bio-marker in predicting remission. Thus, analysis of the bone tumor as a whole is essential for treatment prognosis. Therefore, it is desired that these WSIs are stitched together into an image of the whole bone, called *whole-bone WSI*. We develop an application that takes the gross map and WSIs as input, and stitches the WSIs together into a whole-bone WSI. The whole-bone WSI is stored in PNG format at medium resolution (1 to 20 Mp). A tumor mapping module is also developed, which associates the whole-bone WSI with the tumor classification of each WSI.

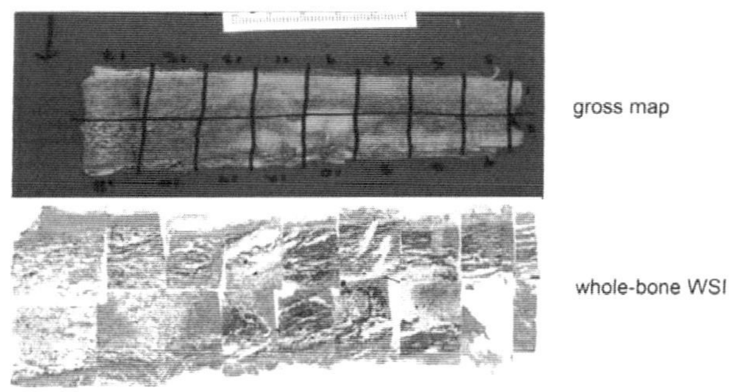

Fig. 1: Top: gross map; Bottom: whole-bone WSI

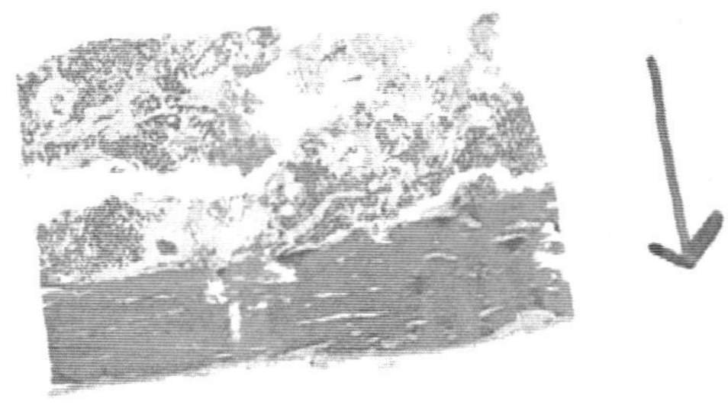

Fig. 2: WSI

1.1 Related Work

The problem of image stitching has been studied by various scientists. Levin et. al [5] presented a method to stitch images of fixed sizes and orientations using gradient difference minimization within overlapping windows of width δ. Rankov et. al [7] came up with an algorithm to stitch images of arbitrary sizes, based on maximizing pairwise cross-correlation of the pixels within a sliding window of overlap. Gallagher [3] presented an approach to solving puzzles with square pieces of arbitrary orientation, using pairwise minimization of the Mahalanobis gradient. Ma et. al [6] developed a seamless stitching algorithm for electronic microscopy images. All these techniques involve small-scale images (up to 1000 x 1000 pixels) and the stitching result is up to 5000 x 5000 pixels. In addition, most of these techniques only work with a small number of input images (2-5).

Armaselu et. al developed an algorithm to stitch small-scale (up to 1 Mp) JPG images of arbitrary orientations and sizes [2]. Later, they extended their algorithm to work with large-scale (up to 5 Gp) SVS images [1].

For large size histological (H&E stained) WSI images stitching, Zerbe et. al [9] produced an image analysis and processing framework, mainly for the purpose of sharpness assessment.

1.2 Our contributions

We improve upon the stitching algorithm in [1] by using a novel approach. First, we introduce a method to flip the WSI such that it matches the rest of the bone when stitching it into the whole-bone WSI. Second, we introduce a method to crop the WSI to tissue, such that it only contains tissue and does not leave white spaces when stitched. Finally, we improve the region detection algorithm in [1] using region growing methods.

We also improve the accuracy of the whole-bone WSI navigation module in [1] by carefully redesigning the stitching and tile fetching pipelines.

Finally, we come up with a tumor mapping module, which reads tumor annotations of individual WSI, and associates them to regions in the whole-bone WSI, in order to produce a whole-bone tumor map on the whole-bone WSI.

The rest of the paper is organized as follows. In Section 2 we present our stitching algorithm and argue how it improves upon the previous one. In Section 3 we describe our navigation module and its improvement upon the previous version. Section 4 introduces our tumor mapping module. Section 5 contains the experimental results and discussion. Finally, in Section 6, the conclusions and future work are stated.

2. Image Stitching Module

We develop a module that stitches a set of input WSIs in order to resemble a given gross map. The output is called the *whole-bone WSI* (Figure 1, bottom).

2.1 Challenges

WSI stitching involves major challenges, such as:

1. WSIs need to be rotated and flipped (mirrored) so that their orientation matches that of the gross map regions.

2. WSIs need to be placed in the correct relative position, according to the gross map region labeling.

3. WSIs need to be stitched together so that they transition smoothly and do not leave gaps in between.

4. There should not be "white" gaps in the interior of the whole-bone WSI.

5. Since the WSI are up to 5 Gp each, stitching them at full size would require up to 750 GB worth of memory and a great amount of processing time.

2.2 Methodology

In order to save the stitching result to a portable file, and perform the image processing efficiently with respect to time and memory, the WSIs are first downscaled so that they don't exceed 0.5 Mp. This is achieved if they are downsized to 0.125X resolution. The labeled gross map regions are then identified. Each region is defined by: id, left-end X coordinate, top-end Y coordinate, width, and height. After that, each WSI is rotated so that the arrow orientation is consistent with the gross map arrow orientation (typically, upwards), and flipped such that the cortex is further to the exterior than the soft tissue. Then, the WSIs are cropped to tissue, so that they do not leave gaps when stitched. Finally, the WSI is placed at its correct position within the whole-bone WSI, according to its corresponding region coordinates, and stitched to the already placed WSIs. The whole-bone WSI is of higher resolution than the gross map, typically on the order of 1 to 20 Mp.

The next subsections detail the region detection, WSI rotation, flip, tissue cropping, and stitching algorithms.

2.3 Region Detection Algorithm

Regions are identified by differentiating among the bone tissue pixels, dark lines, and background. The region detection algorithm is based on a flood-fill-like approach, which works in blocks of pixels, as follows. Denote by $n = W \cdot H$ the number of pixels in the gross map G, where W is the width and H is the height of G.

1. Rescale gross map by a factor of $F = (H \cdot W \cdot LW^2)^{-1/4}$ in both dimensions, where $LW = 0.01$ is the expected ratio between the dark line width and the image width (height). This is done in order for the running time to be linear in the size of the input gross

map image. Denote the width and height of the rescaled gross map by W' and H', respectively.

2. Compute bone bounding box BB by boxing in from the exterior, and stop whenever the standard deviation $\sigma(B(p))$ of the brightness of all pixels p in the current row (column) exceeds a threshold T_σ. In practice, we use $T_\sigma = 15$ on a $[0, 255]$ scale for best results.

3. Divide BB into $|BB|$ overlapping blocks of pixels, of width $LW \cdot W'$, height $LW \cdot H'$, each centered at a pixel of BB. The blocks can be either *background*, *tissue*, or *dark line*. Deciding the type of a block is based on HSB color space thresholding. Perform flood-fill on the set of tissue blocks, in order to obtain the division of the image into regions.

4. Select relevant regions and take their bounding boxes. A region R is considered relevant if all of the following conditions hold.

(i). $area(R) \in [LAT \cdot W' \cdot H', UAT \cdot W' \cdot H']$;

(ii). $width(R) > LWT \cdot W'$;

(iii). $height(R) > LWT \cdot H'$,

where LAT, UAT, LWT denote, respectively, the lower area, upper area, and lower width thresholds. In practice, we set $LAT = 0.001, UAT = 0.333, LWT = 0.03$.

5. Scale regions by $\frac{1}{F}$ in each dimension, in order to match the original gross map coordinates.

The running time of this algorithm is dominated by the running time of the flood-fill operation, which is at most

$|BB| \cdot (LW \cdot W') \cdot (LW \cdot H') \leq (W' \cdot H') \cdot (LW^2 \cdot W' \cdot H') = W'^2 \cdot H'^2 \cdot LW^2 = (W \cdot F)^2 \cdot (H \cdot F)^2 \cdot LW^2 = W^2 \cdot H^2 \cdot F^4 \cdot LW^2 = W^2 \cdot H^2 \cdot (W \cdot H \cdot LW^2)^{-1} = W \cdot H = n.$

That is, the running time is linear is the size of the gross map.

The detected regions are saved to a file "regions.txt". See Algorithm 1 (DetectRegions) for an illustration of the region detection algorithm pseudocode.

The function $Rescale(G, f)$ rescales image G by a factor of f. The function $Division(BB, (x, y))$ divides region BB into $|BB|$ overlapping blocks of size (x, y), each centered at a pixel of BB. The function $FloodFill(Blocks, BB)$ takes a set of blocks and a bounding box BB and returns a division of BB into a list R of regions, such that for every region $R_i \in R$, all blocks $block \in R_i$ have the same type.

2.4 WSI Rotation Algorithm

Similarly to [1], we identify the blue arrow in each WSI, and then rotate the WSI such that the blue arrow points up. If the WSI is in JPEG format, and no blue arrow is detected, it is rotated in such a way as to maximize the pairwise cross-correlation of pixels over a narrow window of overlap (10%) [1]. We present a novel algorithm (Algorithm 2) to decide the horizon-

Algorithm 1 Algorithm DetectRegions

```
procedure DetectRegions(G)
Require: Gross map G
Ensure: List of regions Regions
    (W, H) = (width(G), height(G))
    LW = 0.01, T_σ = 15
    F = (H · W · LW^2)^(-1/4)
    G' = Rescale(G, F)
    (W', H') = (width(G'), height(G'))
    top = min{r : σ{B(p) : p ∈ rows(G')_r} > T_σ}
    bottom = max{r : σ{B(p) : p ∈ rows(G')_r} > T_σ}
    left = min{r : σ{B(p) : p ∈ cols(G')_r} > T_σ}
    right = max{r : σ{B(p) : p ∈ cols(G')_r} > T_σ}
    BB = Rectangle(top, bottom, left, right)
    G_BB = {G'(x, y)|(x, y) ∈ BB}
    Blocks = Division(G_BB, LW · W, LW · H
    for each block block of Blocks do
        HSB = GetHSBThresholdingStatistic(block)
        if isBackground(HSB) then
            type(block) = background
            if isDark(HSB) then
                type(block) = dark
            elsetype(block) = tissue
            end if
    end for
    for each block block_i of Blocks do
        region(block) = R_i
    end for
    R = FloodFill(Blocks, BB)
    LAT = 0.001, UAT = 0.333, LWT = 0.03
    for each region R_i ∈ R do

        if area(R_i) ∈ [LAT·W'·H', UAT·W'·H'] AND
width(R_i) > LWT · W' AND height(R_i) > LWT · H'
then
            RB_i = BoundingBox(R_i)
        end if
        end for
        for each rectangle RB_i do
            Regions_i = Rescale(RB_i, 1/F)
        end for
        return Regions
    end procedure
```

tal/vertical flip (mirror) of the WSIs based on the tissue distribution, which is described below.

Algorithm 2 Algorithm DetectFlip

---

procedure DETECTFLIP($I, index, G, R$)

Require: WSI I of index $index$, gross map G, and region list R

Ensure: flag $flipX$ indicating whether I has to be flipped horizontally, flag $flipY$ indicating whether I has to be flipped vertically

$[vBorder, vOpposite] = getVBorder(index, G, R)$
$[hBorder, hOpposite] = getHBorder(index, G, R)$
$CVB = countCortexPixels(I, vBorder)$
$CVO = countCortexPixels(I, vOpposite)$
$CHB = countCortexPixels(I, hBorder)$
$CHO = countCortexPixels(I, hOpposite)$
$TVB = countTissuePixels(I, vBorder)$
$TVO = countTissuePixels(I, vOpposite)$
$THB = countTissuePixels(I, hBorder)$
$THO = countTissuePixels(I, hOpposite)$
if $CVB > TVB$ and $TVO > CVO$ **then**
  $flipX = TRUE$
else
  $flipX = FALSE$
end if
if $CHB > THB$ and $THO > CHO$ **then**
  $flipY = TRUE$
else
  $flipY = FALSE$
end if
return $flipX, flipY$
end procedure

---

1. Figure out whether the WSI is on the left or right "border" of the bone, according to its region index, the gross map, and the regions file. Count *cortex* and *tissue* pixels in the left and right halves of the WSI. A pixel is considered *cortex* or *tissue* if its HSB color levels lie within certain intervals on a $[0, 255]^3$ scale. In practice, the best results were given by $H \in [224, 248], S > 128$ for *cortex* and $H \in [176, 224], S > 64$ for *tissue*.

2. Flip WSI horizontally if any of the following conditions are satisfied.

(i) WSI is on the left border, and more *cortex* pixels are on the right half than on the left half, and more *tissue* pixels are on the left side than on the right side;

(ii). WSI is on the right border, and more *cortex* pixels are on the left half than on the right half, and more *tissue* pixels are on the right side than on the left side.

The functions $getVBorder(index, G, R)$ (respectively, $getHBorder(index, G, R)$) return a pair $[border, opposite]$, where $border$ is the closest vertical (resp., horizontal) border ("left" or "right", resp. "top" or "bottom") of G where the $index$-th region of R lies, and $opposite$ is the opposite border.

The function $countCortexPixels(I, border)$ counts the number of pixels on the $border$ side (e.g. if $border =$ "$left$", on the left side) of I that are more likely to be cortex than non-cortex. Similarly, the function $countTissuePixels(I, border)$ counts the number of pixels on the $border$ side (e.g. if $border =$ "$left$", on the left side) of I that are more likely to be tissue than non-tissue.

Since the running time of the rotation and flip operations is dominated by counting, rotation and flipping can be done in $O(\sum_i N_i)$ time, where N_i is the number of pixels in WSI I_i.

Figure 3 shows how the WSI in Figure 2 is rotated such that the arrow points up, then flipped so that the cortex is to the exterior of the bone and the soft tissue is to the interior of the bone. The rotation data is saved to a file "anlges.txt".

Flipping the WSIs in the manner described above is an improvement over the rotation algorithm in [1].

When rotating a WSI, we first "square" it, i.e. we shrink the longer dimension (length) to match the shorter dimension (width). This is done in order to avoid issues in image navigation, as we shall see in Section 5.

2.5 Tissue Cropping Algorithm

The WSIs are cropped to the tissue, in order to minimize the amount of extra "white" spaces on the exterior of the WSI. To do that, we box-in from the exterior row-by-row and column-by-column, and stop whenever the fraction of *tissue* pixels in the current row (column) is above the threshold T_{FT}. In practice, we set $T_{FT} = 0.015$ to get the best results.

The tissue crop data is saved to a file "tissue-coords.txt".

Figure 3 illustrates how the WSI is cropped.

The cropping process can be done in $O(\sum_i N_i)$ time.

The tissue cropping is an improvement that was not present in [1], and helps reduce the white spaces, as mentioned in Section 5.

2.6 Seamless Stitching algorithm

When stitching a WSI into the whole-bone WSI, we pair it with every neighboring WSI (which overlaps it according to the region labeling), and apply a gradient-based algorithm [1].

Given two images I_1, I_2 to be stitched, the gradient stitcher finds the approximate optimal seam (i.e. line l that minimizes the gradient difference between I_1, I_2), and then assigns pixels from I_1 on one side of l, and from I_2 on the other side of l.

Let $W = H$ be the width (also height) of the whole-bone WSI (in pixels), which is a square image, and $N =$

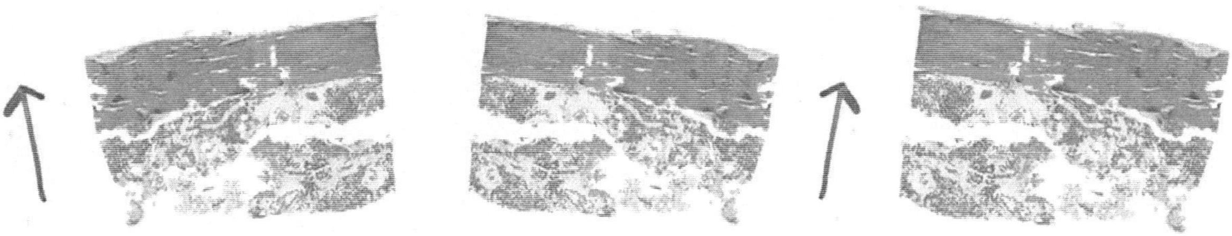

(a) WSI rotated such that the arrow points up (b) WSI flipped horizontally (c) WSI cropped to tissue

Fig. 3: WSI rotation, flipping, and cropping.

$W \cdot H = W^2$.

In this paper, we speed-up the gradient stitcher by a factor of $\Theta((mN)^{1/4})$. This is done at the expense of non-optimality of the seam (that is, the seam is approximately optimal, however, the loss of visual quality of the output is negligible). To achieve this speed-up, for each WSI I_1 of size (W_1, H_1) to be stitched, we sample only $O(\sqrt{W_1 + H_1})$ out of $O(W_1+H_1)$ candidate seams. Since each seam is evaluated in $O(W_1+H_1)$ time, this amounts to $O((W_1 + H_1)^{3/2})$ time per pair. Since there are $O(m)$ pairs per WSI, where m is the number of input WSIs, this gives up $O(m(W_1 + H_1)^{3/2})$ per WSI. Since $\sum_i (W_i + H_i)^{3/2} \leq (\sum_i (W_i + H_i))^{3/2}$, and $\sum_i (W_i + H_i) = O(m^{1/2}(W+H))$, we get a $O(m^{7/4}(W+H)^{3/2}) = O(m^{7/4}N^{3/4})$ running time overall. Note that the algorithm in [1] would take $O(m(W_1 + H_1)^2)$ per WSI, or $O(m^2(W + H)^2) = O(m^2N)$ overall.

The total running time of the stitching algorithm is $O(m^{7/4}N^{3/4}+mN+n)$, since $\sum_i N_i = O(mN)$. Since $m^3 << N, n << N$, this is $O(mN)$.

3. Image Navigation Module

Since the whole-bone WSI is of lower resolution than the input WSIs, we develop a WSI navigation module. This module allows users to visualize small portions of the whole bone at higher resolutions, by navigating the whole-bone WSI. Recall from Section 2 that the WSIs involved in the stitching are scaled down to 0.125X resolution, producing a whole-bone WSI usually no more than 25 Mp. In the navigation, we allow the user to view images at resolutions ranging from 1X to 40X, as well as thumbnail (whole-bone WSI).

When a portion of the whole-bone WSI is selected, the corresponding tile needs to be fetched and displayed from the associated input WSI. Thus, every image coordinate transformation applied in the stitching process is applied in reverse order. For more details, see [1].

Note that, in [1], WSIs are not squared before rotating. Therefore, rotating such a WSI requires allocating an image of size $2\sqrt{2}W \cdot 2\sqrt{2}H$, in order to avoid out-of-image errors when rotating pixels. This causes an unnecessary extra step in the tile fetching process. Furthermore, since the WSIs are stretched to fit the corresponding gross map region, rotating by the specified angle modifies the rotation coordinate system, introducing *skew*. Therefore, in this paper, the WSIs are "squared" before rotating, and we also apply the required transformations before fitting into the corresponding gross map region.

The tile fetching algorithm has improved performance compared to the one in [1]. Note that, the tile fetching algorithm in [1] has an average fetch error of up to $1-2\%$ in both directions. In this paper, we reduce the fetch error to less than 0.1% in both directions. Here the *fetch error* is defined to be the discrepancy, either horizontal or vertical, in whole-bone WSI pixels, between the selected whole-bone WSI location and the whole-bone WSI location corresponding to the view, divided by the whole-bone WSI width or height.

4. Tumor Mapping Module

In this section we describe a method to associate the tumor mapping output from automatic learners (described in [10]) to the whole-bone WSI. The automatic learner saves a heat map for each WSI as a XLS file. This file contains the region coordinates with their classification as row entries. We store, in each WSI, a mapping C that associates each pixel to its original relative coordinates within the WSI, as well as a mapping I to the WSI where it comes from. The mappings of each WSI are updated whenever it is processed (rotated, flipped, cropped, or stitched). This mapping process helps us to associate each whole-bone WSI index to its original WSI and its original location within that WSI. This is helpful when mapping whole-bone WSI regions to tumors heat maps. The tumor mapping module traverses the whole-bone WSI and builds a tumor map image as follows. For each pixel (x, y), it uses the mappings I and C to figure out which XLS file $F(x, y)$ to read (corresponding to a single WSI), and then reads the tumor annotation result $R(x, y)$ from $F(x, y)$ (regions in a WSI). If $R(x, y)$ is viable tumor, we put a red pixel (x, y) on the tumor map. If $R(x, y)$ is necrotic tumor, we put a yellow pixel (x, y) on the tumor map.

Table 1: The WSI dataset

Dataset #	Gross map size	WSI count	WSI input size
1	8.88E+4	12	3.69E+10
2	3.46E+5	21	7.10E+10
3	7.84E+4	15	4.95E+10
4	1.34E+5	10	3.14E+10
mean	2.558E+5	19	6.03E+10

5. Experimental Results

We tested our image stitching algorithms on a sample consisting of 11 datasets. Here we display the results obtained while running on 4 of these datasets. In subsection 5.1, we detail this setup. Then, in subsection 5.2, the performance of the image stitching and image navigation algorithms is reported, performance which will be discussed in subsection 5.3, and compared to the algorithm in [1].

5.1 Experimental setup

Our experimental data consists of 4 relevant osteosarcoma datasets from an archival sample, labeled Dataset 1 through Dataset 4, obtained from the UTSW Medical Center. The datasets consist of a gross map of size on the order of 1 Mp and a set of 6 to 50 SVS WSIs, most of which display a blue arrow. The size of these SVS WSIs is on the order of 1 Gp at 40X resolution. Table 1 shows, for each dataset, the size of the gross map, the number of WSIs, and the total size of the input WSIs.

5.2 Performance

We display, for each SVS dataset, the gross map, followed by the stitching output, i.e. the whole-bone WSI (Fig. 4 and Fig. 5).

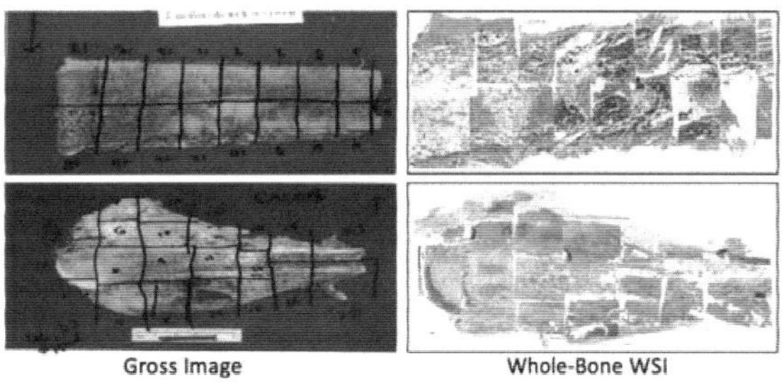

Fig. 4: Stitched WSIs for Datasets 1 and 2

While testing our stitching algorithms and navigation module on the datasets, the following error metrics are considered.

Misplacement of a WSI within the whole-bone WSI is defined as the L_1 distance between the computed location of a corner of the WSI and its correct location, relative to the width and height of the whole-bone WSI, averaged for all four corners.

Misalignment of a WSI within the whole-bone WSI is the maximum of the flip error and the rotation error of the WSI.

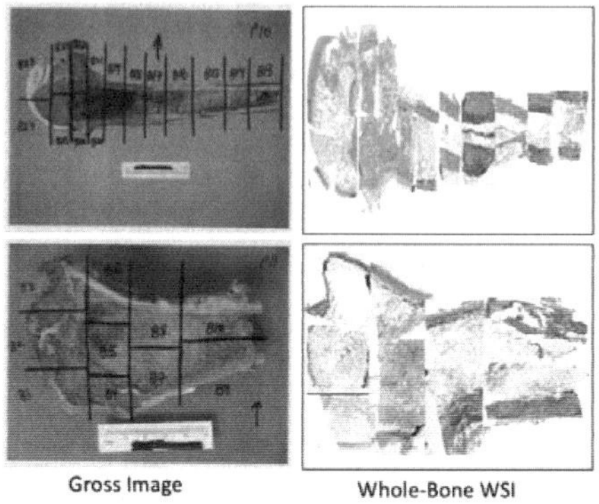

Fig. 5: Stitched WSIs for Datasets 3 and 4

Table 2: FNR, FPR, and $TPRM$ of the data sets.

Dataset	FNR	FPR	TPRM
1	0%	0%	0%
2	0%	0%	0%
3	40%	40%	43%
4	20%	43%	30%
mean	22%	24%	14%

Extra white space on the whole-bone WSI is the amount of white space that was introduced while stitching that was not part of some input WSI.

White space is the fraction of the whole-bone WSI that is white space that lies on the exterior of some WSI.

Loss of tissue is the fraction of the whole-bone WSI that is lost when stitching overlapping WSIs or cutting off WSI tissue when cropping them.

Fetch error, when navigating the whole-bone WSI, measures the distance between the clicked minimap location and its corresponding visualized location, relative to the size of the whole-bone WSI.

Table 2 shows, for each dataset, the performance of the automatic region detection algorithm on the SVS datasets. Specifically, it shows the false negative rate FNR, the false positive rate FPR, and the misplacement of true positive regions $TPRM$. Table 3 shows a comparison between the proposed algorithm and the previous algorithm [1].

5.3 Other Software Performance

For comparison purposes, we tested various off-the-shelf image stitching software, namely AutoStitch, Hugin, FIJI, Image Composite Editor©(ICE), AutoPano Pro©, Panorama Maker 6©(PM6), Panoweaver 9©, and PTGui©. AutoStitch, Hugin, and FIJI are open-source, while ICE, AutoPano Pro, Panorama Maker 6, Panoweaver 9, and PTGui are proprietary software, available with license. For each dataset, we downsampled the SVS images to 0.25X resolution, and then ran each stitching software on the dataset. Table 4 shows the rate R of datasets successfully stitched (without a crash), the time taken to stitch T, the output resolution M, the average misplacement MP, the average misalignment MA, the total relative white space WS, the total relative

Table 3: For each algorithm A, the size of the whole-bone WSI S, the time taken to stitch T, the output resolution M, the average misplacement MP, the average misalignment MA, the total relative white space WS, the total relative extra white space EWS, the time U (in seconds) taken to update the view once the minimap is clicked, and the average fetch error E, averaged over all datasets.

A	S	T	M	MP	MA	WS	EWS	E	U
[1]	3.6E+7	515	0.25	18%	14°	20%	15%	2.15	1.2%
Proposed	1.6E+7	15.2	0.13	2.4%	4°	7%	1.2%	2.15	1.2%

Table 4: For each software SW, the time taken to stitch T, the output resolution M, the average misplacement MP, the average misalignment MA, the total relative extra white space EWS, obtained when running various state-of-the art stitching software, averaged for all datasets

SW	R	T	M	MP	MA	EWS
Hugin	91%	28.8	0.55	87.3%	92°	18.1%
AutoStitch	41.7%	2.83	0.7	65.7%	0°	21.1%
FIJI	100%	6.5	0.45	76.4%	90°	19.6%
ICE	91.7%	4.82	0.05	34%	7.11°	3.33%
AutoPanoPro	41.7%	12.5	0.01	75%	33.8°	12.5%
PM6	0%	-	-	-	-	-
Panoweaver9	0%	-	-	-	-	-
PTGui	100%	22.5	0.57	55%	45°	0%
mean	58%	13	0.39	65.6%	44.7°	12.5%

extra white space EWS, averaged over all datasets successfully stitched, when running each stitching software SW mentioned above.

Thus, our pipeline performs better than the available stitching software.

6. Conclusions and Future Work

We improve the performance and running time of the WSI stitching algorithm in [1] by improving modules such as tissue cropping, region detection, and orientation detection through various image processing techniques. The performance of the image navigation module in [1] is also improved.

We leave for future work investigating possible machine learning or deep learning algorithms to automatically learn the threshold values for the region detection and flip detection, in order to further improve the performance of these algorithms.

References

[1] B. Armaselu and H.B. Arunachalam and O.Daescu and K. Cederberg and D. Rakheja and A. Sengupta and S. Shapek and P. Leavey, Large-Scale SVS Images Stitching for Osteosarcoma Identification, International Conference on Bioinformatics and Computational Biology, 2016, pp. 67–73, ISBN: 1-60132-428-6.

[2] B. Armaselu and H.B. Arunachalam and O.Daescu and J.P. Bach and K. Cederberg and D. Rakheja and A. Sengupta and S. Shapek and P. Leavey, WSI Images Stitching for Osteosarcoma Detection, International Conference on Computational Advances in Bio and Medical Sciences, 2015, ISBN: 9781467396639.

[3] A. C. Gallagher, Jigsaw puzzles with pieces of unknown orientation, Computer Vision and Pattern Recognition, 2012, pp. 382-389.

[4] F. Ghaznavi and A. Evans and A. Madabhushi and M. Feldman, Digital imaging in pathology: whole-slide imaging and beyond, Annual Review of Pathology: Mechanisms of Disease, vol. 8, 2013, pp. 331-359.

[5] A. Levin and A. Zomet and S. Peleg and Y. Weiss, Seamless Image Stitching in the Gradient Domain, ECCV' 2004, pp. 377-389.

[6] B. Ma and T. Zimmermann and M. Rohde and S. Winkelbach and F. He and W. Lindenmaier and K. EJ Dittmar, Use of AutoStitch for automatic stitching of microscope images, Micron 38, 2007, pp. 492-499.

[7] V. Rankov and R.J. Locke and R.J. Edens and P.R. Barber and B. Vojnovic, An algorithm for image stitching and blending, SPIE, vol. 5701, 2005.

[8] F. Wang and T.W. Oh and C. Vergara-Niedermayr and T. Kurc and J. Saltz, Managing and Querying Whole Slide Images, SPIE, vol. 8319, 2012.

[9] N. Zerbe and P. Hufnagl and K. Schluns, Distributed computing in image analysis using open source frameworks and application to image sharpness assessment of histological whole slide images, Journal of Diagnostic Pathology, vol. 6, 2011.

[10] H.B. Arunachalam and R. Mishra and O. Daescu and P. Leavey and D. Rakheja and K. Cederberg and A. Sengupta, Viable and Necrotic Tumor Assessment from Whole Slide Images of Osteosarcoma using Machine-learning and Deep-learning Models, PloS one, 2019, Public Library of Science.

New initialization strategy for nonnegative matrix factorization

Yueyang Wang [1] **and Bahram Shafai** [1]
[1] Department of Electrical and Computer Engineering, Northeastern University, Boston, MA, USA

Abstract— *Nonnegative matrix factorization (NMF) has been proved to be a powerful data representation method, and has shown success in applications such as data representation and document clustering. In this paper, we propose a new initialization strategy for NMF. This new method is entitled square nonnegative matrix factorization, SQR-NMF. In this method, we first transform the non-square nonnegative matrix to a square one. Several strategies are proposed to achieve SQR step. Then we take the positive section of eigenvalues and eigenvectors for initialization. Simulation results show that SQR-NMF has faster convergence rate and provides an approximation with lower error rate as compared to SVD-NMF and random initialization methods. Complementing different elements in data matrix also affect the results. The experiments show that complementary elements should be 0 for small data sets and mean values of each row or column of the original nonnegative matrix for large data sets.*

Keywords: Nonnegative matrix factorization, complementary elements

1. Introduction

Nonnegative matrix factorization (NMF) has become a widely used method in analyzing large datasets, since it extracts features from a large set of data vectors. It is a kind of factorization that constrains the elements of both components and the expansion coefficients to be non-negative.

Non-negative matrix factorization is a useful method in reducing the dimension of large datasets. In the paper Learning the parts of objects by non-negative matrix factorization published by Lee and Seung [5], they presented how NMF could learn parts of objects in facial images. It is intuited by the idea of combining the parts to form the whole. Negative values is admissible, but lose physical meaning in practice.

The factorization of matrices representing complex multidimensional datasets is the basis of several commonly applied techniques for pattern recognition and unsupervised clustering. The objective of non-negative matrix factorization (NMF) is to explain the original data with limited basis components and coefficients, which when combined together approximate the original data as accurately as possible. Because of its definition[5], the NMF method has been successfully applied in several fields including image recognition and pattern recognition, signal processing and text mining[2].

Researchers have also proposed several different algorithms based on the traditional NMF to get better performance such as Least-square NMF[8], Weighted NMF[3] and so on. However, NMF often converges to some local optima because of its random initialization factors. In order to solve this problem, some researchers began to work on the initialization problem. Qiao proposed an initialization method based on singular value decomposition[7]. Wild proposed the initialization method based on spherical k-means clustering to initialize W matrix and apply Nonnegative Least Square to calculate H matrix[9].

NMF can be described as follows: for a non-negative matrix $V_{m\times n}$ of size $m \times n$, each column of V is a sample vector, we can find a non-negative matrix $W \in R_{m\times r}$ and a non-negative $H \in R_{r\times n}$ with respective sizes $m \times r$ and $r \times n$ satisfies:

$$V^{m\times n} = W^{m\times r} \times H^{r\times n} \tag{1}$$

where W is called the basis matrix, and H is called the coefficient matrix and r is the rank of factorization. r should satisfy the rule[6]:

$$(m+n) \times r < m \times n \tag{2}$$

It is important to determine the size of the low rank matrices. For the accuracy of approximation, the larger r is, the higher accuracy will be. On the other hand, we need r to be small to reduce the size of data. Researchers set r randomly at the beginning of other algorithms. In this paper, we set r as different numbers by the choosing rule introduced in SVD-NMF[7].

There are normally two ways to define the cost functions, which can represent the approximation in the NMF reconstruction. One useful measure is simply the square of the Euclidean distance between two matrices[6]:

$$C_1 = ||A-B||^2 = \sum_{ij}(A_{ij} - B_{ij})^2 \tag{3}$$

Another useful measure is the divergence between two matrices[6]:

$$C_2 = D(A||B) = \sum_{ij}(A_{ij}\log\frac{A_{ij}}{B_{ij}} - A_{ij} + B_{ij}) \tag{4}$$

We now consider the update rules of NMF as the following problems:

Problem 1: Minimize $||V - WH||^2$ with respect to W and

H, subject to the constraints $W, H \geq 0$

$$\min f(W,H) = \sum_{i=1}^{n}\sum_{j=1}^{m}(v_{ij} - (WH)_{ij})^2 \\ s.t. W_{ia} \geq 0, H_{bj} \geq 0, \forall i, a, b, j \tag{5}$$

Problem 2: Minimize $D(V||WH)$ with respect to W and H, subject to the constraints $W, H \geq 0$

$$\min D(V||WH) = \sum_{ij}(V_{ij}\log\frac{V_{ij}}{(WH)_{ij}} - V_{ij} + (WH)_{ij}) \\ s.t. W_{ia} \geq 0, H_{bj} \geq 0, \forall i, a, b, j \tag{6}$$

Lee and Seung proposed two update algorithms for solving Problem 1 and 2.

Algorithm 1: The Euclidean distance $||V - WH||$ is non-increasing under the multiplicative update algorithm[6]:

$$H \leftarrow H. \times ((W^TV)./(W^TWH)) \\ W \leftarrow W. \times ((VH^T)./(WHH^T)) \tag{7}$$

Algorithm 2: The divergence $D(V||WH)$ is non-increasing under the divergence-reducing update rules[6]:

$$H_{a\mu} \leftarrow H_{a\mu}\frac{\sum_i W_{ia}V_{i\mu}/(WH)_{i\mu}}{\sum_k W_{ka}} \\ W_{ia} \leftarrow W_{ia}\frac{\sum_\mu H_{a\mu}V_{i\mu}/(WH)_{i\mu}}{\sum_v W_{av}} \tag{8}$$

The paper is organized as follows. We introduce SVD-NMF[7] and the factorization rank choosing rule in Section 2. The SQR-NMF is presented in Section 3. Simulation results in image reconstruction and the comparison with other NMF method is presented in Section 4. Finally, Section 5 presents our conclusion.

2. SVD-NMF

Let $V \in R^{m\times n}$ be a singular value decomposition

$$V = P\hat{\Sigma}Q^T \\ \hat{\Sigma} = diag(\sigma_1, \sigma_2, ...\sigma_p) \in R^{m\times n} \\ p = \min(m,n) \tag{9}$$

where $\sigma_1 > \sigma_2 > ... > \sigma_p$ are the singular values of V, and $P \in R^{m\times m}$ and $Q \in R^{n\times n}$ are orthogonal matrices. There can be negative elements in matrix P and matrix Q , so we cannot directly use these two matrices for initialization. Thus, we set the negative entries to the absolute value of themselves, so we get $|P|$ and $|Q^T|$. We get the initialization formulas of W and H:

$$W_0 = |P| \\ H_0 = |\hat{\Sigma}Q^T| \tag{10}$$

where $|.|$ indicates that all entries of are their absolute values. We set r by the following choosing rule.

2.1 Factorization rank r choosing rule

The singular values obtained by SVD are sorted in the descending order, then the sum of the first few singular values take a large portion of the sum of all singular values, which means they have contained enough information for reconstruction.

We define the sum of all singular values as sum_p and the sum of first few as sum_r, thus we have:

$$sum_p = \sigma_1 + \sigma_2 + ... + \sigma_p \\ sum_r = \sigma_1 + \sigma_2 + ... + \sigma_r \tag{11}$$

Table 1: r of processing 1 image with different extraction ratio

Extraction ratio	Factorization rank				
80 %	10	12	8	7	9
90 %	23	26	20	20	21
100 %	92	92	92	92	92

Table 2: r of processing 5 image with different extraction ratio

Extraction ratio	Factorization rank				
80 %	17	26	18	25	16
90 %	37	47	37	47	37
100 %	112	112	112	112	112

Then we define the choosing rule when the extraction ratio is 90% in the following form:

$$sum_r/sum_p \leq 90\% \\ sum_{r+1}/sum_p \geq 90\% \tag{12}$$

Table 1 gives us the factorization rank r for different facial images using choosing rule. These images are derive from ORL database[4]. The ORL database has 40 different persons and each has 10 different facial images. The size of each image is 112×92. From Section 1, we get that r should satisfies: $r < (m \times n)/(m + n) = 51$ when processing 1 image and $r < (m\times n)/(m+n) = 90$ when processing 5 images for ORL database, where m and n are the number of rows and columns of image matrix. Table 1 and Table 2 show that all of factorization rank satisfy the rule when the extraction ratio is 80% and 90%.

3. SQR-NMF

In this method, we first transform a non-square nonnegative matrix into a square one. We add complementary elements to each row or column to make it a square matrix. The complementary elements can be 0, 1, or the mean values of each row or column. Then we apply eigenvalue decomposition for the square nonnegative matrix and set the factorization rank by the choosing rule introduced in the SVD-NMF. Since there is no randomization in initialization, it can converge to the same solution, which is critical to iterative algorithms. The basic initialization is based on square matrices with eigenvalue decomposition, therefore we title this method as SQR-NMF.

3.1 SQR-NMF based on eigenvalues and eigenvectors

Let $V \in R^{m\times n}$ be a eigenvalue decomposition

$$V_{m\times n} \rightarrow V_{p\times p} = Q\hat{V}Q^{-1} \\ \hat{V} = diag(\sigma_1, \sigma_2, ...\sigma_p) \in R^{p\times p} \\ p = \max(m,n) \tag{13}$$

where $\sigma_1 > \sigma_2 > ... > \sigma_p$ are the eigenvalues of $V_{p\times p}$, and Q is a matrix, consists of the eigenvectors of $V_{p\times p}$.

In this method, we do the initialization with eigenvalue and eigenvectors. The entries of eigenvectors can be negative, we take the positive part for initialization.

We get the initialization formulas of W and H:

$$W_0 = |Q| \qquad H_0 = |\hat{V}Q^{-1}| \tag{14}$$

where $|.|$ indicates that all entries are their absolute values.

3.2 SQR-NMF based on symmetric matrices

Using the Jordan normal form, we can prove that any square real matrix can be written as the product of two real symmetric matrices[1].

$$V_{m\times n} \rightarrow V_{p\times p} = S_1 S_2 \qquad p = \max(m, n) \tag{15}$$

where matrix S_1 and S_2 are symmetric matrices, with size $p \times p$. We generate a symmetric matrix S in the following form:

$$S = QQ^T \tag{16}$$

where matrix Q consists of the eigenvectors of matrix $V_{p\times p}$. Then the square nonnegative matrix $V_{p\times p}$ can be factorized as

$$V_{p\times p} = S_1 S_2 = SV_{p\times p}^T S^{-1} \qquad S_1 = SV_{p\times p}^T \qquad S_2 = S^{-1} \tag{17}$$

We initialize W and H with the positive section of S_1 and S_2 respectively.

$$W_0 = |S_1| \qquad H_0 = |S_2| \tag{18}$$

where $|.|$indicates that all entries are their absolute values.

4. Simulation results and comparison

In this section, we carry out experiments to evaluate different initialization method. Firstly, we use the errors we defined in Section 3 to evaluate them. Then we show the representation images using different initialization methods.

The input data is the ORL face dataset [4], which contains 40 persons and 400 face images in total, each person corresponding to 10 grayscale face image with resolution of 112×92, and the grayscale is $[0, 255]$. In the test, we will present data by matrices. For image data, each pixel value represents a single value in the data matrix. We define the error in the following from to evaluate the approximation:

$$error = \frac{||V - WH||_F}{||V||_F} \tag{19}$$

where $||.||_F$ represents the Frobenius norm of the matrix.

4.1 Numerical results for MU algorithm

The simulation results show the error of reconstruction with fixed factorization rank. r in the title is the rank of factorization. In these cases, the larger the factorization rank is, the lower error rate will be.

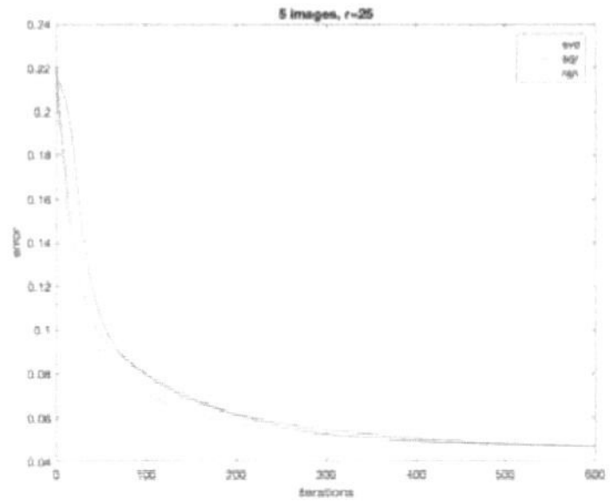

(a) $r = 25$ for 5 images

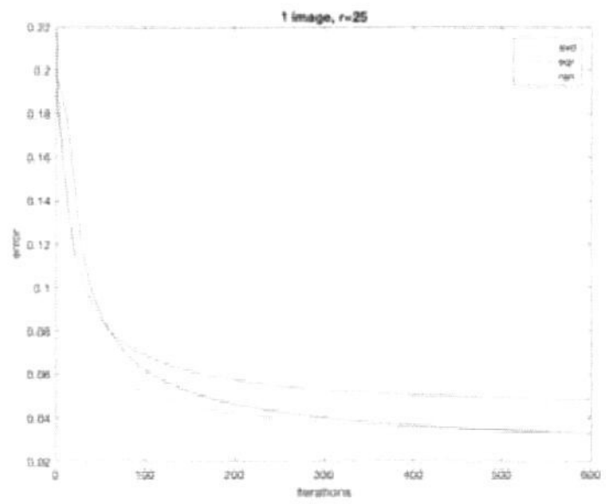

(b) $r = 25$ for 1 image

Fig. 1: Errors of reconstruction using MU algorithm,and sqr represents eigenvalue based NMF

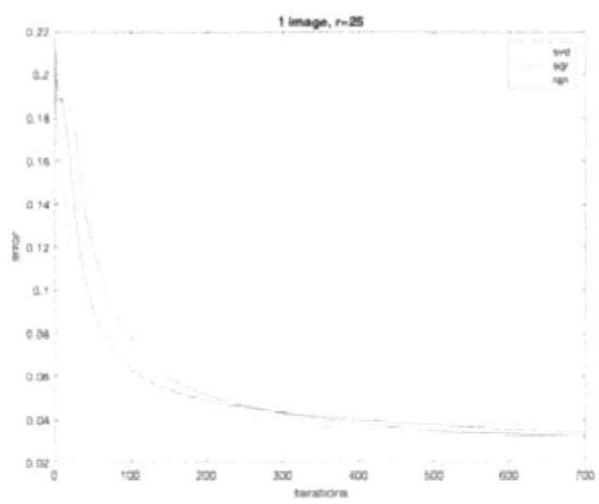

(a) $r = 25$ for 1 image

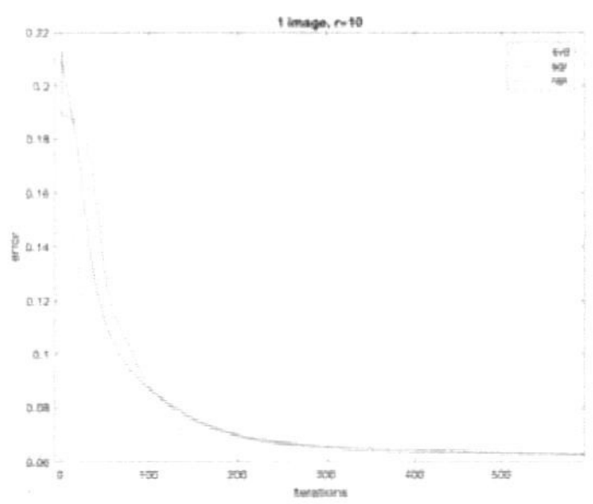

(b) $r = 10$ for 1 image

Fig. 2: Errors of reconstruction using MU algorithm, sqr represents symmetric matrix based NMF

From Figure 1, we can obtain that eigenvalue based SQR-NMF

has lower error rate at the beginning, and it convergence faster than SVD-NMF and random NMF when processing 5 images. However, SQR-NMF based on eigenvalue has a higher error rate when processing 1 image. Thus we do the initialization with symmetric matrix based SQR-NMF instead of eigenvalues based SQR-NMFm, and the result is shown in Figure 2. The performance of this new strategy is convincing, since it has lower error rate when the factorization rank $r = 10$ and $r = 25$, which represent the extraction ratio are 80% and 90% respectively.

From Figure 1 and Figure 2, we conclude that SQR-NMF performs better than the other two methods, and it has significant advantage when the factorization rank is small.

(a) Extraction rate: 80 %, $r = 25$

(b) Extraction rate: 90 %, $r = 45$

Fig. 3: Reconstruction images of SQR-NMF using MU algorithm

Since SQR-NMF has the lowest error rate,thus we show the reconstruction images by using SQR-NMF in Figure 3. The first row shows the reconstruction image when the extraction ration is 80% and the second row 90%. When extraction ratio is 80%, the quality of reconstruction image is good, we can see the details of the facial expression, which means we can represent a image with less data. In our case, this means we can have 80% information about the facial image by using only 49% of its pixel data. When the extraction portion is 90%, the reconstruction image has more details, such as, clearer noses and eyes, and more different expressions, which means we can make better reconstruction when we have more information about the origin data.

4.2 Numerical results for Divergence reducing algorithm

Figure 4 gives us the simulation results by using divergence-reducing algorithm. SQR-NMF has better performance as iteration time goes on in most of the cases. In the case of processing 5 images, SQR-NMF has the lowest error rate compared with random NMF and SVD-NMF. Its advantage is more obvious when the extraction ratio is 80%. Thus, we can conclude that the effectiveness of SQR-NMF is more significant when processing larger dataset with lower factorization rank. When processing 1 image, SQR-NMF has less error though it converges a little bit slower at the first few iterations. However, the its performance is not satisfying, but it converges faster at the beginning. So SQR-NMF can be applied when we try to balance between computational complexity and error rate.

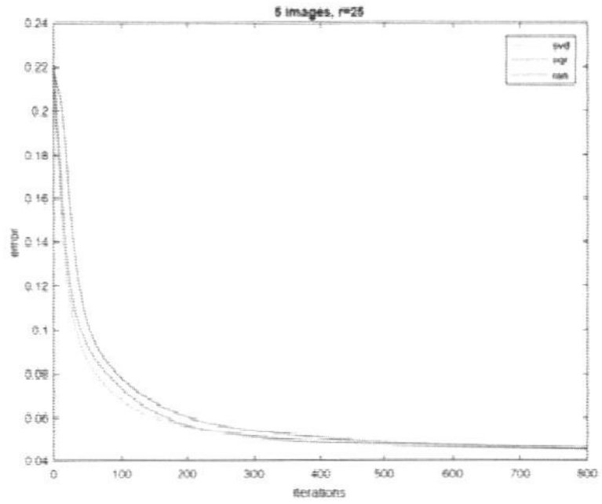

(a) 5 images, $r = 25$, sqr represents eigenvalue based NMF

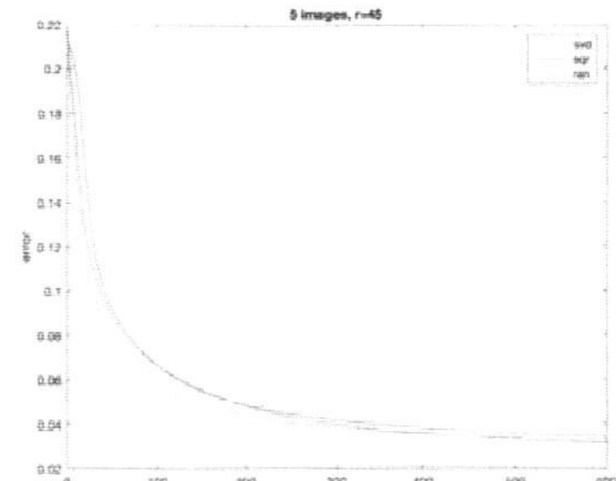

(b) 5 images, $r = 45$, sqr represents eigenvalue based NMF

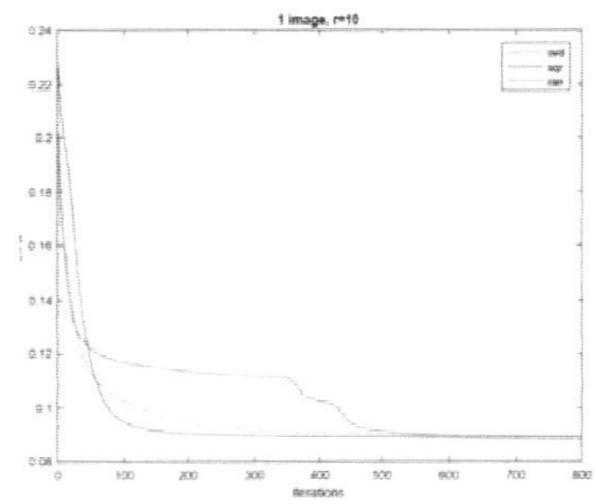

(c) 1 image, $r = 10$, sqr represents symmetric matrix based NMF

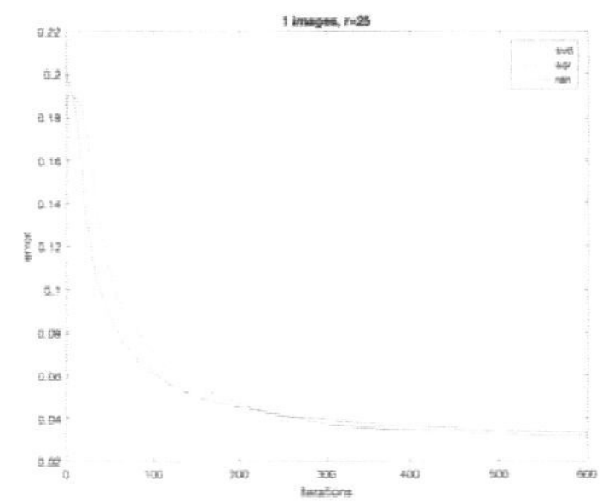

(d) 1 image, $r = 25$, sqr represents symmetric matrix based NMF

Fig. 4: Errors of reconstruction using divergence reducing algorithm

4.3 Numerical results for different complementary elements

The former simulation results show that SQR-NMF performs better than SVD-NMF and random NMF and the error rate is lower when using MU algorithm. Thus, we apply MU algorithm as the iterative algorithm in the following simulation. Then we carry our experiments to show the impact of different complementary elements on the factorization.

In this section, we add different complementary elements to make the original matrix a square matrix. We calculate the errors when the complementary elements are 0 , 1 , and mean values of each row or column.

Figure 5 shows the impact of different complementary elements for processing 1 image. Complementing 0 converges faster than the other elements, and it has lower error rate when r is larger.

Figure 6 gives us the error rate of reconstruction of different complementary elements for processing 5 images. The method of complementing mean values of each row or column have lower error rate and converges faster than adding 0 and 1, the advantage of this method is more significant when r is small.

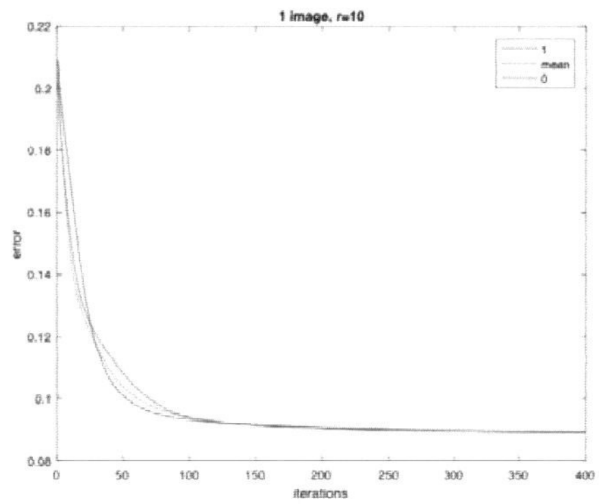

(a) 5 images, $r = 10$

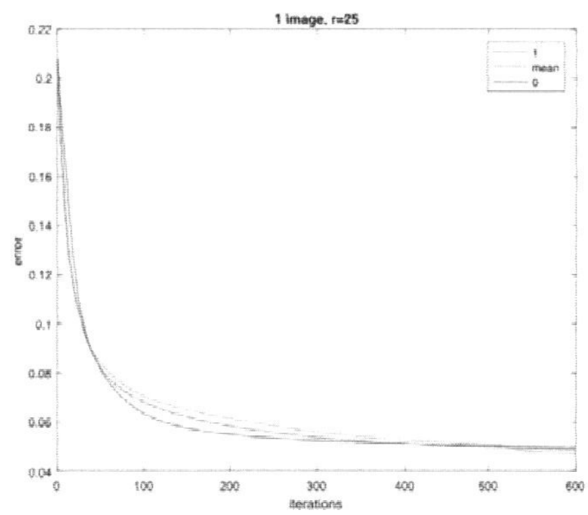

(b) 1 image, $r = 25$

Fig. 5: Errors of adding different complementary elements for 1 image

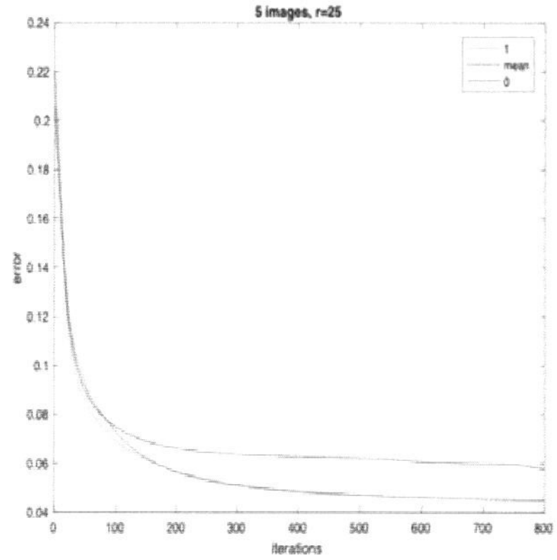

(a) 5 images, $r = 25$

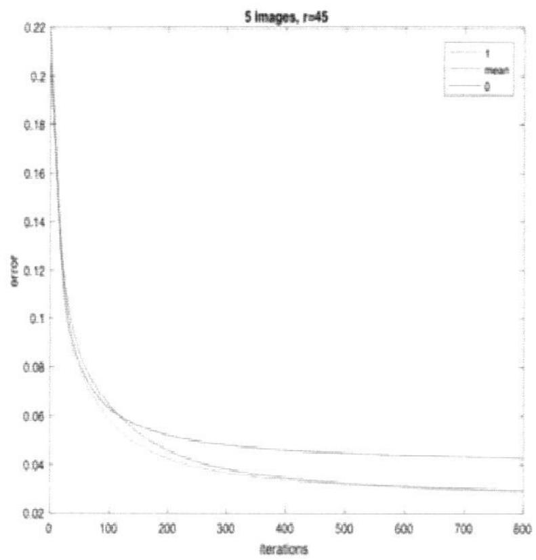

(b) 5 images, $r = 45$

Fig. 6: Errors of adding different complementary elements for 5 images

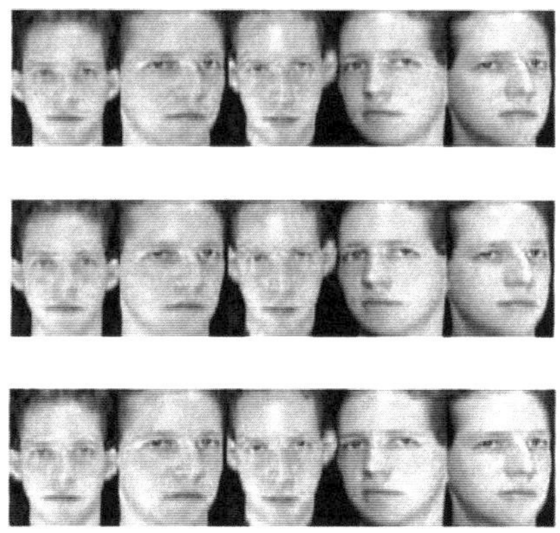

Fig. 7: Reconstruction image of different complementary elements

Figure 7 shows the reconstruction image of the facial image with different complementary elements. The complementary element is 1 for the first row, 0 for the second row and mean values of each column for the third row. We can tell that the third row has clearer facial details than the first two rows.

We also test on another set of facial images. The reconstruction errors of processing 1 image and processing 5 images are shown in Table 3 and Table 4 respectively.

Table 3: Reconstruction error of different complementary elements for 1 image

Complementary element	Reconstruction error
1	0.0250
0	0.0248
mean value of each row	0.0261

Table 4: Reconstruction error of different complementary elements for 5 images

Complementary element	Reconstruction error
1	0.0499
0	0.0495
mean value of each column	0.0491

We conclude that complementing mean values of each row or column performs better especially when the factorization rank is small, because the complementary element is more reliable. Thus, we can get a more approximate result.

5. Conclusion

In this paper, we have proposed a new initialization method for NMF in image representation. The simulation results on facial images show that SQR-NMF can achieve better performance in image representation than SVD-NMF and random NMF. We use eigenvalues and eigenvectors for initialization in SQR-NMF for large data sets and symmetric matrices for small data sets. It is critical to find complementary elements for different data set. We choose 0 for small data sets and mean values for large ones .

References

[1] A. Bosch. Note on the factorization of a square matrix into two hermitian or symmetric matrices. *SIAM Review*, 29(3):463–468, 1987.

[2] K. Devarajan. Nonnegative matrix factorization: an analytical and interpretive tool in computational biology. *PLoS computational biology*, 4(7):e1000029, 2008.

[3] D. Guillamet, M. Bressan, and J. Vitria. A weighted non-negative matrix factorization for local representations. In *Proceedings of the 2001 IEEE Computer Society Conference on Computer Vision and Pattern Recognition. CVPR 2001*, volume 1., pages I–I. IEEE, 2001.

[4] C. U. C. Laboratory. The Database of Faces. https://www.cl.cam.ac.uk/research/dtg/attarchive/facedatabase.html, 1994.

[5] D. D. Lee and H. S. Seung. Learning the parts of objects by non-negative matrix factorization. *Nature*, 401(6755):788, 1999.

[6] D. D. Lee and H. S. Seung. Algorithms for non-negative matrix factorization. In *Advances in neural information processing systems*, pages 556–562, 2001.

[7] H. Qiao. New svd based initialization strategy for non-negative matrix factorization. *Pattern Recognition Letters*, 63:71–77, 2015.

[8] G. Wang, A. V. Kossenkov, and M. F. Ochs. Ls-nmf: a modified non-negative matrix factorization algorithm utilizing uncertainty estimates. *BMC bioinformatics*, 7(1):175, 2006.

[9] S. Wild, W. S. Wild, J. Curry, A. Dougherty, and M. Betterton. *Seeding non-negative matrix factorizations with the spherical k-means clustering*. PhD thesis, University of Colorado, 2003.

Unsupervised Weighed Graph-Based Terrain Filtering Using Terrestrial Laser Scanning Data

Y. Belkhouche[1]
[1]Department of Computing Sciences, Texas A&M University-Corpus Christi, Corpus Christi, Texas, USA

Abstract— *In this paper we establish a simple method for filtering terrestrial laser scanning data. The filtering problem is modeled as graph connected components problem. The proposed method uses weighted k-nearest neighbor graph(knn), it consists of four steps: construction of the knn graph, edge weigh assignment, edge thresholding and finding the graph connected components. In the first step, a knn graph is build using the 3D point cloud. In the second step, we introduce a new scheme for labeling the edges of knn graph. Thresholding is then used to remove edges with certain weights from the knn graph, this leads to disconnecting terrain points from object points. In the last step, a graph connected component algorithm is used to find the connected components and classify the points into either terrain points or object points. We validate our method using visual observation as well as a manually labeled datasets.*

Keywords: Terrestrial laser scanning, Filtering, K-nearest neighbor, Graph connected components, object extraction, digital elevation model.

1. Introduction and literature review

Recent laser scanning instruments collect a very high density 3D point cloud describing the details of the surrounding environment. The collected data are used in many military and civilian applications. Visibility analysis [1], [2] plays an important role for battle field management, in this application the laser scanning data are used to determine what can be seen from a given location, this information is used later to determine strategic locations, positioning of troupes and provide situation awareness. Training soldiers in virtual environments [3] is another military application, where 3D city models are build using laser scanning data of the area of interest, this model is used as virtual environment to train soldiers. Urban planing [4], is another application where laser scanning data are analyzed to determine flood areas, emergency response routes, locations for placing communication antennas, and damage assessment after a disaster event. Infrastructures inspection [5], [6] such as roads, bridges, power lines, rail roads and tunnels are other applications that uses laser scanning data. Other applications that benefit greatly from using laser scanning data are 3D scene reconstruction/understanding, and autonomous robot/car navigation [7], [8], [9], in autonomous robot/car navigation, the 3D point cloud are used to build a 3D map of the environment. This map is used to determine a safe space for navigation by autonomous vehicles. It is important to mention that the 3D LiDAR data cannot be used directly in these applications, the data need to be preprocessed and mined in order to become useful. An important preprocessing task is to separate terrain points and object points, this process is known as filtering. After completing the filtering process, several products are generated using terrain points, among these products are digital elevation models (DEMs) which are used in wide range of applications. Occupancy grid maps used for autonomous vehicles navigation is another product generated using terrain points. On the other hand, object points are further processed and used to detect/classify objects into several categories such as walls, people, street sign, bicycles, cars, trees, ... etc, detecting these objects plays a very important role for 3D scene interpretation and understanding research (for indoors and outdoors scenes). Several terrain filtering(some times called digital elevation model (DEM) extraction) algorithms have been introduced in the past, however the vast majority of these methods are designed and implemented to filter airborne collected LiDAR data (the laser scanner is attached to an airplane). These algorithms do not incorporate the characteristics of terrestrial laser scanning data in the filtering process (terrestrial scanners can obtain laser returns from walls, these returns are missing in airborne collected data, on the other side, airborne scanners can obtain returns from buildings roofs, these returns are missing in the terrestrial collected data), these differences make the adopt these algorithms for filtering terrestrial LiDAR without major modifications a difficult task. Some of the most popular airborne LiDAR filtering methods were introduced in the flowing research papers [10], [11], [12], [13], [14], [15], [16]. Filtering algorithms have been classified into several categories. Segmentation/clustering based methods use a number of selected features to capture the smoothness of the terrain surface (these methods assume that the terrain surface is smooth) which is used to extract terrain points. Other segmentation-based methods use region growing algorithms, these methods require an initialization of the terrain area, the points that are similar (using a certain similarity measures) to the initialized area are added to the terrain points. Morphology-based methods use mathematical morphology operators (opening-closing and dilation-erosion) to remove non-terrain objects, leaving only terrain points. Irregular triangulated network (TIN) based methods build a triangular representation of the area of interest, then manipulate the characteristics of the triangular mesh to separate terrain and object points. Interpolation-based methods convert the LiDAR data into gray level image using the z-value of each point as the gray level color. The produced image is provided as an input to image processing methods to classify each pixel into terrain or object pixel. Another classification of filtering algorithms is based on the characteristics of the area these algorithms are designed to filter (e.g. urban areas, hilly areas, or forests). It is important to note that the methods designed to filter LiDAR data collected in urban areas may not be very successful filtering LiDAR data collected from a forest and vice versa. Most of the research related to terrestrial laser scanning is concerned with either segmentation, classification or object extraction. Segmentation methods have been studied by many researchers [17], [18], [19], [20], [21], these methods are concerned with grouping the 3D point cloud into smaller sections (objects such as cars, trees, walls, people, traffic sign, ...) having similar characteristics according to a predefined similarity measure. Classification methods such as [22], [23], [20], [24], [25] use manually labeled dataset to train a classifier, then use the trained classifier to assign new points to the corresponding class. The most used classifiers are support vector machines, Markov random fields, and neural networks. An important challenge for classification methods is the creation of training datasets. Manually labeling a large data is time and labor consuming, and it induce errors related to miss labeling points due to human errors. Object detection methods [26], [27], [28], [29], [30], [31] use either segmentation or classification to detect and extract objects of interest(cars, road signs, pedestrian, roads, buildings, ...etc). All these methods requires the identification, extraction and computation of large and complex features to be able to successfully identify/classify objects. Large feature vectors may add more challenges to applications that require readtime processing.

The rest of this paper is organized as follows. Section 2 describes the filtering problem and challenges that should be addressed by any filtering algorithm. Our filtering method is introduced in section 3, it consists of three subsections: constructing and labeling the knn graph, thresholding and finding the connected components in the knn graph, and the filtering step. Experiments and results are described in section 4. We conclude the paper and present future considerations in section 5.

2. The terrestrial scanning filtering problem

The filtering problem can be described as follows: Given a collected terrestrial scanning point cloud P_{scan}, the objective of the filtering process is to assign each 3D point in the dataset to either terrain point or object point, such that:

- $P_{Terrain}$: is the set of terrain points.
- P_{Object}: is the set of object points.
- $P_{Terrain} \cup P_{Object} = P_{scan}$
- $P_{Terrain} \cap P_{Object} = \emptyset$

These constraints mean that no point is considered as both terrain and object at the same time. Combining the terrain points and the object points give us the initial dataset. To illustrate the filtering process, consider the 3D point cloud shown in figure 1, these dataset is collected from an urban site, it consists of 79,000 points, and contains small and large buildings, several trees, bushes, and cars. Figure 1(a) shows the raw 3D data before filtering. Figure 1(b) shows an interpolated image of the of this area, in which 3D point cloud is converted into a grid representation, the height (z-value) of each point is converted into gray value(the darkest pixel value represents lower z-values, while the lightest pixel value represents high z-value). The filtered data is shown in figure 1(c), where the red points are terrain points and the blue points are object points.

There are many challenges that must be addressed when developing a filtering algorithms [32]. The most important challenges are the followings:

- Point spatial density: In a low density datasets, only few points are sampled from the surface. This means that many surfaces are not well represented, this leads to the failure of may filtering algorithms. The point spatial density may vary depending on the surface reflectivity (depending on the object material), occlusion, the distance from the surface to the laser instrument (the closer to the scanner the higher the spatial density), as well as the scanner orientation (the density of the areas in the front of the scanner is higher than those area scanned with an angle).
- Scene complexity: Urban scenes are usually complex scenes, they contain several objects with different characteristics. Some of these objects are man-made such are cars, traffic signs, buildings, ...etc. Other are natural objects such trees, bushes, ...etc. These objects vary in sizes, locations, and pose.
- Large size: Most laser scanning instruments collects up one million points per second, the collected data must processed in a very short time in order to be useful for real time applications such as autonomous robots/cars navigation. Real-time processing of LiDAR data is one of the most important challenges, it requires the selection of an appropriate data structure to represent the 3D point cloud as well as the design and implementation of simple and efficient algorithms to process these large datasets.
- Irregularity of LiDAR data: which make it difficult to use image processing algorithms directly on these data. LiDAR data can be interpolated into a gray level image, however, this process leads to losing important

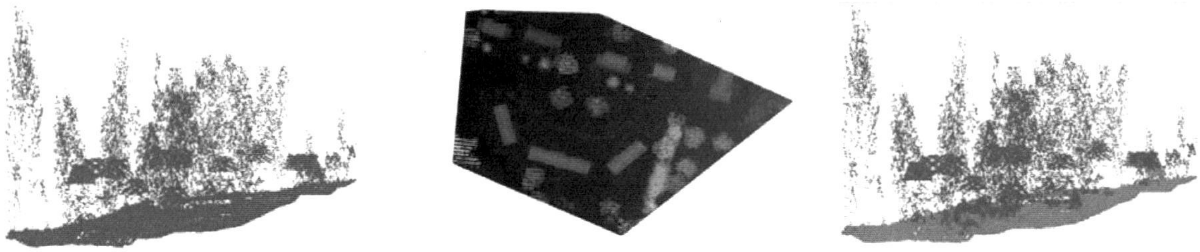

(a) Point cloud (b) Interpolated area (c) Filtered point cloud

Fig. 1: The filtering process.

information about partial occluded objects.

Filtering algorithms may be biased toward terrain or toward object. Depending on the algorithm parameters, it could perform better on correctly identifying terrain points or object points. Some algorithms perform a very high accuracy extracting object points while others achieve better accuracy extracting terrain points.

3. Methodology

The proposed method consists of several steps. IT starts by constructing the knn graph. In the second step, we introduce an edge weighting scheme, this scheme allows us to assign weights to each edge in the knn graph. The next step is thresholding, where we remove all edges smaller than a specified threshold from the knn graph leading to the creation of a new graph. A graph connected components algorithm is used to extract the connected components in the new graph. In the last step, each connected component is classified as either terrain or object. Figure 2 below shows the workflow of the proposed method.

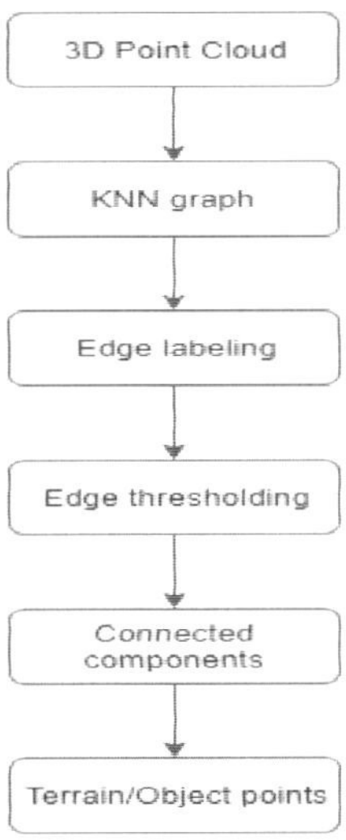

Fig. 2: The proposed filtering method.

3.1 Constructing and weighing the knn graph

A graph is represented as $G(E, V)$ where V is the set of vertices and E is the set of edges connecting these vertices. The proposed filtering method uses the k-nearest neighbor(knn) graph to represent the 3D scanning data. In this paper, we constructed the knn graph in 2D, in which the z-coordinate of each point is ignored (each point is projected onto the $xy-$plane). The initial knn graph is built using the (x, y) coordinates of each point, the Euclidean distance as a similarity metric to decide which points are adjacent to each other. The nearest neighbor criterion described in equation (1) is used to find the first nearest neighbor.

$$NN(p_i) = \{p_j \mid \underset{p_j \in V}{\operatorname{argmin}}\{d(p_i, p_j)\}\} \tag{1}$$

To build the knn graph, equation (1) is applied k times excluding the previously found nearest neighbor point. After constructing the knn graph, we assigned weights to the edges of this graph as follows:

$$w_{ij} = e^{(-|s_{ij}|)} \tag{2}$$

Where w_{ij} is the weight of the edge connecting the points p_i and p_j. s_{ij} is the slope between the points p_i and p_j, it is computed as follows:

$$s_{ij} = \frac{z_i - z_j}{||p_i - p_j||} \tag{3}$$

where z_i and z_j are the z-values for the points p_i and p_j respectively. $||p_i - p_j||$ is the distance between the point p_i and p_j, it is computed using only the x and y coordinates. The weight function in equation (2) maps large slopes to small values. The weight values are in the interval $[0 \;\; 1]$. The edges with value close to 0 are most likely to be located in areas connecting terrain points to object points, while edges with weight values close to 1 lay in terrain areas (relatively flat areas).

To illustrate this weighting scheme, consider the example shown in figure 3. This example consists of four areas with different characteristics. Figure 3(a) shows an area containing three cars and other very small objects. Figure

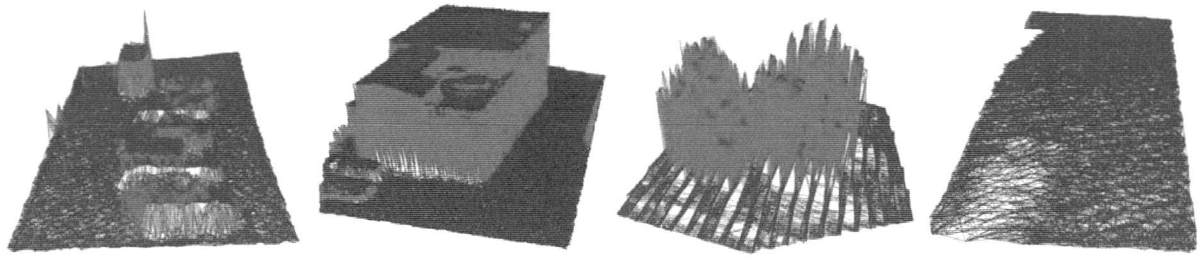

(a) Area 1: three cars and small structures. (b) Area 2: A complex building an small structures. (c) Area 3: two adjacent trees. (d) Area 4: a road segment.

Fig. 3: Lebeling the knn graph.

3(b) shows a large building and some small objects on the side of the building. Figure 3(c) shows an area containing two trees near each other. Figure 3(d) shows a road segment.

For each area we visualize the weighed knn graph using two colors: the red edges lay in the areas connecting terrain points to object points (these edges have a weigh smaller than certain threshold, in this example these edges have weights $w_{ij} \leq 0.2$). The blue edges are found in relatively flat areas (terrain or flat building roofs).

In order to analyze the characteristics of the study areas, we used the weight histogram. Figure 4 below shows the weight histograms for the four areas in figure 3. Even though these histograms are for areas with different characteristics, there are some similarities between them. The left side of each histogram represent the edges with low weights, these edge are located in areas separating the terrain and object points (terrain discontinuity). The right side of the histogram represent edges laying in relatively flat areas areas (terrain, buildings with flat roofs), these edges gives an indication of the flatness of the surface. All weight histograms of areas containing object points, will have high values on the left side (figures 4(a), 4(b), 4(c)). Figure 4(d) shows the weight histogram for a road segment, notice that there are no edges connecting terrain to object points (this is the main reason that the left side of the histogram is empty). These histograms are very useful in the selection of the threshold used to eliminate the the edges connecting terrain points and object points.

3.2 Finding the connected components

In this paper, the filtering problem is modeled as graph connected components problem. Given a graph $G(V, E)$ a connected component of this graph is subgraph where there is at least one path between each two vertices belonging to that subgraph, and no path from any vertex of the subgraph to the any vertex outside that subgraph. The key idea behind the proposed method is to generate a graph containing several connected components, this is achieved by disconnecting object points from terrain points. In order to do that we need remove all edges connecting terrain and object components (these are the red edges shown in figure 3) from the knn graph. These edges are the ones represented on the left side of the histograms in figure 4. Removing these edges from the knn graph leads to creating new graph with several components. A threshold value is selected and all edges smaller than that value are removed from the initial knn graph. After removing these edges, a connected components algorithm is applied to the new graph to find all connected components. To illustrate this concept, consider the area shown in figure 3(b), The connected components are shown using different colors (figure 5). There is one large component (points in blue color) representing the terrain points and may other small components representing object points.

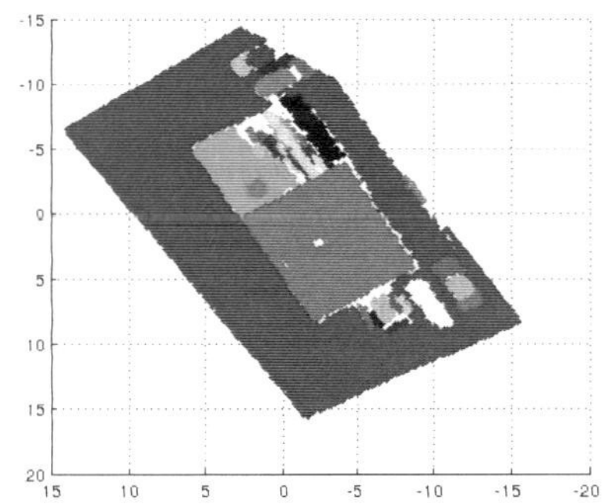

Fig. 5: Connected components for area in 3(b)

3.3 Filtering

In this step, the connected components detected in the previous step are classified as either terrain components or object components. The largest component is classified as terrain, which represents the terrain points. The main reason for selecting the large component as terrain is mainly because there is no discontinuities in the points sampled from the terrain surface, and the change between neighboring

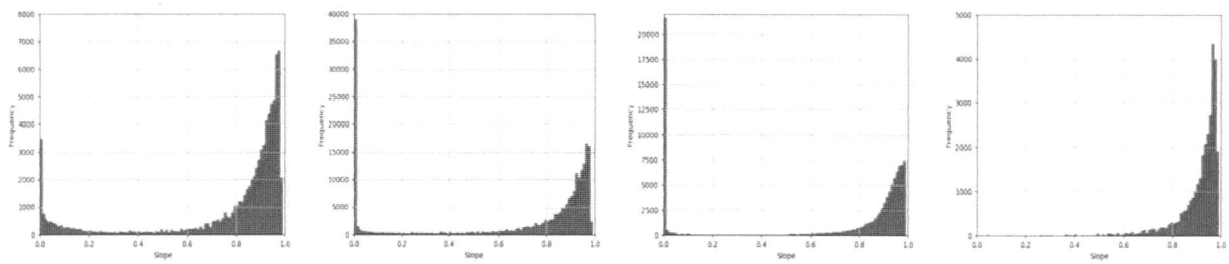

(a) Weights histogram for area 1. (b) Weights histogram for area 2. (c) Weights histogram for area 3. (d) Weights histogram for area 4.

Fig. 4: Edge weights histograms

points is usually smooth, leading to one large connected component. All other components are classified as object components.

4. Experimental Results

To validate the efficiency of the proposed method, we conducted two experiments. In the first experiments, we used visual observation of the filtered area to validate the results. In the second experiment, we used a manually labeled dataset to assess the accuracy of our filtering method. The measures used to evaluate the filtering results are the total accuracy, the object accuracy, and the terrain accuracy. These measures are shown below:

Table 1: Confusion-matrix

		Classified	
		Terrain	Object
Reference	Terrain	a	b
	Object	c	d

Table 2: Accuracy measures

Accuracy	%
Total accuracy	$\frac{a+b}{a+b+c+d}$
Object accuracy	$\frac{d}{c+d}$
Terrain accuracy	$\frac{a}{a+b}$

Where:

- a: is the number of correctly classified terrain points.
- b: is the number of miss classified terrain points.
- c: is the number of miss classified object points.
- d: is the number of correctly classified object points.
- Object accuracy: the accuracy of correctly classified object points.
- Terrain accuracy: the accuracy of correctly classified terrain points.
- Total: is the total accuracy of correctly classified points.

The proposed method requires two parameters, the k value used to construct the knn graph, and threshold value used to remove certain edges from the knn graph. In order to gain an insight to how the k and the threshold values affect accuracy of our filtering method, we designed an experiment in which we changed the values of k and the threshold and calculate the accuracy. Figure 6 shows how the accuracy change when changing the parameters. This experiment demonstrate that the highest accuracy is obtained with higher k values and low threshold values.

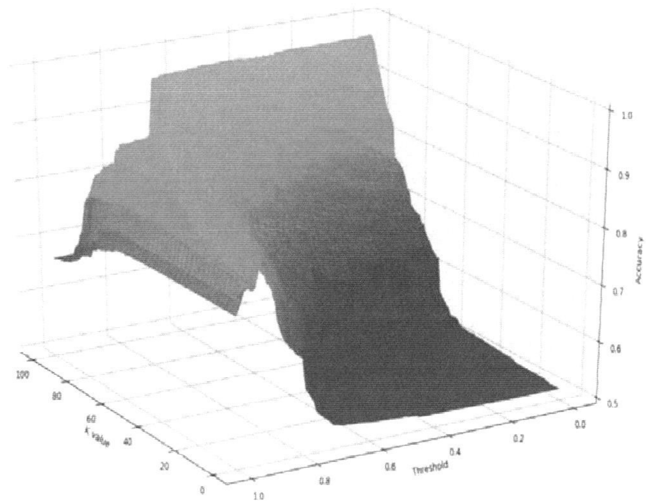

Fig. 6: The relationship between k, edge threshold and the accuracy.

4.1 Experiment 1:

In this experiment we used a dataset collected using Velodyne laser scanner. The scanned area is an urban street scene, it contains building walls, cars, trees, power lines, power posts and may other objects. The area is 168 m by 168 m, it contains 3,200,000 points. The filtering results for this area is shown in figure 7. The red point are terrain points while the blue are object points.

Fig. 7: LiDAR data used in experiment 1: blue points are objects, red points are terrain.

4.2 Experiment 2:

In this experiment, we used the LiDAR dataset provided by [33], [34]. These datasets were collected in urban areas using Velodyne LiDAR scanner. Each dataset is a single scan collected form a rotating scanner, with no overlap between the scans. These datasets were manually labeled and contain several objects with different characteristics. Table 3 below summarizes the characteristics of each dataset.

Table 4 summarizes the result of our experiments. The table contains the k value and the threshold value used to filter each dataset. It also contains the total accuracy, the object accuracy, and the terrain accuracy. The table shows that on most datasets the total accuracy was more than a 95%.

5. Conclusion and future work

We established a simple and efficient method for filtering terrestrial laser scanning data. We modeled the filtering process as a graph connected components problem. We proposed a graph edge weighing scheme that allows the characterization of edges connecting terrain and object points. The removal of these edges led to disconnecting objects from the terrain surface. Experimental results demonstrate the effectiveness of our method. Ten manually labeled datasets were used, the proposed method achieved more that 95% accuracy on all the datasets used in the experiments. In future we will consider developing an automatic technique for selecting the value of k used for constructing knn graph as well as selecting the threshold value used for disconnecting the graph.

References

[1] R. M. Marino and J. William R. Davis, "Jigsaw: A foliage-penetrating 3D imaging laser radar system," *Lincoln Laboratorry Journal*, vol. 15, no. 1, pp. 189–206, 2005.

[2] P. L. Guth, "Probabilistic line-of-sight with LiDAR point clouds," in *ASPRS 2012 Annual Conference*, Sacramento, CA, March 2012.

[3] X. You, W. Zhang, M. Ma, C. Deng, and J. Yang, "Survey on urban warfare augmented reality," *ISPRS International Journal Geo-Information*, vol. 7, p. 46, 2018.

[4] R. Garnett and M. D. Adams, "LiDAR a technology to assist with smart cities and climate change resilience: A case study in an urban metropolis," *ISPRS International Journal Geo-Information*, vol. 7, p. 161, 2018.

[5] X. Qin, G. Wu, J. Lei, F. Fan, X. Ye, and Q. Mei, "A novel method of autonomous inspection for transmission line based on cable inspection robot LiDAR data," *Sensors*, vol. 18, no. 2, p. 596, 2018.

[6] Y. Zhou, S. Wang, X. Mei, W. Yin, C. Lin, Q. Hu, and Q. Mao, "Railway tunnel clearance inspection method based on 3D point cloud from mobile laser scanning," *Sensors*, vol. 17, no. 9, p. 2055, 2017.

[7] T. Zemánek, M. Cibulka, P. Pelikán, and J. Skoupil, "The use of terrestrial laser scanning for determining the driverâĂŹs field of vision," *Sensors*, vol. 17, no. 9, p. 2098, 2017.

[8] S. Ito, S. Hiratsuka, M. Ohta, H. Matsubara, and M. Ogawa, "Small imaging depth LiDAR and DCNN-based localization for automated guided vehicle," *Sensors*, vol. 18, no. 1, p. 177, 2018.

[9] A. Hornung, K. M. Wurm, M. Bennewitz, C. Stachniss, and W. Burgard, "Octomap: an efficient probabilistic 3D mapping framework based on octrees," *Autonomous Robots*, vol. 34, no. 3, pp. 189–206, April 2013.

[10] Z. Chen, B. Gao, and B. Devereux, "State-of-the-art: DTM generation using airborne LiDAR data," *Sensors*, vol. 17, no. 1, p. 150, 2017.

[11] M. Bartels and H. Wei, "Towards DTM generation from LiDAR data in hilly terrain using wavelets," *In Proceedings of 4th International Workshop on Pattern Recognition in Remote Sensing in conjunction with the 18th International Conference on Pattern Recognition*, pp. 33–36, 2006.

[12] N. A. Akel, K. Kremeike, S. Filin, M. Sester, and Y. Doytsher, "Dense DEM generation aided by roads extracted from LiDAR data," *Workshop Laser scanning*, pp. –, Sept. 2005.

[13] C. Qi, "Airborne LiDAR data processing and information extraction," *Photogrammetric engineering and remote sensing*, vol. 73, no. 2, pp. 109–112, 2007.

[14] W. Lu, "A hybrid conditional random field for estimating the underlying ground surface from airborne LiDAR data," *IEEE Transactions on Geoscience and Remote Sensing*, vol. 47, no. 8, pp. 2913–2922, 2009.

[15] D. Mongus and B. Žalik, "Parameter free ground filtering of LiDAR data for automatic dtm generation," *ISPRS Journal of Photogrammetry and Remote Sensing*, vol. 67, pp. 1–12, January 2012.

[16] D. Mongus, N. Lukač, and B. Žalik, "Ground and building extraction from LiDAR data based on differential morphological profiles and locally fitted surfaces," *ISPRS Journal of Photogrammetry and Remote Sensing*, vol. 93, pp. 145–156, July 2014.

[17] F. Moosmann, O. Pink, and C. Stiller, "Segmentation of 3D LiDAR data in non-flat urban environments using a local convexity criterion," in *IEEE Intelligent Vehicles Symposium*, Xi'an, China, Jun 2009, pp. 215–220.

[18] B. Douillard, J. Underwood, N. Kuntz, V. Vlaskine, A. Quadros, P. Morton, and a. Frenkel, "On the segmentation of 3D LIDAR point clouds," in *2011 IEEE International Conference on Robotics and Automation (ICRA)*, May 2011, pp. 2798–2805.

[19] D. Anguelov, B. Taskar, V. Chatalbashev, D. Koller, D. Gupta, G. Heitz, and Y. Andrew, "Discriminative learning of Markov random fields for segmentation of 3D scan data," in *IEEE conference on computer vision and pattern recognition (CVPR)*, San Diego, CA, USA, 2005, pp. 169–176.

[20] A. K. Aijazi, A. Serna, B. Marcotegui, P. Checchin, and L. Trassoudaine, "Segmentation and classification of 3D urban point clouds: Comparison and combination of two approaches," in *10th Conference on Field and Service Robotics (FSR)*, Toronto, Canada, Jun 2015.

Table 3: Characteristics of study areas

	#Points	Buildings	Trees	Fences	Humans	cars	street signs	Others
Area 1	65554	Yes	Yes	Yes	Yes	Yes	Yes	Yes
Area 2	65432	Yes	Yes	Yes	No	Yes	Yes	Yes
Area 3	63363	Yes	Yes	Yes	Yes	Yes	Yes	Yes
Area 4	65858	Yes	Yes	Yes	Yes	Yes	Yes	Yes
Area 5	65398	Yes	Yes	Yes	Yes	Yes	Yes	Yes
Area 6	66044	Yes	Yes	Yes	No	Yes	Yes	Yes
Area 7	63783	Yes	Yes	Yes	Yes	Yes	Yes	Yes
Area 8	66416	Yes	Yes	Yes	Yes	Yes	Yes	Yes
Area 9	65023	Yes	Yes	Yes	Yes	Yes	Yes	Yes
Area 10	67085	Yes	Yes	Yes	No	Yes	Yes	Yes

Table 4: Experimental Results

	k	Threshold	Total Accuracy	Terrain Accuracy	Object Accuracy
Area 1	51	0.07	97.38	96.49	97.82
Area 2	46	0.06	97.20	95.95	98.21
Area 3	70	0.03	91.34	93.77	90.05
Area 4	45	0.05	96.51	90.52	98.99
Area 5	45	0.08	96.63	95.64	97.11
Area 6	70	0.1	91.84	97.31	90.51
Area 7	40	0.06	96.46	94.71	97.56
Area 8	50	0.04	96.61	90.70	99.48
Area 9	45	0.06	94.46	91.75	95.69
Area 10	80	0.08	97.00	90.14	98.69

[21] R. Shapovalov and A. Velizhev, "Cutting-plane training of non-associative Markov network for 3D point cloud segmentation," in *3DIMPVT*, Hangzhou, China, May 2011.

[22] J. Niemeyer, F. Rottensteiner, and U. Soergel, "Contextual classification of LiDAR data and building object detection in urban areas," *ISPRS Journal of Photogrammetry and Remote Sensing*, vol. 87, pp. 152–165, 2014.

[23] Z. Jixian, L. Xiangguo, and N. Xiaogang, "SVM-Based classification of segmented airborne LiDAR point clouds in urban areas," *Remote Sensing*, vol. 5, no. 8, pp. 3749–3775, 2013.

[24] D. Munoz, N. Vandapel, and M. Hebert, "Onboard contextual classification of 3D point clouds with learned high-order Markov random fields," in *International Conference on Robotics and Automation ICRA*, Kobe, Japan, May 2009.

[25] J. Lalonde, , R. Unnikrishnan, N. Vandapel, and M. Hebert, "Scale selection for classification of point-sampled 3D surfaces," in *Fifth International Conference on 3D Digital Imaging and Modeling 3DIM'05*, 2005, pp. 285–292.

[26] J. Zhang, M. Duan, Q. Yan, and X. Lin, "Automatic vehicle extraction from airborne LiDAR data using an object-based point cloud analysis method," *Remote Sensing*, vol. 6.

[27] W. Xiao, B. Vallet, K. Schindler, and N. Paparoditis, "Street-side vehicle detection, classification and change detection using mobile laser scanning data," *ISPRS Journal of Photogrammetry and Remote Sensing*, vol. 114.

[28] C. Premebida, O. Ludwig, and U. J. Nunes, "LiDAR and vision-based pedestrian detection system," *Journal of Field Robotics*, vol. 26, no. 9, pp. 696–711, 2009.

[29] A. Asvadi, L. A. da Silva Garrote, C. Premebida, P. Peixoto, and U. J. Nunes, "Multimodal vehicle detection: fusing 3D LiDAR and color camera data," *Pattern Recognition Letters*.

[30] F. Zhang, D. Clarke, and A. Knoll, "Vehicle detection based on LiDAR and camera fusion," in *17th International IEEE Conference on Intelligent Transportation Systems (ITSC)*, Oct 2014, pp. 1620–1625.

[31] M. Himmelsbach, A. Muller, T. Luttel, and H. J. Wunsch, "LiDAR based 3D object perception," in *First International Workshop on Cognition for Technical Systems*, Munchen, Germay, October 2008.

[32] X. Liu, "Airborne LiDAR for DEM generation: some critical issues," *Progress in Physical Geography*, vol. 32, pp. 31–49, 2008.

[33] K. Lai and D. Fox, "Object recognition in 3D point clouds using web data and domain adaptation," *The International Journal of Robotics Research*, vol. 29, no. 8, May 2010.

[34] K. Lai and D. Fox, *3D laser scan classification using web data and domain adaptation.* MIT Press Journals, 2010, vol. 5, pp. 169–176.

Singular level curves of harmonic functions, conformal mappings and emerging applications to shape recognition of planar-domains

S. Hersonsky[1] **and E. Perkerson**[2]
[1]Department of Mathematics, University of Georgia, Athens, Georgia, USA
[2]Department of Mathematics, University of Georgia, Athens, Georgia, USA

Abstract— *In spite of significant advances in computer graphics and computer vision for description and recognition of rigid shapes and objects, the problem of description and recognition of non-rigid shapes and objects is still open (see for instance [12]). In earlier studies [8], [9], [10] and [3], we proposed an approach, based on complex and harmonic analysis, aiming to describe and analyze non-rigid shapes. In this note, we describe a step in our program to supply a* canonical *set of shapes, very much like a dictionary with mathematical structures, that intrinsicially determine the shape and its classification. Our goal is to provide a computational method of representing 2D shapes where every planar shape will be assigned a unique fingerprint, which is a conformal map of the shape to a canonical shape in the plane or in space. We believe that the study presented in this paper can be extended to describe and recognize both rigid and non-rigid shapes and objects. The main focus of this article is the case of planar domains of high genus since the case of simply-connected and doubly-connected domain was treated in the references mentioned above.*

Keywords: Domain decomposition, Image processing, Conformal mappings

1. Introduction

We are concerned with research problems that belong to the field of Shape Recognition, which is an important and active topic within the scope of Computational Science. For instance, The study of 2D shapes and their similarities is of a central importance in the field of computer vision. It includes the classification and recognition of various kinds of shapes that appear in pictures and videos, defining natural distances between 2D shapes, and creating a *canonical set* of shapes, very much like a dictionary with mathematical structures that are inherently relevant to the classification task.

Conformal maps have had central applications in Pure Mathematics. These maps preserve the angles between any two intersecting curves in the plane. However, the *existence* theory of such maps depends on delicate theorems from the field of Partial Differential Equations in Pure Mathematics, and the computational aspects of their approximation remains an area of active research.

In the 19th and the beginning of the 20th century, the recognition of Riemann surfaces and the conformal structures defined on them was an important milestone in the development of Mathematics. This motivated the formulation of the *uniformization theorem*.

The uniformization theorem [2] implies that any simply connected Riemann surface is *conformally equivalent* to one of three known Riemann surfaces: the open unit disk, the complex plane or the Riemann sphere. This remarkable theorem is a vast generalization of the celebrated *Riemann mapping theorem* asserting that a non-empty simply connected open subset of the complex plane (which is not the whole of it), is conformally equivalent to the open unit disk in the complex plane.

Conformally equivalent means that there exists an angle-preserving map from the given set (the domain surface) to the open disk (other model surfaces) which is one-to-one and onto, and that map has an inverse with the same properties. Such a map preserves the shape of any sufficiently small figure, while possibly rotating and scaling (but not reflecting) it.

These theorems are important in other fields such as Physics and Computer Science. Usually, the input is a 2-dimensional surface, such as the surface of a ball with many corners, or a donut (with one hole or more). These objects often show up in applications, and Uniformization allows one (in principle) to put a set of global coordinates on the input surfaces, thereby allowing useful computations.

In this note, by introducing *singular level curves discrete harmonic functions*, we advance our results in [8], [9], [10], [3] towards our goal of representing 2D shapes: every planar shape will be assigned a unique *fingerprint*, which is a *conformal map* of the shape to a *canonical* shape in the plane or in space, where a *finite* and computable set of parameters determine if the shapes are conformally equivalent or not.

2. Domain decomposition along singular level curves of harmonic functions

There is a classical theory of conformal uniformization for domains in the Riemann sphere that are not simply connected. Keeping our previous notation, let Ω be a domain in the Riemann sphere. Koebe proved that Ω is conformally homeomorphic to some domain Ω^* whose boundary components are circles (or points). Furthermore, Ω^* is unique up to Möbius transformations. Such a domain is called a *circle domain*. This is an existence theorem and a concrete description of such a conformal map is desirable.

It is reasonable to first construct a *discrete uniformization map*, that is a rough approximation to the desired conformal map. This approximation is quite hard to achieve since the input is usually a coarse type of information (such as a triangulation of the domain), and the output should consist of a map from the domain to a surface with some geometric structure. This map should have nice properties (see for instance [8], [9]). Once this step is complete, one then tries to prove convergence of maps and convergence of the output objects attained to concrete geometric objects, under suitable conditions.

In [10, Theorem 4.7], such a scheme in the case of doubly-connected domains (i.e., when the input is a planar annulus) was proved. Specifically, it was shown that given *any* planar annulus, say with a polygonal boundary, there exists a scheme of discrete approximation which yields the best possible approximation (i.e., in the L_∞ norm) to the conformal map of this annulus to a round one.

The scheme is based on constructing a sequence of pairs of discrete harmonic functions where each pair is defined on a triangulation of the given annulus. As the triangulations get finer and finer, it is shown in [10] that the limiting pair converges to the real and imaginary parts, respectively, of the conformal map. The reader is invited to view [10] and [3] for the details.

With the above structure in place, a natural extension that comes up is: What are the analogous results when the domain under consideration has two holes? One hundred holes? One should note that these questions are related to applications. For example, a face can be roughly drawn as a non-planar domain with several holes (eyes, mouth, and nostrils).

To address this situation we are setting forth the mathematical and computational foundations. One novel idea is to decompose the given domain into simpler regions that can be assembled together to create a uniform model. However, as the case of one hole (i.e., annulus) shows, there is an increasing level of difficulty as the number of holes is increased. For instance, it turns out that the canonical images (even in the case of domains with two holes) will no longer be planar.

Indeed, in [8, Section 2] is was shown that even if the planar domain has many holes, there is a procedure to decompose it into simpler regions by cutting along singular level curves of certain discrete harmonic functions, where each region is either an annulus or very close to being an annulus. The procedure is based on successively cutting the region along singular level curves of a discrete harmonic function that approximates the real part of the conformal mapping of the domain. The following figures show two polygonal annuli and the approximation for their conformal images.

3. Algorithmic and Computational approach for a decomposition of a domain along singular level curves

First, we introduce two important definitions: A *region object* needs to contain a subset of $\mathbb{R}^2$ by giving the piecewise-linear outer boundary and two piecewise-linear inner boundaries giving the boundaries of the two holes in the subset.

A *triangulation object* needs to contain the coordinates of the vertices in a triangulation, the indices of the edges drawn between these vertices, and the triplets of indices of the triangles in the triangulation. In addition, another data structure we will call the *triangulation topology* needs to be calculated and included as well, which stores which triangles are adjacent to other triangles along an edge.

The algorithm works as follows: first we need to compute the triangulation object from the region object. This is done using the function `triangulate_acute(R)`. We compute an *acute triangulation* (a triangulation where every triangle is acute) of the region, which is done using the aCute software. This gives an initial acute triangulation of the region, but to construct a sequence of acute triangulations with diminishing mesh, we need to also have a way of refining this triangulation. To preserve the angles of the triangulation, which will then preserve the acuteness of the triangulation, we use what we will call the Hojo refinement [11]. To apply this refinement to a single triangle, take the midpoint of each edge and connect them to form a new triangle, which then partitions the original triangle into four sub-triangles with the same angles as the original.

We now solve the Dirichlet problem on the region using our acute triangulation. This is mostly based on the Mathematica function `NDSolveValue` [13] which is well documented. We let `f` denote the function which solves this PDE, which is 0 on the inner boundaries and 1 on the outer boundary.

To compute the singular level curve, we first need to find the vertex which lies in the singular level curve by extensively using the index formula (5.1) in [8] which is taken from [4]. For every vertex v in the triangulation T, we use the edge information to compute the neighbors of v so that the number of sign changes between those neighbors can be computed as well. This is denoted $\mathrm{Sgc}_f(v)$, and with this computed we can compute the index of the vertex v using the formula:

$$\mathrm{Ind}_f(v) = 1 - \frac{\mathrm{Sgc}_f(v)}{2}.$$

Compute this index for every vertex, and the singular vertex can be identified by having an index different than zero. With

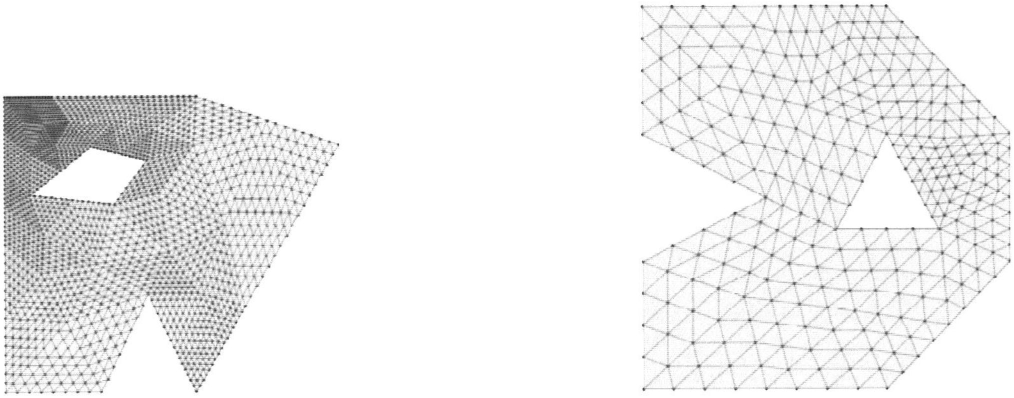

Fig. 1: The triangulated polygonal annuli

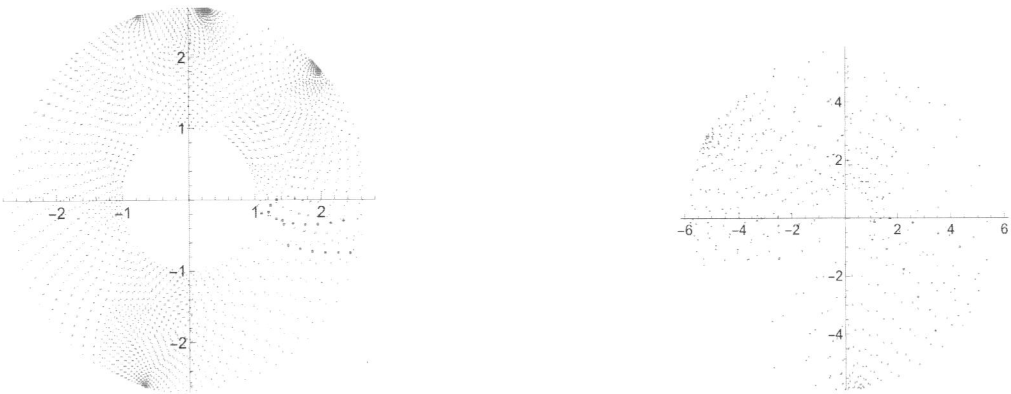

Fig. 2: The images of the polygonal annuli under the conformal map

the singular vertex, say v_s in hand, we can compute $f(v_s)$ to compute the height of the singular level curve, and then the singular level curve can easily be computed by finding the piecewise-linear curve at that height (remembering that the function f is linear on each triangle in the triangulation).

4. The algorithm

Let us provide a short description of the algorithm used to compute and produce the examples in this article. Our algorithm relies on the aCute software to generate acute triangulations, which are defined as triangulations where every triangle is acute. References for this package can be found in the bibliography, and the contact author for the software is Alper Üngör.

5. Numerical Results

In the next page, several figures depict the way we decompose such domains into simper regions via the *singular* level curves of the discrete harmonic functions we discussed in previous sections. The work of assembling the resulting regions (each one is an annulus) into a canonical family of domains is under our current research.

Algorithm 1: Algorithm to Compute the Singular Level Curve

Input: A region object R with genus two
Output: The singular level curve of the region object R

```
T = triangulate_acute(R)
f = solve_pdf(T)
singular_vertex = find_singular_vertex(T)
singular_height = f(singular_vertex)
singular_level_curve = compute_level_curve(T,
  singular_height)
```

Fig. 3: Planar domain with two holes

Fig. 4: The triangulations of the domains

Fig. 5: The singular curves of the harmonic function

References

[1] A.Üngör *https://www.cise.ufl.edu/~ungor/aCute/*

[2] L. V. Ahlfors, *Conformal Invariants: Topics in Geometric Function Theory*, McGraw- Hill, New York, 1973.

[3] H.R. Arabnia, S. Hersonsky and T.R. Taha, *A Novel Approach to the Approximation of Conformal Mappings and Emerging Applications to Shape Recognition of Planar-Domains* , Proceedings of the 2017 International Conference on Computational Science and Computational Intelli- gence, Publisher: IEEE CPS, Editors: Hamid R. Arabnia, Leonidas Deligiannidis, Fernando G. Tinetti, Quoc-Nam Tran, Mary Qu Yang, (2017), 532-534.

[4] T. Banchoff, *Critical points and curvature for embedded polyhedra*, J. Differential Geometry, **1**, (1967), 245–256.

[5] E. Bendito, A. Carmona, A.M. Encinas, *Solving boundary value problems on networks using equilibrium measures*, J. of Func. Analysis, **171** (2000), 155–176.

[6] F.R. Chung, A. Grigoŕyan and S.T. Yau, *Upper bounds for eigenvalues of the discrete and continuous Laplace operators*, Adv. Math. **117** (1996), 165–178.

[7] H. Erten and A. Üngör *Quality Triangulations with Locally Optimal Steiner Points, SIAM Journal of Scientfic Computing, Vol.31, No.3: 2103-2130 (2009).*

[8] S. Hersonsky, *Boundary Value Problems on Planar Graphs and Flat Surfaces with integer cone singularities, I: The Dirichlet problem*, J. Reine Angew. Math. **670** (2012), 65–92.

[9] S. Hersonsky, *Boundary Value Problems on Planar Graphs and Flat Surfaces with integer cone singularities, II: The Dirichlet-Neumann problem*, Differential Geometry and its Applications **29** (2011), 329-347.

[10] S. Hersonsky, *Approximation of conformal mappings and novel applications to shape recognition of planar domains*, The Journal of Supercomputing **74** (2018), 6333-6368.

[11] *https://en.wikipedia.org/wiki/Hojo_clan*

[12] A. Mukhopadhyay, A.T. New, H.R Arabnia and S.M. Bhandarkar, *Non-rigid Shape Correspondence and Description Using Geodesic Field Estimate Distribution*, Proceedings of ACM SIGGRAPH 2012, ISBN: 978-1-4503-1682-8, August 2012.

[13] Wolfram, *https://reference.wolfram.com/language/ref/NDSolveValue.html*

Vision Based Coastline Detection for Autonomous Unmanned Aerial Systems

Wei Chen
Department of Computer Science
Cal Poly Pomona
Pomona, CA 91768, USA
wqchen@cpp.edu

Dulal Kar
Department of Computing Sciences
Texas A&M University-Corpus Christi
Corpus Christi, TX 78412, USA
dulal.kar@tamucc.edu

Simon Merheb
Department of Comp. and Math. Sciences
Lewis University
Romeoville, IL 60446, USA
simonjmerheb@lewisu.edu

***Abstract*—Autonomous tracking of the coastline using an Unmanned Aerial Vehicle (UAV) can provide valuable data for research. However, the dynamic nature of the coastline present numerous problems for such task. To tackle such difficulties, many have proposed to use a machine learning approach. However a machine learning approach requires an extensive pre-learning phase that is time-consuming. This paper proposes a real-time coastline detection algorithm that requires very little pre-processing. Through the use of simple image processing techniques, an UAV will be able to detect the coastline and provide parameters for flight control. For testing the algorithm, data was collected using a commercial quadcopter and processed after flight. Results show that the algorithm is able to identify the coastline through minor calibrations of the algorithmic parameters using images of the target coastal region.**

I. INTRODUCTION

The acquisition of high quality videos and pictures of coastlines is of interest to many scientific and engineering fields. For example, coastal data can be used to estimate land resources and provide the basis for urban planning, conservation, and environmental protection [3]. The current methods of acquiring coastal data primarily includes the use of either manned aircrafts or satellite imagery technology. While these methods may be fitting for some applications involving large geographical areas, the use of Unmanned Aerial Vehicles (UAV) can be advantageous to extend the domain of applications particularly for small geographic areas. For example, monitoring coastal regions with manned aircrafts is costly due to the operation cost of the aircraft and the labor cost of the personnel. Furthermore, despite the fact that satellite imagery is relatively cheap to obtain, the resolution of these images may not be sufficient enough for some applications. The image spatial resolution of satellite and manned aircraft images ranges between 10 cm to 100 cm, while the resolution achievable by UAVs are between 2 cm to 5 cm [4]. The relatively low operation cost of UAVs and the good resolution of images that can be obtained using UAVs make them a good option for similar task involving monitoring or security of a coastal region.

Our ultimate goal is to develop an autonomous system for monitoring coastal regions using UAVs. An autonomous system for monitoring the coastal regions using an UAV has many applications. An autonomous coastline tracking system using an UAV can be broken up into two distinct sub-systems or components:

- *Coastline Detection*: It involves identifying the boundary between water and land from a video stream and correspondingly extracting information for flight control.
- *Flight Control and Navigation*: It involves coordinating the flight path for an UAV using information from the coastline detection algorithm and guiding the UAV accordingly in real-time.

This work presents an coastline detection algorithm that is fast enough for an UAV to execute in real-time. Given a coastal region, the algorithm can identify the coastline by highlighting the threshold between land and water using two techniques. The coordinates of these pixels can be applied to flight control purposes.

In section II, we discuss related works on coastline detection, detection of rivers, and detection of major structures. In section III, we present our proposed algorithm for coastline detection. In section IV, experimental results are presented and discussed. Section V concludes the paper and provides further directions for future work.

II. RELATED WORKS

A wide variety of techniques are available in literature for coastline detection and extraction that utilize various forms of data including aerial photographs, satellite images, SAR images, LIDAR data, and aerial videos. We focus on the techniques that are similar to ours and very relevant for real-time applications. The method presented in [3] utilizes several well-known image processing techniques to extract coastline information from satellite images. The five main steps in the proposed approach in [3] include: 1) image extraction, 2) histogram matching, 3) applying Gaussian blur filter 4) applying locally adaptive thresholding technique, and 5) edge detection using Canny's algorithm. The proposed coastline detection method in [3] was tested with satellite images of two artificial islands Palm Jebel and Palm Jumeirah in Dubai. The results show that the method is effective and accurate even with complex coastal images.

A similar work regarding the use of small autonomous UAVs to follow structures is presented in [1]. A fixed wing

UAV is used to search and map the coordinates of a two-mile stretch of a river in Camp Roberts, California. The river detection algorithm is based on machine learning and is composed of two phases: 1) a learning phase and 2) the real time detection algorithm. A test video obtained by a helicopter is used for the learning phase of the algorithm. The extracted parameters from the learning procedure is then used for pixel classification in the real time algorithm. For flight control, a state transition diagram is proposed. Experimental results show that the UAV is able to detect and follow the river with an average cross track error of 9 meters with respect to the centerline of the river.

A similar vision based work that can track structures using UAVs is presented in [2]. Specifically in [2], a control system as well as an image processing system for autonomous UAVs is proposed. It is a vision based control algorithm that can track structures such as roads, bridges, canals, and so on. Similar to the work in [1], the work presented in [2] makes use of two algorithmic components: 1) a semi-supervised learning algorithm and 2) a real time detection algorithm for structures. The proposed algorithm was tested at Crows landing Naval Auxiliary Landing Field, Patterson, California. The fixed wing UAV equipped with an onboard camera tracked a 700 meter canal. Results show the average cross track error is approximately 10 meters.

A. Objectives and Challenges

The dynamic nature of a coastline presents many challenges for a vision based autonomous UAV to determine its flight path while flying. Some of these challenges are:

- Waves
- Reflection of Sunlight
- Winds
- Local Ecology

In conditions of high winds when waves are crashing on the shores or beaches, tracking and following the coastline using an UAV becomes a tedious task. Accordingly, any algorithm we develop for the purpose must be tested rigorously under varying environmental conditions. We find the method of coastline extraction from satellite imagery in [3] is simple, efficient, and straight-forward. On the contrary, the machine learning approaches in [1] and [2] are more complex. The structure tracking algorithm [2] requires a learning phase that is tedious and time consuming. Inspired by the method proposed in [3], in this work, we present a real-time coastline detection algorithm that requires minimal learning and pre-processing phase. The algorithm will work with flight control to plan the path for an autonomous UAV. The following section discusses the methodology along with the detection algorithm.

III. Methodology

The main contribution of this paper is to develop a shoreline detection algorithm. This algorithm will produce information that is needed for flight control in tracking coastlines with an autonomous UAV. There are five key steps in this algorithm:

A) Parameter Extraction
B) Video Frame Processing
C) Region of Interest Marking
D) Canny Edge Detection
E) Hough Line Transformation and Contours

A. Parameter Extraction

The detection algorithm requires different thresholding parameters due to the diversity of coastal regions to classify pixels in images. The parameter extraction phase of the proposed algorithm utilizes images from the target coastal region that the autonomous UAV will eventually track. Images of a coastal region can be obtained from a satellite or using an UAV through an on-site visit. For our purpose, we obtain videos of several coastal regions using UAVs. Given the water color and lighting, a unique set of parameters must be chosen for pixel classification. These parameters are used to decide on the threshold value for shoreline detection. Pixels greater than the threshold value is assigned a binary pixel value, and pixels smaller is assigned the other. After processing a video frame, the algorithm outputs a binary image of the frame showing the threshold between land and water. The thresholding technique is further discussed in the next subsection.

B. Video Frame Processing

After obtaining the necessary parameters for thresholding, the UAV video is processed using various image processing techniques. In this process, frames are extracted from the video and is processed individually. The thresholding function requires information on pixel intensity to separate important pixels. Given most videos are captured in the RGB color space, a standard video is to be converted to a different color space for thresholding purposes. The RGB format represents colors using three primary colors: red, green, and blue. These values are dependent on each other and the required pixel intensity information cannot be extracted. A color space widely used in image processing is known as HSV (hue, saturation, and value). In the HSV color space, the value component is similar to intensity or luminance. Therefore, the intensity information can be easily extracted from the color values [5]. The transformation from RGB color space to HSV color space is carried out using eqns. (1)-(3).

$$H = cos^{-1}\frac{\frac{1}{2}(2R-G-B)}{\sqrt{(R-G)^2-(R-B)(G-B)}} \tag{1}$$

$$S = \frac{max(R,G,B)-min(R,G,B)}{max(R,G,B)} \tag{2}$$

$$V = max(R,G,B) \tag{3}$$

The next step is to convert video frames to gray scale images and apply the Gaussian blur filter on them. The Gaussian blur filter creates a blurring effect which effectively reduces the noise and speckles in a video frame. This is a common technique used in the pre-processing stage of computer vision algorithms to help remove noise without eliminating the key

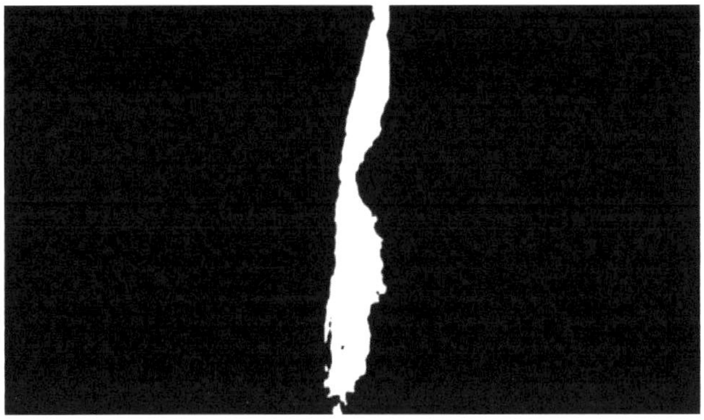

Fig. 1. Video frame processed with Thresholding. The white pixels represent the shore.

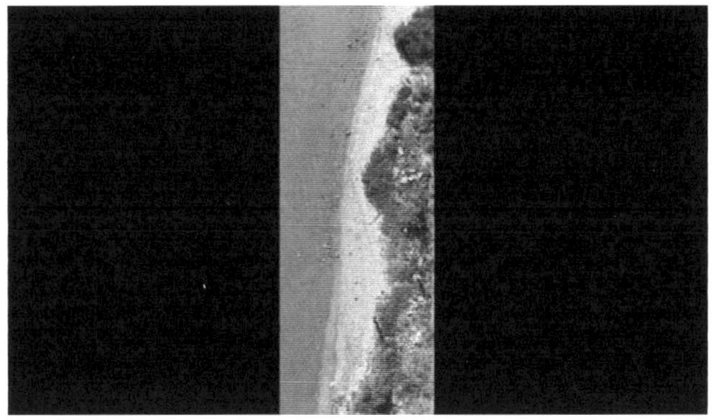

Fig. 2. Region of interest applied to video frame.

features [3]. A kernel size is to be determined to alter the blur effect i.e., this kernel size is to be chosen judiciously depending on the amount of noise or irrelevant features that generally occur in video frames obtained from a coastal region. Thresholding is the last phase in the process. Given the parameters obtained from the coastal images, the thresholding function differentiates the pixels of land from the pixels of water. The function compares the pixel intensity value with respect to a threshold established by the parameters. Each pixel is assigned a value of either 0 (black) or 255 (white) based on its intensity [7]. The result of this phase is a binary video with black pixels for land and white pixels for ocean water. Fig. 1 shows a resultant binary image on a video frame of a coastal region.

C. *Delineating Region of Interest*

Specifying the region of interest (ROI) in a frame can increase the accuracy of the algorithm as it can ignore the noisy or unnecessary regions in the frame from processing. This can reduce computation time to process a frame. The use of ROI is found in many driving assistance and lane detection systems. Determining ROI is important in these systems because road environments is often complex and unnecessary information can derail a lane detection system. Identifying ROI in a frame can isolate the important regions before computation and reduce the processing time [6]. The region of interest (ROI) technique is utilized in our algorithm in order to reduce the ill effect of noise or undesirable information in a video frame. This approach of using ROI also reduces computation time needed by the algorithm. To incorporate ROI to our algorithm, the shoreline must be relatively centered in the video frame. The tracking algorithm will lose the shoreline if the UAV is unable to keep the shoreline relatively centered. It is important to note this for the flight control portion of the system and a search feature will be beneficial if the shoreline falls out of the ROI. An example on the ROI technique applied to a video frame is shown in Fig. 2.

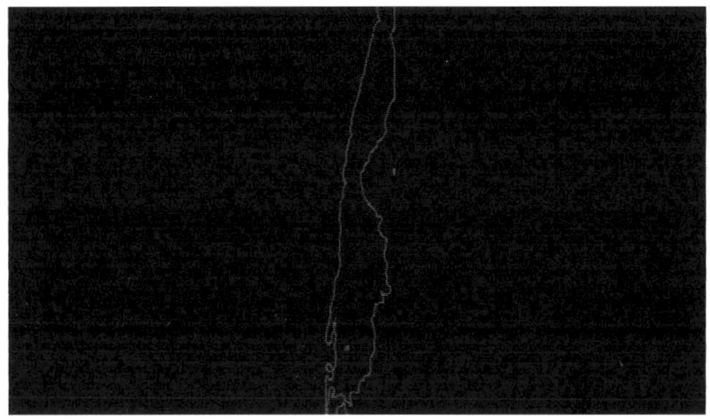

Fig. 3. Output of video frame after Canny edge detection. The edge line represent the boundary of shore

D. *Canny Edge Detection*

For simple and reliable edge detection, the Canny edge detection method is widely applied and used to extract edges between different vision objects [3]. The binary video created from thresholding is converted to a video consisting of edge lines using the Canny edge detection method. As shown in Fig. 3, these lines represent the coastal boundary between the black and white pixels i.e., between land and water.

E. *Hough Line Transformation and Contours*

The Canny edge detection method provides the necessary points for the Hough line transformation. The edges found on a frame using the Canny edge detection method is used for the Hough line transformation method in our approach [8]. The pixel coordinates for these edge lines are utilized and represented using Hough lines as shown in Fig. 5. The Hough line transform keeps track of intersections between curves of all points in each video frame. The points for these intersections correlate to the original UAV video where the lines are to be displayed.

Contouring is a useful method for shape analysis and object detection in an image [9]. Accordingly, finding contours in a frame can be an effective way to identify shoreline boundaries in coastal video. Essentially, a contour line in a coastal image can be used as a guide to identify a shoreline boundary. In the

Fig. 4. Boundary of shoreline highlighted with Hough line. At Corpus Christi Bay, Corpus Christi, TX

Fig. 5. Video frame with Contour function highlighting shore boundary. At Corpus Christi Bay, Corpus Christi, TX

binary image obtained after applying the threshold technique, the shore can be defined as the area consisting of entirely black or white pixels (depending on threshold settings). A contour line can be obtained by joining all continuous points along the boundary of this area. Fig. 5 shows the highlighted shore obtained after using the contouring technique.

IV. Experimental Results

We test our proposed algorithm with videos taken from multiple coastal locations with varying environmental and geographic conditions. Specifically, the coastline detection algorithm is tested using video clips captured by a DJI Phantom 4 Pro. As shown in Fig. 6, the camera angle of the DJI Phantom 4 Pro is set to 90 degrees to obtain a top-down view of the coastline. The video recording is carried out along a coastline of the Corpus Christi Bay, Corpus Christi, Texas. The UAV is flown at a height of about 165 feet in a wind condition of 13 miles per hour. The height of 165 feet is chosen to reduce the effect of water movement during processing of the video frames by the algorithm. During flying of the UAV along the shoreline, the captured frame of the DJI video feed application is centered at the boundary between water and land as much as possible.

When processing the video, the shoreline detection algorithm is able to identify the boundary between land and water by creating a line along the boundary using the Hough line transformation technique. Furthermore, the algorithm can highlight the boundaries of the shoreline with contours correctly. The algorithm is also tested with the video footage obtained from Padre Island, Corpus Christi, Texas. The setup of the equipment is identical as above. However, the beach conditions on Padre Island are more disruptive and irregular due to randomness of waves crashing on the shore. The algorithm is affected by disruptions caused by the incoming random waves and excessive water movement along the shoreline which cause shifting of the boundary line between land and water constantly. Fig. 7 shows the result from an attempt using the Hough transform, in which a clear depiction of the separation of land and water is not visible. As shown in Fig. 8, the contouring technique also fails to produce any boundary showing separation of land from water.

Fig. 6. Camera set up for DJI Phantom 4 Pro. Camera angle set at 90 degrees (top-down view).

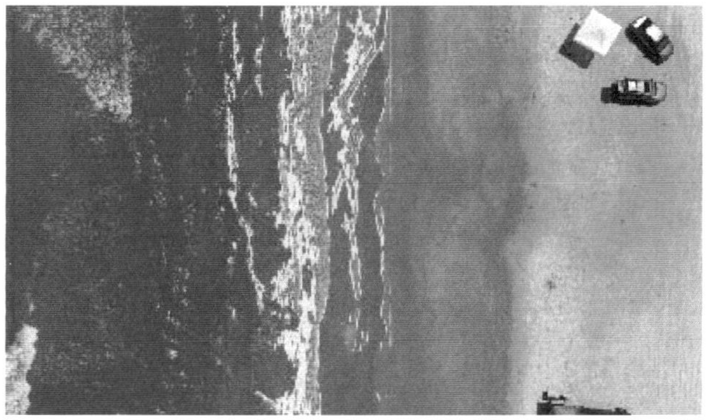

Fig. 7. Result on Hough line technique with video from Padres Island, Corpus Christi, Texas.

V. CONCLUSIONS

In this work, we propose a coastline detection algorithm that can be used for flight control of an UAV. The proposed algorithm utilizes images from the target coastal region to

Fig. 8. Result on contour technique with video from Padre Island, Corpus Christi, Texas.

calibrate the algorithm and is able to detect the shoreline using the calibration parameters. The algorithm works effectively in calm coastal conditions. However, the algorithm does not perform well in conditions with excessive wave interferences. Areas of future work include improving the thresholding technique used in this algorithm to tackle the conditions of high wave movements. Furthermore, this algorithm should be tested in different coastal regions, especially regions where the water is clear enough to see the ocean bottom. Detecting separation of land from water can be challenging in this situation. A possible solution for this could be utilizing an infrared camera where water absorbs the near-infrared wavelength, giving it a black appearance in images. In more challenging conditions, machine learning approach will be more effective. Lastly, the flight control algorithm must be efficient enough to execute in real-time along with this algorithm on an onboard processing unit. This should not be a challenge for a quadcopter but it could be for a fixed-wing UAV which is capable of traveling much longer distances. In our future work, we plan to develop the flight control algorithm that can utilize the results of the coastline detection algorithm to guide an UAV.

References

[1] S. Rathinam, et al., "Autonomous searching and tracking of a river using an UAV," 2007 American Control Conference, New York, NY, pp. 359-364, 2007.

[2] S. Rathinam, Z. Kim, and R. Sengupta, "Vision-based following of structures using an unmanned aerial vehicle (UAV)," 2006 Institute of Transportation Studies, University of Texas, pp. 1-13, 2006.

[3] D. Vukadinov, R. Jovanovic and M. Tuba. "An algorithm for coastline extraction from satellite imagery," 2017 International Journal of Computers, 2 ,pp. 8-15, 2017.

[4] A. Papakonstantinou, K. Topouzelis, and G. Pavlogeorgatos, "Coastline Zones identification and 3D coastal mapping using UAV spatial data," ISPRS Int. J. Geo-Inf. 5, 75, 2016

[5] P. Ganesan and V. Rajini, "Assessment of satellite image segmentation in RGB and HSV color space using image quality measures," 2014 International Conference on Advances in Electrical Engineering (ICAEE), Vellore, pp. 1-5, 2014.

[6] D. Ding, C. Lee and K. Lee, "An adaptive road ROI determination algorithm for lane detection," 2013 IEEE International Conference of IEEE Region 10 (TENCON 2013), Xi'an, pp. 1-4, 2013.

[7] Bradski, and Kaehler, "Basic thresholding operations," OpenCV: Image Thresholding, docs.opencv.org/2.4/doc/tutorials/imgproc/threshold/threshold.html.

[8] Bradski, and Kaehler. "Hough line transform," OpenCV: Image Thresholding, docs.opencv.org/2.4/doc/tutorials/imgproc/imgtrans/hough_lines/hough_lines.html

[9] "Contour approximation method," OpenCV: Image Thresholding, docs.opencv.org/3.4.0/d4/d73/tutorial_py_contours_begin.html.

Acknowledgements

This work was supported in part by the Division of Computer and Network Systems of the National Science Foundation under NSF Cooperative Agreement No. CNS-1757940. Any Opinions, findings and conclusions or recommendations expressed in this material are those of the authors and do not necessarily reflect those of the National Science Foundation.

No-Reference Video Quality Assessment Using Spatial, Temporal, Transform, and Spatiotemporal Features

Yi-Lun Chiang and Jin-Jang Leou

Department of Computer Science and Information Engineering
National Chung Cheng University, Chiayi 621, Taiwan, ROC

Abstract – *In this study, a no-reference (NR) video quality assessment approach using spatial, temporal, transform, and spatiotemporal features is proposed. First, three different resolutions of each video sequence by down-sampling are generated and then spatial, temporal, transform, and spatiotemporal features are extracted. Spatial, temporal, and transform feature maps are converted into feature vectors using histogram statistics, whereas principal component analysis (PCA) is employed to perform dimension reduction on spatiotemporal feature vectors. After normalization and concatenation, support vector regression (SVR) is employed to perform machine learning and video quality assessment score estimation. Based on the experimental results obtained in this study, in terms of PLCC and SROCC, the performance of the proposed approach is better than those of eight comparison approaches.*

Keywords: no-reference video quality assessment, spatial, temporal, transform, and spatiotemporal features, feature extraction, dimension reduction, support vector regression.

1 Introduction

Nowadays, a lot of video contents are transmitted over the Internet or wireless networks. Due to video compression, noise corruption, and transmission medium properties, various types of distortions may be introduced, which will degrade the quality of experience (QoE) of human users (human perception). Video quality assessment (VQA) (subjective or objective) is very important for video providers and users. Although subjective VQA can achieve higher accuracy of video quality assessment, it is time-consuming and expensive. Additionally, in terms of the use of original video information, objective VQA approaches can be partitioned to three categories, namely, full-reference (FR) [1-2], reduced-reference (RR) [3], and no-reference (NR) [4-7]. For FR VQA approaches, such as peak-signal-to-noise ratio (PSNR), structural similarity index (SSIM), and multi-scale SSIM, the original video sequence and the distorted video sequence are employed (compared) to estimate the video quality assessment score. For RR VQA approaches [3], partial information of the original video sequence and that of the distorted video sequence are used to estimate the video quality assessment score. For NF VQA approaches [4-7], only the distorted video sequence is directly used to estimate the video quality assessment score. In this study, a no-reference video quality assessment approach using spatial, temporal, transform, and spatiotemporal features is proposed.

This paper is organized as follows. The proposed no-reference video quality assessment approach is described in Section 2. Experimental results are addressed in Section 3, followed by concluding remarks.

+ This work was supported in part by Ministry of Science and Technology, Taiwan, Republic of China under Grant MOST 106-2221-E-194-057-MY2.

2 Proposed approach

2.1 System Architure

As shown in Fig. 1, the proposed no-reference video quality assessment approach contains four main stages. First, three different resolutions of each input video sequence by down-sampling are generated and then spatial, temporal, transform, and spatiotemporal feature maps are extracted. Spatial, temporal, and transform feature maps are converted into feature vectors using histogram statistics, whereas principal component analysis (PCA) is employed to perform dimension reduction on spatiotemporal feature vectors. After feature vector normalization and concatenation, support vector regression (SVR) with polynomial kernel is employed to perform machine learning and video quality assessment score estimation. In this study, including the original video sequence, two corresponding video sequences of reduced resolutions by down-sampling are generated for feature extraction and video quality assessment score estimation by SVR.

2.2 Feature Extraction

To extract beneficial features from a video sequence, based on the characteristics of the human visual system (HVS), four (spatial, temporal, transform, and spatiotemporal) different types of features will be extracted.

Assume that a video sequence contains n frames of size $M \times N$, $f_i(x,y)$, $i = 1,2,\dots,n$, $1 \le x \le M$, $1 \le y \le N$. Let $f_i^1(x,y)$, $i = 1,2,\dots,n$, $1 \le x \le M/2$, $1 \le y \le N/2$, denote the first down-sampled video sequence and $f_i^2(x,y)$, $i = 1,2,\dots,n$, $1 \le x \le M/4$, $1 \le y \le N/4$, denote the second down-sampled video sequence. Four different types of features, namely, spatial, temporal, transform, and spatiotemporal, are extracted, which will be described as follows.

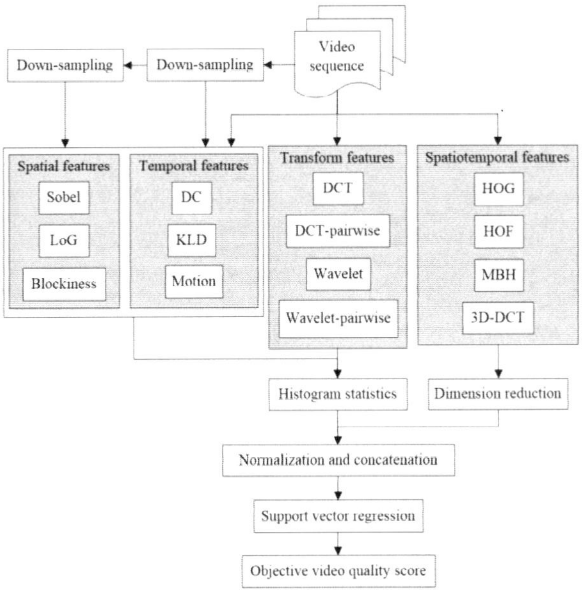

Fig. 1. Flowchart of the proposed approach.

Both edges possessing strong intensity contrasts in a frame and blockiness being a type of distortion are usually attractive to human visual perception. Here, Laplacian of Gaussian (LoG) filter with zero crossing is employed to construct three LoG edge maps $L_i(x,y)$, $L_i^1(x,y)$, and $L_i^2(x,y)$, for $f_i(x,y)$, $f_i^1(x,y)$, and $f_i^2(x,y)$, respectively, $i = 1,2,\ldots,n$. To generate six edge maps from $f_i(x,y)$, $f_i^1(x,y)$, and $f_i^2(x,y)$, $i = 1,2,\ldots,n$, Sobel operator is employed, i.e.,

$$S_{i,x} = f_i * g_x, S_{i,y} = f_i * g_y;$$
$$S_{i,x}^1 = f_i^1 * g_x, S_{i,y}^1 = f_i^1 * g_y; \quad (1)$$
$$S_{i,x}^2 = f_i^2 * g_x, S_{i,y}^2 = f_i^2 * g_y,$$

where * denotes the convolution operator and

$$g_x = \begin{bmatrix} -1 & -2 & -1 \\ 0 & 0 & 0 \\ 1 & 2 & 1 \end{bmatrix}, \quad (2)$$

$$g_y = \begin{bmatrix} -1 & 0 & 1 \\ -2 & 0 & 2 \\ -1 & 0 & 1 \end{bmatrix}. \quad (3)$$

Based on entropy defined as

$$E_{i,k} = -\sum p_{i,k}(x) \log_2 p_{i,k}(x), \quad (4)$$

where $p_{i,k}(x)$ is the probability mass function of luminance in the k-th block of frame i, six edge maps are converted into six edge entropy feature maps, namely, $E_{L,i}$, $E_{L,i}^1$, $E_{L,i}^2$, $E_{S,i}$, $E_{S,i}^1$, and $E_{S,i}^2$ by entropy computation.

In this study, blockiness measure proposed in [8] is employed. As shown in Fig. 2, blockiness measure of block A is based on the horizontal block difference between blocks A and B and the vertical block difference between blocks A and C. The horizontal block difference between blocks A and B is defined as

$$B_{i,k,h} = \begin{cases} N_h/S_h, \text{if } S_h \neq 0, \\ 0, \text{if } S_h = 0 \text{ or } |\bar{b} - \bar{a}| < lm(\bar{b} - \bar{a}/2), \end{cases} \quad (5)$$

where

$$N_h = r_D \times \sum_{i=1}^{8} |a_{i1} - b_{i8}|, \quad (6)$$

$$S_h = \sum_{i=1}^{8} \left(\sum_{j=5}^{7} |b_{i(j+1)} - b_{ij}| + \sum_{j=1}^{4} |a_{i(j+1)} - a_{ij}| + |a_{i1} - b_{i8}| \right), \quad (7)$$

$$\bar{a} = \left(\sum_{i=1}^{8} \sum_{j=1}^{4} a_{ij} \right)/32, \quad (8)$$

$$\bar{b} = \left(\sum_{i=1}^{8} \sum_{j=5}^{8} b_{ij} \right)/32, \quad (9)$$

$$lm(X) = \begin{cases} 17 \times \left(1 - \sqrt{X/127}\right) + 3, \text{if } X \leq 127, \\ 3 \times (X - 127)/128 + 3, \text{if } X > 127, \end{cases} \quad (10)$$

where r_D, a control coefficient, is set to 10. The vertical block difference $B_{i,k,v}$ between blocks A and C can be calculated similarly. The blockiness measure of block A (the k-th block of frame i) is defined as

$$B_{i,k} = \left(B_{i,k,h} + B_{i,k,v}\right)/2. \quad (11)$$

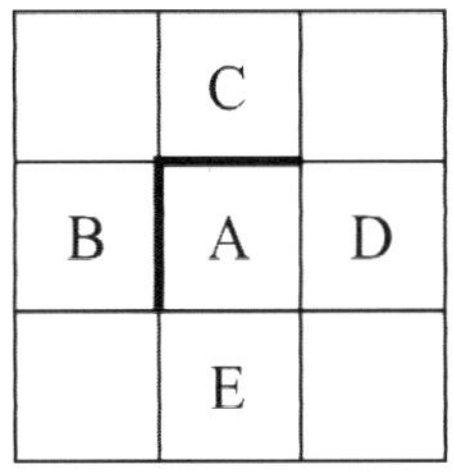

Fig. 2. Blockiness measure of block A.

All block difference values of frame i are combined as its blockiness feature map. Finally, blockiness feature maps for $f_i(x,y)$, $f_i^1(x,y)$, and $f_i^2(x,y)$ are obtained and denoted as $B_{block,i}$, $B_{block,i}^1$, and $B_{block,i}^2$, respectively.

Because intensity variations in a video sequence is sensitive to human visual perception, the absolute DC coefficient difference between two adjacent frames is computed as

$$Diff_{i,k} = |DC_{i+1,k} - DC_{i,k}|, \quad (12)$$

where $DC_{i+1,k}$ and $DC_{i,k}$ denote DC coefficients of the k-th blocks of frames f_{i+1} and f_i, respectively. Then, we can obtain three absolute DC coefficient difference feature maps, namely, $Diff_i$, $Diff_i^1$, and $Diff_i^2$, for $f_i(x,y)$, $f_i^1(x,y)$, and $f_i^2(x,y)$, respectively. In addition, to track temporal variations between two adjacent frames, Kullback Leibler distance (KLD) calculating the distance between two probability distributions is employed, which is defined as

$$KLD_i = \sum p_i(u) \log(p_i(u)/p_{i+1}(u)), \quad (13)$$

where μ denotes the luminance and $p_i(u)$ denotes the probability distribution of luminance for frame f_i. Tree KLD feature maps, namely, KLD_i, KLD_i^1, and KLD_i^2 for $f_i(x,y)$, $f_i^1(x,y)$, and $f_i^2(x,y)$, respectively, can be obtained.

Additionally, motion is an important cue in a video sequence. Here, nearest neighbor field and random sample consensus (RANSAC) algorithm are employed to generate a dominant similarity matrix ***d*** for the motion correspondences between two adjacent frames. By subtracting the corresponding backgrounds of two adjacent frames, motions between two adjacent frames are obtained. By entropy computation, three motion track maps, namely, M_i, M_i^1, and M_i^2 for $f_i(x,y)$, $f_i^1(x,y)$, and $f_i^2(x,y)$, respectively, can be obtained.

By using DCT (discrete cosine transform), we can obtain the DCT feature map DCT_i for $f_i(x,y)$. To obtain temporal variations of local phase structures [9], continuous wavelet transform with 8 orientations $\theta \in \{0^\circ, 45^\circ, 90^\circ, 135^\circ, 180^\circ, 225^\circ, 270^\circ, 315^\circ\}$ is employed and the average of all oriented subbands of continuous wavelet transform is calculated as continuous wavelet transform map CWT_i, which may be converted into continuous wavelet transform energy feature map $EG_{CWT,i}$ for $f_i(x,y)$. In this study, pairwise products [10] are used to obtain relationships between neighboring feature map values along four orientations, namely, horizontal H, vertical V, diagonal ND, and off-diagonal FD. Thus, DCT pairwise feature maps along four orientations, namely, $H_{DCT,i}$, $V_{DCT,i}$, $ND_{DCT,i}$, and $FD_{DCT,i}$, and continuous wavelet transform pairwise feature maps along four orientations, namely, $H_{CWT,i}$, $V_{CWT,i}$, $ND_{CWT,i}$, and $FD_{CWT,i}$, are obtained.

To extract spatiotemporal features, based on improved dense trajectories, histogram of oriented gradients (HOG), histogram of optical flow (HOF), motion boundary histogram (MBH) [11], and 3-D (three-dimensional) spatiotemporal DCT [12] are employed. First, HOG based on gradient orientations can extract static information of local appearance and shape of a frame. Second, HOF based on orientations of optical flow can extract motion information for a video sequence. MBH can suppress camera motions in a video sequence, which can be extracted by using the horizontal and vertical components of optical flow separately.

Due to inherent multidimensional statistical characteristics and excellent spatiotemporal decorrelation ability [12], 3-D DCT is utilized to extract 3-D features in spatiotemporal volumes. In this study, the averages of all 3D-DCT coefficients for spatiotemporal volumes are extracted as 3D-DCT feature vector *ThrDCT*.

2.3 Histogram statistics

After spatial, temporal, and transform feature maps are obtained, histogram statistics are used to convert these feature maps into feature vectors. First, each mean feature map is obtained as the average feature map over all frames in a video sequence. Second, each mean feature map is quantified into histogram with 40 bins. Feature vectors, $E_L, E_L^1, E_L^2, E_S, E_S^1, E_S^2$, B_{block}, B_{block}^1, B_{block}^2, $diff$, $diff^1$, $diff^2$, KLD, KLD^1, KLD^2, DCT, EG_{CWT}, H_{DCT}, V_{DCT}, ND_{DCT}, FD_{DCT}, H_{CWT}, V_{CWT}, ND_{CWT}, and FD_{CWT} are obtained by histogram statistics. Additionally, HOG, HOF, and MBH feature maps are quantified into histograms with 96, 96, and 192 dimensions, which are denoted as HOG, HOF, and MBH, respectively.

2.4 Dimension reduction, normalization, and concatenation

In this study, principal component analysis (PCA) is employed to perform feature vector dimension reduction and maintain feature variability as much as possible. Since feature vector values may have different ranges and distributions, a simple normalization is employed, which is realized as

$$V' = \big(V - \min(V)\big)/\big(\max(V) - \min(V)\big), \tag{14}$$

where V' and V denote the normalized and original feature vectors, respectively, and $\min(\cdot)$ and $\max(\cdot)$ return the minimum and maximum feature vector values, respectively. After normalization, the final feature vectors for machine training and video quality assessment score estimation are

$$V'_{con} = [E_L, E_L^1, E_L^2, E_S, E_S^1, E_S^2, B_{block}, B_{block}^1, B_{block}^2, diff, diff^1, diff^2, KLD, KLD^1, KLD^2, DCT, EG_{CWT}, H_{DCT}, V_{DCT}, ND_{DCT}, FD_{DCT}, H_{CWT}, V_{CWT}, ND_{CWT}, FD_{CWT}, HOG, HOF, MBH, ThrDCT]. \tag{15}$$

Finally, based on the final feature vectors, linear SVR support vector regression with polynomial kernel LIBSVM [13] is used to perform machine learning and video quality assessment score estimation.

3 Experimental results

The proposed approach is implemented on an Intel Core i7-4790K 4GHz CPU with 32GB main memory for Windows 10 64-bit platform using MATLAB 9.0 (R2016a). LIVE video quality assessment database [14] containing 150 distorted video sequences is employed, which includes four distortion categories, namely, MPEG-2 compression, H.264 compression, transmission over IP network, and transmission over wireless network. To evaluate the performance of the proposed approach, eight comparison approaches including three FR VQA approaches, one RR VQA approach, and four NR VQA approaches are employed. In terms of Pearson linear correlation coefficients (PLCC) and Spearman rank correlation coefficients (SROCC), performance comparisons of the eight comparison approaches and the proposed approach are illustrated in Table 1.

4 Concluding remarks

In this study, a no-reference video quality assessment approach using spatial, temporal, transform, and spatiotemporal features is proposed. Based on the experimental results obtained in this study, in terms of PLCC and SROCC, the performance of the proposed approach is better than those of eight comparison approaches.

Table 1. In terms of PLCC and SROCC, performance comparisons of the eight comparison approaches and the proposed approach.

Categories	Approaches	PLCC	SROCC
FR	PSNR	0.715	0.694
FR	SSIM [1]	0.646	0.652
FR	MOVIE [2]	0.852	0.807
RR	STRRED [3]	0.767	0.813
NR	NVIE [4]	0.620	0.604
NR	Video-BLIINDS [5]	0.853	0.741
NR	Galea and Farrugia [6]	0.732	0.703
NR	Video-CORNIA [7]	0.693	0.740
NR	Proposed	**0.861**	**0.833**

5 References

[1] Z. Wang, et al., "Image quality assessment: from error visibility to structural similarity," *IEEE Trans. on Image Processing*, vol. 13, no. 4, pp. 600-612, Apr. 2004.

[2] K. Seshadrinathan and A. C. Bovik, "Motion tuned spatio-temporal quality assessment of natural videos," *IEEE Trans. on Image Processing*, vol. 19, no. 2, pp. 335-350, Feb. 2010.

[3] R. Soundararajan and A. C. Bovik, "Video quality assessment by reduced reference spatio-temporal entropic differencing," *IEEE Trans. on Circuits and Systems for Video Technology*, vol. 23, no. 4, pp. 684-694, Apr. 2013.

[4] A. Mittal, M. A. Saad, and A. C. Bovik, "Zero shot prediction of video quality using intrinsic video statistics," in *SPIE Proceedings*, vol. 9014, Feb. 2014, pp. 90140R-1-90140R-13.

[5] M. A. Saad, A. C. Bovik, and C. Charrier, "Blind prediction of natural video quality," *IEEE Trans. on Image Processing*, vol. 23, no. 3, pp. 1352-1365, Mar. 2014.

[6] C. Galea and R. A. Farrugia, "A no-reference video quality metric using a natural video statistical model," in *Proc. of 2015 IEEE Int. Conf. on Computer as a Tool*, Sept. 2015, pp. 1-6.

[7] J. Xu, et al., "No-reference video quality assessment via feature learning," in *Proc. of 2014 IEEE Int. Conf. on Image Processing (ICIP)*, Oct. 2014, pp. 491-495.

[8] X. Hu, et al., "A hybrid no-reference video quality assessment based on region of interest," in *Proc. of 2014 Int. Symposium on Wireless Personal Multimedia Communications (WPMC)*, Sept. 2014, pp. 1-5.

[9] A. K. Moorthy and Q. C. Bovik, "Blind image quality assessment: from natural scene statistics to perceptual quality," *IEEE Trans. on Image Processing*, vol. 19, no. 12, pp. 3350-3364, Dec. 2011.

[10] A. Mittal, A. K. Moorthy, and A. C. Bovik, "No-reference image quality assessment in the spatial domain," *IEEE Trans. on Image Processing*, vol. 21, no. 12, pp. 4695-4708, Dec. 2012.

[11] H. Wang and C. Schmid, "Action recognition with improved trajectories," in *Proc. of IEEE Int. Conf. on Computer Vision (ICCV)*, Dec. 2013, pp. 3551-3558.

[12] M. Servais, G. Jager, "Video compression using the three dimensional discrete cosine transform (3D-DCT)," in *Proc. of 1997 South African Symposium on Communicaitons and Signal Processing*, Sept. 1997, pp. 27-32.

[13] C. C. Chang and C. J. Lin, "LIBSVM: a library for support vector machines," *ACM Trans. on Intelligent Systems and Technology (TIST)*, vol. 2, no. 3, pp. 1-39, April 2011.

[14] K. Seshadrinathan, et al., "Study of subjective and objective quality assessment of video," *IEEE Trans. on Image Processing*, vol. 19, no. 6, pp. 1427-1441, Jun. 2010.

A System for the Detection and Identification of Objects and Their Distances to Aid Blind People

Abdelfatah A. Tamimi, Alaa A. Abu Hammad, Ayman M. Abdalla, Omaima N. Al-Allaf
Faculty of Science and Information Technology, Al-Zaytoonah University of Jordan, Amman, Jordan

Abstract - *This paper presents a novel system to help blind people detect and identify objects and their locations. This system represents visual objects with audio through a simulator to inform blind people about objects' names and locations. The system captures images with a portable camera device. Then, the system obtains the location of each object through a fixed indoor position system. In the next step, the system employs real-time image recognition to detect and identify objects. After that, object distances from the person are computed. Existing objects inside the room are stored in a Reference Database using an Indoor Positioning System. For object detection and identification, the input images are compared with the objects in the Reference Database. Finally, the names and locations of the recognized objects are read audibly through speakers. Test results showed the system's effectiveness in recognizing and identifying commonly used objects and computing their distances.*

Keywords: Image detection, Image identification, IPS, SIFT, SURF

1 Introduction

Recent studies have shown that at least 217 million people have moderate to severe vision impairment and 36 million people are blind [1]. In addition, more than 826 million people live with near-vision impairments [2]. These visually impaired people, especially the blind, generally face burdens in finding their way through unknown places and have to overcome further difficulties to recognize objects and people and their locations.

This paper provides an analysis and evaluation for the technologies used in the object identification task, and then proposes a system for the Detection and Identification of Objects and their Distances to aid Blind people (DIODB) through image to sound conversion. The proposed DIODB system uses the Scale Invariant Feature Transform (SIFT) and Speeded-Up Robust Features (SURF) robust algorithms in the detection and recognition of objects in images. These methods provide more matching, good processing speed, and robustness to variations with respect to illumination, rotation, and scaling to identify objects. Then, the output of these methods are processed further for converting the information of the recognized object to the speech form. Feature-detection, matching, and mosaicking with SIFT and SURF was discussed and implemented in details by [3].

DIODB employs an Indoor Positioning System (IPS) to locate objects inside the room. IPS works in a way similar to Global Positioning System (GPS), but rather than utilizing a satellite signal, IPS exchanges signals between the location devices and sensors of smart devices.

2 Related work

Since the 1970s, systems based on portable cameras have been evolving considerably, continuously creating new tools for the visually impaired [4]. The visual world is very complex, as objects may be added or relocated within the visual field at any time. It is difficult to represent objects mentally in the visual world because of world and object complexity. Each object comprises many features such as line edges, orientations, colors, luminance intensities, and moving parts. Although many applications were developed for this task, such applications are often not very robust because machine vision does not offer a robust and actual representation of the real world [5]. For example, biometric recognition modalities may be used in identifying people [6,7,8,9,10] where different methods are needed for object identification [4].

A system was developed by [11] to provide safety assistance to car drivers. This system was able to recognize objects, signs, and road surface to make decisions on warning or acting on behalf of a driver. However, this system was not suited to aid walking visually impaired people, and it did not concentrate on identifying the detected objects or people.

Several general methods for object recognition were considered by [12] as they developed a novel segmentation system. An excellent real-time object detection system is named YOLO [13]. This system performs fast object-recognition with high accuracy. Even though it was not designed for blind people, it could be modified or combined with another system to suit blind people and to provide extra features such as computing distances and giving voice notifications for designated objects.

A method for object and scene detection for blind peoples using vocal vision was presented by [14], but implementation results were not discussed and the system's effectiveness was not demonstrated. Reference [15] developed an automatic algorithm for object recognition and detection based on Affine SIFT (ASIFT) key points. They presented an ASIFT method to identify objects with full boundary detection by combining a fixed constant scale and a zone integration algorithm. A strong integration algorithm is used in the region to identify the object with full boundaries and detect it in other images based on the Aseptic key points and measure the similarity of the areas merged into the image. Their experimental results showed that this method was effective in recognizing and detecting the object.

Reference [16] proposed a system to provide blind people with real-time visual recognition to transform the visual world into 3D audio to inform blind people of names of objects and their locations.

Modern mobile phones have strong communication capabilities and are equipped with different types of integrated sensors for various functions. A survey of systems for finding indoor position of a person using Wi-Fi and a smartphone is available [17]. These systems are not sufficient for aiding visually impaired people find their way and they do not detect objects and people unplugged from the system. However, such systems may be used in conjunction with recognition and identification methods to provide the visually impaired with a more helpful system.

Reference [18] suggested that IPS uses multiple signals from location devices in addition to sensors including motion sensors to accurately calculate user position. Some IPS systems analyze the system's underlying data generated while the system is running. These processes can predict future user traffic even in multi-story buildings [18].

Reference [19] proposed an object recognition method to help blind people find missing items using SURF. The proposed recognition process matches the individual features of the user-queried object to a database of features that contain different pre-saved personal items. The matching was performed under various conditions including image scale, partial occlusion, translation, rotation, and change in viewpoint.

3 Methodology of proposed system

3.1 System overview

The proposed DIODB system identifies objects and computes their distances from the user, and then it relays this information by sound to benefit visually impaired users. The system starts with activating the portable camera and capturing an image of the scene in which objects are to be discovered. Then, the system analyzes this image by specifying feature points that identify key properties of this image. These feature points are used in image matching with reference images previously stored in the DIODB database. This is performed by finding the common characteristics between the scanned image and reference images. If a matching is found for three or more feature points of the scanned image, the system will detect the object. After the process of matching and detecting objects in the scene image, the system copies the matched images from the database to a specific folder of discovered images and then stores the names of the recognized objects in a text file. Finally, the system will read this text file audibly. Next, the IPS system responsible for locating objects in the closed place starts to locate the positions of the discovered objects and stores their coordinates. After that, the system will compute the distances to these objects and outputs them audibly through the speakers. Figure 1 shows a general diagram of the system.

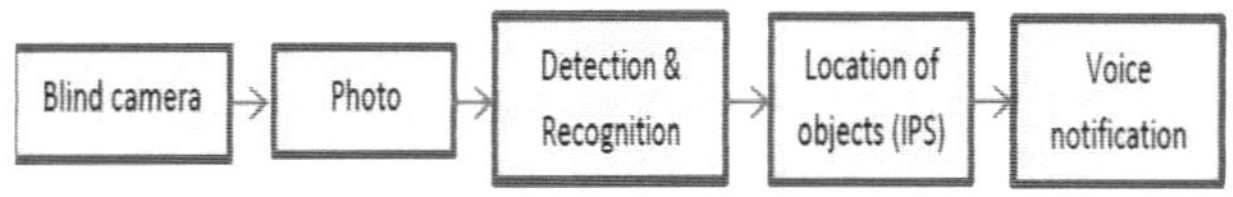

Figure 1: A general diagram of the DIODB system.

3.2 Phase 1: Scene shooting

Figure 2 illustrates the scene shooting phase of the DIODB system. This phase starts with shooting a given number (J) of images of the scene with a portable camera and saves them into the testing database. Figure 3 shows an example of a scene obtained at the scene shooting phase.

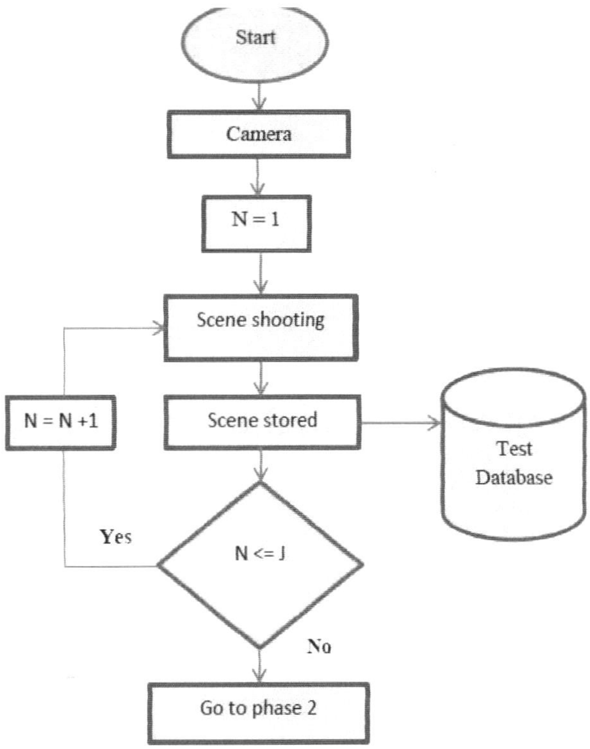

Figure 2: Flowchart of the scene shooting phase.

Figure 3: An example of a scene obtained at the scene shooting phase.

3.3 Phase 2: Object detection and recognition

A flowchart of the object detection and recognition phase is shown in Figure 4. After obtaining J images of the scene in Phase 1, Phase 2 detects and recognizes the objects in the scene to match them with the objects in the Reference Database. When implemented, DIODB started with extracting 300 key points for each image stored in the database of reference images. Figure 5 shows an example of a scene image with 300 feature points. Then, DIODB selected the strongest 100 key points for each of these objects. Figure 6 shows the box image from the Reference Database after selecting the 100 strongest feature points.

The algorithm tries to match the objects in the scene image with those in the reference images database by making a linear connection between the key points of each object in the scene and the reference data. When three or more links are found between a scene object and a reference object, the object is identified. Figure 7 shows matched points of the object identified and shown in Figure 8.

After objects' detection, the IPS system is applied to determine the location of the objects in the room. The final step is to convert all objects' names and locations to voice by an existing text-to-speech conversion system.

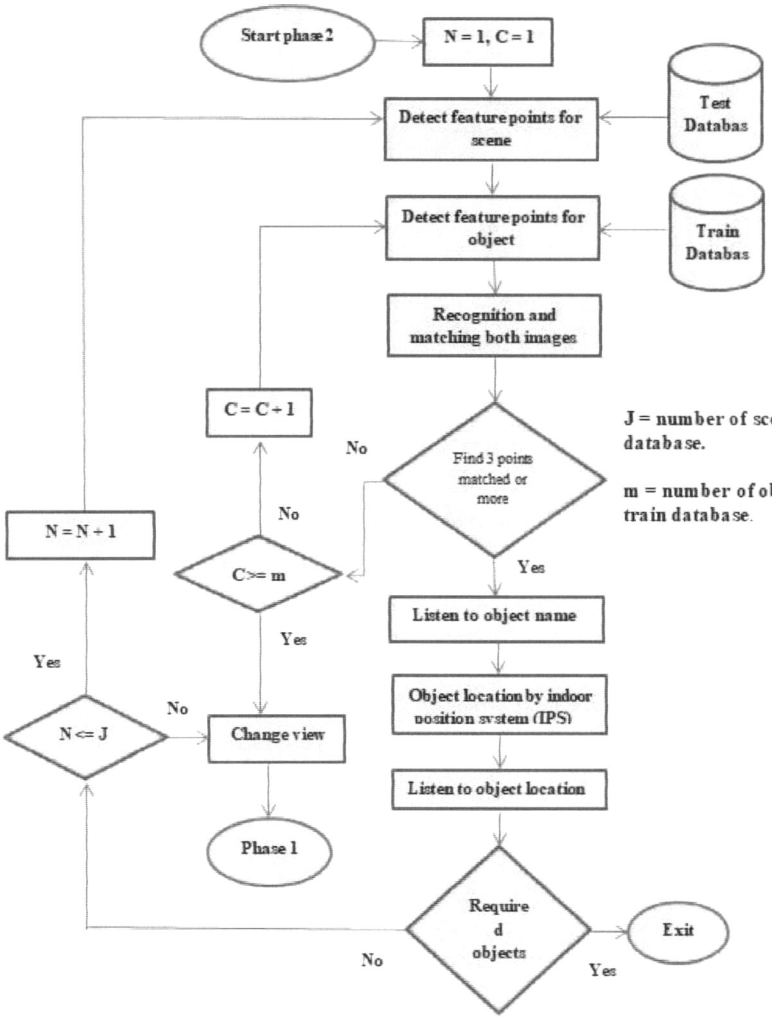

Figure 4: Object detection and recognition phase.

Figure 5: An example of a scene image with 300 feature points.

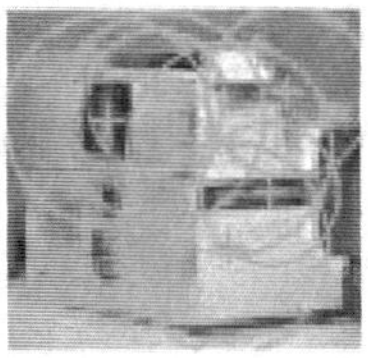

Figure 6: An example image of a reference object with 100 strongest feature points.

Figure 7: Matched points.

Figure 8: Identified object.

3.3.1 Indoor position system

In DIODB, we replace the sensors in an indoor position system (IPS) with cameras having IPS capabilities located inside the room. When taking a picture of objects through the camera on the blind glasses, the cameras inside the room take a full picture of the room. At the same time, processing the image begins to identify the objects in the room and locate them using the image taken by the cameras inside the room and the IPS. Once the objects have been detected, identified and positioned, their locations are convert to voice. The blind person can be directed to the intended object using the building map and the IPS.

Steps for determining object distances using IPS in the DIODB system:

1. Initialize each object's location (x_1,y_1,z_1) by using fixed IPS cameras, where z_1 = object height from the ground.
2. The user enters the room with an IPS-enabled camera to locate his position.
3. The user searches for needed items by executing Phase 1 and Phase 2.
4. If object (x_1,y_1,z_1) is detected and recognized, the IPS system will compute its distance from user's location (x_2,y_2,z_2) with (1).

$$d = \sqrt{(x_2 - x_1)^2 + (y_2 - y_1)^2} \quad (1)$$

Figure 9 shows initialized coordinates for all objects' locations on the map of the room by using IPS.

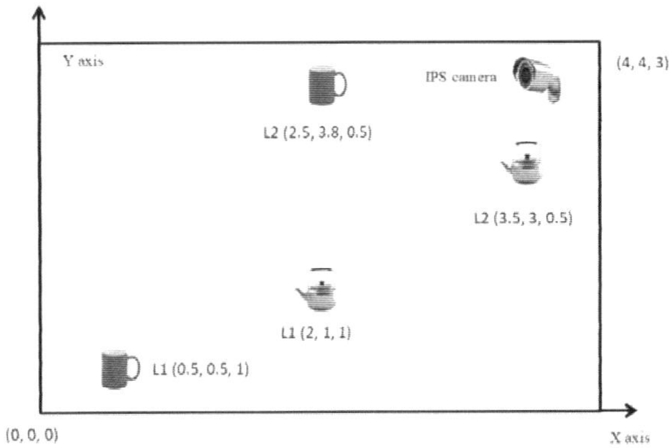

Figure 9: Initialize coordinates for all objects location .

3.3.2 Voice notification

In this phase, the system gives information about the name and location of the object by playing the audio files for the blind person and directing that person through IPS to reach the required object.

4 Implementation results and analysis

The program was executed and samples were taken from different distances and angles. The number of objects detected, the number of matched objects, and the accuracy calculations were computed for matching the objects. The following assumptions were made:

1. The features of the camera do not have accuracy zooming.
2. There is no representation from angle 90° on the Y axis vertically.

3. The amount of lighting should be taken into account.

To choose an appropriate value of the number of captured input scene images (J), the DIODB algorithm was tested with values of J from 1 to 5. As shown in Table 1, the values ($J \geq 3$) gave the maximum number of recognized images, so ($J = 3$) was the optimal number.

Table 1. Multiple trials for J = 1 to 5.

No. of Scenes	No. of Objects	No. Recognized
1	6	1
2	6	3
3	6	5
4	6	5
5	6	5

Table 2 shows a general comparison between DIODB and some related systems in terms of the features they provide, where DIODB appears to offer relatively good features for users. More features could be added to the system in future work. The test results of [19], shown in Table 3, showed that the overall percentage of detected elements was 84%.

In the DIODB system, the first step is to detect objects in images by using the speed up robust feature (SURF) algorithm for one or more objects that have multiple images in different scenes. Object detection in DIODB uses SURF as a robust speed up feature. Every object has 10 2D images where these images were taken from multi-view scenes.

Table 2. General comparison between DIODB and some related systems.

Systems	Camera	Detection	Recognition	IPS	Ultrasonic sensor	Voice	Vibration	Distance
Electronic Travel Aids	No	No	No	No	Y	No	Y	No
Augmented Reality	Y	No	No	No	No	No	No	Y
Navigation Assistance for Visually Impaired	Y	Y	Y	No	Y	Y	No	Y
Deep-See	Y	Y	Y	No	No	Y	No	No
DIODB	Y	Y	Y	Y	No	Y	No	Y

Table 3. Recognition accuracy for reference objects by [19].

Objects	No. of Images	Correctly Detected	False Positive	Accuracy
Keys	20	19	0	95%
Cell	20	12	0	60%
Wallet	20	17	0	85%
Sunglasses	20	17	0	85%
Sneaker	20	19	0	95%
Total	100	84	0	84%

Figure 10: Object detection by DIODB.

Figure 11: Sample Reference Database Images.

Figure 10 shows object detection using one image of one scene as input to our system. Using the SURF algorithm on this image detected each object by itself and stored the data in a table.

Figure 12: A Selected Test Image.

Figure 13: Identifying an Object.

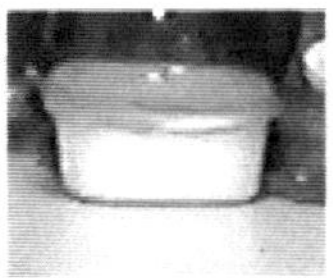

Figure 14: Identified Object.

Object recognition is the process of identifying an object in a digital image or video. The proposed DIODB system creates a reference database that has 510 images for many objects with different poses for each object. The Reference Database is used in the learning phase of the object recognition. In addition, a Test Database was used for comparing the results with images in the Reference Database. The Test Database images were not identical to the images in the reference database, but generally similar object were recognized and unknown objects were not. Figure 11 shows a sample of selected images from the Reference Database where Figure 12 shows a selected test image.

To recognize the test image, the system uses the geometric transformations method in SURF and compares this image with images in the Reference Database to be identified. As shown in Figure 13, a linear mapping is made between the identified object in the scene (on the right-hand side of Figure 13) and the object (on the left-hand side of Figure 13) coming from the Reference Database. The identified object, which was extracted from the scene in Figure 13, is shown in Figure 14.

Tables 4, 5, and 6 are multiple results with different objects and with angles (ax) degrees on the x-axis, (ay) degrees degree on the y-axis, and (d) distances in centimeters. As seen in these tables, the DIODB system was able to recognize objects with relatively high accuracy, even with rotated objects.

5 Conclusions

In this research, a new system employing the indoor position system was introduced to identify objects and their locations and to convert obtained information into audio. Implementation results showed that this system could help the visually impaired to track various indoor objects. The system could be enhanced by identifying objects from multi-view scenes and accounting for more factors such as occlusion and distortion. More features could be added to enhance the system's usability. Extended future work may use video to account for object's motion characteristics where it could benefit from existing software such as YOLO [13]. Related future work may combine this system with augmented reality software such as Google Tango and ARCore.

Table 4. (d = 25 cm, ax = 0, ay = 0).

No. objects	Detection	Recognition	Accuracy
1	1	1	100%
2	2	2	100%
5	5	5	100%
10	10	9	90%
15	15	13	86%
20	20	19	95%

Table 5. (d = 50 cm, ax = 0, ay = 0).

No. objects	Detection	Recognition	Accuracy
1	1	1	100%
2	2	2	100%
5	5	5	100%
10	10	8	80%
15	15	12	80%
20	20	17	85%

Table 6. (d = 100 cm, ax = -90, ay = 30).

No. objects	Detection	Recognition	Accuracy
1	1	1	100%
2	2	2	100%
5	5	4	80%
10	10	8	80%
15	15	10	67%
20	20	14	70%

6 References

[1] R.R.A. Bourne, S.R. Flaxman, T. Braithwaite, M.V. Cicinelli, A. Das, J.B. Jonas, et al. "Vision Loss Expert Group. Magnitude, temporal trends, and projections of the global prevalence of blindness and distance and near vision impairment: a systematic review and meta-analysis"; Lancet Glob Health, Vol. 5, No. 9, 888–897, Sep 2017.

[2] T.R. Fricke, N. Tahhan, S. Resnikoff, E. Papas, A. Burnett, M.H. Suit, T. Naduvilath, K. Naidoo. "Global Prevalence of Presbyopia and Vision Impairment from Uncorrected Presbyopia: Systematic Review, Meta-analysis, and Modelling"; Ophthalmology, May 2018.

[3] Shaharyar A.K. Tareen and Zahra Saleem. "A Comparative Analysis of SIFT, SURF, KAZE, AKAZE, ORB, and BRISK"; International Conference on Computing, Mathematics and Engineering Technologies – iCoMET, 2018.

[4] Kirti P. Bhure and J.D. Dhande. "Object Detection Methodologies for Blind People"; International Journal on Recent and Innovation Trends in Computing and Communication, Vol. 5, Issue 1, 194-198, 2017.

[5] Mitchell. R.P. Lapointe and Bruce Milliken. "Influences of Context on Object Detection and Identification in Natural Scenes"; Ph.D. Thesis, McMaster University, 2016. http://hdl.handle.net/11375/20265

[6] O.N. Al-Allaf, A.A. Tamimi and M.A. Alia. "Face Recognition System Based on Different Artificial Neural Networks Models and Training Algorithms"; International Journal of Advanced Computer Science and Applications, Vol. 4, No. 6, 40-47, 2013.

[7] M.A. Alia, A.A. Tamimi and O.N. Al-Allaf. "Integrated System for Monitoring and Recognizing Students During Class Session"; International Journal of Multimedia & Its Applications, Vol. 5, No. 6, 45-52, 2013.

[8] D.R. Ibrahim, A.A. Tamimi and A.M. Abdalla. "Performance Analysis of Biometric Recognition Modalities"; International Conference on Information Technology (ICIT'2017), pp. 980-984, Amman, Jordan, 17-18 May 2017.

[9] A.A. Tamimi, O.N. Al-Allaf and M.A. Alia. "Real-Time Group Face-Detection for an Intelligent Class-Attendance System"; International Journal of Information Technology and Computer Science, Vol. 6, pp. 66-73, 2015. doi: 10.5815/ijitcs.2015.06.09.

[10] A. Tamimi, O.N.A. Al-Allaf and M.A. Alia. "Eigen Faces and Principle Component Analysis for Face Recognition Systems: A Comparative Study"; International Journal of Computers & Technology, Vol 14, No. 4, 5650-5660, Feb. 2015.

[11] Meiyuan Zhao. "Advanced Driver Assistance Systems"; Technical Paper, Security & Privacy Research, Intel Labs, 2015. https://www.semagarage.com/assets/pdf/advanced-driver-assistant-system-paper.pdf.

[12] Kiana Ehsani, Roozbeh Mottaghi and Ali Farhadi. "SeGAN: Segmenting and Generating the Invisible"; 2018 IEEE/CVF Conference on Computer Vision and Pattern Recognition, Salt Lake City, UT, USA, 18-22 June 2018. https://dx.doi.org/10.1109/CVPR.2018.00643.

[13] https://pjreddie.com/darknet/yolo/

[14] Nalawade M. Rajendra, Wagh Vrushali and Kamble Shradha. "An Approach for Object and Scene Detection for Blind Peoples Using Vocal Vision"; Int. Journal of Engineering Research and Applications, Vol. 4, Issue 12, Part 5, 1-3, Dec. 2014.

[15] Reza Oji, "An Automatic Algorithm for Object Recognition and Detection Based on ASIFT Key Points"; Signal & Image Processing: An International Journal, Vol. 3, No. 5, 29-39, 2012.

[16] Rui Jiang, Qian Lin and Shuhui Qu. "Let Blind People See: Real Time Visual Recognition with Results Converted to 3D Audio"; Technical Report, Stanford University, 2016. http://cs231n.stanford.edu/reports/2016/pdfs/218_Report.pdf

[17] Gajanan D. Bonde, Pooja U. Barwal, Sandhya R. Pal, Sumaiya I. Khan and Kiran Ablankar. "Finding Indoor Position of Person Using Wi-Fi & Smartphone: A Survey"; International Journal for Innovative Research in Science & Technology, Vol. 1, Issue 8, January 2015.

[18] Marin Kaluža, Kristina Beg and Bernard Vukelic. "Analysis of an Indoor Positioning System"; Zbornik Veleučilišta u Rijeci, Vol. 5, No. 1, 13-32, 2017.

[19] Ricardo Chincha and YingLi Tian. "Finding Objects for Blind People Based on SURF Feature"; 2011 IEEE International Conference on Bioinformatics and Biomedicine Workshops, Atlanta, GA, USA, 12-15 Nov. 2011.

3D surface reconstruction of trees using a region-based active contour model

Shijun Tang[1] and Sihai Tang[2]

[1]Department of Science and Mathematics
Alvernia University, Reading, PA, USA 19607

[2]Department of Computer Science and Engineering
University of North Texas, Denton, TX, USA 76203

Abstract— **In this paper, a novel method is proposed for 3D surface reconstruction of trees using a region-based active contour model. Both individual tree crowns and clusters of trees are first segmented for further exploration. Multiple horizontal slices corresponding to different heights are obtained. The 3D structure is built using raw data from light detection and ranging (LiDAR) point clouds. The results indicate that this approach is effective for 3D surface reconstruction of trees including individual trees and clusters of trees.**

Keywords*— *LiDAR, a region-based active contour model, 3D surface reconstruction, segmentation

I. INTRODUCTION

Forests are closely related with the development of life and human civilization. Through the use of light detection and ranging (LiDAR), forest attributes (such as tree height, canopy closure, and diameter at breast height) can be effectively estimated. These attributes are often employed to evaluate forest growth, competition, and photosynthesis [1], carbon sequestration, standing timber volume, and biomass of trees [2],[3],[4].

Canopy height models (CHMs) are often used to represent horizontal and vertical distribution of tree canopies. Once a digital elevation model (DEM) and a digital surface model (DSM) are interpolated from LiDAR point clouds, a CHM can be obtained by subtracting the DEM from the DSM [5]. However, CHMs are limited in their capacity to accurately retrieve individual tree and crown attributes[6] [7] [8]. The CHMs' limitations are often due to applying inappropriate crown shapes, overlap with adjacent trees, or canopy gaps [9] [10]. Also, contained surface irregularities [5], tree top dislocation in the CHMs [11], and underestimation of tree height are commonly reported [12][13].

Parametric height models (PHM) describe the forest canopy as a series of cones fitted to the LiDAR point clouds. From it, tree crowns can be extracted through simple geometric operations [8]. However, for parametric height models, the negative height bias or positive height bias still exists in the results. When fitting cones to the LiDAR point clouds, there exists matching errors depending on the property and distribution of LiDAR point clouds.

In order to overcome the weaknesses and limitations of the above models, in this paper, we propose a new 3D surface reconstruction method for tree canopy using a region-based active contour model.

II. METHODOLOGY

A. Study area

The study area is located in the Soquel Demonstration State Forest in California, USA. The LiDAR data were collected on March 29, 2007 by the GeoEarthScope Northern California LiDAR project (Prentice et al. 2009), and downloaded from the OpenTopography Facility at the San Diego Supercomputer Center. The LiDAR point density is approximately 9.6 points m^{-2}. Major tree types in the study area include Douglas fir, redwood, and oak.

B. Data processing

Preprocessing of LiDAR data is necessary before separating data points into height layers. A digital elevation model (DEM) was created from ground points using inverse distance weighted (IDW) interpolation. The height from ground for each LiDAR point was then obtained by subtracting the DEM-derived ground elevation beneath the point from the elevation of the point.

C. Segmentation using a region-based active contour model

The active contour model along with level set technology has been widely applied to many research fields including computer vision and medical image processing[14][15][16]. Chan and Vese [17] introduced a variational model based on the level set function ϕ(t,x,y), for which the zero level set segments the image domain into several intensity homogenous regions by minimizing the following function. The level set function ϕ(t,x,y) presents the zero-level curve at time t or the evolution of the curve.

$$
\begin{aligned}
F(c_1, c_2, \phi) &= \mu \int_\Omega \delta(\phi(x,y)) \,|\, \nabla \phi(x,y) \,|\, dxdy \\
&+ v \int_\Omega H(\phi(x,y)) dxdy \\
&+ \lambda_1 \int_\Omega | u_0(x,y) - c_1 |^2 H(\phi(x,y)) dxdy \\
&+ \lambda_2 \int_\Omega | u_0(x,y) - c_2 |^2 (1 - H(\phi(x,y)) dxdy \qquad \text{..........(1)}
\end{aligned}
$$

where u: $\Omega \longrightarrow R$ is an image defined on Ω, c_1 and c_2 are constants, and $H(\cdot)$ is the Heaviside function and $\delta(\cdot)$ is Kronecker delta function. Of the four terms in equation (1), the first is the length of the contour; the second is the area within the contour; the third and fourth terms are proportional to the energy within and outside the contour, respectively.

This minimization problem is solved by taking the Euler-Lagrange equations and updating the level set function ϕ by gradient descent.

$$
\frac{\partial \phi}{\partial t} = \delta(\phi)[\mu \cdot div\left(\frac{\nabla \phi}{|\nabla \phi|}\right) - \lambda_1 (u_0 - c_1)^2 + \lambda_2 (u_0 - c_2)^2] \qquad \text{............(2)}
$$

For a 3D reconstruction, each slice of an object must first be obtained. The slice is related with detection and location of the object in each 2D image. As an effective model, the level set technology provided by Chan and Vese [17] can detect the locations of boundaries very well, and is insensitive to placement of the initial curve in the image. We use this model to separate the individual trees or clusters of trees from their backgrounds and to obtain the contours of the individual trees or clusters of trees.

D. 3D reconstruction of individual trees or clusters of trees

For each height, we utilize the above active contour method to complete the segmentation. So, at different heights, the contours of individual trees or clusters of trees may be obtained.

After obtaining a series of tree slices (boundaries) from different heights, a 3D canopy of trees is reconstructed by putting all slices together following their height orders.

Using interpolation or MESH function in Matlab, 3D reconstruction with finer and smoother canopy surface is obtained for individual trees or clusters of trees.

III. EXPERIMENTAL RESULTS AND ANALYSIS

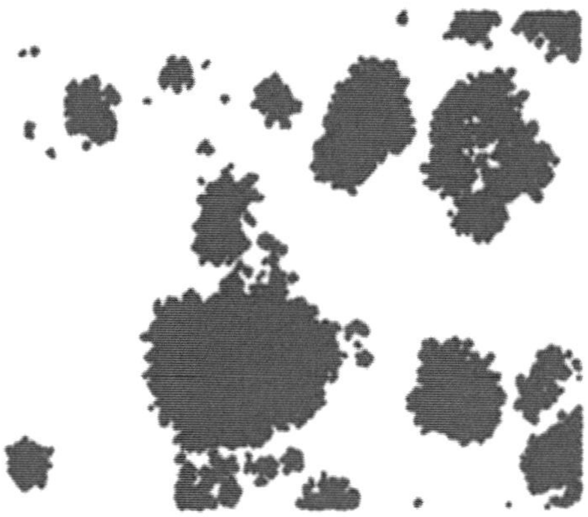

Figure 1(a). 2D image of trees at height (h ≥25 m) is obtained from 3D raw LiDAR data.

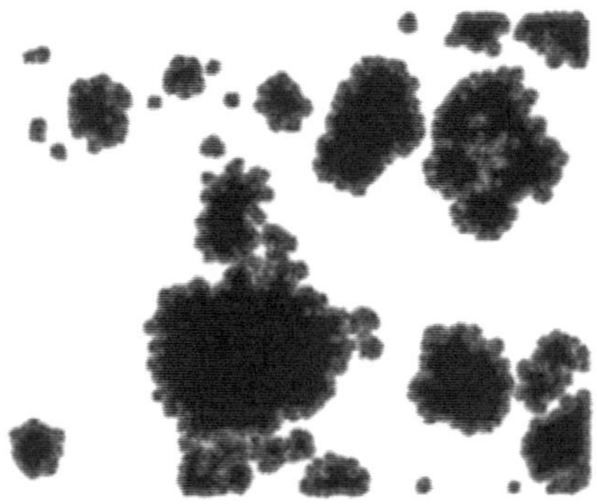

Figure 1(b). 2D image of trees at heights (h ≥25 m) is obtained from 3D raw LiDAR data (black area); Boundaries of trees in 2D image are segmented using a region-based active contour model (Green color).

Fig. 1(a) shows a 2D image of trees from LiDAR data at heights (h ≥25 m). By employing the region-based active contour model to separate individual trees or clusters of trees from their backgrounds, the contours of individual trees or clusters of trees are obtained and shown in Fig. 1(b) and 1(c).

A 3D canopy surface is reconstructed by putting together a series of tree slices (boundaries) corresponding to different heights following their height orders. After using interpolation or the MESH function in Matlab, a finer and smoother canopy surface is achieved.

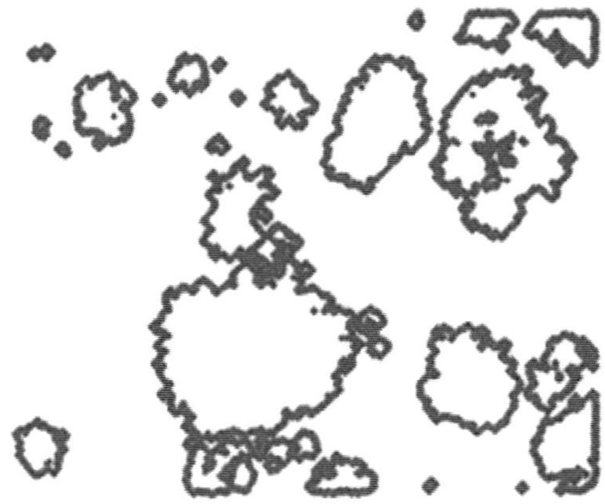

Figure 1(c). The contours of individual trees or clusters of trees are obtained by using a region-based active contour model.

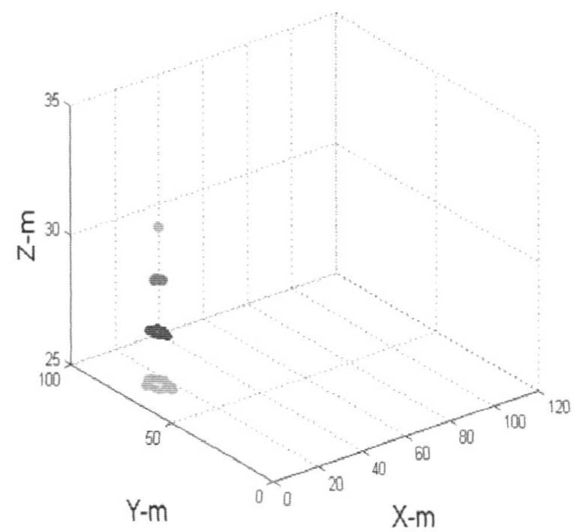

Figure 2(a) exhibits a stack of individual tree slices from different heights.

Fig. 2(a) shows a series of slices for an individual tree. Fig. 2(b) is a 3D canopy surface reconstruction with smoother surface for the tree.

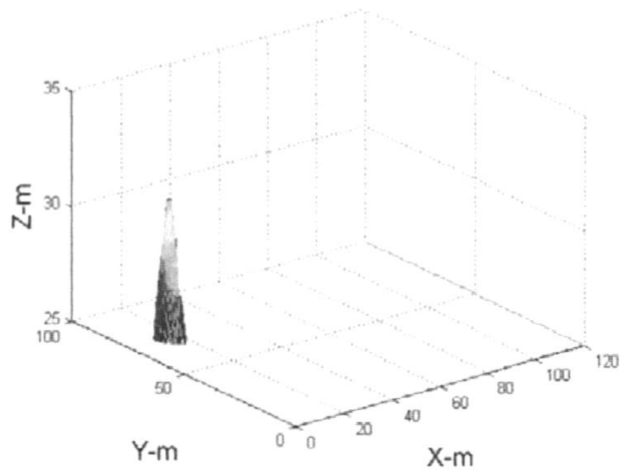

Figure 2(b) shows 3D canopy reconstruction with smoother surface for individual tree.

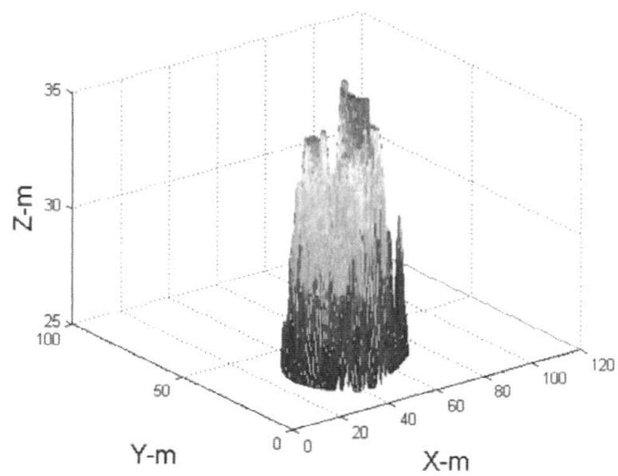

Figure 3(b) displays 3D canopy reconstruction with smoother surface for a cluster of trees.

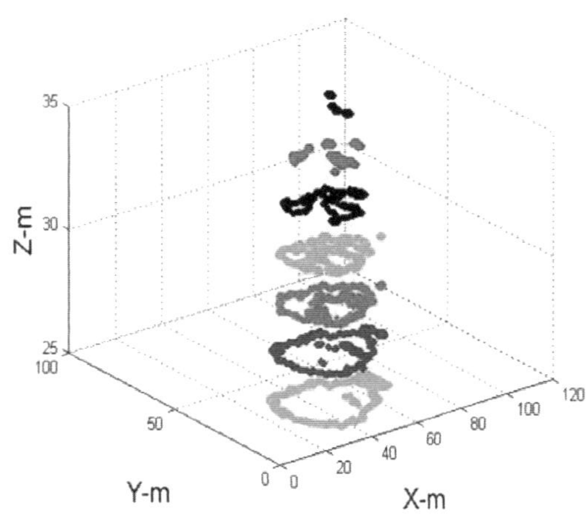

Fig. 3(a) exhibits the slices stack of a cluster of trees.

Fig. 3(a) displays a series of slices for a cluster of trees. Fig. 3(b) exhibits 3D canopy surface reconstruction with smoother surface for the cluster of trees.

In the Fig. 1, boundaries of trees in 2D image at heights (h ≥25 m) are segmented using a region-based active contour model. Using the same methods and process, boundaries of all trees in 2D image at different heights are also segmented and obtained. After putting all trees' slices at different heights in the study area together, 3D canopy

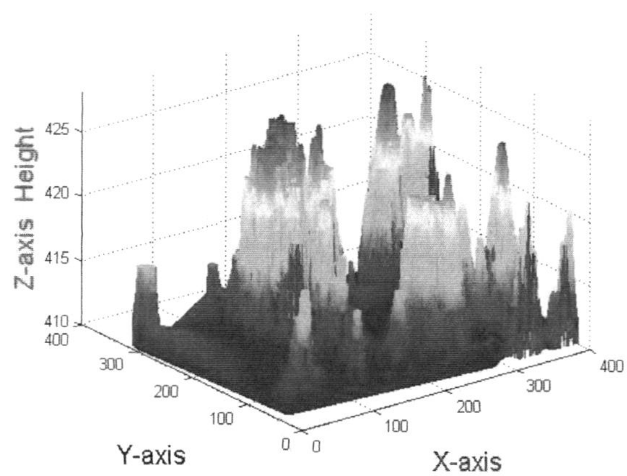

Fig.4 shows the 3D canopy surface reconstruction with smoother surfaces from different heights for individual trees and clusters of trees. This includes all trees (individual trees and clusters of trees) in the studied area.

surface reconstruction with smoother surfaces of trees, including individual trees and clusters of trees, has been obtained and displayed as Fig. 4.

IV. CONCLUSIONS

In this paper, based on a region active contour model, we propose a new method for 3D canopy surface reconstruction of individual tree crowns and clusters of trees from LiDAR point clouds. The proposed method allows for delineations of 3D forest canopy naturally from the contours of raw LiDAR point clouds.

The proposed model is suitable not only for a series of ideal cone shapes, but also for other kinds of 3D shapes. More importantly, several contours corresponding to different heights are very useful to quantitatively describe attributes and categories of trees.

V. REFERENCES

[1] Meng, S. X., Lieffers, V. J. and Huang, S., Modeling crown volume of lodgepole pine based upon the uniform stress theory, Forest Ecology and Management, 251, pp. 174–181, 2007

[2] Lim, K., Treitz, P., Wulder, M. and Stonge, B., LiDAR remote sensing of forest structure, Progress in Physical Geography, 27, pp. 88–106, 2003

[3] Patenaude, G., Hill, R. A., Milne, R., Gaveau, D.L.A., Briggs, B.B.J., Dawson, T. P., Quantifying forest above ground carbon content using LiDAR remote sensing, Remote Sensing of Environment, 93, pp. 368–380, 2004

[4] Hese, S., Lucht, W., Schmullius, C., Barnsley, M., Dubayah, R., Knorr, D., Neumann, K., Riedel, T., Schrfter, K., Global biomass mapping for an improved understanding of the CO_2 balance - the Earth observation mission Carbon-3D, Remote Sensing of Environment, 94, pp.94–104, 2005

[5] Ben-Arie, J. R., Hay, G. J., Powers, R. P., Castilla, G. and Stonge, B., Development of a pit filling algorithm for LiDAR canopy height models. Computers & Geosciences, 35, pp. 1940–1949, 2009

[6] Nelson, R., Jimenez, J., Schnell, C.E., Hartshorn, G.S., Gregoire, T.G. and Oderwald, R., Canopy height models and airborne lasers to estimate forest biomass: two problems, International Journal of Remote Sensing, 21, pp. 2153–2162, 2000

[7] Weinacker, H., Koch, B., Heyder, U. and Weinacker, R., Development of filtering, segmentation and modeling modules for LIDAR and multispectral data as a fundament of an automatic forest inventory system, In International Archives of Photogrammetry, Remote Sensing and Spatial Information Sciences XXXVI-8/W2, 3–6 October 2004, Freiburg, Germany (The Netherlands: GITC bv), pp. 50–55, 2004

[8] Leeuwen, M. V., Coops, N. C. and Wulder, M., Canopy surface reconstruction from a LiDAR point cloud using Hough transform, Remote Sensing Letters, Vol. 1, No. 3, September 2010, pp.125–132, 2010

[9] Mei, C. and Durrieu, S., Tree crown delineation from digital elevation models and high resolution imagery, In International Archives of Photogrammetry, Remote Sensing and Spatial Information Sciences XXXVI-8/W2, 3–6 October 2004, Freiburg, Germany (The Netherlands: GITC bv), pp. 7–13, 2004

[10] Rahman, M.Z.A. and Gorte, B.G.H., Tree crown delineation from high resolution airborne lidar based on densities of high points. In International Archives of Photogrammetry, Remote Sensing and Spatial Information Sciences XXXVIII-3/W8, 1–2 September 2009, Paris, France (The Netherlands: GITC bv), pp. 123–128, 2009

[11] Pitkanen, J., Maltamo, M., Hyyppa, J. and Yu, X., Adaptive methods for individual tree detection on airborne laser based canopy height model, In International Archives of Photogrammetry, Remote Sensing and Spatial Information Sciences XXXVI-8/W2, 3–6 October 2004, Freiburg, Germany (The Netherlands: GITC bv), pp. 187–191, 2004

[12] NÆsset, E., Determination of mean tree height of forest stands using airborne laser scanner data. ISPRS Journal of Photogrammetry and Remote Sensing, 52, pp. 49–56, 1997

[13] Holmgren, J., Nilsson, M. and Olsson, H., Estimation of tree height and stem volume on plots using airborne laser scanning, Forest Science, 49, pp. 419–428, 2003

[14] Tang S., Buckles B.P. and Namuduri K., 3D surface reconstruction of brain based on level set method, The 2012 International Conference on Image Processing, Computer Vision, & Pattern Recognition (IPCV'12), Vol. I, pp.64, 2012

[15] Tang S., Dong P. and B.P. Buckles, Three-dimensional surface reconstruction of tree canopy from LiDAR point clouds using a region-based level set method, International Journal of Remote Sensing, Vol. 34, No. 4, pp.1373, 2013

[16] Tang, S. H., Alex, R., and Tang S., Spatial Location of 3D Reconstructed Subthalamic Nuclei, the 2018 International Conference on Image Processing, Computer Vision, & Pattern Recognition (IPCV'18), pp.78, 2018

[17] Chan, T. F., Vese, L., Active contours without edges, IEEE Trans. Img. Process. 10 (2), pp.266–277, 2001

Visible and NIR Image Blending for Night Vision

Tae-Young Jung, Dong-Min Son, Sung-Hak Lee
School of Electronics Engineering, Kyungpook National University, Daegu, Korea

Abstract – *In this paper, the image blending method with visible and near infrared (NIR) images obtained by switching IR lighting under low-light conditions is proposed, the image blending is first performed by using a weighting map generated by surround parameters, then tone mapping based on human visual system balances the luminance of the blended image. Finally, color-scaling and correction compensates the noise and color distortion. In the qualitative comparison with conventional methods, the performance of the proposed method has good detail, low-level noise and color accuracy with respect to other methods*

Keywords: visible and near infrared image, image blending, night vision, image enhancement, high dynamic range, tone compression

1 Introduction

Surveillance cameras such as CCTVs are required to provide enough information to provide sufficient information under varying conditions such as underground, tunnels, vehicle headlights, daylight conditions and no-light dark rooms etc. Recently, there is an increasing interest in high resolution, high sensitivity of an image sensor, and an LED sub-lighting system for the performance improvement of surveillance cameras. In particular, cameras used at low-light condition have adopted an IR LED light to recognize objects while avoiding security or visual interference.

In the last decade, related researches based on the multi-spectral imaging with NIR images have been proposed[1-2]. These researches have still difficulty to control the camera properly depending on the distance of objects and the amount of lights under various visible-light illuminations, and the hardware system is also complicated. Figure 1 shows the result of image blending with visible and NIR image based on the conventional method[2] under a low-light condition. The result image shows the noise at lower level and color distortion at higher level. In this paper, we propose the enhancement image blending algorithm for the night vision image using visible and NIR images obtained by switching IR-light under dark or dim surrounds.

2 Proposed Algorithm

NIR images are very useful for complementing image information because they have more details for edges and texture information than visible images in low light conditions. In this research, the image fusion is performed using the visible image and the NIR image as the input image as shown in Fig. 2. The proposed algorithm consists of four stages: image decomposition with the bilateral filter[3], luminance blending with a weighting map, tone mapping with multi-scale luminance adaptation, and color correction with color scaling & correction. The image processing of these stages is performed in the *CIELAB* color space. The luminance value (radiance map) of the output image is constructed through the weighted blending. The color components of the output image are obtained by color scaling and compensation of the *a, b* values of the input visible image in the *Lab* color space. Finally, the obtained luminance and color values are converted to the *RGB* color space. The flow chart of the proposed algorithm is shown in Fig. 3.

2.1 Image Decomposition

For the majority of diffuse objects, the pixel values can be regarded as a product of incoming illumination (irradiance) and the surface reflectance[4]:

$$intensity = reflectance \times illumination$$

Fig. 1. Result of conventional visible and NIR image blending[2].

(a) (b)

Fig. 2. Input images: (a) Visible input image, (b) NIR input image.

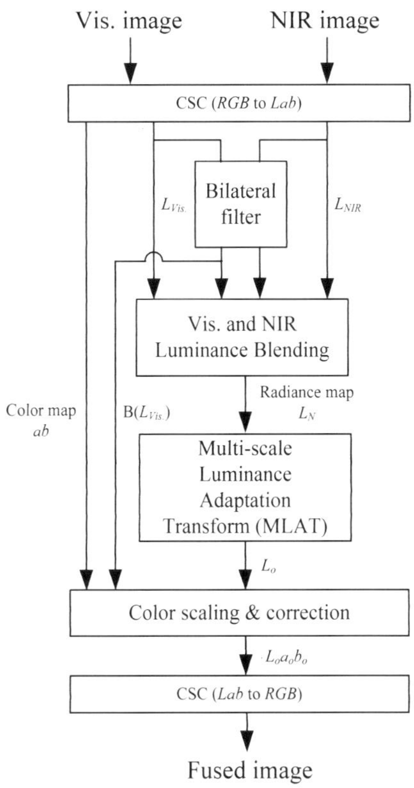

Fig. 3. Flow chart of proposed algorithm.

In a dark environment, the NIR image has much more details and texture information than the visible image. To use the useful information of the NIR image, it is necessary to separate the reflectance and illumination from the intensity of the input image. In this part, the input intensity is decomposed into the illumination component using an edge-preserving filter called the bilateral filter proposed by Durand and Dorsey[3]. The bilateral filter is the effective method to separate illumination from reflectance while keeps sharp edges and to avoid halo artifacts.

$B(L_{Vis.})$: *illumination(surround) of visible image*

$B(L_{NIR})$: *illumination(surround) of NIR image*

The notation of B in this paper refers to the bilateral filtering. Some of the weighting parameters are constructed using $B(L_{Vis.})$ and $B(L_{NIR})$.

2.2 Luminance Channel Blending

In this part, a weighting map for image blending is constructed using three surround parameters. The weighting map has values in the range from 0 and 1. If the value is 1, the intensity of the NIR image is not used for image blending. First W_1 provides the relative surround intensity of the visible image, that is, a visibility parameter from the base layer level of the visible image. Second W_2 is a surround difference parameter between NIR and visible images and third W_3 is an activity difference parameter obtained by the standard variation of base layer images. W_2 and W_3 provide relative difference of local intensity and contrast of the two input images. The parameters are normalized from 0 to 1, and the value closer to 1 indicates that the components of the visible image are dominant. The parameters for a weighting map are defined as following:

$$W_1 = N(B(L_{vis})) \quad (1)$$

$$W_2 = N(B(L_{NIR}) - B(L_{Vis.})) \quad (2)$$

$$W_3 = N(Var(L_{vis}) - Var(L_{NIR})) \quad (3)$$

Where, the notations of 'N' and 'Var' refer to the normalizing function and the variance function, respectively. Through compromising the three parameters, the final weighting map is obtained as following:

$$W_{Map} = \sum_{i=1}^{N} W_i / N, for\ N = 3 \quad (4)$$

The radiance map is obtained through the weighting map and the luminance channels of the input images as following:

$$L_N = W_{Map} \times L_{vis} + (1 - W_{Map}) \times (E_R) \times L_{NIR}$$

$$E_R = average(L_{vis}) / average(L_{NIR}) \quad (5)$$

where, E_R is relative exposure gain of visible and NIR images.

2.3 Tone Balance with Luminance Adaptation.

After image blending processing, luminance adaptation transform(LAT)[5] is applied based on the brightness perception of human vision suitable for changes in light source and luminance. The LAT based tone-mapping method enhances the local contrast and the saturation of the blended image. In local tone-mapping method, the single-scale LAT(SLAT) structure may lead to trade-off problems with the scale of blur functions. Here, multi-scale LAT (MLAT)[6] method is applied for increasing both local and global rendering qualities.

Human visual system (HVS) is more influenced by contrast of image than intensity of physical brightness. To obtain the contrast of the image, the minimum and maximum levels of perceived luminance are modeled from the Stevens' brightness function and the Bartleson-Breneman's brightness function [7-8] as following:

$$L_{min} = 0.0212 + 0.0185 G(L_N)^{1.0314} \quad (6)$$

$$L_{max} = 25.83 + 30.82 G(L_N)^{0.6034} \quad (7)$$

Where, L_{min} and L_{max} are the minimum and maximum luminance level, respectively. $G(L_N)$ is the surround map achieved from Gaussian blurring for L_N with the maximum value of 100.

The HVS is adapted to a level of adaptation that depends on the luminance of the visual field. The visual gamma (γ_v) changes with the adaptive luminance of the HVS and can be described as following:

$$\gamma_v = 0.444 + 0.045\ln(G(L_N) + 0.6034) \qquad (8)$$

Using the local operators derived above, the local tone mapping function is as following:

$$SLAT: \; L_o = I_{o\_gain} \times N([|L_N|]^{\gamma_v} + I_{o\_offset}) \; (9)$$

where L_o is the output image of the luminance channel. I_{o_gain} and I_{o_offset} are operators to control the output range. And the multi-scale method is used to balance between the local and global renditions, as following:

$$MLAT = \sum_{n-1}^{N} \omega_n SLAT_n \qquad (10)$$

where MLAT is the output of multi-scale LAT, SLAT is the output of the nth single-scale LAT, and ω_n is the nth weighting factor.

2.4 Color Compensation

After image blending and MLAT process, the color scaling and correction(CsC) is applied for color compensation. CsC uses a scaling factor to minimize the noise and color distortion caused by image blending and MLAT. The scaling factor consists of color correction according to luminance and tone scaling according to the ratio of surrounds. CsC is applied to obtain a color similar to the visible image as following:

$$\begin{aligned} a_o &= T_S \times R_S \times B(L_{VIS}) \times a \\ b_o &= T_S \times R_S \times B(L_{VIS}) \times b \\ T_S &= L_o / L_N \\ R_S &= B(L_N) / B(L_{Vis}) \end{aligned} \qquad (11)$$

Where, (a, b) in *CIELAB* color space are the color components of the input visible image and (a_o, b_o) are the output value of CsC processing. T_S is a scaling factor for toning and obtained by the ratio of change for the luminance components. R_S is the scaling factor for radiance, which is obtained as the ratio of surround change of the visible image before and after the tone processing. The result of the CsC processing is shown in Fig.4. The CsC applied image shows the decrement of low level noise and enhancement of color details, visible color fidelity, and white balance in dim areas.

3 Experimental Results

We evaluated the overall image quality through qualitative comparisons with conventional methods. The proposed algorithm has been compared with blending and toning methods, in two combinations: Debevec's radiance map[9] & iCAM06[10] (DRiC) and soft-mixing & Monobe's local contrast range transform[11] (SMML).

The input and result images are shown in Fig. 5. The results show significant differences in the details and colors in view of low-level noise, color distortion, de-saturation/over-saturation and white balance change. Specially, the continuity of the level cross region is unnatural in the compared methods.

4 Conclusions

The proposed algorithm provides the NIR and visible image capturing and good fused image visibility at low-light conditions. In our future work, we plan to evaluate the image quality for daylight and the quantitative comparisons.

5 Acknowledgment

This research was supported by Basic Science Research Program through the National Research Foundation of Korea (NRF) and the BK21 Plus project funded by the Ministry of Education, Korea (NRF-2017R1D1A3B03032807, 21A20131600011).

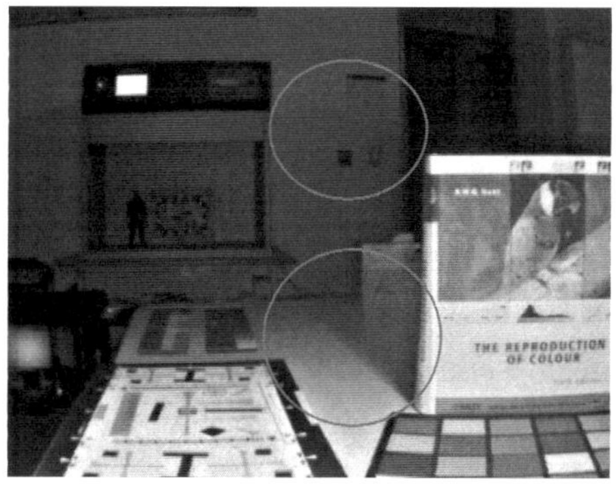

(a)

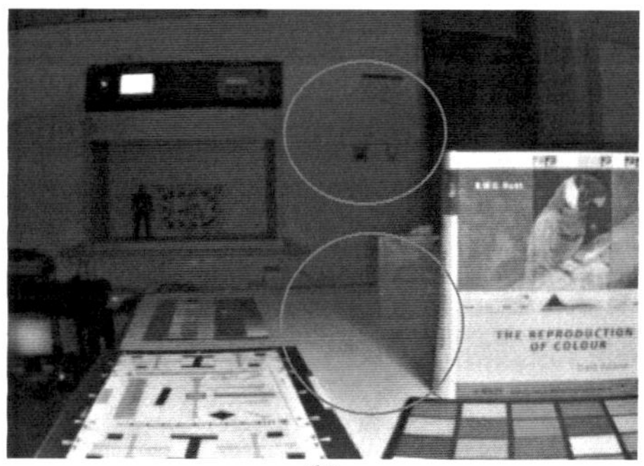

(b)

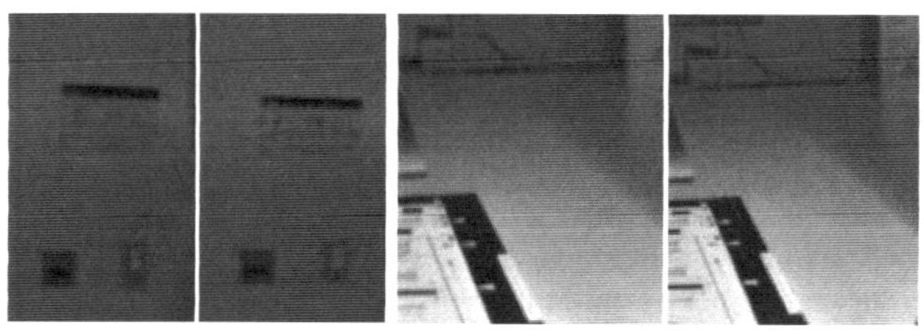

(c)

Fig. 4. CsC processing comparison: (a) before CsC, (b) after CsC, (c) enlarged parts in results.

6 References

[1] Zhuo S., Zhang X., Miao X., and Sim T. "Enhancing Low Light Images using infrared Flash Images", IEEE 17th International Conference on Image Processing, 2010.

[2] A.V. Vanmali, V.M. Gadre, "Visible and NIR image fusion using weight-map-guided Laplacian–Gaussian pyramid for improving scene visibility", Sadhana 42(7), pp. 1063-1082, 2017.

[3] Frédo Durand and Julie Dorsey, "Fast bilateral filtering for the display of highdynamic-range images", ACM Transactions on Graphics (Proc. SIGGRAPH), 21(3), pp. 257–266, 2002.

[4] Rafal K. Mantiuk, Karol Myszkowski, and Hans-Peter Seidel, High Dynamic Range Imaging. In Wiley Encyclopedia of Electrical and Electronics Engineering. Wiley, pp. 1-81. E, 2015.

[5] Kwon, H.J., Lee, S.H., Lee, G.Y., Sohng, K.I.: "Luminance adaptation transform based on brightness functions for LDR image reproduction", Digital Signal Processing, 30, pp. 74–85, 2014.

[6] Kwon, H.J., Lee, S.H., Lee, G.Y., Sohng, K.I.: "Enhanced high dynamic-range image rendering using a surround map based on edge-adaptive layer blurring", IET Computer Vision, 10(7), pp. 689–699, 2016.

[7] Stevens, J.C., Stevens, S.S.: "Brightness function: effects of adaptation", J. Opt. Soc. Am., 53(3), pp. 375–385, 1963.

[8] Bartleson, C.J., Breneman, E.J.: "Brightness perception in complex fields", J. Opt. Soc. Am., 57, (7), pp. 953–957, 1967.

[9] P. E. Debevec and J. Malik, "Recovering high dynamic range radiance maps form photographs," SIGGRAPH'97, pp. 369-378, 1997.

[10] J. Kuang, G. Johnson, and M. Fairchild, "iCAM06: A refined image appearance model for HDR image rendering,"J. Vis. Commun. Image R.,18 (5), pp. 406-414, 2007.

[11] Y. Monobe, H. Yamashita, T. Kurosawa, and H. Kotera, "Dynamic range compression preserving local image contrast for digital video camera," IEEE Tans. on Consumer Electronics, 51 (1), pp. 1-10, 2005.

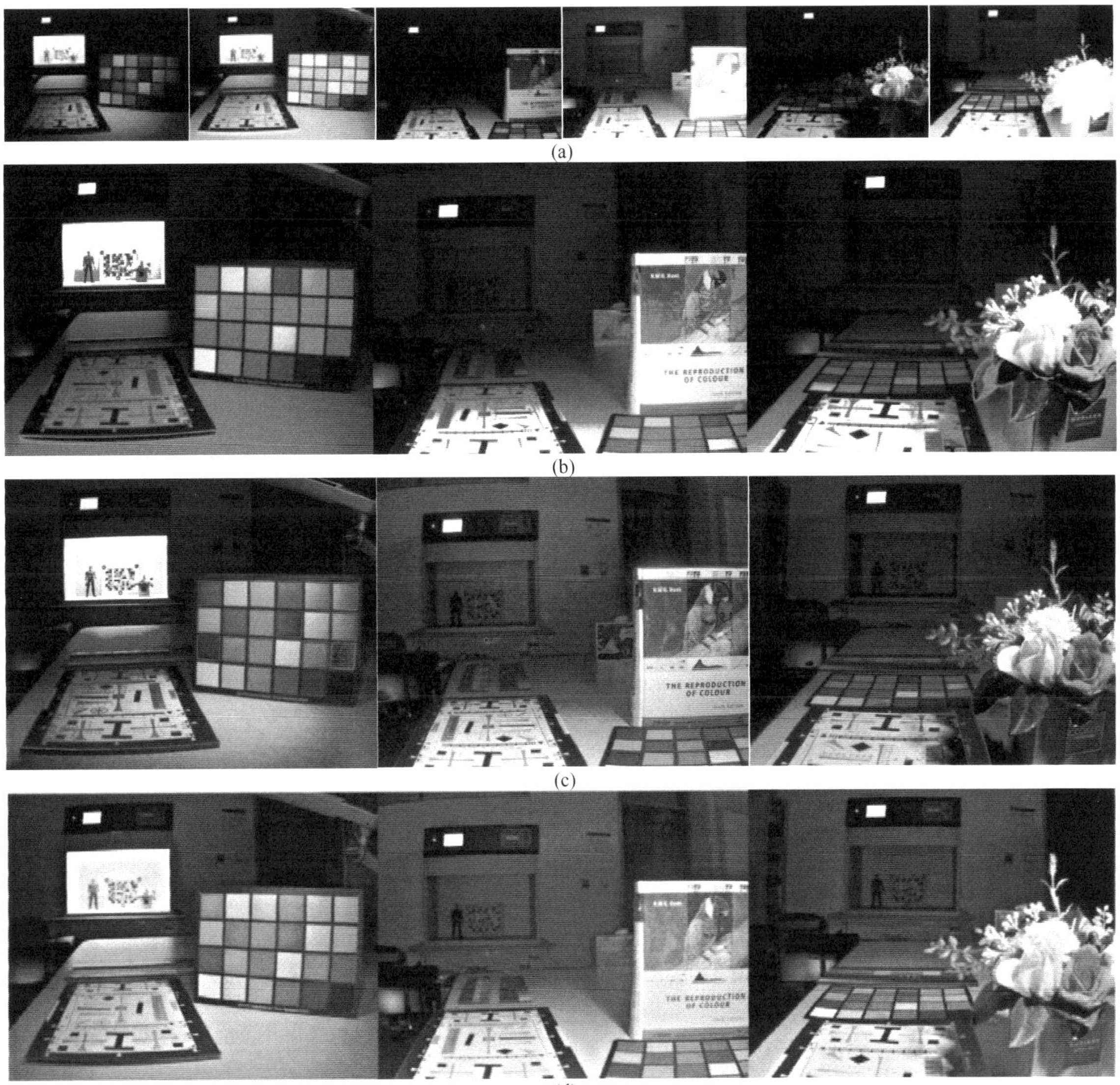

(a)

(b)

(c)

(d)

Fig. 5. Input(visible and NIR image) and resulting images: (a) input images, (b) SMML, (c) DRiC, (d) proposed

Sports Skill Analysis for Motion Data Focused On Frequency

Toshiyuki MAEDA
Department of Management Information
Hannan University, Japan
Email: maechan@hannan-u.ac.jp

Chikako MITSUYASU
Department of Management Information
Hannan University, Japan
Email: cmitsuyasu@hannan-u.ac.jp

Akiyoshi WAKATANI
Faculty of Intelligence and Informatics
Konan University, Japan
Email: wakatani@konan-u.ac.jp

***Abstract*—This paper presents data analysis for sports skill, focused on volleyball attack skill motion frequency. We try to justify a assumption that expert skills have relatively low frequency motions rather than novice skills as the similarity of human postural control. To this end, we use volleyball to attack the time series of moving images for experimentation and exercise techniques to analyze the movement frequency. In our research, volleyball play is analyzed with motion image data recorded by hi-speed cam-coder, where we do not use physical information such as body skeleton model. The time series data is measured from moving image data with four marker points and analyzed by fast Fourier transform (FFT) as well as Mel-frequency cepstral coefficients (MFCC), using clustering methods. The experimental results show that novice data has higher frequency data, which means that novice moves with high frequency motion, which may help us to assume that expert players use low frequency motion.**

Keyword: Sports skill, Motion frequency, Fast Fourier Transform, Mel-frequency cepstral coefficients

I. INTRODUCTION

For sports skills, most of researches treat structure models retrieved from body information, for instance, activity or bio-mechatronical data [7]. Those are possibly because of those belief that technical skill models consist of some skill hierarchies, which are environmental adjustment, human intention, and so on [10].

A research of Matsumoto et al. presents crafts-mens skill architecture model, and in the paper crafts-men select action procedure adapted with environments [6]. It is as though hard for expert workers to clarify their models by themselves. They treat unconsciously and achieve expert skill technique with their own models.

On the other hand, there are some researches for human postures. For instance, Nomura et al. [9] present that reaction force of human stance on the ground is modulated in hemodynamic cardiac cycle synchronously. They also implies that deterministic slow oscillations, which have intermittent features of control strategy, might be a basic mechanism to generate postural sways.

This implies that motor skills and normal motion control may have similar posture controls, which means that expert skills have lower frequency motions than novice ones. We had researched sports skills, and classify skill models by motion image analysis. This paper addresses a personal sports skill classification focused on volleyball play motion frequency using some analyzing methodologies.

II. BACKGROUND

As for the background of this research, we introduce some related works, and our previous works.

A. Our Previous Works

We have researched some of sports skill analyses. In [4], we focus on table tennis action, especially fore-hand strokes, as sports play, and classify skill models by time series motion image data analysis without physical structure models. We had investigated three play levels as expert, intermediate and novice, and try to discriminate the models by knowledge retrieval technologies. This research is a attempt to retrieve skill models only from motion image data. In this paper, we carry out experiments and the results suggests that the expert or intermediate subjects may group some categories as for technical skills, but there might not be "novice category," and that is because novice players' skills varies to each other. Moreover, reconstruct time series data are reconstructed from the original data, and apply the data into knowledge retrieval techniques as J48 (a C4.5 implementation), Naive Bayes Tree, and Random Forest. The recognition rate to evaluate data is quite bad, but that of J48 is better as for learning and test than the others. We thus make an attempt for two-class analysis, and that implies Intermediate class might be sorted as Novice class.

In [5], we present sports skill discrimination by motion image data for volleyball attack skill. This study aims to demonstrate that expert skills have lower frequency motions than novice skills as a hypothesis of human gesture control similarity. To this end, we examine through the volleyball attack time series of moving images to experiment and analyze the movement of motor skills frequency. In this research, we use high-speed cam encoders to record motion image data to analyze volleyball matches, and we do not deal with physical data like body skeleton models. The time series data is measured from moving image data with four marker points and analyzed by fast Fourier transform (FFT) using clustering methods. The experimental results show that the novice data of the y-axis has higher frequency data, which means that the novice action may have high-frequency motion, which may contribute to our hypothesis.

Based on these researches, this paper furthermore addresses analysis on motion frequency in various methodologies.

B. Related Works

A research by Kirschenbaum et al. [2] is that positive self-monitoring, more than the negative monitoring or control processes, might improve average scores of bowling for sixty unskilled league bowlers, by self-regulated laboratory researches.

However, negative self-monitoring seemed to produce relatively the best result for sixty seven skillful league bowlers. In partial support of the assumptions, positive self-monitoring makes significant progress for bowling averages, more than all other groups of low-skilled bowlers. In addition to other results in cognitive therapy and sports psychology, these results suggest they describes the circumstances in which the self-monitoring facilitates positively with self-regulation.

Smeetona et al. [11] show that the performance in team sports is based on the ability to recognize patterns of plays. Skills of pattern recognition might reuse from a sport to another one when there are some similarities in strategies, relations, and perceptual features. They might encode and decode useful information. In this research, expert and less expert volleyball, field hockey and soccer players' abilities for pattern recognition are investigated.

Subjects watch well-formed and ill-formed play sequences for all sports, and half of them are randomly showed with clips not previously viewed. Here they have to identify previous action sequence quickly and accurately. Pattern recognition skills are dependent to transfer on the skills of participants, practiced sports, the essence of tasks and extent of structures. In this research, expert soccer and hockey players are quicker than volleyball players to recognize soccer and hockey action plays. Performance is not different from the well-formed volleyball trials between the expert volleyball, field hockey and soccer players to each other. The expert field hockey and soccer players can reuse perceptual information or strategies among the respective sports. The results of novice participants are not so relevant. They discuss the transfer and diversity cross-over the domains for domain-specific skills.

Nomura et al. [9] report human being modulates ground reaction force with the quiet stance with cardiac cycles synchronously. In this research, periodic hemodynamic force almost causes small disturbance torque to ankle joints, and they are thought as a source of internal perturbation which causes postural sway. They hence consider dynamics of postural sway for reversed pendulum models for intermittent control strategy by comparison to usual feedback controller in continuous time sequence. They have investigated that each control model can exhibit human-like postural sway, featured by the behavior at low frequency band, on weak perturbation by periodic and randomly mimicking forcing hemodynamics.

They suggest that not continuous control with typical feedback gain but intermittent control exists in the human-like sway pattern. Furthermore, for generating the postural sway, there might a certain mechanism for deterministic, including chaotic, slow oscillations, and those are by intermittent control strategy in addition to the tiny hemodynamic perturbation.

Those researches are the basis of our researches, and among them, Nomura's work especially inspires us much and then this paper focuses on motion frequency.

III. Mel-frequency cepstral coefficients

For analysis of motion frequency, we introduce Mel-frequency cepstral coefficients (MFCCs) [3], [8] in addition to Fast Fourier transform.

The mel-frequency cepstrum (MFC) is a representations of the short-term sound power spectrum, and it is based on a log power spectrum with linear cosine transform, and thus on nonlinear mel scale of frequency in the field of sound processing.

MFCCs are coefficients which make up an MFC collectively. Those are derived from type of cepstral representations of audio clips, or a nonlinear "spectrum-of-a-spectrum."

The cepstrum and mel-frequency cepstrum is the most significantly different from the frequency bands in the MFC, and they are equally spaced on the mel scale. That looks after the response of human auditory system more closely than the linearly-spaced frequency bands in the normal cepstrum. For example, this frequency warping may show for better sound representation in the field of audio compression.

The Mel scale relates pitch, or perceived frequency, of pure tones to the actual measured frequency [1]. Human being is much better to discern small changes in pitch at low frequencies rather than at high frequencies. To introduce this scale may make the features fit more closely what human being listens.

The formula to convert from frequency to Mel scale is as follows:

$$M(f) = 1125 \ln(1 + \frac{f}{700})$$

To get from Mel scale back to frequency is as follows:

$$M^{-1}(m) = 700(e^{\frac{m}{1125}} - 1)$$

Brief steps to calculate MFCCs are as follows:

1) Make frames of the signals into short ones.
2) Take the periodogram estimate of power spectra for all frame.
3) Apply the mel filterbank to each power spectrum, then sum the energy for all filters.
4) Calculate logarithms of all filterbank energies.
5) Calculate DCT of all log filterbank energies.
6) Keep DCT coefficients two to thirteen, then discard the rest.

We introduce this methodology in addition to FFT as variation of feature retrieval from motion frequency data.

IV. Experiment and discussion

A. Experiment condition

We here make a target on volleyball attacks as well as the previous research [5], and attempt further analysis of volleyball attack.For this analysis, we use the same subjects who are six university students. In terms of skill analysis as representation of plays, we set up two levels as below;

- Expert class: members of university volleyball club, and
- Novice class: inexperienced students.

The subjects are three expert and three novice-level players in this experiment. All subject players are marked at four points as:

- Right elbow
- Right shoulder
- Right waist
- Left knee

FIGURE 1. Measurement markings.

Figure 1 presents the positions of markings for measuring. We record several motion images, or movies, for swing traces of attacks by a cam-corder. The recording situation is as follows:

- The cam-corder has a resolution of 512 × 384 pixels, and a frame-rate of 300 frames per seconds.
- It is installed besides of the players.
- Subjects play in several minutes, and during that time, some attack motions are recorded for each subject player.

B. FFT and MFCCs Analysis

In this research, we have an attempt to classify six subjects to each other. 300 frames (one minute) in the recorded movies are extracted from the start of the take-back till the end of the attack motion as well as previous research. After that, We retrieve two dimensional axes position data of four marking points for each frame shown as pixel values. The beginning point is fixed, for the basis of the coordinates, at the shoulder position of the first frame. We reconstruct feature vector data from time series data of each axis by MFCCs as well as FFT.

In the previous research [5], we use hierarchical clustering, but in this research, we attempt to classify each subject by logistic regression with cross validation.

The reason to apply logistic regression to this analysis is because:

- Clustering is a task to group sets of objects by similarity to each other.
- Logistic regression is one of appropriate regression analyses for conduction of dependent variables.
- One of objectives of this research is to investigate the possibility of classification for multi dependent variables data, and then logistic regression should be fit better than clustering.

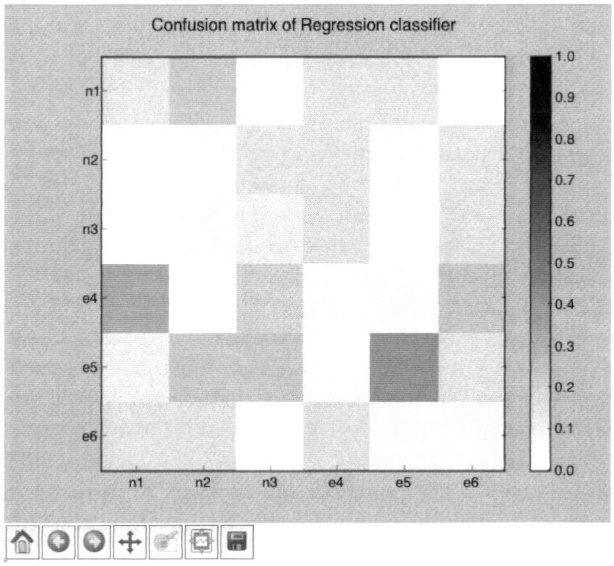

FIGURE 2. Confusion matrix of Regression classifier.

At first, we apply the logistic regression classifier to the draft time serial data. Figure 2 shows the classification result as confusion matrix using the draft data.

In this figure, the vertical axis is for "true class", and the horizontal axis for "predicted class." Moreover, 'n1','n2','n3' are from the data of novice subjects, and 'e4','e5','e6' are of expert subjects. Densities of squares indicate the percentage of correct prediction as shown in the right side of the figure, and so a denser diagonal square means a better classification result.

This diagram indicates the result is quite bad as for classification, though 'e5' may be classified correctly to a certain degree. The accuracy rate is 19.1%.

Figure 3 is the classification result by the FFT-based data.

This diagram indicates the result is also bad as for classification, though 'e4' and 'e5' may be classified correctly to a certain degree. The accuracy rate is 23.6%.

Figure 4 is the classification result by the MFCC-based data. Comparing to the above FFT-based classification, this result does not show so good, but a little better than the above result by FFT, as the accuracy rate is 51.6%.

In both cases, 'e5' is classified more clearly rather than the others, and that may indicate the skill of 'e5' is quite special,

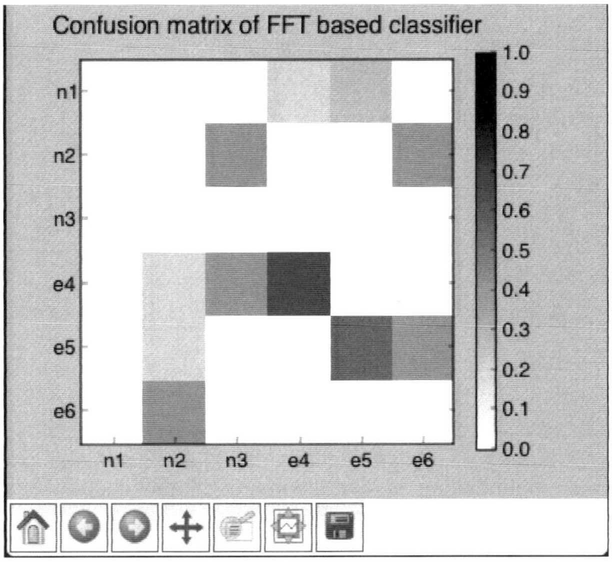

FIGURE 3. Confusion matrix of FFT based classifier.

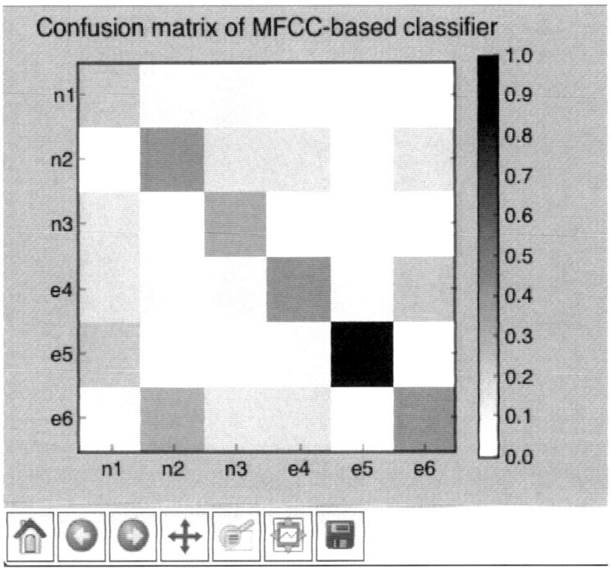

FIGURE 4. Confusion matrix of MFCC-based classifier.

though further experiments are needed as we don't think we have enough amount of data for this sort of analysis.

V. Conclusion

This paper presents motion frequency data analysis for sports skill, focused on volleyball attack skill. Volleyball play is analyzed with motion image data recorded and time series data are obtained from motion image with marking points.

We analyzed those data with view of motion frequency by using MFCCs and FFT methods, and then logistic regression techniques. We have the better classification result by MFCCs than that by FFT, and that suggests a possibility of skill research methodology by MFCCs, though further investigation is required.

For the future plans, we must have more experiments and research more precise data for identification. Moreover, we might use other classification technologies such as Recurrent Neural Network (RNN), and so forth.

Acknowledgment

Part of this research is supported by JSPS KAKENHI Grant Number 18K02920 and 19K0318. This research is partially assisted by Mr. Y. Tamari and Mr. Y. Tsujino at Hannan University, especially for data management. The authors greatly appreciate those.

References

[1] Practical Cryptography. Mel frequency cepstral coefficient (mfcc) tutorial. http://practicalcryptography.com/miscellaneous/machine-learning/guide-mel-frequency-cepstral-coefficients-mfccs/, 2016.

[2] A. M. Ordman D. S. Kirschenbaum, A. J. Tomarken, and R. Holtzbauer. Effects of differential self-monitoring and level of mastery on sports performance: Brain power bowling. *Cognitive Therapy and Research*, 6(3):335–341, 1982.

[3] B. Logan et al. Mel frequency cepstral coefficients for music modeling. In *ISMIR*, 2000.

[4] T. Maeda, M. Fujii, I. Hayashi, and T. Tasaka. Sport Skill Classification Using Time Series Motion Picture Data. In *Proceedings of the 40th Annual Conference of the IEEE Industrial Electronics Society (IECON 2014)*, pages 5272–5277, Dallas (TX, USA), 2014.

[5] T. Maeda and M. Yajima. Sports skill discrimination with motion frequency analysis. In *Proceedings of The 2016 Future Technologies Conference (FTC 2016)*, pages 250–253, San Francisco, CA (USA), 2016.

[6] Y. Matsumoto. *Organization and Skill – Organization Theory of Preservation of Technique (in Japanese)*. Hakuto Shobo, 2003.

[7] Y. Mochizuki, R. Himeno, and K. Omura. Artificial Skill and a New Principle in Sports (Special Issue on Digital Human : Measurement and Modeling of Human Functions) (in Japanese). *System, Control, and Information*, 46(8):498–505, 2002.

[8] S. Molau, M. Pitz, R. Schluter, and H. Ney. Computing mel-frequency cepstral coefficients on the power spectrum. In *Proceedings on IEEE International Conference on Acoustics, Speech, and Signal Processing (ICASSP'01)*, pages 73–76. IEEE, 2001.

[9] T. Nomura, S. Oshikawa, Y. Suzuki, K. Kiyono, and P. Morasso. Modeling human postural sway using an intermittent control and hemodynamic perturbations. *Mathematical Biosciences*, 245, iss.1:86–95, 2013.

[10] T. Shiose, T. Sawaragi, K. Kawakami, and O. Katai. Technological scheme for the preservation of technique from ecological psychological approach (in japanese). *Ecological Psychology Research*, 1(1):11–18, 2004.

[11] P. Wardb and A. M. Williamsa. Do pattern recognition skills transfer across sports? a preliminary analysis. *Journal of Sports Sciences*, 22(2):205–213, 2004.

SESSION

IMAGING SCIENCE, SECURITY AND SURVEILLANCE APPLICATIONS + WATERMARKING

Chair(s)

TBA

Robust Digital Watermarking and Recovery via Deep Residual Learning

Alwyn Aswin and Yanzhen Qu
School of Computer Science, Colorado Technical University, Colorado Springs, CO, USA

Abstract - *The internet age has led to an explosion of technologies that has made digital copying of media relatively easy, compared to the cost of production, often leading to widespread piracy. One mitigation to this problem is through watermarking. An ideal watermark should be invisible and robust, so it can be left behind on the host image as a poison pill, possibly laced with collateral to deter distribution. Common watermarking techniques often rely on spatial domain embedding, which often requires difficult tradeoffs between robustness and visibility. The closer the watermark to the center, the more robust, but also the more conspicuous. The closer to the margin, the easier to crop off without requiring major tradeoffs in viewing quality. The visibility also attracts the attention of many would be attackers. To ensure invisibility and robustness, this paper will focus on frequency domain embedding and robust recovery of attacked image by using deep residual learning, then explore the relationship between embedding strength and accuracy of detection. Should automatic detection fail, a manual verification is explored.*

Keywords: deep learning, Fourier, frequency domain watermarking, non-blind watermarking, robust watermarking

1 Introduction

One of the concerns that keeps artists from sharing their work digitally is the difficulty in controlling the mean of distribution after publication. When it comes to images this concern is often alleviated by watermarking the free copy. Nevertheless, traditional watermarking techniques usually does not go far enough to prevent unauthorized distribution after sales at which point traditional watermark is removed.

Fig. 1. A watermarked image sample [1].

In Fig. 1, the watermark in the image is located in the small area at the top left corner. A malicious attacker can simply crop the image to exclude the watermark or use one of the available watermark removal tools to circumvent it, without damaging the quality of the subject in the picture, consequently setting it up for unauthorized distribution.

Alternatively, a traditional watermark can be placed squarely on top of the subject itself, which makes it significantly harder to remove via cropping. This, however also prevents the viewing enjoyment of the subject. Consequently, such watermark will have to be removed at sales, after which point the image is unprotected. Some of the more sophisticated and free tools also allow watermark removal even when placed on top of the subject as seen below.

Fig. 2. Show three steps to quickly remove watermark through common tools (a) the original watermarked picture, (b) watermark location highlighted, (c) watermark removed [2].

Tools such as the one found at Theorex (n.d.) and shown in images 2 (a) – (c) can also help with quickly removing watermark, even one that stretches across the entire image as shown above.

2 Problem Statement, Hypothesis Statement and Research Questions

One of relatively effective mitigation methods of fighting the widespread digital art work piracy problem is through watermarking. An ideal watermark should be invisible and robust, so it can be left behind on the host image as a poison pill, possibly laced with collateral to deter distribution.

2.1 Problem Statement

Conventional watermarking techniques often rely on spatial domain watermark embedding which often requires difficult tradeoffs between robustness and invisibility because these two properties of the watermark are directly conflict in the spatial domain.

2.2 Hypothesis Statement

If we can find a method which can transfer the embedding watermarking from the spatial domain to the frequency domain where the tradeoff between two properties of the watermark, robustness and invisibility, is gradual and measurable, then we should be able to find a solution which can produce a relatively robust and invisible watermarking.

2.3 Research Questions

In this research, to prove the hypothesis statement, we have proposed the following five research questions:

"How will the Peak Signal to Noise Ratio (PSNR) of the host image change when watermark is embedded in the frequency domain compared to the spatial domain?"

"How will the PSNR of the recovered watermark change when watermark is embedded in the frequency domain compared to when it is embedded in the spatial domain after being subjected to common attack vectors such as compression, rotation, stretch, and skew?"

"How will the recovery and recognition of the watermark be automated?"

"How can manual intervention be attempted to save the identification process should automation process fail?"

"How will the watermark survive common medium transfer such as between a monitor and a phone camera, which likely undergoes convolution with a new point spread function?"

3 Related Work

Two desirable characteristics of digital watermarking are invisibility and robustness. Digital watermark should be invisible so that it detracts little from the normal enjoyment of the host content. Digital watermark also must be robust, so it can protect the host through possible tampering and removal attempts.

3.1 Invisible Fragile Watermarking

Singh, Shaw and Alam provide a great summary of the various watermarking techniques currently known [5]. The earliest known watermarking techniques are embedded in the spatial domain [5]. However, these techniques suffer due to the almost binary tradeoff between visibility and robustness that is also difficult to quantify [5]. The spatial domain techniques simplicity makes them among the most widely used digital watermarking techniques. After the spatial domain techniques, the frequency domain techniques were developed. The most well-known of these are the Discrete Cosine Transform (DCT), which is a type of quantized Fourier transform and Discrete Wavelet Transform DWT [5]. Singh, Shaw and Alam proposed using least significant bit substitution [5], which makes the watermark largely invisible at the expense of its fragility to common affine transformation attack vectors that does not require appreciable image quality degradation. Unlike Singh, Shaw and Alam, the technique described in this paper is a hybrid application of both frequency domain and spatial domain techniques. One of the greatest advantages of spatial domain technique is the robustness in watermark recovery when the embedding is specifically designed for such. Nevertheless, many of the more advanced embedding techniques usually ignore spatial properties and hence resort to linear distance functions such as correlation coefficient to recover watermark, which is insufficient if the watermark has been damaged beyond that which can be linearly correlated. Additionally, our ability to recognize symbols such as letters, characters, and alphabets are much more sophisticated than a simple correlation between two signals. Worst perhaps, is that embedding with correlation-based recovery tends to remove the option of manual intervention in case of systemic failure. Instead of using maximum correlation to match a scanned watermark and its origin, this paper advocates using deep learning techniques to relate the two.

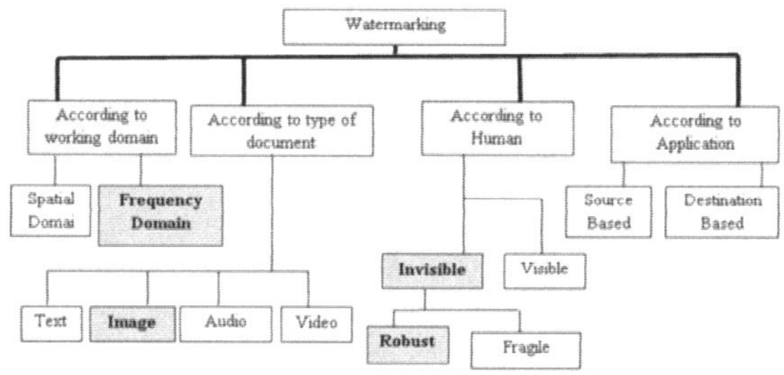

Fig. 3. Classification of watermarking [5].

3.2 Alpha Blending Robust Watermarking

Patra, Saha and Chakraborty elaborate another spatial domain watermarking schema with a summary over the most recent trends in digital watermarking an information hiding [3]. The evolution of invisible watermarking started from LSB scheme previously highlighted, moving towards jpeg compression based DCT domain embedding, and consequently jpeg2000 DWT [3]. DCT is essentially Fourier transform without the phase component or imaginary vector. DWT is a discrete decomposition of images into a tree like structure based on the delta of adjacent pixels of an image. In their paper, Patra, Saha, Chakraborty exploit the poor sensitivity of the HVS to red and blue colors in comparison to green [3]. However, like any watermarking in the spatial domain, visibility of the embedded image is fairly high as can be seen in the Figure 4, below. Additionally, in this paper the host image is conveniently rich in green, which provides a lot of cover to hide images in the respective red and blue channels. Frequency domain embedding proposed in this paper works even in grayscale images in addition to colored ones.

3.3 Invisible and Robust Watermarking

Riad, Harba, Douzi, Ros, & Elhajji in a collaboration between IRF-SIC laboratory in Morocco and PRISME laboratory in France described a Fourier based watermark embedding for ID images in smart cards [4]. Fourier based embedding was chosen because of its simplicity and proven robustness against affine transform, reprinting and noise-based attacks [4]. It was necessary that the watermark can survive both incidental and intentional tampering of a printed id card such as from wear and tear for up to 5 years, bending, and affine transforms during scanning process, as well as intentional reprinting and unauthorized copying [4]. Just like this paper, Riad, Harba, Douzi, Ros, & Elhajji simulated various common attack vectors that could affect the detection of the watermarks embedded in the frequency domain of host image [4]. Nevertheless, while the embedding scheme in this paper is similar to the proposal by Riad, Harba, Douzi, Ros & Elhajji [4], the watermark choice and its extraction as well as scoring mechanisms differ in that watermark recommended here should be both humanly verifiable and machine automatable through deep residual network. The deep network is expected to capture non-linear relationship between the pixels of the rasterized symbols to that of the original watermark using trained convolutional filters.

4 Research Design

This research will combine both frequency domain and spatial domain watermark embedding with proven robustness. In this scheme, a humanly recognizable watermark is inserted into the frequency domain of the host image. Upon reverting the host image back into the spatial domain, the watermark is consequently converted into its frequency representation. The two images essentially swap domains. In this scheme recovery of the watermark can be done using deep learning techniques or through manual human interventions.

To make the watermark robust and tamper proof, it will be generated from a symbol that is then rasterized and turned into an image. Rasterized image exists in multiple domains at the same time. It exists in the spatial domain and also in the lexical-symbolic domain if it contains letter and words and potentially content rich inferential knowledge graph. As a result, the human brain and a trained system can quickly recover missing information by building knowledge graph that can infer the missing information from the intact evidence. For example in a word scramble ω = "Ap_le", the Pr(ω' == "Apple" | ω) >> Pr(ω' != "Apple" | ω) where $\omega' \in W$, W is the universe of all English words and ω is the surviving evidence of ω'. Similarly, each pixel in a raster image can be treated as evidences and predictors that generate letters, then words, which can be used to infer the identity of the watermark given a set of possible watermarks.

The proposed robust watermarking technique must have self-inferential property such that: Let I be the original image and w` be the watermarked image after it was tampered. And L, are letters in the watermark and D, are words spanned by the letters, then we want a watermarking scheme such that:

$$\Pr(w|D, L, w', I) \gg \Pr(w_i|D, L, w', I) \text{ for all } I, w_i \subset W \quad (1)$$

where W is the set of all possible watermarks.

And that Pr(w | D, L, w`, I) should follow a Bayesian inference such that using the chain rule:

$$Pr(w|D,L,w`,I) \propto Pr(D|L,w',I,w) \times Pr(L|w',I,w)Pr(w'|I,w) \times Pr(I|w)Pr(w) \quad (2)$$

This inferential property is useful, because even when part of the information is missing or corrupted, as is typical when the image is attacked, the remaining pixels, letters can still be used to ascertain the most likely watermark among prospective candidates.

To prove the hypothesis that in frequency domain embedded watermark can create a watermark that is invisible and measurably robust against removal attempts the following experiment is designed.

4.1 Watermark Embedding Procedure

Below are the details of the procedure of watermark embedding.

a. Given an image I(x,y), we want to find the corresponding image in frequency domain F(p,q) using Fourier transform *F*. Hence:

$$\mathcal{F}(I(x,y)) \rightarrow F(p,q) \quad (3)$$

b. A watermark image W containing semi randomly placed letters or symbols is generated.

c. A smarter attack vector such as the one described in Google's paper, detects the geometry of the watermark to compromise the most valuable evidence pixel, potentially undermining the symbol inference proposed in this paper [6]. Hence. We want to randomize the geometry of the watermark by randomizing its placement [6].

d. We will define the embedding technique in the host frequency domain as:

$$F'(p,q) = F(p,q) + \delta \times \sqrt{\left(p-\frac{pmax}{2}\right)^2 + \left(q-\frac{qmax}{2}\right)^2} * F(p,q)W(x,,y) \quad (4)$$

   a. δ is the embedding strength.
   b. The Euclidian distance function from the center of the Fourier frequency representation:

$$d(p,q) = \sqrt{\left(p-\frac{pmax}{2}\right)^2 + \left(q-\frac{qmax}{2}\right)^2} \quad (5)$$

   ensures that embedding is proportional to the increase in frequency. This embedding is designed so that the watermark signal strength is stronger at the higher frequencies as these frequencies can carry more information.
   c. $F'(p,q)$ is the frequency domain image with watermark embedded.

e. The resulting watermarked image in the spatial domain will then be found by applying inverse Fourier transform $\mathcal{F}'$.
   a. Hence the watermarked image:

$$\mathcal{F}'(F'(p,q)) \rightarrow I_w \quad (6)$$

f. The watermark W and I will be persisted in a data store, to be used as class prior probability, when computing the most probable watermark for a given surviving pixels.

g. Why this is expected to work:
   a. Human eyes are not sensitive to images in frequency domain.
   b. Embedding watermark image in the frequency domain through pixel wise operation is equivalent to convolution with the watermark frequency image with that of the original image.

$$\mathcal{F}(F'(p,q)) = \mathcal{F}(F(p,q) + \delta \times d(p,q) \times F(p,q) \times W(p,q)) for \forall p \forall q \in I$$
$$= \mathcal{F}\big(F \odot (1 + \delta \times d \times W)\big)$$
$$= \mathcal{F}(\mathrm{F}) * \mathcal{F}\big((1 + \delta \times \mathrm{d} \times \mathrm{W})\big)$$
$$= \mathcal{F}(F) * \mathcal{F}\big((1 + \delta \times d \times W)\big) \quad (7)$$

h. Hence the watermarked image I_w, is a convolution of the original image with the frequencies of the watermark embedded with linearly increasing strength at distance from center.

$$I_w = I * \mathcal{F}\big((1 + \delta * d * W)\big) \quad (8)$$

4.2 Extraction Procedure

Below are the details of the Extraction Procedure:

a. In a real environment, we will need to solve the inverse of the attack functions carried out in the previous subsection. For linear transformation, this can be done by minimizing the Least Squared Error (LSE) of the overdetermined system and solving for the inverse matrix of the affine transform using the SURF or SIFT feature points between the original and the compromised image.

b. Image matrix of the watermark will also have to be standardized against the original. That is:

$$I''_w = I'_w - \big(\mathrm{Average}(I'_w) - \mathrm{Average}(I_o)\big) \quad (9)$$
$$I'''_w = I''_w * \mathrm{StdDev}(I_o)/\mathrm{StdDev}(I''_w) \quad (10)$$

c. We take the potentially compromised watermarked image I'''_w, and convert it back to frequency domain to recover the watermark, we apply the inverse of the embedding process.

$$W(p,q) = ((\mathcal{F}(I'''_w) - F(p,q)) / (\delta \times d \times F(p,q)) \quad (11)$$

d. We then find the most probable watermark using residual neural network as a proxy for Bayesian inference.

e. The result of the classification is recorded so they can be plotted against the PSNR of the watermark, which is affected by the embedding factor δ, and the PSNR of the watermarked image, after it was compromised in a possible attempt to remove the watermark.

4.3 Overview of Watermark Robustness Test

Below are the steps of the Watermark Robustness Test.

a. 200 unique watermarks are generated.

b. For each watermark, we apply 1000 affine transformations and salt and pepper noises of varying pseudo random strength generated using Box-Muller algorithm around a reasonable normal.

c. The PSNRs of the images before and after the attempted attacks vs. the original are recorded.

d. After minor filtering, watermark is extracted.

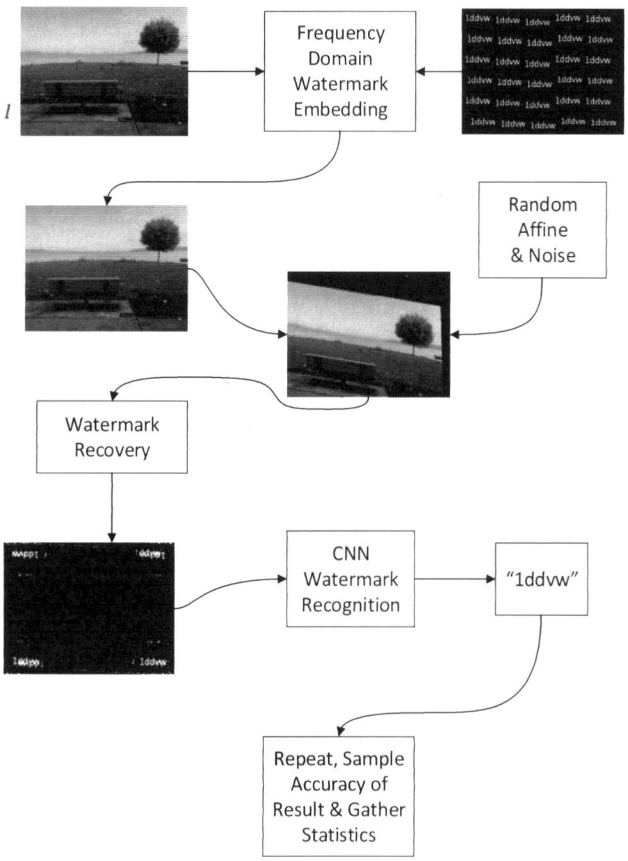

Fig. 4. Experiment Workflow. A workflow of the watermark embedding, attack simulation and recovery experiment.

e. ½ of the 200,000 extracted watermarks is used to train 8 layers residual network. The residual neural network is made up of 5 residual, convolutional layers and 4 fully connected layers, all with rectifier linear unit aka. ReLu activation functions and trained using cross entropy loss function and stochastic gradient descent (SGD) learner. The resulting model is then applied to the entire extracted watermark images, to predict the original watermark.

f. A manual test will be included in the experiment. Watermarked image is copied from a monitor using a cell phone camera to ensure that the surviving watermark is recognizable despite the change of medium.

4.4 A Deep Residual Convolutional Neural Network for Watermark Detection

A deep residual Convolutional Neural Network (CNN) was trained to classify over 200 distinct watermark symbols recovered each altered from 1000 distinct damages applied to the host image in a pseudo random manner while simulating common attack vectors.

Preprocessing steps:

a. Reverse affine transform is applied to the watermarked image. The inverse matrix can be commonly found by solving the least squared error equation of the affine transform that maps the post-attack to pre-attack SIFT or SURF feature points.
b. Images are downscaled to 150x150 pixels.
c. Median filter is applied on 4x4 squares.
d. Grayscale image is turned into binary image with threshold of 0.0000000001 luminance value.
e. Because the surviving watermarks come from the high frequency corners, the images are further shrunk into 64x64 pixels with four channels, each channel coming from a distinct corner.

Training Steps:

a. Convolutional Neural Network with kernel width and height of 7 pixels.
b. Stride size of 1.
c. Each residual layer is made up of 3 layers: ReLu skip layer with Glorot activation and bias parameter 0. A batch normalization layer, and a summation layer that adds the output of the normalization layer to the output from 2 layers prior.
d. The number of output filters for each of the 5 residual layers are: 64, 128, 256, 512, and 512 respectively.
e. The residual layers are aggregated using max value pooling layer with 4 x 4 window and a stride size of 1.
f. The result of the pooling layer is fed into 4 dense (fully-connected) layers with 512, 384, 384 and 256 ReLu nodes.
g. The chosen classification error function is Cross Entropy with Softmax.
h. Learning rate is 0.048 with minibatch size of 40 picked at random. Training is continued indefinitely until it exceeds 60% accuracy.

Validation steps:

a. We validate against all 200,000 sample watermarks recovered after the attack simulations and then record the values expected and the predicted by the network.
b. Only 100,000 (50%) was previously seen by the deep network and used in the training set. The remaining 100,000 is new and will require the network to infer the proper classification.

5 Experiments and Results

5.1 Result Evaluation of the Watermarking Technique

We use peak signal to noise ratio PSNR as a proxy to measure the tradeoffs between the quality of the watermarked image and the subsequent robustness of the watermark in resisting attempts of removal without similarly destroying the quality of the original content.
Hence:

$$\frac{PSNR_{post-attack}}{PSNR_{watermarked}} \propto Accuracy \quad (12)$$

The resulting fraction indicates the ratio of the quality introduced from attempted watermark removal divided by the quality after the watermark embedding. These fractions are binned and plotted using R against the probability of correct watermark detection (accuracy) using the residual neural network discussed before. The result is as follow:

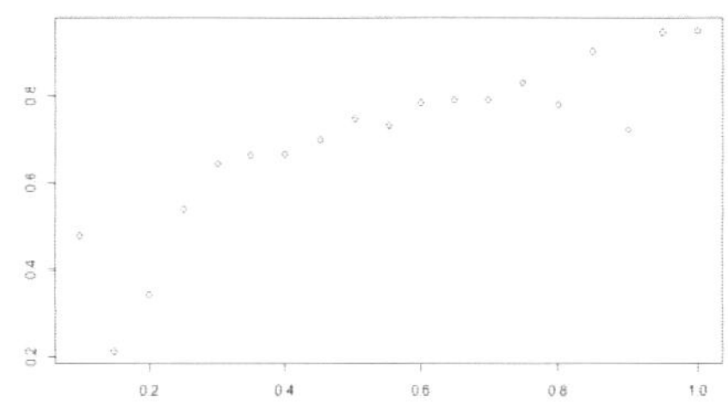

Fig. 5. Scatter plot between PSNR ratio and chance of detection. Generated in R from the command: plot(as.numeric(truncated2$postAttack/truncated2$psnrWatermark), truncated2$isPredicted)

From the graph above, the detection rate follows logarithmic rate from the ratio of the PSNR. Using R to confirm the relationship of the two:

```
> model <- lm(aggregated1$detection.rate ~
log(aggregated1$group.max),data=aggregated1)
> summary(model)

Call:
lm(formula = aggregated1$detection.rate ~
log(aggregated1$group.max), data = aggregated1)
Residuals:
      Min        1Q    Median        3Q       Max
-0.187998 -0.009383  0.009788  0.044250  0.181041
Coefficients:
            Estimate Std. Error t value Pr(>|t|)
(Intercept) 0.89783  0.03094  29.021 6.36e-16 ***
log(aggregated1$group.max) 0.26084 0.03092 8.437
1.76e-07 ***
---
Signif. codes:
0 '***' 0.001 '**' 0.01 '*' 0.05 '.' 0.1 ' ' 1
Residual standard error:
0.08653 on 17 degrees of freedom
```

```
Multiple R-squared:
0.8072,  Adjusted R-squared:  0.7959
F-statistic:
71.18 on 1 and 17 DF,  p-value: 1.756e-07
```

The findings indicate significant correlation between the logarithmic model and the original scatter plot as indicated by the low Std. Error and P-Value. The adjusted R-Squared and R-Squared show considerable correlation between the model and dataset. Plotting model with its upper and lower bound of std. deviation:

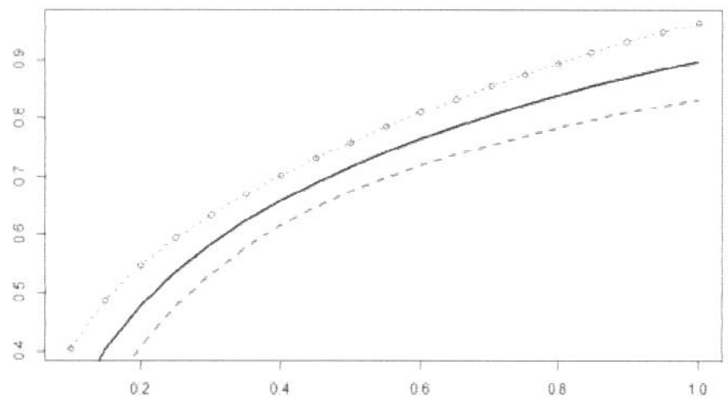

Fig. 6. Model plot between PSNR ratio and chance of detection. Generated in R with upper and lower std deviation bounds.

The formula that predicts the probability of successful recovery of the original watermark when using a residual network employed in this experiment is as follow:

$$Pr(Success) = 0.20684 \times \log(\frac{PSNR_{post-attack}}{PSNR_{watermarked}}) \quad (13)$$

There are 3 levers in this watermarking scheme to improve robustness, described in this equation. Embedding factor can be increased at the cost of additional error from the original image. Alternatively, preprocessing can be attempted to reduce the error in the watermarked image. An image preprocessing technique can be employed to fold the symbols back into one, although this will require knowing their pseudo random placements. The last option is to write a better neural network that improves on the accuracy of the detection and thereby improving the coefficients in the formula above. The curvature of the model indicates that the power of the neural network in identifying the watermark drops precipitously when the attack degrades the image quality as measured using PSNR by a factor of 1/0.14626~7X worse than the original.

5.2 Visualization

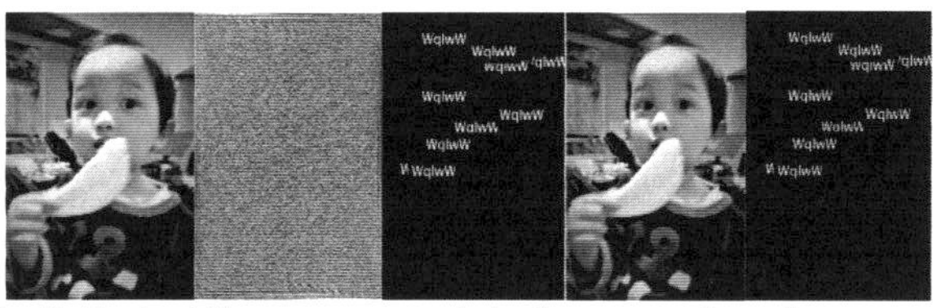

Fig. 7. Embedding a watermark in frequency domain

From left to right. Fig. 7 (a). The original image, unwatermarked. Fig. 7 (b). The image from Figure 7 (a) after undergoing Fourier transform to frequency domain. Fig. 7 (c). A watermark, which is a 5 letters randomly generated string, placed in random location, to avoid detection through aggregation and to ensure that watermark is unique. Fig. 7 (d). The image from 7 (a), now embedded with the watermark. The PSNR of this is 42.6774 dB, compared to the original. This falls right between 35 dB and 54 dB of the typical and ubiquitous JPEG compression scheme [7]. Fig. 7 (e). The watermark extracted from Figure 7 (d). This watermark has a noise level of 21.32 dB compared to the original.

5.3 Surviving an Attack

Visual verification can also be done to ensure that the watermarking scheme can survive random attacks such as affine transforms and noise addition. The following set of images describe a common attack scenario.

Fig. 8. Example of surviving an attack

In clock-wise direction. Fig. 8(a). Shows the watermark image to be inserted to the image into 8(b). Fig. 8(b). Shows the original image to be protected. Fig. 8(c). After watermarking. Fig. 8(d). Shows the host image after possible scaling, translation, cropping, rotation, shear, and salt & pepper noise attacks. This image is barely useable as far as content is concerned. A traditional watermark in the right corners of the image would not be recognizable at this point. Fig. 8(e). Most of the watermark was destroyed in the attack, but the identification string "Z8WM8" is still recognizable if only barely.

5.4 A Real-World Attack Surviving Test

Surviving a transfer of medium between a monitor and a camera is a difficult test for this watermarking scheme. Digital camera and LCD monitor just like our watermarking scheme applies convolution with the device characteristic point spread function to render or capture the image, adding significant amount of noise in the same space as the one used to embed the watermark.

Fig. 9. An example of real-world attack surviving test

From left to right. Fig. 9(a). Original B&W image watermarked. Fig. 9(b). The same image after it was copied through a digital camera from the monitor. Fig. 9(c). The watermark recovered from the camera copied image. The amount of noise makes it necessary to normalize the size, standard deviation and mean of the pixel values. Which is done by the following Matlab code.

```
copy1 = rgb2gray(imresize(copy1, [height, width]));
copy1 = (std(double(base),0,'all')/std(double(copy1),0,'all')) * copy1;
copy1 = copy1 - (mean(copy1, 'all') - mean(base,'all'));
```

The watermark recovered from the copied image is very faint, but again a few letters stand out. This is where the inferential property of the watermark is important. The surviving letters that can still be made out are z_sCF. Nevertheless 4 of 5 letters are enough to narrow down the original watermark.

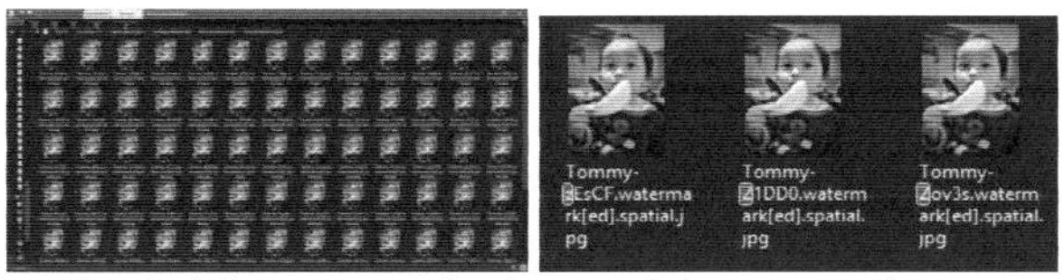

Fig. 10. Find the watermark after surviving an attack

Left to right. Fig. 10(a). A proxy for a file system containing all the possible image watermarks. Searching for watermark that starts with "z", narrows down the search to only 3 images out of 81, and only one of them ends with "sCF". Fig. 10(b). Searching the most likely watermark.

6 Conclusion

Watermark can have many values including tracking the original customer who made available the first unauthorized distribution. Watermark can also be used to embed collateral information such as credit card number, name and address into the purchased image to create a poison pill to discourage redistribution. An invisible and robust watermark is important because the watermark can continue to protect the content after the content is transferred to the customer.

In this research, we have demonstrated that the watermark embedded in the frequency domain can be not only invisible and robust, but also easily recovered by applying deep residual learning even after an attack. The tradeoff between image quality and robustness can be predicted by simulating attacks and automating the detection using deep learning network. Using this knowledge, a weighted cost-benefit analysis can be performed to decide the quality threshold below which point protecting the watermarked content is no longer deemed worthwhile.

7 References

[1] A modern way of watermarking, at your fingertips. (n.d.). Retrieved from https://www.watermark.ws/features/watermarking

[2] Teorex. (n.d.). Easily Remove Watermark from a Photo. Retrieved from https://www.theinpaint.com/inpaint-how-to-remove-watermark-from-a-picture.html

[3] Patra, A., Saha, A., Chakraborty, A. K., & Bhattacharya, K. (2018, March). A new approach to invisible water marking of color images using alpha blending. In *2018 Emerging Trends in Electronic Devices and Computational Techniques (EDCT)* (pp. 1-4). IEEE.

[4] Riad, R., Harba, R., Douzi, H., Ros, F., & Elhajji, M. (2016). Robust fourier watermarking for id images on smart card plastic supports. *Advances In Electrical and Computer Engineering*, *16*(4), 23-30.

[5] Singh, R. K., Shaw, D. K., & Alam, M. J. (2015). Experimental studies of LSB watermarking with different noise. *Procedia Computer Science*, *54*, 612-620.

[6] Dekel, T., Rubinstein, M., Liu, C., & Freeman, W. T. (2017, July). On the Effectiveness of Visible Watermarks. In *Proceedings of the IEEE Conference on Computer Vision and Pattern Recognition* (pp. 2146-2154).

[7] Saffor, A., Ramli, A. R., & Ng, K. H. (2001). A Comparative study of image compression between JPEG and wavelet. Malaysian Journal of computer science, 14(1), 39-45.

Designing a Robust Image Steganography Algorithm Using the Discrete Cosine Transform

Jemilade Longe[1], Gahangir Hossain[1], and Ayush Goyal[1]
[1]Department of Electrical Engineering and Computer Science, Texas A & M University - Kingsville, Texas, USA

Abstract - *There is a great need to overcome the increasingly difficult challenge of using digital mediums to transfer sensitive data including images in a fast but secure way. Previous solutions to this challenge have been centered around cryptography mostly data encryption. This paper involves a more recent developed solution which can be used on mobile devices, known as steganography to augment the failures of encryption. Many of the previous image steganographic schemes use complex algorithms to embed pictures known as payload images, into image files known as cover images to get stego images. Hence, this research aims at developing a novel method to embed and recover payload images in cover images. The novel steganography method employed here is based on the discrete cosine transform (DCT) combined with the least significant bit (LSB) method, and it has been shown to give better signal to noise ratio of the recovered payload image as compared to previous discrete wavelet transform (DWT) and LSB based methods.*

Keywords: Cybersecurity, Signal-to-noise-ratio, Image Processing, Steganography, Least Significant Bit, Discrete Cosine Transform.

1 Introduction

Since the internet and digital age were birthed, transmission of images and their data has been easier and faster, but also less secure. The problem with securely transmitting information in digital media has recently become a challenge to be taken more seriously for the sake of security. The more information that is made available on the Internet, the more owners of such information need to protect themselves from theft and false representation [1]. There is a great need to overcome the increasingly difficult challenge of using digital mediums to transfer sensitive data and images in a fast but secure way.

This is because in the digital age, many more computing devices are getting designed to use cloud computing platform rather than the do the computation themselves. Hence transmission of sensitive digital information between personal computing devices and the cloud servers over networks [2].

Previous solutions to this challenge have been to encrypt sensitive image data before transmission and decrypt upon receival of the data. Although encrypted data may not be interpreted by illegal information hunters, this method has been proved to be unsafe because it is difficult to conceal. This is not very helpful as encryption can sometimes be illegal in some circumstances. Furthermore, it is nearly impossible to develop and implement an encryption-decryption scheme that will not be compromised over time. While encryption and cryptography are frequently used in information security systems, a newer and relatively more secure approach of transmitting securely, called Steganography has recently began to develop.

Steganography has been developed to augment the failures of encryption. Its goal is to covertly embed and retrieve hidden data in a carrier [3]. Steganography seems more secure as eavesdroppers may not know that the valuable data that they are looking for to steal is being transmitted. This makes it possible for steganography to be able to hold its own against attacks from unintended recipients with a significantly large amount of time and computing resources.

There are many various steganography techniques. Though each steganography technique may have its relevance, trade-off and applications. Some of these steganography techniques may be more complex with respect to others. For example, some applications may require total imperceptibility of the secret information which is usually small in size, while other applications demand a larger secret message to be hidden but under a fair amount of invisibility [4].

The challenges involved in previous image steganographic schemes is that they use extremely and unnecessarily complex algorithms to embed pictures and text known as stego images, into image files known as cover images.

The following sections of this paper are ordered as follows: in Section 2, a literature review of steganography techniques and schemes is discussed. Previous implementations of relevant image steganography schemes are discussed and analyzed in Section 3. Then a new and effective image steganography scheme based on the combination of the Least Significant Bit (LSB), and the Discrete Cosine Transform (DCT) methods is proposed in Section 4. In Section 5, details and results of designed experiments from the proposed methods are presented. Finally, the conclusion and analysis of the results, are discussed in Section 6.

2 Literature review

The word "Steganography" was derived from the Greek language. It is literally translated as "covered writing" [1]. Steganography was quoted to be used as far back as 440 BC, by the Greek historian, Herodotus who tattooed on the shaved heads of some of his slaves, some secret message. After the slave's hair regrew with passing time, Herodotus would order his slave with the secret message to go to the intended receiver. During the second World War, the Germans applied a technique known as Microdots. The aim of this technique was to decrease the size a secret information image or message until it was about the size of the typed period. As time went on, the Microdots technique was applied to shrink the secret message, the secret message was then put on a wooden piece after which the secret message was hidden by covering it with wax. Another application of steganography developed during World War II was a technique known as invisible ink. The invisible ink technique was implemented by writing the secret message on a paper using a certain kind of ink referred to as invisible ink. The retrieval of the secret message was possible only when the paper was heated [5].

The author of the prisoner's problem explained the concept of steganography in a more understanding manner [6]. The purpose of digital steganography is therefore to hide a secret digital message in a digital carrier or cover medium which could be an image, a video, a body of text, a wireless communication channel or an audio signal. To effectively hide data, one is required to understand the characteristics of the cover medium that is being used [7].

Although many digital file formats may be applied in steganography, there are four main categories of file formats that can be used for steganography are shown in Figure 1 below. The formats that are best applicable for steganography are those with a significant amount of redundancy data. Redundancy can be defined in [8] as the bits of an object that provide accuracy far greater than necessary for the object's use and display. The research in [9] described the redundant data bits of a medium as those bits within that medium that can be altered in a way that the medium is not noticeably altered. Digital image, video and audio files may easily have a large amount of redundant data. For this reason, digital images are frequently used for hiding secret information. Hence, this work will focus on hiding information in images in the next sections.

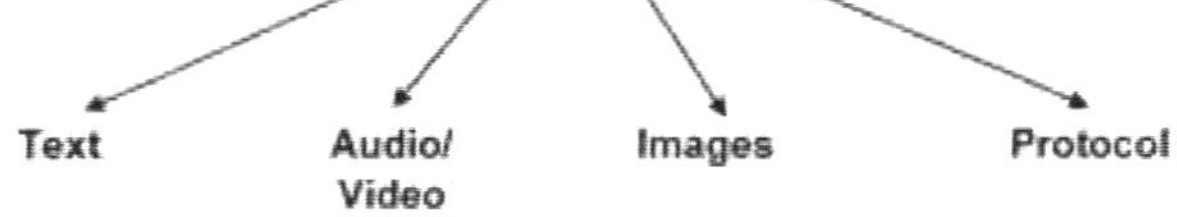

Figure 1: An overview of carrier media that can be used for steganography.

2.1 Image steganography

There are two main classifications of techniques used in image steganography:

1. Spatial Domain Techniques
2. Frequency Domain Techniques

Each technique within these classifications above has its strengths and weaknesses. Frequency domain techniques may be highly robust, have higher capacity to hide more information, and be much harder to detect, but will require a lot of computing resources to implement. On the other hand, spatial domain techniques may be simpler to implement, but may have a smaller capacity to hide information in images. The tradeoff between image steganographic techniques depend on the situation in which image steganography is to be applied. Figure 2 below shows the classification of image steganography techniques.

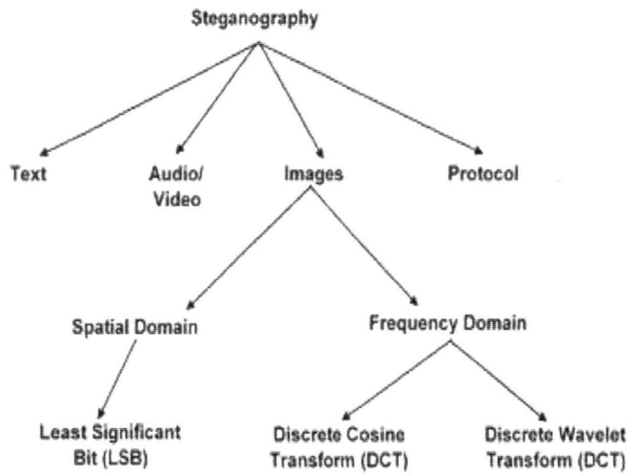

Figure 2: An overview of steganography with emphasis on image steganography.

2.1.1 *Spatial domain techniques*

Spatial domain techniques are centered on hiding information in images, by slightly changing the absolute values of certain pixels in an image. Usually, the least significant bits (LSB) of the pixels' value are the ones that are changed. They are relatively easier to implement and may not require much computational power to implement. The challenge with spatial domain techniques is that the human eye may be sensitive enough to detect a direct absolute value change exceeding the four least significant bits (±16) in pixels that are very close to each other. For this reason, spatial domain techniques do not have a high capacity to hide information in images. Spatial domain techniques are also called LSB methods.

2.1.2 *Frequency domain techniques*

To understand how frequency domain techniques work, the concept of image compression must be revised. Image compression is the process of reducing irrelevant and redundant information of the image to be able to store or transmit that image data in an efficient form. Image compression is minimizing the size in bytes of an image file, which may degrade the quality of the image slightly, but not to an unacceptable level [10].

Frequency domain techniques are the reason why steganography is possible in JPEG images which are widely common but have a lossy compression. The LSB method can have some distortion in the information that it intends to hide in JPEG images due to lossy compression. Unlike spatial domain techniques, frequency domain techniques do not directly affect or change the absolute values of certain pixels in an image. Frequency domain techniques rather manipulate how computers remove non-trivial information from an image when storing that image. Computers use image transformations techniques to store most of the information of an image at a fraction of the memory size of that image. They are relatively more complex to implement and may require much computational power to implement. Frequency domain techniques have a high capacity to hide information in images and they are much harder to detect compared to the LSB method [11]. The common frequency domain techniques used are the Discrete Cosine Transform (DCT) and the Discrete Wavelet Transform (DWT).

The DCT domain technique is used more frequently. The reason for this is that the digital images are usually compressed using widely known DCT based techniques by digital cameras [11]. DCT-based steganography is implemented by hiding information in an image either by manipulating the DCT quantization table, or by altering the DCT coefficients of that image, for example by changing the least significant bit of each coefficient. The variances between the transmitted payload image and extracted payload are largely affected by the method used to calculate DCT [10].

DWT domain technique is relatively newer. It was used in the JPEG2000 compression technique. It is implemented by modifying certain wavelet coefficients of the image [12].

It is assumed the digital images do not vary with time, hence wavelet transform coefficients may not be noticeably more accurate than the DCT coefficients. Hence, the DCT is still the more popular compression technique applied on digital images.

3 Previous work

In "A Novel Approach of Color Image Hiding using RGB Color planes and DWT" the authors used the Discrete Wavelet Transform (DWT) to split the cover and secret images into four blocks/bands (LL1, LH1, HL1, HH1). The LL1 band was then again split using the Discrete Wavelet Transform, into four bands (LL2, LH2, HL2, HH2). The LL2 band was split again using DWT into another four bands (LL3, LH3, HL3, HH3). The cover, payload and stego images were the same size. The authors used a technique called the alpha blending technique to blend the cover image and the secret image together to create a stego image. The alpha blending technique has a formula below:

Stego Image pixel = (alpha * cover image's pixel) + ((1.0-alpha) * (secret image's pixel))

Extraction of secret image is gotten from the formula below:

Extracted secret image's pixel = (Stego Image pixel - (alpha * cover image's pixel) ÷ (1.0-alpha)

The authors performed image quality checks using the Signal to Noise Ratio (PSNR) to compare the relationship between the cover image and stego image. The PSNR was also used to compare the payload and extracted payload images [13].

In "Performance Evaluation of DWT Based Image Steganography", The authors used the Discrete Wavelet Transform (DWT) to split the cover images into four blocks/bands: Approximation (CA), Horizontal detail (CH), Vertical detail (CV) and Diagonal detail (CD). Embedding of the secret image was done in the CV, CH and CD bands to reduce the difference between the cover and the stego images. The DWT was also implemented on the secret image to get four blocks which were similar to that of the cover image. The approximation (SA) was the only band to be embedded and extracted. The authors compared the recovered embedded image to the actual payload by measuring the SNR. The stego and cover images were also compared by measuring the SNR [14].

The challenge with this paper is that it involves a complex error matching scheme to produce a secret-key which determines which pixel in the cover image that each pixel in the secret image will be embedded in, this approach is more complex compared with proposed algorithm in this paper. The approach by the authors also produces a SNR that is barely as good as the proposed algorithm in this paper.

4 Proposed steganography algorithm

In the method, a spatial technique and a frequency domain technique are combined to implement image steganography. There are three steps in the proposed image steganographic algorithm:

1. Data Hiding Algorithm
2. Data Recovery Algorithm
3. Signal to Noise Ratio (SNR) estimation

4.1 Data hiding algorithm

First, an image **M** to be hidden in a cover image **C** is first resized to the dimensions of **C** to get **M_resized. M_resized** is then darkened by dividing all its values by a positive integer (in this case 2) to get **M_dark**. Then the DCT is applied to the darkened image (**M_dark**) to get a new matrix **Diff_Transmit.** Then **Diff_Transmit** affects the LSBs of the cover image by being added to, or subtracted from the cover image **C** to get a stego image **C_stego** which is then transmitted over an unsecure channel. It should be noted that the maximum value of **Diff_Transmit** is relatively small (≤ 8) and hence, **C_stego** looks very much like **C**.

$$\boldsymbol{M\_resized} = \boldsymbol{imresize}(\boldsymbol{M}, \boldsymbol{size}(\boldsymbol{C})) \quad (1)$$

$$\boldsymbol{M\_dark} = \boldsymbol{M\_resized} \div \boldsymbol{4} \quad (2)$$

$$\boldsymbol{Diff\_Transmit} = \boldsymbol{DCT}(\boldsymbol{M\_dark}) \quad (3)$$

$$\boldsymbol{C\_Stego} = \boldsymbol{C} \pm \boldsymbol{Diff\_Transmit} \quad (4)$$

4.2 Data recovery algorithm

The receiver receives the stego image **C_stego** which is transmitted over an unsecure channel. It is assumed that the receiver has a copy of the original cover image **C**. The receiver then subtracts the pixel values of **C_stego** from **C** to get a matrix called **False_Diff**. Then the Inverse DCT is applied to **False_Diff** to get a new matrix **M_rec_dark**. **M_rec_dark** is then brightened by multiplying all its values by a positive integer (in this case 2) to get **M_reconstruct**. **M_reconstruct** is very much identical to **M_resized** which is just a resized version of the hidden image **M**.

$$\boldsymbol{False\_Diff} = \boldsymbol{C} - \boldsymbol{C\_stego} \;\; \boldsymbol{OR} \;\; \boldsymbol{C\_stego} - \boldsymbol{C} \quad (5)$$

$$\boldsymbol{M\_rec\_dark} = \boldsymbol{inverse\_DCT}(\boldsymbol{False\_Diff}) \quad (6)$$

$$\boldsymbol{M\_reconstruct} = \boldsymbol{M\_rec\_dark} \times \boldsymbol{4} \quad (7)$$

4.3 SNR measurement algorithm

The SNR was used to measure a noisy signal with a noiseless signal. The idea behind it is that the noisier a signal is, the more that signal's values will deviate from its noiseless version. In this algorithm, the two images that are to be compared to measure SNR are termed as matrices ***A*** and ***B*** respectively. ***A*** and ***B*** must have the same size. ***B*** is subtracted from ***A*** to get a matrix called ***Image_diff***. All the elements in ***Image_diff*** are raised to the power of 2 to get a matrix called ***Square_Image_diff***. Then all the elements in ***Square_Image_diff*** matrix are summed up to get the mean square error (MSE). The MSE is then applied in the formula below.

$$PSNR = 10 \times \log\left(\frac{255 \times 255}{MSE}\right) \quad (8)$$

$$\boldsymbol{MSE} = \sum_{i=1}^{len} \sum_{k=1}^{width} \| \boldsymbol{A}_{i,k} - \boldsymbol{B}_{i,k} \|^2 \quad (9)$$

To measure the quality of the data hiding algorithm, the SNR algorithm is applied to the cover image and stego image.

To measure the quality of the data hiding algorithm, SNR algorithm is applied to the payload image and reconstructed payload image.

When the SNR is estimated, the steganographic algorithms in this paper can be compared to the steganographic algorithms used in the previous works

5 Results

The figures below show the similarity between the Stego image and the cover image.

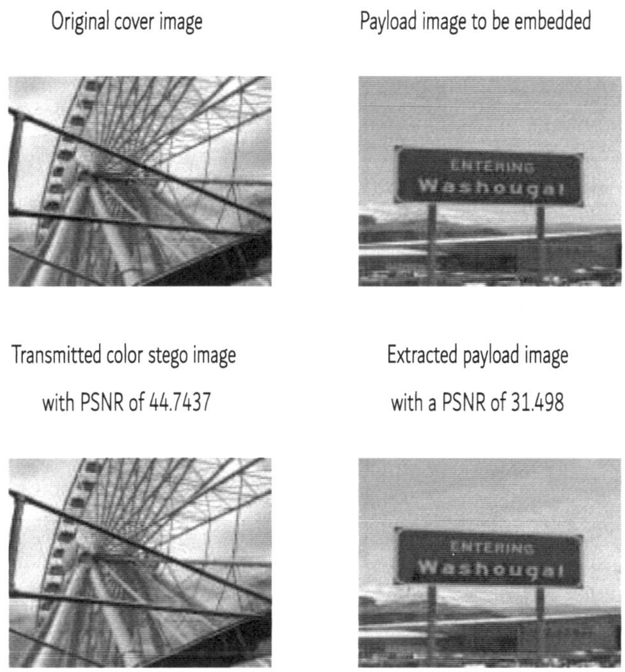

Figure 5: Sample implementation of image steganography algorithm

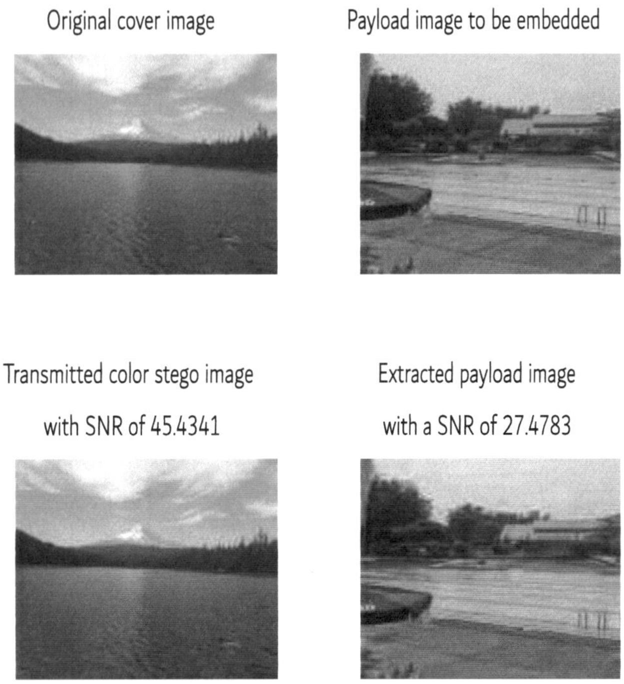

Figure 6: Sample implementation of image steganography algorithm

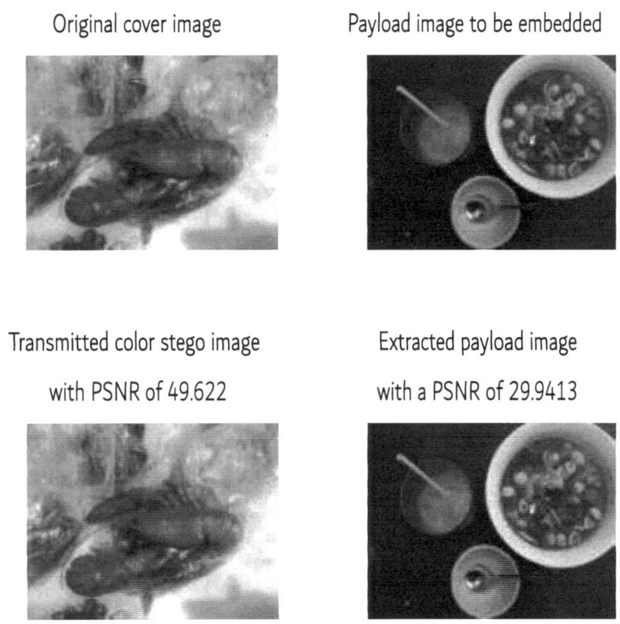

Figure 7: Sample implementation of image steganography algorithm

The signal to noise ratio between the stego and cover image is measured to estimate similarity between the two images. The signal to noise ratio between the transmitted hidden image and reconstructed hidden image is measure as well even though in practical cases, the receiver will have access to the reconstructed hidden image and will not be able to compare that image to the transmitted hidden image. The proposed method and the standard LSB steganography method were applied to fifteen (15) images to compute the average SNR as a basis of comparison with other methods.

The table below shows a comparison of different approaches to image steganography using SNR

Table 1: Comparison of results using SNR for different approaches to image steganography

Author	Cover/Stego SNR	Secret/Extracted SNR	Basis of Method
Dey, Roy & Dey	16.9680	14.2321	**DWT**
Kumar & Kumar	30.9055	28.8251	**DWT**
Standard LSB	37.8795	26.1168	**LSB**
Proposed Method	44.7742	26.8485	**DCT and LSB**

6 Conclusion

This paper proposes a simple but effective image steganography algorithm. The recovered payload image looks very similar to the original payload image. Due to the relatively high SNR between the recovered payload image and the original payload image, filtering is not necessary in the recovered payload image to have the original image. Hence, the proposed algorithm does not require much computational power - very simple. Due to the simplicity and effectiveness of this algorithm, it is suitable for mobile devices.

However, the main limitation of this algorithm is the method used, the DCT-based steganography method, is that the stego image to be transmitted over the cyberinfrastructure platform should be compressed in a lossless format, in this case, .png format, to retain and not lose the crucial embedded information needed to recover and reconstruct the payload image. Since modern cyberinfrastructure platforms are designed to store and rapidly data with large memory space, the use of lossless compressed images is not so much of a challenge.

Another point worth noting is that the payload and cover images needed to have copies of them that were compressed in a lossless (.png) format. The idea behind this, is to be able to have well defined cover image and payload image to make an accurate estimation of the SNR of the stego image with respect to cover image, as well as the SNR estimation of the reconstructed payload image with respect to payload image respectively.

References

[1] N. F. Johnson and S. Jajodia, "Exploring steganography: Seeing the unseen," *IEEE Computer Society,* vol. 31, no. 2, pp. 26-34, 1998.

[2] K. Kumar and Y.-H. Lu, "Cloud computing for mobile users: Can offloading computation save energy?," *IEEE Journal of Computer,* vol. 43, no. 4, pp. 51-56, 2010.

[3] Y. J. Chanu, T. Tuithung and K. M. Singh, "A short survey on image steganography and steganalysis techniques," in *2012 3rd National Conference on Emerging Trends and Applications in Computer Science*, Shillong, 2012.

[4] H. B. Bahar and A. Aboutalebi, "Image Steganography, a New Approach for Transferring Security Information," *Computing Research Repository (CoRR),* vol. arXiv preprint arXiv:0808.1410, 2008.

[5] P. Kumari, K. Chetna and J. Bhushan, "Data Security Using Image Steganography And Weighing Its Techniques," *International Journal Of Scientific & Technology Research 2,* vol. 2, no. 11, pp. 238-241, 2013.

[6] G. J. Simmons, "The prisoners' problem and the subliminal channel," *In Advances in Cryptology,* pp. 51-67, 1984.

[7] D. E. Stevenson, W. Michael. R and S. J. Ratering, "Steganography and cartography: interesting assignments that reinforce machine representation, bit manipulation, and discrete structures concepts," *ACM SIGCSE Bulletin},* vol. 37, no. 1, pp. 277-281, 2005.

[8] D. L. Currie and C. E. Irvine, "Surmounting the effects of lossy compression on Steganography," in *19th National Information Systems Security Conference*, Baltimore, MD, 1996.

[9] R. J. Anderson and F. A. P. Petitcolas, "On the limits of steganography," *IEEE Journal on Selected Areas in Communications,* vol. 16, no. 4, pp. 474-481, May 1998.

[10] S. Kaur, S. Bansal and a. R. K. Bansal, "Steganography and classification of image steganography techniques.," in *Computing for Sustainable Global Development (INDIACom), 2014 International Conference on. IEEE*, New Delhi, 2014.

[11] T. Morkel, J. H. P. Eloff and M. S. Olivier, "An overview of image steganography," in *Proceedings of the Fifth Annual Information Security South Africa Conference*, Sandton, South Africa, 2005.

[12] H. Ge, M. Huang and Q. Wang, "Steganography and steganalysis based on digital image," in *2011 4th International Congress on Image and Signal Processing*, Shanghai, 2011.

[13] N. Dey, A. B. Roy and S. Dey, "A Novel Approach of Color Image Hiding using (RGB) Color planes and Discrete Wavelet Transform (DWT)," vol. 36, no. 5, pp. 19-24, December 2011.

[14] V. Kumar and D. Kumar, "Performance Evaluation of DWT Based Image Steganography," in *2010 IEEE 2nd International Advance Computing Conference (IACC)*, Patiala, 2010.

Image Steganography: Review Study

Haval Muhammed Sidqi[1] , Prof. Dr. Muzhir Shaban Al-Ani[2]

University of Sulaimani Polytechnic, Institute of Computer, Department of Database, KRG Iraq
University of Human Development, College of Science Department of Information Technology,Sulaimania,KRG Iraq

ABSTRACT *Steganography is the science and art of covert communication. it allows the undercover information transmission and conceal the existence of message itself in content such as video, audio, or image to protect the transmitted information from intruders and unwanted recipients.. This paper presents a relative study of many procedure steganalysis techniques. It investigated and compared the performances of each technique in the detection of embedding methods considered. Based on the results of our analysis, this paper provides information as to which specific steganalysis technique needs to be used for a particular steganography method. Finally, we suggest a procedure which may help a legal examiner to agree an order in which different steganalysis methods need to be measured in the detection process to complete the best finding results in terms of together time and accuracy.*

Keywords: Security; Information Hiding; Steganography.

1 Introduction

The concept of information hiding is ancient technique which is traced back to a thousand years ago. It is merely based on dimming messages content by a process called encryption, which is sometimes not practically effective. In many competitive cases, it is highly demanded to suppress the initial existence of a communication in order to avoid suspicion from adversaries [1]. Recently, the information hiding techniques have become an important practice in a wide areas and applications, including digital audio, video, and pictures which are equipped dramatically with imperceptible marks that possibly contain a existence [2]. The information hiding refers to two concepts steganography and digital watermarking. The steganography is defined as the attempt to hide the fact that information is being transmitted at the first place, while watermarking is usually referred to the involved methods by which an identified information is being hidden in a data object, and accordingly, the information will be kept robust against modification [3]. Steganography is considered as a kind of a hidden communication which means literally the “covered writing”. Originally, it has been derived from the two Greek words stegano which refers to “covered” and graphos which refers to “to write”. The goal of applying the steganography is to hide the information message inside a harmless cover medium by a certain way that makes it impossible to detect the secret information and even its existence in the cover medium [4]. Secrete information hiding is a method of steganography that works by hiding secrete information into digital image for the purpose of identification, annotation, and copyrighting. In fact, several manacles affect such a process and this is including, the quantity of the proposed data to be hidden, the need for invariance of these data under conditions where a “host” signal is subjected to distortions, e.g., lossy compression, in addition to the degree to which the data must be immune to an interception, a modification, or a removal by a third party [5]. The three main aspects regarding information hiding systems are capacity, security and robustness as represented in figure 1.1. Generally, steganography requires a high security and capacity levels, i.e. hidden information are usually a fragile ones which can be destroyed by even slight modifications. On the other hand, watermarking mostly relies on achieving a robustness status where it is impossible to remove the watermark without causing severe cover content quality degradation[6].

2 Background

2.1 Steganography and Cryptography

Cryptography and Steganography are members of the detective skill family, both aiming at providing secret communication. Cryptography secretes only the meaning or fillings of a message from an attics dropper, but the encrypted message still exists and can be seen. Steganography, on the other hand, deals more secrecy than cryptography, since it hides the meagre existence of secret message rather than only trust the message contents [11]. A Cryptography system is jeopardized. If a malicious attacker can read the insides of a secret message, while a steganography system is risked if the existence of the message is detect by an attacker. In other words, a stegonagraphic system is considered exposed even without decoding the message, if an attacker suspects the file carrying the secret message or the steganography method used for encoding the secret message[7].

Hence, steganography can complement cryptography to avoid educating the feeling of system attackers and not to substitute cryptography. Steganography is a subdivision of information hiding technology which includes applications for protection against discovery and protection against removal such as copyright protection for digital media, watermarking, fingerprinting and data embedding. In these applications, information is hidden within a host data set, which is purposely corrupted in a covert way, so that it could be sent secretly to an intended receiver.

Cryptography is one of the old-style ways used to surety the privacy of communiqué between parties. This method is the skill of secret text, which is used to encrypt the plaintext with a key into cipher-text to be transferred between parties on an insecure channel. Using a valid key, the cipher-text can be decrypted to the original plaintext. Deprived of the information of the key, nobody can recover the plaintext. Cryptography shows an important role in many aspects essential for secure communication across an insecure channel, like: secrecy, isolation, non-repudiation, key exchange, and authentication. Figure 1 illustrates the cryptography system [10].

There are two types of cryptographic schemes for securing the data. These schemes are often used to extent the objective: public-key cryptography, secret key cryptography, and hash functions. The length and type of the keys used depend on the kind of encryption algorithm [10]. Cryptography not only keeps data from robbery or alteration, but can also be used for user validation.

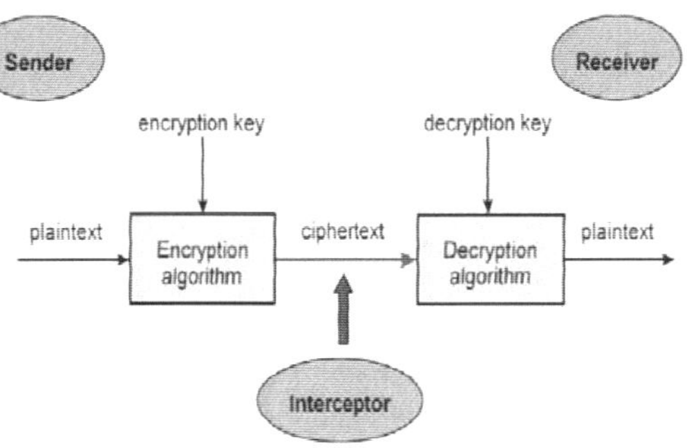

Fig. 1 Cryptography System [11]

2.2 Steganography and Watermarking

Steganography and watermarking are a way of data hiding and share common features. The aim of watermarking is to embed a single signature to indicate the origin or rights of a digital media for the purpose of copyright protection, while the aim of steganography is to protection the existence of the communication taking place within a digital media. Watermarking is a mechanism used to show that illegal copying or any minor modification of the watermarked file is done. One of the main features of watermarking is knownas''robustness'', if somebody knows that a digital mark happens (i.e. visible watermarking) and attempts to remove the watermark from the watermarked media, he/she should consequently cause distortions or destroys the original watermarked media [13].

Watermarking is protect message for verify the identity and authenticity of the owner of a multi media. It is a way in which the information which verifies the owner is inserted into the digital image or signal. These signal could be either videos or pictures or audios. For sample, illustrious watermark their pictures and images. If somebody tries to copy the image, the watermark is derivative along with the image. [13] Watermarking classify into two group; visible and invisible.

.Visible : visible watermarking refers to the information can be seen on the image or video or picture. Visible watermarks are typically logos or text. For example, in a TV show, the symbol of the broadcaster is visible at the right side of the screen. [14] Invisible : Invisible watermarking refers to embedding information in a video or picture or audio as digital data. It is not show or visible, but it can be noticed by different means. It can be a type of steganography and is has been used for widespread use. Secret information can be extracted easily. [14]

Watermarking is used in many 1pplications such as: copyright protection, source tracing, and annotation of photographs.

In summary we can say Watermarking is a process in which the information which verifies the owner is embedded into the digital image or signal. These original signals could be either videos or pictures or audios, steganography process will be change the cover image in a way that only the sender and the authorized receiver are able to detect the message sent through it.

2.3 Steganography Terminology

Steganography contains of two terms that is message and original image. Message is the secret data that needs to hide and original image is the carrier that hides the message in it, the below figure 2 illustrate it.[16]

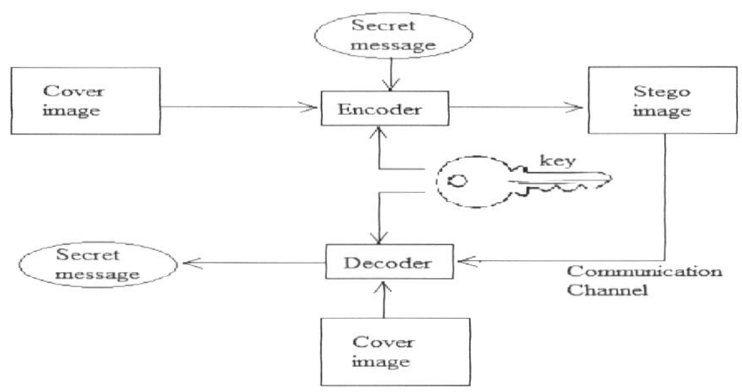

Fig.2 Steganography Diagram

2.4 Adaptive Steganography

Statistics - aware embedding are the two earlier special case discussed methods of an adaptive steganography [20] The image before trying to interact with its LSB/DCT coefficients will takes statistical global features. It is described by a random adaptive selection of pixels depending on the cover image and the selection of pixels in a block with large local STD, standard deviation. Adaptive steganography try to find images with existing or deliberately added noise and images that establish color complexity, avoiding areas of uniform color. However, in order to maintain the image's quality, it is necessary to take the human visual system (HVS) into consideration and ensure that the distortion introduced by embedding is imperceptible to the human eye.

One of the embedding strategies in the spatial and frequency domain trusts on image thresholding. Thresholding is one of the methods used in image segmentation where a binary image is created from a grayscale image. One of its main functions is to separate objects from the background such as printed characters, graphical content and map processing where lines, legends and characters are to be detected.[20], thresholding methods are categorized according to the information they obtain from the data into:

Histogram-shaped-based: these analyses the form and shape of image histogram such as the peaks, valleys and curvatures.

Grouping-based: these rely on making two cluster objects (background and foreground) from grey-level information.

Entropy-based: these use the entropy of the distribution of grey levels in the picture.

Object attribute-based: these are methods that extract a threshold value based on similarities between the original image and the binaries one using some attribute quality or similarity measure.

Spatial methods: these use higher-order chance distribution and/or correlation between pixels.

Between the first adaptive thresholding methods was the algorithm evolving by Nakagawa and Rosenfeld[22] , who planned a variation on the original method of variable thresholding by Chow and Kaneko [22]. In their method, the image is shared into several windows of the original image with the locality property. Those windows with histograms are selected and a threshold is calculated. Then the edge from altered windows is incorporated to calculate a final threshold for the whole image. Their results were successfully applied to the TV images of machine components with substantially better results than those that applied a fixed threshold to the whole image. [23] established an algorithm that adapts threshold selection from a local window by calculating a local mean and standard deviation. This method was later enhanced [23] to recognize letters in stained documents or documents with bad clarification by adjusting the impact of the standard deviation in the algorithm. Such methods are known as local variance methods method of variable thresholding [23]. In their technique, the image is shared into several windows of the original image with the locality property. Those windows with histograms are selected and a threshold is calculated. Then the threshold from different windows is incorporated to calculate a final threshold for the whole image. Their results were successfully realistic to the TV images of machine components with substantially better results than those that applied a fixed threshold to the whole image.

3 Analysis and Discussion

Steganography methods and several article are discussed in this paper. The mixing method of encryption techniques with steganography may be useful to obtain stegoimage and it will become more powerful and hard to break from attackers. Based on the many research studies, the table below illustrates the literature comparison with the advantage, disadvantage and result. The paper studies the different kinds of Steganography and methods to find the steganography. In this study basically image steganography techniques are discussed. All the methods debated in this paper are able to secure the embedding information. On the other hand some algorithms have a very high time complexity and very less amount of data stored in the images. So, there is a need to grow capable and accurate Steganography procedures, either by combining the existing methods or by rising new methods.

In this study, analyzed the different methodologies of various researchers in the area of image steganography is to ebbed the actuality of the data from illegitimate intention. Different carrier file types would be used, but digital images are great enough used due to the frequency and massive users on the worldwide Internet. To hide the secret data in images, there are large ranges of steganography methodologies exist some are complex in used than others method. Every method has respective strong and weak points, has been showed in table 1. The diagram below collected many research's from 2009 to 2018.First step found 216 article in Science Director, 329 article in IEEE and 32 article in Springer all of them under title "Hidden Image or Steganography or cryptography or watermark, hidden information."

From 2000 until 2018.Second step selected 327 articles of 512 articles from 2010 until 2018. Third step deleted 211 articles out of domain and chose 106 articles in domain. Fourth step after reading body of articles, 9 articles has been selected and mentioned in this review paper.

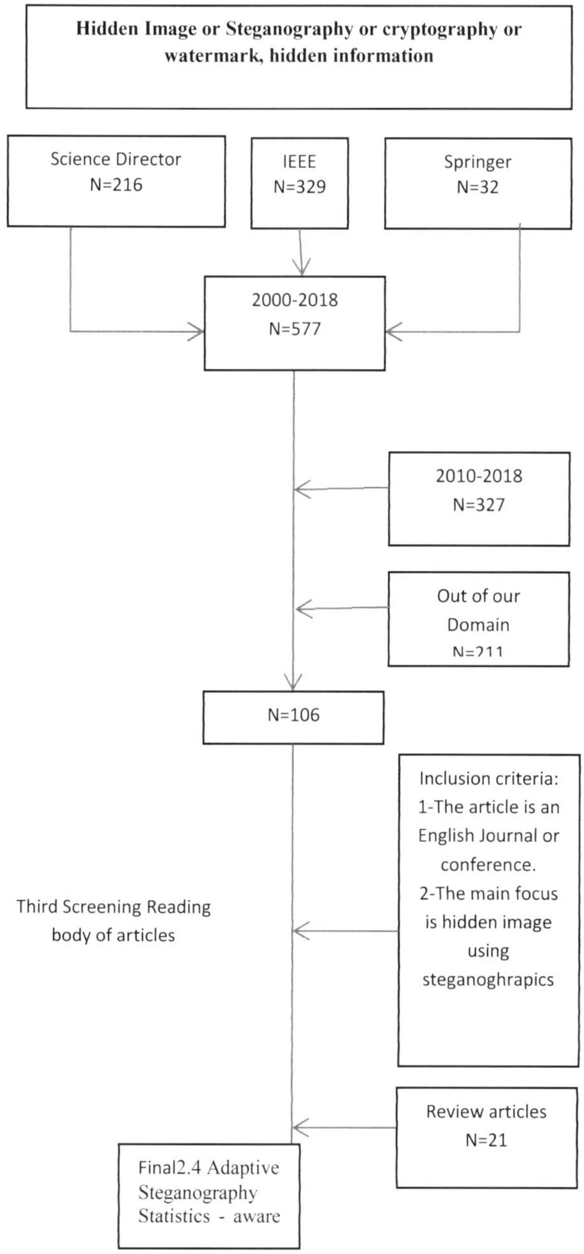

Fig. 3 Steps of survey papers

4 CONCLUSION

This paper debates several parts of cryptography and steganography with their works and improvements based on the analysis and observations. Powerful results are obtained by hybridizing different encryption technique. The increasing in key size with random attribute leading to better and powerful security improvement. Steganography develops an interested field of data hiding techniques. This paper offers an overview of different steganography methods that satisfy the most important features of steganography design. Haar wavelet transform method has a high-capacity image steganography that is able of embedding many type of data of different size has been presented. All these of secretive secrete image are concealed in stego-images. The stego-image is formed to be always equal to the cover image. In this paper, we reviewed some of the fundamental concepts, performance measures and other significant parameters that impact image steganography. With the survey papers pre-sented earlier, some of the important aspects that contribute to steganography system such as cover image selection, image quality metrics etc. are relatively less investigated. Hence, we have focused on such issues. Different ways to embed secret bits with various types, their merits and demerits are discussed. There are three different approaches to design secure, high capacity image steganography system: (a) Choose suitable cover image form the database. (b) Select appropriate embedding locations (c) Use encrypted version of secret data for embedding.

5 REFERENCES

[1] M.B.Ould MEDENI and El Mamoun SOUIDI, (2010) "A Generalization of the PVD Steganographic Method", International Journal of Computer Science and Information Security, Vol.8.No.8, pp156-159

[2] S.Arivazhagan, W.Sylvia Lilly Jebarani, and S.Bagavath (2011) "Colour Image Steganography Using Median Maintenance", ICTACT Journal on Image and Video Processing, Vol. 2, Iss:01, pp.246-253.

[3] Sathishkumar GA,Ramachandran S, Bagan KB. (2012) Encrypt Image using random pixel permutation by chaotic mapping. In IEEE symposium on computers & informatics (pp. 247-51).

[4]Hemalatha.S, U.Dinesh Acharya , (2013) "Comparison of Secure and High Capacity Color Image Steganography Techniques in RGB and YCBCR domains", International Journal of Advanced Information Technology, Vol.3, No.3, pp.1-9.

[5] Praneeta Dehare, Padma Bonde (2014) "Hiding Image in Image by using FMM with LSB Substitution in Image Steganography ", International Journal on Recent and Innovation Trends in Computing and Communication ISSN: 2321-8169 Volume: 2 Issue: 11,pp 3663 – 3667.

[6] Ahmed Shihab, (2015) "Image Steganography Based on Discrete Wavelet Transform and Enhancing Resilient Backpropogation Neural Network", master thesis 2015 Department of Computer Science Faculty of Information Technology Middle East University Amman-Jordan.

[7] R. Rejani,D.Murugan and Deepu. (2016) "DIGITAL DATA PROTECTION USING STEGANOGRAPHY "ICTACT JOURNAL ON COMMUNICATION TECHNOLOGY, MARCH 2016, VOLUME: 07, ISSUE: 01 ISSN: 2229-6948(ONLINE) DOI: 10.21917/ijct.2016.0183.

[8] Ashwini W, Archana Patankar (2017) "QR Code Based Image Steganography" International Journal of Advance Research, Ideas and Innovations in Technology. ISSN: 2454-132XImpact factor: 4.295(Volume3, Issue3).

[9] Govind R. Suryawanshi, Suresh N. (2018) "Analysis of Effect of Spatial Domain Steganography Technique on DCT Domain " international Journal of Applied Engineering Research ISSN 0973-4562 Volume 13, pp. 634-640.

[10] N. F. Johnson, (1998) "Exploring Steganography", IEEE Computer vol. 31, issue 2, pp. 26-34.

[11] J. C. Judge (2001) "Steganography: Past, Present, Future", SANS Publications.

[12] D.Artz. (2001) "Digital Image Steganography, Hiding Information within Information", ieee vol. 5, issue 3, pp. 75-80,.

[13] Jar no Mielikainen (2006) "LSB Matching Revisited", Signal Processing letters, ieee, vol. 13, issue 5, pp. 285-
287, May 2006.

[14] L-C. Lin (2009) "Hiding Data in Spatial Domain with Distortion Tolerance", Computer Standard & Interfaces, 2009, 31, pp. 458-464.

[15] C-C. Chan (2007) "Reversible Hiding in DCT based Compressed Images", Information Sciences, 2007, 177, pp. 2768-2786.

[16] Anjali A. Shejul, Prof. U. L. Kulkarn (2010) "A DWT based Approach for Steganography using

Biometric" International Conference On Data Storage and Data Engineering, IEEE,2010, pp. 39-43.

[17] Provos and Honeyman (2003) "An Introduction to Steganography", IEEE Security and Privacy, vol. 01, issue 3, pp. 32-44.

[18] Shaveta Mahajan, Arpinder Singh (2012) "A Review of Methods and Approach for Secure Steganography", International Journal of Advanced Research Computer Science and Software Engineering, October 2012, vol.2, issue 10, pp. 67-70.

[19] K. Gopalan. (2003) "Audio steganography using bit modification", IEEE International Conference on Acoustics, Speech, and Signal Processing, (ICASSP '03), April 2003, vol2 , pp. 6-10.

[20] D. Kirovski and H. Malvar (2003) "Spread spectrum Watermarking of Audio Signals," IEEE Transactions on Signal Processing, April 2003, vol. 51, no. 4, pp. 1020 –1033.

[21] Tomáš Pevný, Jessica Fridrich, And Andrew D. Ker (2012) "From Blind To Quantitative Steganalysis," IEEE Transactions On Information Forensics And Security, 2012, Vol. 7, No. 2, pp. no 445-454.

[22] Jan Kodovský, Jessica Fridrich (2012) "Ensemble Classifiers For Steganalysis Of Digital Media," IEEE Transactions On Information Forensics And Security,2012, Vol. 7, No. 2, pp no. 432-444.

[23] I. Avcibas, M. Nasir, and B. Sankur (2001) "Steganalysis Based on Image Quality Metrics," IEEE 4th Workshop on Multimedia Signal Processing, 2001, pages 517–522.

[24] K. Sullivan, U. Madhow, S. Chandrasekaran, and B. Manjunath (2006) "Steganalysis for Markov Cover Data With Applications to Images," IEEE Transactions on Information Forensics and Security,2006, 1(2):275–287.

[25] R.J. Anderson (1996) "Stretching the Limits of Steganography," 1st International Workshop on Information Hiding, 1996 1174:39–48.

[26] R. J. Anderson and F. A. P. Petitcolas (1998) "On the limits of Steganography," IEEE Journal of Selected Areas in Communications, 1998, 16(4):474–481.

[27]S. Badura and S. Rymaszewski (2007) "Transform Domain Steganography in DVD Video and Audio Content," IEEE International Workshop on Imaging Systems and Techniques, 2007, pp. 1–5.

[28] X.Chen, Y. Wang, T. Tan, and L. Guo (2006) "Blind Image Steganalysis Based on Statistical Analysis of Empirical Matrix," International Conference on Pattern Recognition, 2006, 3:1107–1110.

[29] G. Xuan, Y. Q. Shi and W. Chen (2005) "Steganalyzis Based on Multiple Features Formed by Statistical Moments of Wavelet Characteristic Functions," International Workshop pages:262–277.

[30] Y. Q. Shi, and C. Chen (2005) "Image Steganalyzis Based on Moments of Characteristic Functions Using Wavelet Decomposition, " IEEE International Conference , pages 269–272.

[31] C. Chen, Y. Q. Shi, W. Chen, and G. Xuan (2006) " Statistical Moments Based Universal Steganalysis using JPEG 2-D Array and 2-D Characteristic Function," IEEE International Conference on Image Processing, 2006, pages 105–108.

[32] H. Farid (2001) "Detecting Steganographic Messages in Digital Images," TR2001-412, Department of Computer Science, Dartmouth College.

SESSION

POSTER PAPERS AND EXTENDED ABSTRACTS

Chair(s)

TBA

Arm control of a tele-existence robot by correcting the influence of the vision system

Shunya Suzuki, Yuki Matsui, Yuki Mori, and Hideo Furuhashi
Dep. Electrical and Electronics Eng.
Aichi Institute of Technology
Toyota, Japan

Abstract— *Herein, the arm of a tele-existence robot has been controlled by correcting the influence of the vision system. There are many types of tele-existence robot arms that use a stereo camera and a head mounted display (HMD). Owing to the camera angle, the inter-camera distance and the physical structure of the arms are different on the operator and robot sides. Therefore, natural operation cannot be performed. Herein, the inconsistency between the inter-camera distance and the structure has been corrected, and the operator's arms are controlled to move the robot's arm to the exact position. Thus, natural operation is performed.*

Keywords—tele-existence robot, vision system, head mounted display

1. Introduction

Various types of tele-existence robots have been reported recently. Many of these robots use a stereo camera and a HMD for their vision system [1,2]. The interpupillary distances and the view angles of an operator differ from the inter-camera distance and the view angle of the stereo camera, respectively. Therefore, at a particular point in space, the position of the operator in the virtual space is different from the real position of the target. Furthermore, as the physical structure of a robot does not correspond to the physical structure of the operator, the robot arm and the operator's arm perform different operations if the joint angles are controlled using the same angles with the operator's arm. Therefore, natural operation of the robot cannot be obtained.

In this study, a tele-existence robot having a humanoid upper body equipped with a stereo camera has been developed, the influence of the vision system on the operation of the robot arm has been studied, and finally, the influence and difference in the arm structure between the robot and the operator have been corrected.

2. System

Figure 1 presents the developed tele-existence robot comprising 11 degrees of freedom (DOF). The head has 3 DOF while each of the two arms has 4 DOF. The head of the robot is equipped with a stereo camera (two web cameras; HD WEBCAM C525, Logicool Co Ltd.). The operator wears the HMD (Oculus Rift CV1, Facebook Technologies, LLC) and operator's arms are fitted with motion sensors (PERCEPTION NEURON, Noitom Ltd.). The robot head and arms are controlled by the posture of the HMD and the motion sensors, respectively.

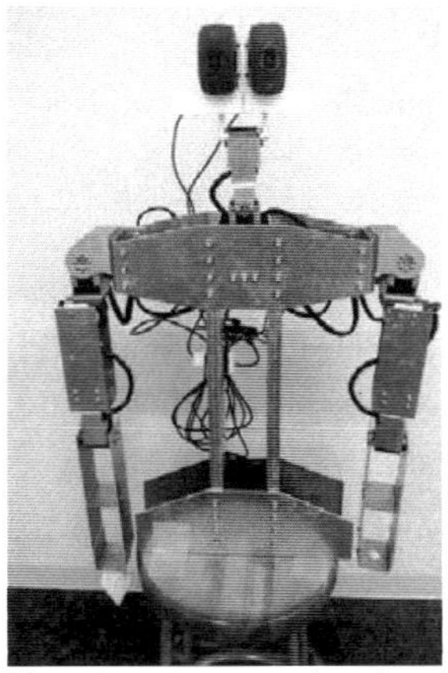

FIGURE 1.The tele-existence robot developed herein

The operator moves his arm to place the robot's arm at the target position perceived using the vision information. The hand position of the operator is evaluated by applying forward kinematics on the joint angles of the operator's arm fitted with the motion sensors. By considering the influence of the vision system mismatch on the operator's hand position, the real space position of the robot corresponding to the operator's hand position is corrected. The robot is controlled by evaluating the angle of the actuators through inverse kinematics such that the corrected position becomes the hand position of the robot. The flowchart of these processes is shown in Figure 2.

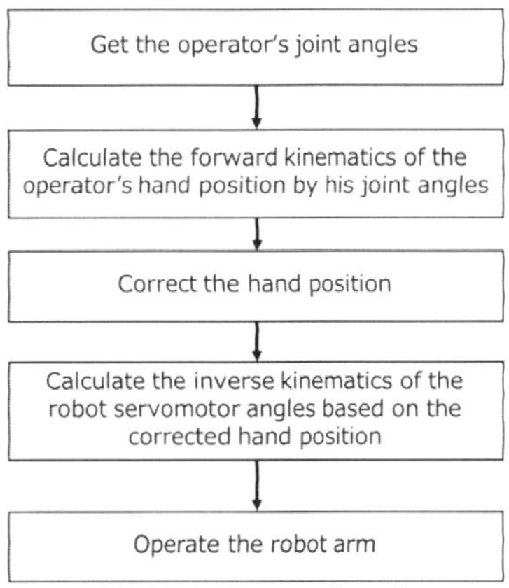

FIGURE 2. System flowchart

The relationships between the real position determined by the robot and the position perceived by the operator can be defined as follows [3]:

$$x_0 = \frac{x_r}{\rho_d}, \quad (1)$$

$$z_0 = \frac{\rho_\varphi}{\rho_d} z_r, \quad (2)$$

where (x_r, z_r) denotes the real position (horizontal axis and depth axes); (x_0, z_0) denotes the perceived position; ρ_d denotes the ratio between the inter-camera distance of the robot and the interpupillary distance of the operator; and ρ_φ denotes the ratio of the tangents of the view angle between them. The vertical axis is 0 in this experiment.

3. Result

First, the influence of the vision system was measured by applying equations 1 and 2. The operator closed his eyes after perceiving that the position dots were plotted on a paper placed in front of the robot to avoid the influence of visual feedback. Figure 3 shows the experimental results. The triangular marks indicate the real position, whereas the circular marks show the position perceived by the operator after the corrections using equations 1 and 2. Errors of few centimeters were observed in the results. This is caused by the errors of the interpupillary distance and the operator's view angle. Furthermore, setting errors, such as the direction of the camera influence the results.

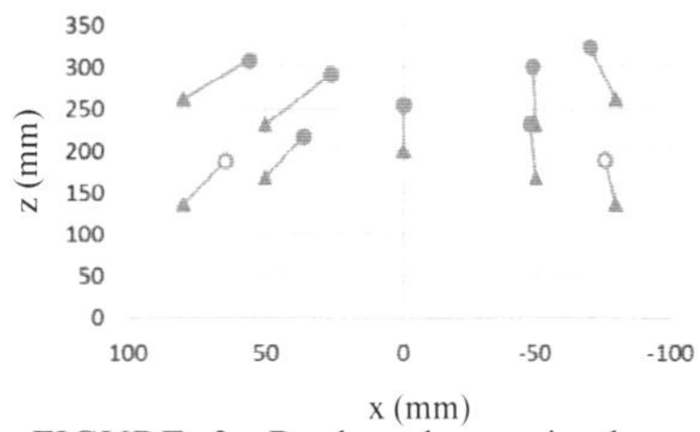

FIGURE 3. Real and perceived positions with theoretical error corrections.

Therefore, the parameters ρ_d and ρ_φ in equations 1 and 2 were estimated from the above experimental data. The robot's arm was controlled by the correction of the vision system. The target was set at two points: (x, z) = (−100, 350) and (−100, 450). The height of both targets was set to the height of the stereo camera. The X–Z plane of the target arrangement is shown in Figure 4, whereas the Y–Z plane is shown in Figure 5. The operator perceives the target from the stereo image displayed in the HMD. Then, the operator closes his eyes and operates his right arm to indicate the target. Thus, the right arm of the robot is moved following the signal of the operator, and the robot's right arm also indicates the target. The difference between the target position and the position indicated by the robot hand was observed. The experiment was conducted using an inter-camera distance of 55–90 mm. The average values of the errors in the X and Z directions are shown in Table 1.

At any inter-camera distance, the errors were observed to be relatively small in both the X and Z directions, and the control of the robot's arm was corrected with the influence of the visual system.

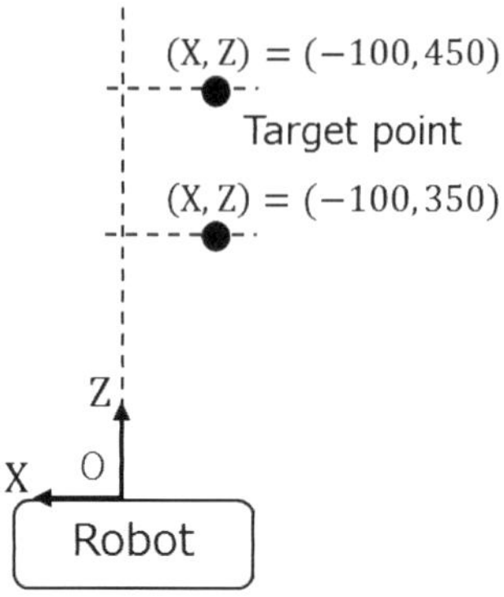

FIGURE 4. Experimental setup (X–Z plane)

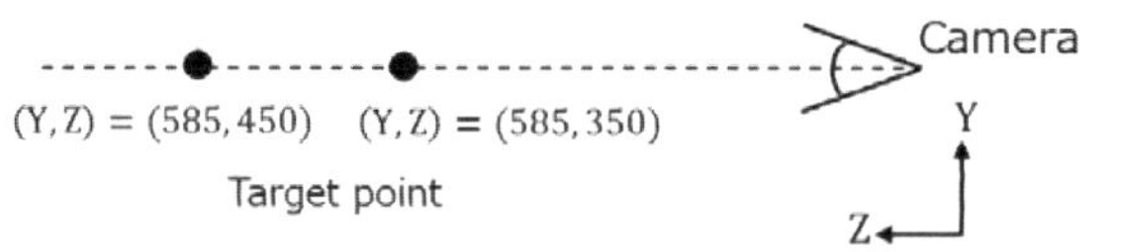

FIGURE 5. Experimental setup (Y–Z plane)

TABLE 1. Errors of the robot arm controlled through the correction of the vision system using the experimentally obtained parameters.

	Inter-camera distance [mm]				
	55	60	70	80	90
X	−5	−8	6	−13	−2
Z	1.5	−1.0	1.6	−2.1	−1.6

4. Conclusion

In this study, a system to control a tele-existence robot's arm at a real space point corresponding to the position perceived by the operator using the stereo camera and the HMD has been developed. Precise control of the robot arm was achieved by correcting the influence caused by the vision system.

For further improvement of natural control, correction in the vertical direction and consideration of the perceived distortion of the vision system's shape is required. These topics will be covered in future works.

5. References

[1] Higuchi Keita, Jun Rekimoto, "Flying head: a head motion synchronization mechanism for unmanned aerial vehicle control," CH'13 Extended abstracts on Human Factors in Computing Systems, pp. 2029–2038, 2013.

[2] Martinez-Hernandez, Uriel, Luke W. Boorman, Tony J. Prescott, "Multisensory wearable interface for immersion and telepresence in robotics," IEEE Sensors Journal, vol. 17, no. 8, pp. 2534–2541, 2017.

[3] Yasuyuki Yanagida, Susumu Tachi, "Dynamic effects of inconsistent field of view in HMD-based telexistence systems," Transactions of the Virtual Reality Society of Japan, vol. 7, no. 1, pp. 69–78, 2002.

Chroma Uniformity Assessment of LED Display Based on HVS

Baixiu Ding* [1,2], Yingnan Geng[2,3], Mi Lu[2]
[1]School of Electrical Engineering and Computer, Jilin Jianzhu University, Changchun,Jilin,China,
2 Department of Electrical and Computer Engineering, Texas A & M University, College Station, Texas,USA,
3College of Electrical and Information Engineering,Changchun Institute of Technology, changchun,Jilin,China.

Abstract – *Chroma uniformity assessment of LED displays is important for LED assessment. In this paper, we propose a method to assess the chroma uniformity of LED displays based on HVS. We set three feature factors to assess the partial feature including chroma characteristic, texture details and spatial location feature factors. Images of LED displays are captured by a CCD camera. These images will be partitioned into several parts with same sizes after certain image processing procedures. The feature factors of each part will be calculated. We multiply them together to obtain the final feature value. This method fuses objective assessment results and subjective assessment results. It is a proficient way to assess chroma uniformity which is approaching the assessment of human's eyes.*

Keywords: chroma, HVS, assessment, feature factor.

1 Introduction

LED (light-emitting diode) displays are becoming more and more widely used. LED displays should be assessed before selling and after using for certain time. Uniformity assessment includes a few indexes. Chroma uniformity is one of the most important indexes. Chroma uniformity refers to the chromatic aberration uniformity when each pixel and module of the same display shows the same color. This is a foundation to recover the source information. The core of LED display assessment is human. Human vision system is of great significance to the research of evaluation algorithm. The research on the characteristics of human vision involves physiological and psychological aspects, but so far it has not been fully understood. In particular, it is difficult to find a quantitative description method for the psychological characteristics of vision, so there is still lack of a comprehensive and unified image quality evaluation systems. There are few articles on LED chroma uniformity assessment. Nagamine developed a quantitative evaluation method for luminance and color uniformity of a liquid crystal display (LCD) screen based on human perception [1]. Gui suggested a luminance uniformity evaluation for LED display panel based on human vision system (HVS) [2]. We will propose an evaluation method for LED chroma uniformity based on HVS.

2 Traditional chroma uniformity assessment method for LED displays

Traditional chroma uniformity assessment includes subjective assessing and objective assessing.

2.1 Subjective assessing method

A group of specialized persons assess the chroma uniformity of an LED display in the same environment of darkness. Each person provides a score between 0 to 10. After all persons complete their evaluation, the average value of all persons' scores will be calculated to obtain the final assessed value of that LED display. Even though an average value is used, it is too versatile to get a stable value because even if the given condition is fixed, the same person can generate different results.

2.2 Objective assessing method

The RGB information of every LED point is extracted by a CCD (Charge Coupled Device) camera. The RGB information can be converted to color coordinate parameters. The mean value and standard deviation value will be counted out. The mean and standard deviation can be used in assessing methods.

3 Chroma uniformity assessing method based on HVS

3.1 Image preprocessing

Images captured by a CCD camera include image boundaries which are not useful for collecting information. They will be cut off from the original images. LED points will be located in appropriate locations. An equal interval division for all the LED points will be processed to get a threshold segmentation. The summation of all pixels in one LED point can be computed out to obtain the RGB value of the LED point. The RGB values of each LED point, three separate values, will be used [3].

3.2 Feature factors extraction

From the point of view of psychology, vision is a kind of positive feeling behavior. It is not only related to physiological factors but also psychological factors to a large extent. When persons are looking at and understanding an image, they will

This research was supported in by Jilin Jianzhu University Project: "Study on luminance and chroma uniformity assessing system of LED displays" focus on certain interesting areas subconsciously. The uniformity of the whole image will change to the uniformity of certain areas. They will not notice the unevenness of the area they are not interested in.

We partition an LED image into N $(N \leq 25)$ subareas with the same size. Let "j" be the serial number of subareas, and each subarea Q_j $(1 \leq j \leq N)$ contains M × N pixels. The chroma characteristic feature factor, texture details feature factor and spatial location feature factor of each subarea will be computed out respectively [4].

3.2.1 Chroma characteristic feature factor

The reflection of the stimulus signal by the human visual system is not dependent on the absolute value of the signal, but on the degree of stimulus the signals exert to the average value. Fechner's law states that the subjective sensation is proportional to the logarithm of the stimulus intensity. It is shown as follows:

$$s_j = \mathrm{k}\lg\frac{ca_{jmax}}{ca_{javg}} \quad (1)$$

where ca_{jmax} and ca_{javg} are the maximum and average chroma in subarea j respectively.

3.2.2 Texture details feature factor

To deal with the texture details feature, we should generate new images which can be used to extract texture features as follows:

$$R_{mean} = \frac{1}{n}\sum_{j=1}^{n} R_j \quad (2)$$

$$R_{newj} = R_j - R_{mean} \quad (3)$$

where n is the number of LED points in an LED image, R_{mean} is the average value of all the LED points when the LED display is showing red, R_{newj} is the pixel value of the jth pixel in the newly generated image. This new R image is used to extract texture feature. G (green) and B (blue) images are produced with the same method. A texture feature library is then set up. We will use the method of machine learning to obtain the texture details feature factor. A texture feature assessment value of part j named d_j will be given out [5].

3.2.3 Spatial location feature factor

Photosensitive cells are more closely distributed in the macular area of the retina, so in the center of the central macular area, the human eye has the highest resolution, while the retina peripheral vision, which is composed of rods, is of low resolution, and the details of the image cannot be seen clearly. When viewing an image, the human eye can only have a good resolution of the details of one part of the image, and cannot distinguish other parts of the image at the same time. When persons look at an image, they look at the center first because the so called importance of an image decreases from the center to the boundary. The spatial location feature factor can be described as follows:

$$r_j = 1 - B_r \times \frac{\sqrt{(x_{j0}-x_c)^2-(y_{j0}-y_c)^2}}{r} \quad (4)$$

where (x_c, y_c) is the coordinate of the central point of the whole image to be assessed, and (x_{j0}, y_{j0}) is the coordinate of the central point of the subarea j [2].

3.3 Final chroma uniformity assessment result

Based on the above analysis of chroma feature factor s_j, texture detail feature factor d_j and spatial location feature factor r_j in subarea j, the uniformity evaluation w_j of each block based on HVS is defined as follows:

$$w_j = \sqrt{s_j^2 \times d_j^2 \times r_j^2} \quad (5)$$

The final assessment result of the whole LED display will be calculated as follows:

$$c_{HVS} = \sqrt{\frac{\sum_{j=1}^{N}(w_j-\overline{w_j})^2}{N-1}} \quad (6)$$

where $\overline{w_j}$ is the average assessment value of all the subareas' assessment values. c_{HVS} is the final assessing result of the whole LED display. The smaller c_{HVS}, the better the chroma uniformity of LED display.

4 Conclusions

In this paper, a new method is proposed to assess the chroma uniformity of the LED display. It fully considers the complex characteristics of human visual system, and makes a comprehensive modeling analysis and quantitative calculation of the influence of image relative chroma, texture details and spatial location on human visual interest. Compared with the traditional method of using mean square deviation, the HVS index can distinguish the image characteristics of different regions in the image, which is consistent with the human visual characteristics and approximated to the evaluation results of subjective evaluation, and can be used to evaluate the image uniformity. It will provide a reference for the quantitative test of the future chroma correction work and improve the efficiency and display quality of the full-color LED display.

5 References

[1] K. Nagamine. "A quantitative evaluation method for luminance and color uniformity of a display screen based on human perception"; IEICE TRANS.ELECRON, Vol. E95_C No. 11, 1699—736, November, 2012.

[2] J. Gui. "Luminance uniformity evaluation for LED display panel based on HVS"; Chinese Journal of Liquid Crystals and Displays, Vol. 27 No. 5, 658—665, October 2012.

[3] I. Moreno. "Illumination uniformity assessment based on human vision"; Optics Letters, Vol. 35 No. 23, 4030—4032, December, 2010.

[4] S. Roelandt, L. Bogaert. "Color uniformity in compact LED illumination for DMD projectors"; Proc. SPIE 7723, Optics, Photonics, and Digital Technologies for Multimedia Applications, 77230X (5 May 2010); doi: 10.1117/12.854333.

[5] Y. Hu, M. R. Luo and Y. Yang, "A study on lighting uniformity for LED smart lighting system"; 2015 12th China International Forum on Solid State Lighting (SSLCHINA), Shenzhen, pp. 127-130, 2015.

Real-Time Embedded System for Human Detection and Tracking

Chun-Chieh Lee, Chih-Yu Wang, Chiao-Wen Kao, and Kuo-Chin Fan
Department of Computer Science & Information Engineering,
National Central University, Taoyuan City 32001, Taiwan.

Abstract - In the past few years, various excellent object detection methods using deep learning techniques have been proposed, for example, the region proposal series and the single shot series. However, it is difficult to well apply these methods in the embedded platforms which are only equipped with finite memory and low-end CPU. In this paper, we propose a lightweight, reliable human detection model, named Brisk-YOLO. In the test of PASCAL VOC 2007 dataset using Raspberry Pi 3B platform, the detection speed of our proposed model is 22fps, which is about 55 times faster than the Tiny-YOLO. Moreover, in the experiments on the benchmarking BoBoT dataset, our detection and tracking system show its favorable performance and accuracy.

Keywords - Deep Learning, Object Detection, Human Tracking, Embedded System

1. Introduction

The performance of object detection via computer vision has been dramatically enhanced using deep learning techniques. Recently, the Faster R-CNN [1] and the YOLO family [2] have greatly improved the detection speed and accuracy. However, to apply these models usually needs quite a lot of computing resources, said larger memory requirements, high-end CPU and/or GPU. In some real-time embedded system applications, for example, to developing a mobile robot to follow a walking people, we might not be able to apply these models smoothly. In general, this kind of embedded platform usually has only limited hardware capacity. But, the detection and tracking performance should be kept at an acceptable level in spite of the constrained resources. In this paper, we propose a real-time embedded system for reliable human detection and tracking. The system is implemented on the Raspberry Pi 3B platform which is only provided with one 1.2GHz ARM CPU and 1GB RAM.

2. The proposed system

The architecture of our proposed system consists of three main components: Detector(YOLO), Tracker(KCF) and Re-Identification, as shown in Figure 1. In the following, we will briefly describe each component.

2.1. Detector(YOLO)

The accuracy of the detector has a significant impact on the overall performance of the system. The Tiny-YOLO was chosen as the baseline model of the detector. To estimate its performance, we implement the Tiny-YOLO on the Raspberry Pi 3B platform and its detection speed can only reach about 0.4fps, which is not fast enough for the real-time application. Therefore, we redesign the network architecture and try to maintain the balance between the acceptable accuracy rate and the detection speed. Figure 2 shows the layer structure of the proposed network model called Brisk-YOLO. In order to achieve faster detection performance, we cut down the model parameters mainly by reducing the number of the convolution kernels and thus decreasing the size of feature maps. But, merely reducing the filter channels might decrease the detection accuracy. Therefore, we design a new structure called Blaze layer as shown in Figure 3. The concept of Blaze layer is similar to the Fire layer proposed in [3]. The experiment shows that it can reduce the model parameters and at the same time still maintain the desired accuracy.

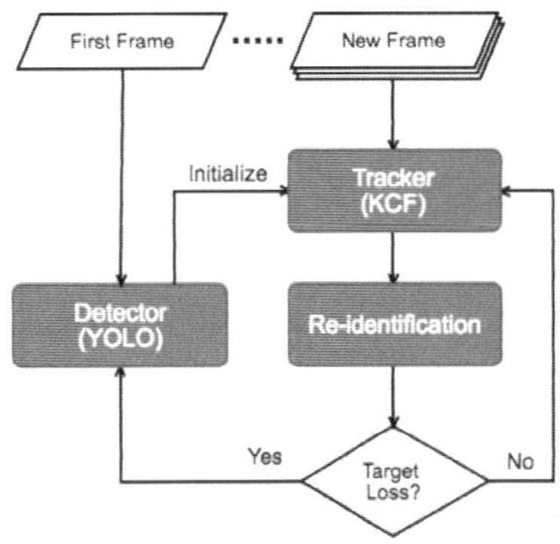

Figure 1. The process of the proposed system.

	Type	# of Filters	Size/Stride	Output
	Input			320 × 320
1	Convolutional	16	3 × 3/2	160 × 160
2	Maxpool		2 × 2/2	80 × 80
3	**Blaze**	4, (12, 12, 8+12)	1 × 1/1, 3 × 3/1	80 × 80
4	Maxpool		2 × 2/2	40 × 40
5	**Blaze**	8, (24, 24, 8+24)	1 × 1/1, 3 × 3/1	40 × 40
6	Maxpool		2 × 2/2	20 × 20
7	**Blaze**	16, (32, 32, 24+32)	1 × 1/1, 3 × 3/1	20 × 20
	Convolutional	24	1 × 1/1	20 × 20
8	Maxpool		2 × 2/2	10 × 10
9	Convolutional	32	3 × 3/1	10 × 10
10	Convolutional	24	1 × 1/1	10 × 10
11	Convolutional	64	3 × 3/1	10 × 10
12	Convolutional	24	1 × 1/1	10 × 10
13	Convolutional	72	3 × 3/1	10 × 10
14	Convolutional	30	1 × 1/1	10 × 10

Figure 2. Brisk-YOLO model.

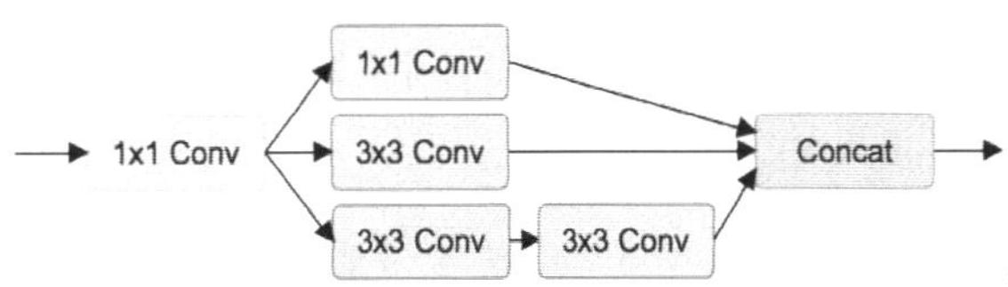

Figure 3. The Blaze layer.

To obtain the demanding performance, we replace some convolution layers by Blaze layers. In order to train our model more effectively, various techniques for training deep neural networks are applied. The periodical triangular learning rate and batch normalization are used. We also apply the Dense->Sparse->Dense(DSD) training procedure to train our model. The DSD method can speed-up model convergence and improve detection accuracy.

2.2. Tracker(KCF)

To solve long-term tracking problems and consider the balance between speed and accuracy, the Kernelized Correlation Filters (KCF) tracker[4] is adopted in our tracking component. The Brisk-YOLO detector will redetect the target human and initialize the KCF tracker in case of tracking failure. Because the KCF cannot be adaptive to the target size, the system will also initialize the KCF by executing the detector periodically (every 30 frames) to attain the multi-scale adapting capability.

2.3. Re-Identification

The color histogram technique is used in feature matching in re-identification task. We divide the bounding box of detected human into six equal parts horizontally and the resulting feature vector is 660-dimension. The Bhattacharyya distance is used to measure the similarity between feature vectors. If the distances to all candidate regions are greater than the defined threshold, the target is considered lost and the detector will be executed to initialize the tracking process.

3. Experimental results

Table 1 shows the experimental results between the Tiny-YOLO and our proposed Brisk-YOLO on the PASCAL VOC 2007 dataset. The model size of the Brisk-YOLO is only 0.283 MB and its detection speed can achieve 22fps. In terms of mAP and IoU, our detection accuracy is a little lower than the Tiny-YOLO, but it still keeps at the desired level. The fast detection speed and acceptable accuracy performance make it possible to adopt the Brisk-YOLO for real-time embedded applications.

The Bonn Benchmark on Tracking (BoBoT) is a public dataset providing a benchmark for comparing different visual tracking algorithms. The frame size is of 320×240 pixels. Our proposed method is compared with four tracking methods. We evaluate the performance on the sequences of D, F, and I of the dataset. The experimental results shown in Table 2 indicate that the proposed tracking method has superior performance in most video sequences, especially it exhibits excellent robustness under complicated situation with severe occlusion (video sequence I).

Figure 4 shows some samples of our tracking results. The red box indicates the ground truth and the tracking result is presented by the green box. The number within the upper part of the bounding box shows the value of IoU.

4. Conclusions

We propose a lightweight model Brisk-YOLO for human detection. Combining the Brisk-YOLO and reliable tracking method we construct an integrated human detection and tracking system. The proposed system has been implemented on the embedded platform and the experimental results show that it can achieve near real-time performance while keeping acceptable detection accuracy. In the future, we plan to continue improving our model capacity, increasing its detection accuracy rate as well as enhancing its detection speed to meet more real-time needs.

Table 1. The comparisons between Tiny-YOLO and Brisk-YOLO

Model	mAP	IoU	FPS	Size
Tiny-YOLO	**59.59%**	**56.59%**	0.4 fps	63.5MB
Brisk-YOLO	58.56%	45.46%	**22 fps**	**0.283 MB**

Table 2. The average IoU of different human tracking methods

Seq.	average IoU[%]				
	[5]	[6]	[7]	[8]	ours
D	71.12	76.39	**80.6**	72.61	70.63
F	60.82	40.02	56.1	53.86	**68.93**
I	75.02	47.63	77.7	70.77	**80.63**
Avg.	68.98	54.34	71.46	72.41	**73.39**

(a) Partial occlusion

(b) Successful tracking after severe occlusion

Figure 4. Tracking samples under various conditions.

Acknowledgment

This research is partially supported by the Ministry of Science and Technology under Grant Number MOST 108-2634-F-008-002 through Pervasive Artificial Intelligence Research (PAIR) Labs, Taiwan.

References

[1] S. Ren, K. He, R. Girshick, and J. Sun, "Faster R-CNN: Towards Real-Time Object Detection with Region Proposal Networks," *IEEE Trans. Pattern Anal. Mach. Intell.*, vol. 39, no. 6, pp. 1137–1149, Jun. 2017.

[2] J. Redmon and A. Farhadi, "YOLO9000: Better, Faster, Stronger," *IEEE CVPR* Vol. 1, pp. 6517–6525, 2017.

[3] F. N. Iandola, S. Han, M. W. Moskewicz, K. Ashraf, W. J. Dally, and K. Keutzer, "SqueezeNet: AlexNet-level accuracy with 50x fewer parameters and <0.5MB model size," *ArXiv160207360 [cs.CV]*, Feb. 2016.

[4] J. F. Henriques, R. Caseiro, P. Martins, and J. Batista, "High-Speed Tracking with Kernelized Correlation Filters," *IEEE Trans. Pattern Anal. Mach. Intell.*, vol. 37, no. 3, pp. 583–596, Mar. 2015.

[5] D. Klein, D. Schulz, S. Frintrop, and A. Cremers, "Adaptive real-time video-tracking for arbitrary objects," *IEEE/RSJ International Conference on Intelligent Robots and Systems*, pp. 772–777, 2010.

[6] S. Frintrop, "General object tracking with a component-based target descriptor," *IEEE International Conference on Robotics and Automation*, pp. 4531–4536, 2010.

[7] A. Kolarow et al., "Vision-based hyper-real-time object tracker for robotic applications," *IEEE/RSJ International Conference on Intelligent Robots and Systems*, pp. 2108–2115, 2012.

[8] D. Kumlu and B. Gunsel, "Variable rate adaptive color-based particle filter tracking," *IEEE International Conference on Image Processing*, pp. 1679–1683, 2016.

SESSION

LATE BREAKING PAPERS: IMAGING SCIENCE AND APPLICATIONS

Chair(s)

TBA

Non-Contact Surface Displacement Measurement for Concrete Samples Using Image Correlation Technique

Hector Cruz, Siavash F. Aval, Keyur Dhawan, Mohammad Pourhomayoun, Tonatiuh Rodriguez-Nikl, Mehran Mazari *California State University Los Angeles*

Abstract—**Concrete stress-strain analysis provides an understanding of the response of the material under different loading conditions and is a measure of strength as well as structural capacity. Current laboratory methods to extract displacement and strain values require precise equipment with high accuracy and complex data acquisition systems. A simplified non-contact methodology to estimate surface displacement and micro crack initiation will be highly beneficial in terms of enhancing laboratory and field evaluations. Advancements in image analysis and correlation algorithms have allowed for the development of methods to estimate surface displacement and strain through video recordings. The process involves deconstructing a video into individual images per frame, which are then processed for feature detection and monitor those features over time. In this study, a preliminary algorithm was developed to perform the aforementioned tasks on a series of laboratory images. In this paper, video recordings of cylindrical concrete specimens, prepared in the laboratory under standard compression testing, are processed by the proposed surface displacement measuring algorithm and then compared to displacement gauge readings.**

I. Introduction

THE application of computer-based image correlation and analysis has been gaining popularity with increasing availability of advanced optical devices. Programs have been developed to follow movement by detecting key features in the image and comparing frame-by-frame images to track the features of interest. Those programs can benefit researchers to improve on existing inspection methods and structural health monitoring processes. Currently there are numerous applications for image-based analysis such as deformation monitoring of bridge elements, pavement surface crack detection, and crack identification on tunnel lining surfaces. Improvements being made for these applications and more practical image capturing methods such as unmanned aerial systems, can be pursued.

The image correlation algorithms can also be employed for evaluating the hardened property measurements of concrete specimens in the laboratory conditions and further applied in the field. Currently strain gauges are used to collect displacement data for compression testing. However, they require high-precision linear variable transducer connected to a data acquisition system to record the specific points on interest on the specimen surface. These measurements are usually localized and limited to a specified surface area. The need for a non-contacting strain measurement for concrete surfaces is highly sought after for both laboratory applications that could be further calibrated and expanded to field applications. These methods allow for unlimit ed tracking on any visible point on the captured image of the concrete surface and can produce a more in-depth analysis of the surface deformations.

The main objective of this study was to develop a method for utilizing video recordings of concrete specimen surface in the laboratory to estimate the surface displacement and strain. Several concrete cylinder samples were prepared and analyzed during both compression and splitting tensile strength tests to evaluate the preliminary results. There are various factors that contribute to the ability of the algorithm to accurately detect features and analyze them. An optimal test setting will be achievable upon availability of different testing conditions and refinement of the developed algorithm.

II. Background

There has been a growing interest for non-contact test methods for evaluating the health and performance of structures throughout the literature. Concrete is a common material used in construction and understanding its properties ensure the safety and health of structures. The recent techniques that utilize image correlation and analysis, such as Speckle statistics, are being tested to eliminate the need for conventional methods [1]. Speckle statistics is a form of digital image correlation in which speckle patterns, with random intensity distribution, are compared during before and after images to evaluate displacement and deformation. The surface of a specimen is illuminated by a laser light to generate a speckled appearance. The speckled appearance is compared between frames and images to determine correlations between those patterns through superimposition. The displacement of the surface can then be measured by tracking the speckle patterns over time [2]. The setup consisted of a Diode-Pumped Solid-State laser, positive lens, screen, and a high-resolution video camera. The captured images were then processed for strain calculations and compared with results from three compression tests. Overlaying graphs from different methods demonstrated that the results were fairly accurate with a 5.6 percent average uncertainty, making this method a fairly reliable technique for measuring strain. That study established the potential of speckle statistics for measuring strain [2].

Another technique is Digital Image Correlation (DIC) which compares before and after images to measure deformation of an object surface. Introduced in the 1980s, DIC algorithms focus on increasing correlation speed and accuracy. DIC is highly sensitive to lighting conditions, requiring a specific setup in order to maintain consistent results during testing. Correlation between images is determined by tracking matching pixel subsets. An image has a constant dimension size that is represented by number of pixels in the vertical and horizontal directions. Subsets are determined within this region and tracked throughout the deformation process. Recently DIC has been implemented to aid in problems such as fracture mechanics investigation and high temperature deformation analysis [3]. Developing strain and displacement measurement techniques that are accurate and cost effective are highly desirable. Studies on DIC attempt to achieve this by providing a method that is simple and practical for laboratory and field applications [4]. Although there are other techniques, such as laser shearography and speckle interferometry, DIC is simpler to apply in field conditions since required equipment is mainly an image capturing device. However, there are still challenges with accuracy due to effects from the environment and potential changes to surfaces being observed. Studies have demonstrated the potential applications of DIC but further work required to produce a method that is reliable for field conditions [3].

Deformation on concrete structure surfaces leads to crack formation which is an indication of failure thus requiring a monitoring system to ensure structural health. Image correlation techniques can be applicable to this situation to reduce manual inspections and improve detection rates. The validity of these techniques was investigated in a study reviewing 50 papers to evaluate the quality of image processing for crack detection and potential use in field conditions [5]. Typically, those studies have used image correlation and analysis methods following the procedure of capturing images, pre-processing, image processing, feature detection, and parameter estimation. Various methods were investigated such as DIC, morphological approach, speckle statistics, photogrammetric technique, and reconstruction technique to name a few. Each study attempted to measure various features of cracks on surfaces with varying results. The range of accuracy was between 70 to 95 percent with a few cases achieving higher than 95 percent accuracy. That review study demonstrated the potential that image analysis techniques have for practical use as well as shortcomings that need to be improved to increase accuracy [5].

Other applications of optical techniques include measurements of deformation in bridge elements. A study utilizing moiré photography and photogrammetry demonstrated the potential benefits of applying image analysis compared to existing monitoring and testing methods. A destructive load test on a bridge structure was measured and compared to the conventional technique [6]. The method required the surface be covered in dotted patterned paper. Sequential images were then collected with various cameras, using a point of intersection to calculate the position of feature being focused. Displacements in the x and y directions could then be measured by comparing images. Limitations of that method were target recognition and measurements of precise positions. Further development in that technique can lead to simpler evaluation and monitoring methods for structures while increasing accuracy [6].

The image correlation process is generally broken down into two parts, the detector and the descriptor. The detector process is meant to consistently detect interest points such as corners, blobs, and T-junctions. The ability of the detector should be robust with respect to changes in viewpoint. The neighborhood of the selected features is represented as feature vectors or descriptors. Ideally, captured sections should represent the most distinctive features. The descriptor is then compared and matched with different images. There are various algorithms that achieve this with varying results. Some algorithms process the images quickly (i.e. lower computational cost) with low accuracy while others require higher computation power but are more reliable.

The main objective of this study was to develop a preliminary algorithm to detect and track features in sequential images (or frames) of a concrete surface in laboratory conditions to estimate the surface displacement and deformations. The initial algorithm was evaluated with different image resolution and quality under different lighting conditions and various surface annotation. The optimum algorithm was then partially validated using a digital strain gauge during a compression test. The following sections include the details of algorithm development as well as discussion of preliminary results.

III. Methodology

For this research Speeded-Up Robust Feature (SURF) combined with and Binary Robust Invariant Scalable Keypoints (BRISK) methods were employed in order to achieve a robust algorithm for multiple applications. The initial detector-descriptor algorithm was SURF which is based on the Hessian matrix concept. Utilizing integrated images, computation time can be reduced. Although the detector implements the Hessian matrix, computation is improved by utilizing the determinant of the matrix for the scale and location. The descriptor is then composed of a distribution of Haar-wavelet responses within the neighborhood of the interest point. The Haar-wavelet is a rescaled sequence of square-shaped wavelets utilized by SURF to detect contrast in dark and light pixels from left to right, and top to bottom [7]. The BRISK algorithm utilizes a scale-space key point detector, key point descriptors, and matching algorithm for feature detection. The BRISK sampling patterns are concentric circles used to construct pairwise brightness comparison which help in increasing processing speed [8]. Attempts to improve image quality through better lighting impact the results of SURF and BRISK methods due to changes in lighting contrast. The algorithm utilizes the Hessian matrix $H(x, \sigma)$ to determine instance in images where there is a change in lighting. Given a point $x = (x, y)$ in an image I, the Hessian matrix $H(x, \sigma)$ in x at scale σ is defined as follows [9]:

$$H(x,\sigma) = \begin{bmatrix} L_{xx}(x,\sigma) \; L_{xy}(x,\sigma) \\ L_{xy}(x,\sigma) \; L_{yy}(x,\sigma) \end{bmatrix} \qquad (1)$$

where $L_{xx}(x,\sigma)$ is the convolution of the Gaussian second order derivative $\frac{\partial^2}{\partial x^2} g(x)$ with the image I in point x, and similarly for $L_{xy}(x,\sigma)$ and $L_{yy}(x,\sigma)$.

Assuming that the reference pixel in the original frame is located at (x_0,y_0) and the point of interest at the location of (x_i,y_j), after deformation and displacement of the concrete surface, these two point will be relocated to (x'_0,y'_0) and (x'_i,y'_j), respectively. The correlation between the aforementioned points can be expressed as follows [10]:

$$x_i' = x_i + \alpha(x_i, y_j) \qquad (2)$$

$$y_j' = y_j + \beta(x_i, y_j) \qquad (3)$$

where α and β are the displacement mapping or shape functions. Assuming a rigid body transition, the following equations can be used to represent the deformed location of the interest points in terms of $\Delta_x = x_i - x_0$ and $\Delta_y = y_j - y_0$ [*11*]:

$$\alpha_2(x_i, y_j) = a + a_x\Delta x + a_y\Delta y + 0.5a_{xx}\Delta x^2 + 0.5a_{yy}\Delta y^2 + a_{xy}\Delta x\Delta y \quad (4)$$

$$\beta_2(x_i, y_j) = b + b_x\Delta x + b_y\Delta y + 0.5b_{xx}\Delta x^2 + 0.5b_{yy}\Delta y^2 + b_{xy}\Delta x\Delta y \quad (5)$$

where *a* and *b* are directional displacement components of the reference interest point in *x* and *y* directions, respectively. The first and second order gradients of the reference are denoted as subscript of *x* (or *y*) and *xx* (or *yy*), respectively. Figure 1 shows a schematic of the BRISK algorithm.

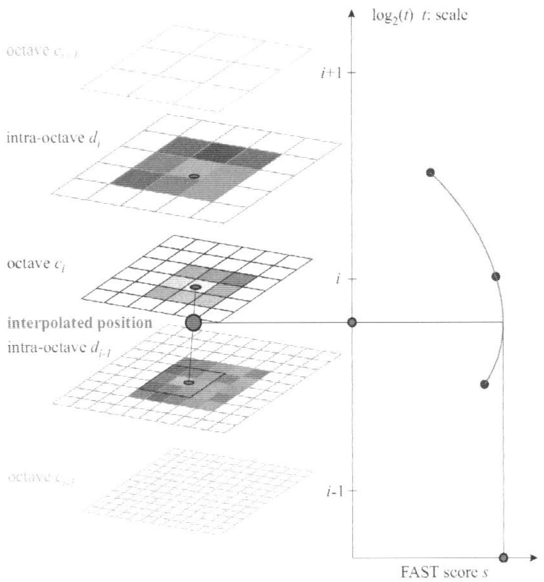

Fig. 1 Detection and tracking of the interest point between image octaves using Binary Robust Invariant Scalable Keypoints [*8*].

In this study, an algorithm was developed to detect and extract the features of interest from a series of images to estimate the surface displacement on a cylindrical specimen undergoing compression test. This algorithm deconstructs the video into individual images (frames) that are later scanned and checked for feature detection. Black dots on the surface of each sample were designated features to be detected. The surface area of the concrete sample was painted white to reduce the color distortion caused by concrete surface cavities and texture. Black dots were then marked on the painted surface to use as reference features for tracking during testing. Different detection methods, such as gridded dots and speckle patterns, were explored. Gridded dots consisted of a collection of hand drawn black dots in a specified matrix form with varying spacing size. Speckle patterns were sprayed on using a spray can and the speckles were randomly applied on the specimen surface. Figure 2 illustrates examples of speckled and gridded dot surfaces prepared for the image acquisition process.

(b)

Fig. 2 Preparing the surface of concrete sample: (a) Speckle paint, and (b) Matrix format.

For testing purposes, optimal environment settings were set to increase the ability to detect features. A digital camera capable of recording 30 frames per second at 1080p quality were used in this study to ensure that the number of pixels available for analysis are optimized. Stability is required to reduce the effect of noise in measuring displacements, however minor ground motion was inevitable. Optic Lens was utilized to further focus on the specimen at a safe distance in order to avoid damaging the camera during compression test while increasing size of focused image. The lens assists in optimizing the number of pixels available per frame. Lighting is controlled throughout the process with an LED source to ensure consistency. Placement of lighting source was at an angle to reduce reflection off the concrete sample surface which negatively effects the detection process. Figure 3 shows the laboratory setup for image capturing process.

Once the video is recorded, it is divided into individual frames for analysis. The algorithm then compares before and after images to determine the surface displacement and deformation by tracking the points of interest in the consequent images. The images would be cropped to focus on the interest area to reduce the number of false feature detection. A false detection could occur at edges where light and dark contrast are significantly higher. A base frame was analyzed to determine the initial locations of each feature on the specimen surface to create a matrix of interest points. Upon completion of the analyses, the strain along x and y directions were calculated and visualized in both graph and heatmap format. The image capturing process was performed at a frequency of 30 frames per seconds.

Fig. 3 Setup for image capturing process.

IV. DATA PROCESSING AND ANALYSIS

Data was collected from cylindrical concrete samples prepared in the laboratory. Upon preparing the concrete surface for gridded or speckled marking, the specimens were capped and undergone a compression test at a constant loading rate. The imaging apparatus was setup to capture consequent images of the testing process for further analyses. Upon completion of the test and retrieval of images, the initial feature detection algorithm was performed on the series of captured images. Figure 4a illustrates the results of an initial feature detection process that was performed on a frame during testing. Figure 4b shows a series of features that were located and annotated by the algorithm on one of the initial frames. An area of interest was identified by the user to focus the feature detection and tracking within a specified area of the sample surface. One of the advantages of this algorithm over conventional strain measurement devices is that the user is able to track the movement of many specified points on the surface during the test. Figure 5 shows the images extracted from different stages of the compression test at different focus settings. The algorithm was able to plot a movement trajectory for all the point of interest on the specified images. This features enables the user to track and monitor the surface displacement at almost every point on the specimen surface during testing. The plots of accumulated strain in x-direction at 9 points of interest on the surface were illustrated in Figure 6. Most of the tracked features show a consistent pattern for displacement except for one of them. This could be due to false detection of features between some frames during the analysis period. Improving the lighting conditions and better preparation of surface before testing will reduce the possibility of false positives.

(a)

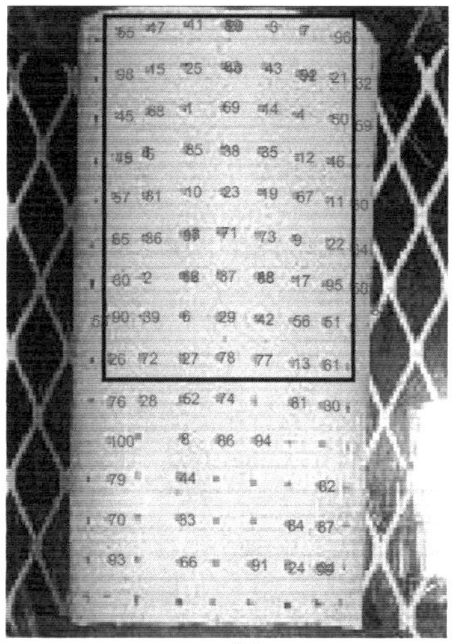

(b)

Fig. 4 (a) Detection and matching the image features, and (b) Annotating points of interest and cropping the selected section for displacement monitoring.

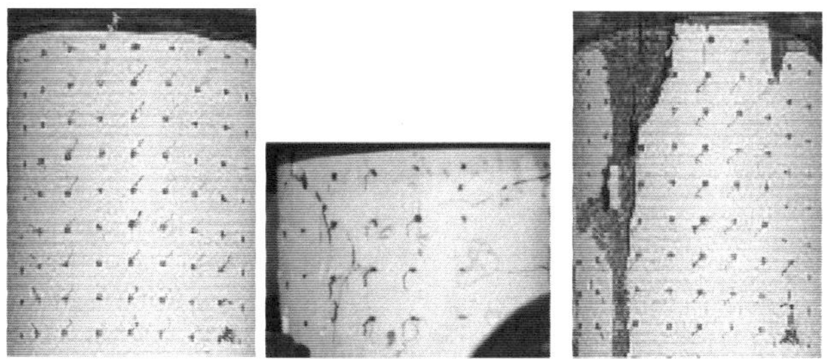

Fig. 5 Trajectory of detected features on the concrete surface.

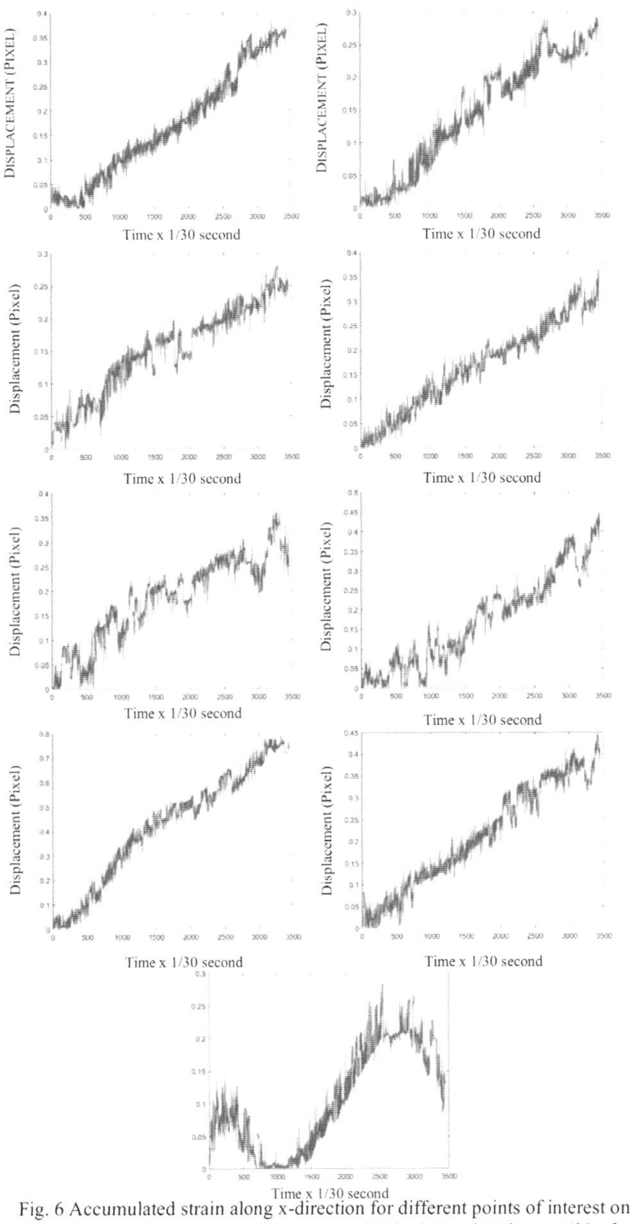

Fig. 6 Accumulated strain along x-direction for different points of interest on specimen surface. (Y axis: displacement in Pixel, X axis: Time x 1/30 of second)

The displacement signal obtained from the initial analyses of the images also reflect some noise due to the missing features or proximity of pixels during the analysis. These noisy signals could be smoothened using a moving average or other smoothing algorithms to produce a more uniform response.

To better represent the trend of developing displacements and surface deformations from the image correlation algorithm, a nested interpolation of strain data was performed on the specimen surface that was captured during imaging process. Superimposing the contour plots of surface deformation during the testing period, generates an animated representation of strain development on the sample surface in form of a heatmap. Figure 7 illustrates a screen captured of the animated strain heatmap during the compression test. The lighter areas in these figures represent higher strains and in some locations cracking of the specimen surface. A higher resolution of this heatmap enables the user to extract meaningful information regarding the crack initiation and propagation on the concrete surface under loading conditions.

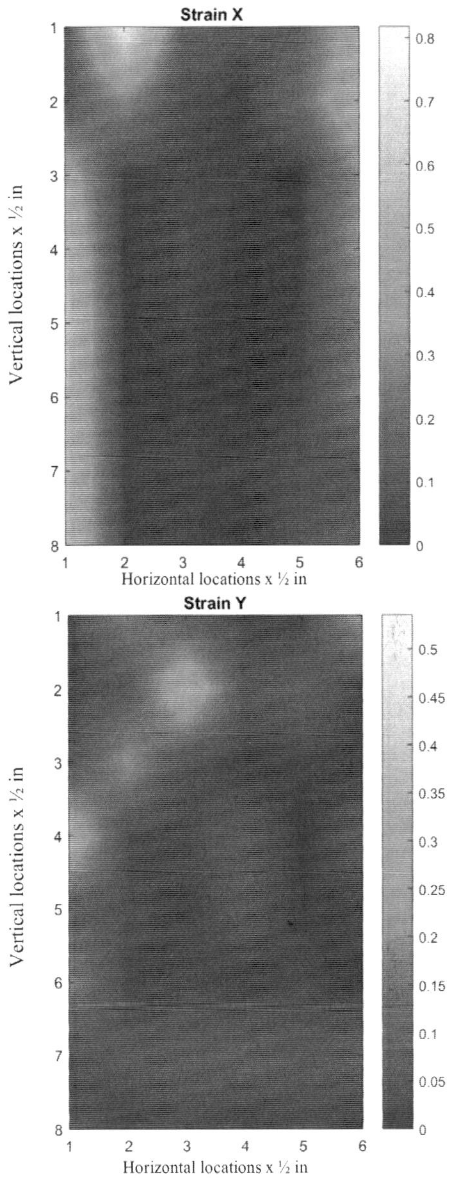

Fig. 7 Heatmap of strain measurement in the x- and y-directions.

The next step in this study was to partial validate the results of image correlation algorithm with measured deformations using mounted local strain gauges. To perform the validation process, two linear strain gauges were installed on a frame around the cylindrical specimen to measure the extension and compression of the sample during the compression strength test. At the same time, the image capturing device was setup to acquire images of the sample during the testing process. The strain values calculated from both image correlation algorithm and strain gauge data were plotted on a stress-strain graph to compare the results. Within a reasonable accuracy range, the results of strain measurements from image correlation algorithm are comparable to those captured by digital strain gauges. Figure 8 shows the results of this partial validation. A more in-depth validation and calibration process are undergoing. The discrepancy between measured and estimated displacements in these figures is mostly due to the unmatched timing of the image capturing process and the unsynchronized frequency of data collection between the gauge and image correlation algorithm. The more in-depth validation of the results from this algorithm is undergoing.

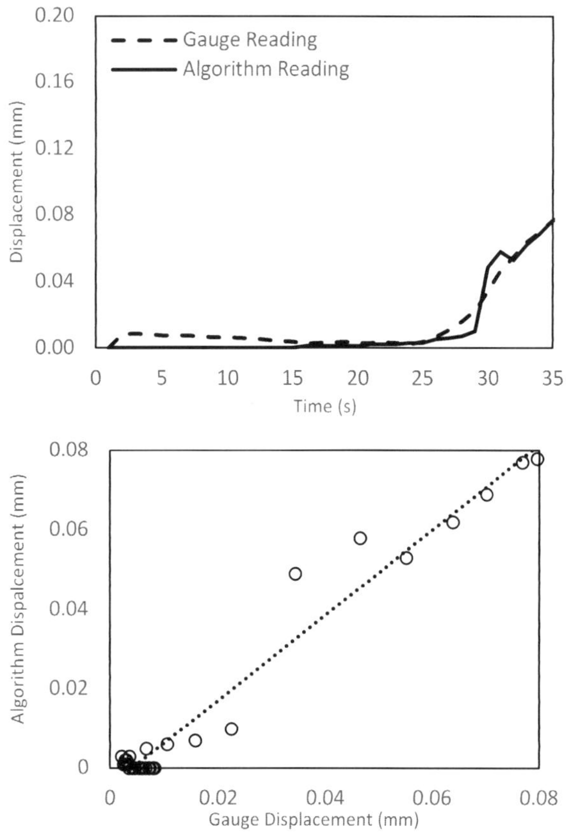

Fig. 8 Displacement measurement comparison between gauge reading and algorithm calculation.

V. SUMMARY AND CONCLUSIONS

A preliminary version of an image correlation algorithm was developed to capture the surface properties of concrete samples in the laboratory conditions. The accuracy of the developed algorithm is dependent on the stabilization of the image capturing device, lighting source and preparation of surface for proper feature detection. The preliminary results show potential of using this non-contact method to estimate the surface deformation and displacement of concrete samples.

Based on current version of the algorithm, it can be observed that the strain measurements are relatively close to those measured from a digital gauge. Further improvement is being explored in terms of increasing accuracy and speed of calculations. Further investigation into factors that can improve detection of features will improve accuracy of the algorithm.

VI. ACKNOWLEDGMENT

This study was carried out with the support from the University Transportation Center for Underground Transportation Infrastructure (UTC-UTI), funded by a grant from the U.S. Department of Transportation's University Transportation Centers Program. The contents of this paper reflect only the views of the authors, and not necessarily those of the sponsors.

REFERENCES

[1] Sadana, H.A., P.A. Marquez Aguilar and O.A. Molina. "Concrete Stress-Strain Characterization by Digital Image Correlation." J Appl Mech Eng 4 (2015): 189

[2] Leendertz, J. A. (1970). "Interferometric displacement measurement on scattering surfaces utilizing speckle effect." Journal of Physics E: Scientific Instruments, 3(3), 214.

[3] Kai Zhang. "Digital Image Correlation Analysis of Alkali Silica Reaction in Concrete with Recycled Glass Aggregate." Masters Thesis, University of Illinois at Urbana-Champaign. (2014)

[4] McCormick, Nick, and Jerry Lord. "Digital image correlation." Materials today 13.12 (2010): 52-54.

[5] Mohan, Arun, and Sumathi Poobal. "Crack detection using image processing: A critical review and analysis." Alexandria Engineering Journal (2017).

[6] Forno, C., et al. "The measurement of deformation of a bridge by Moirè photography and photogrammetry." Strain 27.3 (1991): 83-87.

[7] Bay, Herbert, Tinne Tuytelaars, and Luc Van Gool. "Surf: Speeded up robust features." European conference on computer vision. Springer, Berlin, Heidelberg, 2006.

[8] Leutenegger, Stefan, Margarita Chli, and Roland Y. Siegwart. "BRISK: Binary robust invariant scalable keypoints." Computer Vision (ICCV), 2011 IEEE International Conference on. IEEE, 2011.

[9] Bay, H., Ess, A., Tuytelaars, T., & Van Gool, L. (2008). Speeded-up robust features (SURF). Computer vision and image understanding, 110(3), 346-359.Pan et al. 2009

[10] Jin, H., Lu, W. Y., & Korellis, J. (2008). Micro-scale deformation measurement using the digital image correlation technique and scanning electron microscope imaging. The Journal of Strain Analysis for Engineering Design, 43(8), 719-728.

[11] Fu, Gongkang, and Adil G. Moosa. "An optical approach to structural displacement measurement and its application." Journal of Engineering Mechanics 128.5 (2002): 511-520.

Author Index